Automotive Global Value Chain

Today, some suppliers have grown increasingly powerful and in certain cases, earn revenues that rival or even exceed that of their automaker clients. In the pre-globalisation period, automakers wielded absolute power over their significantly smaller suppliers. This book reveals the upending of this relationship, with the gradual shift in the balance of power from automakers to their suppliers in this era of globalisation.

The book examines how suppliers in the global tyres, seats, constant velocity joints (hereafter 'CVJs'), braking systems and automotive semiconductor industries have evolved into powerful oligopolies through a mix of acquisition and organic growth strategies. It also highlights how joint ventures could be strategically deployed as springboards to acquisition, as they enable firms to familiarise themselves with their partners' markets and operations. Moreover, the book analyses the disruption stirred by the entry of well-resourced technology titans into this industry and their inevitable clash with the traditional incumbents.

This book is an invaluable reference for anyone interested in learning more about the automakers' and now their suppliers' relentless quest to create market-dominating intelligent driving systems.

Wilson Kia Onn Wong completed his PhD at the Centre of Development Studies, University of Cambridge, under the supervision of Professor Peter Nolan, who holds the Chong Hua Chair in Chinese Development. His PhD research focused on the factors driving the formation of oligopolies in the global automotive components industry, specifically in the tyres, car seats, constant velocity joints, braking systems and automotive semiconductor subsectors. Moreover, his research interests span both quantitative and qualitative studies, with particular emphasis on the empirical analysis of the impact of corporate takeovers on acquirers' stock returns and the economic history of the rise of key automotive manufacturers and their suppliers over the last five decades.

Routledge Advances in Management and Business Studies

Automotive Global Value Chain

The Rise of Mega Suppliers

Wilson Kia Onn Wong

Routledge
Taylor & Francis Group

LONDON AND NEW YORK

First published 2018 by Routledge

2 Park Square, Milton Park, Abingdon, Oxfordshire OX14 4RN

52 Vanderbilt Avenue, New York, NY 10017

Routledge is an imprint of the Taylor & Francis Group, an informa business

First issued in paperback 2019

British Library Cataloguing-in-Publication Data
A catalogue record for this book is available from the British Library

Library of Congress Cataloging-in-Publication Data
Names: Wong, Wilson Kia Onn, author
Title: Automotive global value chain : the rise of mega suppliers / by Wilson Kia Onn Wong.
Description: Abingdon, Oxon ; New York, NY : Routledge, 2018. | Series: Routledge advances in management and business studies ; 71 | Includes bibliographical references and index.
Identifiers: LCCN 2017015839 | ISBN 9781138237049 (hardback) | ISBN 9781315300993 (ebook)
Subjects: LCSH: Automobile supplies industry.
Classification: LCC HD9710.3.A2 W66 2018 | DDC 338.8/876292—dc23
LC record available at https://lccn.loc.gov/2017015839

ISBN: 978-1-138-23704-9 (hbk)
ISBN: 978-0-367-37472-3 (pbk)

Typeset in Galliard
by Apex CoVantage, LLC

Contents

Figures

Tables

Foreword

Since the 1980s the global business system has gone through a revolutionary transformation. The automobile industry has been at the forefront of this process. A dramatic process of cross-border mergers and acquisitions has contributed to high-speed industrial consolidation of the leading 'system integrator' firms in both the passenger vehicle and the closely related commercial vehicle sector. A handful of firms now control almost the entire global vehicle market. The market in the high-income countries is stagnant. Vehicle ownership in developing countries is far behind that in the developed countries. In the decades ahead almost all of the growth in vehicle markets will take place in the developing countries. A small group of companies with their headquarters in the high-income countries are poised to take advantage of this huge and fast-growing market.

Alongside the greatly increased level of industrial consolidation among the 'system integrator' firms, pressure from these firms has stimulated a revolutionary transformation of the entire supply chain. Through their vast procurement spending the system integrator firms have forced a comprehensive transformation of the industrial structure of the huge supply chain of this industry. Intense pressure from the system integrator firms has forced their leading suppliers to build just-in-time global supply chains, invest heavily in research and development, and place pressure on their own supply chains to lower costs. Every part of the supply chain of global vehicles has now become controlled by a handful of giant sub-system integrator firms. Ferocious oligopolistic competition has driven unprecedentedly rapid technological change across the entire supply chain of this vast industry.

The automobile industry is entering another era of revolutionary change, which is being driven by the penetration of the vehicle industry by information technology. Traditional assemblers and manufacturers in the vehicle supply chain face potentially severe competition from leading firms in the information technology hardware and software industry. The nature of the relationship between information technology and traditional manufacturers is still in its infancy. It remains to be seen whether the relationship will be one of deep cooperation or ferocious competition. The way in which this relationship evolves will be at the heart of institutional and technological change in this massive industry in the years ahead.

Wilson Wong's research offers great insight into this process. Few scholars have penetrated so deeply into the texture of this revolutionary transformation of a hugely important part of the global business system. His path-breaking research deep in the supply chain of this industry will assist scholars and business practitioners to understand better not only the revolutionary transformation of recent decades but also helps to deepen their understanding of the even more revolutionary changes that lie ahead. His unique in-depth research into the supply chain of this immensely important industry will form a key text for scholars and business practitioners attempting to understand better the evolution of this industry in its transition from traditional manufacturing to a new world in which information technology is deeply embedded within every vehicle and each vehicle is directly connected to the material world around it.

Peter Nolan
Chong Hua Professor of Chinese Development,
Director,
Centre of Development Studies,
University of Cambridge.

1   Introduction

1. Research objectives

The arrival of the automobile has been one of the defining hallmarks of the twentieth century. With the proliferation of the automobile through the pioneering mass production efforts of Henry Ford, industrial titans such as Volkswagen, Ford, Toyota and General Motors (hereafter 'GM') have emerged in this relentless race to move the world's growing masses. After decades of consolidation, these firms have become the leaders of an exclusive coterie of automakers (also known drolly as 'assemblers'), churning an approximate 90.1 million vehicles annually (International Organization of Motor Vehicle Manufacturers, 2015). Despite the generally misperceived mature nature of this industry, the global production of vehicles is expected to reach a staggering 110 million by 2021; as this book unfolds, it would become apparent that the industry is on the cusp of a major technological revolution, incorporating while concurrently advancing the development of the various emerging electronics, networking, communications, artificial intelligence and microchip technologies. Today the automotive industry is valued to be in excess of US$2 trillion and is directly and indirectly responsible for the employment of at least 50 million people worldwide (PwC Autofacts, 2015; Reuters, 2009; First Research, 2015).

The automotive industry's value chain also stretches far beyond public perception, as it extends from gargantuan automakers headquartered in affluent developed countries to the humble rubber suppliers spread across Indonesia, Thailand and Malaysia. This industry is at once associated with our immediate future (e.g., hyper-efficient intelligent electric vehicles, impeccable driverless technology and artificial intelligence powered safety systems) yet firmly rooted in our past through the seemingly backward rubber industry. In the past few decades, a great deal of research and media attention has been focused on the global automotive industry and their leading brands (i.e., Volkswagen, Ford, Toyota and GM) whose products now choke the world's ever-increasing roads and expressways. However, relatively scant research has been done on the automotive components industry, which over the decades has become the bedrock of the industry. Today, there are about 16 automakers that sell more than a million cars annually. However, these 16 carmakers procure their parts from about ten global suppliers, which are expected to provide unrelenting support to their increasingly multi-national empires, with their ever-expanding production and R&D facilities that bestride the globe.

Over the past 30 years, the automotive components suppliers have steadily assumed ownership over the actual vehicle making process, reducing the automakers to mere assemblers, more focused on what they perceive to be higher value-added activities such as branding, marketing and international business expansion. This trend has resulted in the automotive components players becoming responsible for 85 percent of the value of today's automobile (up from 65 percent a decade or two earlier), leaving only the production of engines in the purview of their automaker clients (Foy, 2014; Bratzel, 2011). More importantly, the carmakers by outsourcing the production of increasingly important automotive semiconductors (the 'brains' of the vehicle) to a few select suppliers may already have ceded the future leadership of this industry; today's vehicles are experiencing unprecedented computerisation, spurred by the introduction of electric and autonomous vehicle technologies. These suppliers and not their automaker clients are now the primary forces driving the revolution in automotive technology.

Even non-traditional automotive players such as Intel, Apple and Google, enticed by the potentially exponential profits in driverless car systems and related technology (i.e., the microchips residing in them) are making considerable headway in the development of such technologies. The automakers are in danger of becoming mere assemblers, the 'Foxconns' of the automotive industry[1] (McGee, 2016). The automotive components suppliers have become irrepressible entities breaking free from the control of their automaker paymasters. Through a ruthless cycle of consolidation, many of these suppliers are now multinationals in their own right, with multi-billion-dollar revenues and R&D expenditures. For instance, the world's leading automotive components supplier, Robert Bosch GmbH (hereafter 'Bosch') posted 2015 revenues of €70.6 billion, supported by R&D spend of €6.378 billion, simply overshadowing key automaker clients such as Renault in these aspects; in 2015, Renault recorded revenues of €45.3 billion along with R&D expenditure of €2.075 billion (Bosch, 2015; Renault, 2015). In a rare display of rising supplier power, a seats supplier Magna even attempted, albeit ultimately unsuccessfully, to acquire GM's German subsidiary, Opel in 2010. The recent spate of events suggests that the automotive industry is now possibly entering the age of the mega suppliers; an age where there is a shift in the balance of power from the automakers to their suppliers.

Like their automaker clients, the automotive components industry has also undergone significant change and consolidation over the past few decades. This state of affairs is because some suppliers were able to launch international acquisitions and forge joint ventures and strategic alliances, even in once closed markets (e.g., China). Moreover, this pace of consolidation accelerated in the 1990s, with the removal of cross-border restrictions on acquisitions in most countries. Over the past four decades, the number of components manufacturers to the automakers went from over 40,000 in 1970 to less than 5,000 in 2000, and possibly less than 3,000 by 2015 (DaimlerChrysler, 2005). With the consolidation juggernaut barrelling virtually unimpeded over this stretch of business history, one would imagine an inevitable deceleration to a relatively moderate trend in recent years. However, the pace of consolidation in today's automotive components industry is anything but moderate. From 2010 to 2015, this seeming throwback from a bygone industrial era saw the value of mergers and acquisitions (hereafter 'M&A') rise from a modest US$4.4 billion to a considerable US$32.9 billion; a remarkable compound annual growth rate (hereafter 'CAGR') of approximately 50 percent (PwC, 2015). This book aims to address the gap in the literature with regard to the institutional change that has taken place in the global automotive components industry since the 1980s. It aims to ascertain the extent and determinants of change in industry structure (i.e., the degree of industrial concentration) in the global components industry with specific reference, to the tyres, seats, CVJs, brakes and automotive semiconductor subsectors. This book is by no means all-encompassing but focuses on what are commonly perceived as critical components in today's vehicles.

Over the last three decades, these five subsectors were not only able to grow exponentially but also managed to secure unprecedented market power. This was largely due to the 'cascade effect' generated by the tremendous consolidation among the global automakers which has compelled them to actively select their most competent components suppliers, in a form of 'industrial planning'. They pick 'aligned suppliers' who can support their global growth strategies and meet ever-increasing requirements in quality and service standards (e.g., lean requirements,[2] worldwide technical support). This strategy also enables automakers to free up resources for higher value-added activities such as marketing, next-generation R&D and international expansion. Further this cascade effect generates intense pressures for first-tier suppliers covered in this book to themselves merge and acquire, and develop leading global positions. These suppliers subsequently pass on this intense pressure to their own supplier networks (Nolan, 2008). Buffeted by the powerful forces of the cascade effect, even traditionally small third-tier suppliers (e.g., rubber suppliers in chapter 3) are compelled to merge to not only augment their ability to meet the increasingly stringent quality and service demands of their first-tier supplier customers but also to bolster their position in price negotiations. In short, the cascade effect has not only led to rising industrial concentration (i.e., forming oligopolistic and even duopolistic market structures) among the first-tier suppliers but has also spilled over to the second and third-tier suppliers (Nolan, Zhang and Liu, 2008).

The five subsectors in this book were chosen for the pivotal role they play in the automotive industry. Further, for each subsector, the top two to four companies covered in this book account for 40 percent or more of their respective markets. Rapid technological progress, along with increasing safety and environmental concerns since the 1980s has led to the deployment of increasingly sophisticated technologies to the seemingly traditional tyres, seats, CVJs and brakes subsectors. This has generated tremendous cost pressures and an ever-growing demand for economies of scale and scope. The relatively recent automotive semiconductor sector is now assuming unprecedented significance due to rising electronic content across all automotive components from brakes to tyres; the average vehicle rolling off today's production lines has between 50 to 100 microchips, capable of processing millions of lines of code. Its increasing importance is underscored by the following statement from an industry analyst: 'it would be easy to say the modern car is a computer on wheels, but it's more like 30 or more computers on wheels' (Motavalli, 2010; Pagliery, 2014). This sector has witnessed tremendous consolidation, resulting in the creation of powerful oligopolists with unprecedented market power. As evidenced in Table 1.1, the oligopolists across the five subsectors have significant market shares ranging from approximately 40 percent to nearly 80 percent of their respective markets; in the case of the CVJs subsector, it is effectively a duopoly, as

Table 1.1 2015 Market shares of leading oligopolists across the five subsectors

Subsectors	Industry Oligopolists	Combined Market Share (%)
Tyres	Bridgestone Corporation (hereafter 'Bridgestone'), Goodyear Tire & Rubber Co (hereafter 'Goodyear'), Michelin Group (hereafter 'Michelin')	38.2
Automotive Seats	Johnson Controls, Inc.* (hereafter 'JCI'), Lear Corporation (hereafter 'Lear'), Faurecia	77.3
CVJs	GKN Plc (hereafter 'GKN'), NTN Corporation (hereafter 'NTN')	65.0
Braking Systems	Continental AG (hereafter 'Continental'), Bosch, ZF Friedrichshafen (hereafter 'ZF')	76.7
Automotive Semiconductors	NXP Semiconductors N.V. (hereafter 'NXP'), Infineon Technologies (hereafter 'Infineon'), Renesas Electronics Corp. (hereafter 'Renesas'), STMicroelectronics (hereafter 'STM')	40.4

*JCI spun off its Automotive Experience (includes seats) division in October 2016, resulting in the creation of a new company known as Adient.

Source: Company Annual Reports

only two companies control nearly two-thirds of this market, with the remaining players holding negligible stakes.

The seemingly humble tyres sector is not only the largest (worth US\$187.2 billion) among the five sectors covered but has also witnessed one of the fiercest takeover battles in modern corporate history. In the US alone, approximately 75 percent of tyre companies (accounting for 90 percent of the value of the US tyre subsector) experienced acquisition attempts or were compelled to restructure due to such takeover bids in the period 1982–1989; this resulted in a shift of ownership across half these US tyre companies, with the majority of them falling into foreign ownership (Chapter 3) (Mitchell and Mulherin 1996; Rajan, Volpin and Zingales, 2000). Leading tyre makers, Bridgestone and Pirelli & C. S.p.A. (hereafter 'Pirelli') both viewed the acquisition of US tyre maker, Firestone Tire & Rubber Company (hereafter 'Firestone'), as critical in dominating the highly profitable US tyre market and bolstering their international presence; Bridgestone emerged the victor in this bidding war. The acquisitions strategies of tyre companies such as Bridgestone and Goodyear have also made them more than just tyre manufacturers, as they now offer comprehensive tyre management services (Chapter 3). In effect, these mega suppliers have also positioned themselves as premium solutions providers to steal a march on their rivals in this era of intensifying, oligopolistic competition.

The genesis of the global automotive seats subsector was triggered by the unprecedented outsourcing by the leading automakers and the acquisitive strategies of the then emerging seat makers (i.e., JCI (now Adient), Lear and Faurecia) to build the global machinery needed to service the surging needs of this undulating subcontracting torrent. It could be argued that the demand by the automakers for entire seating systems compelled once disparate suppliers of covers, cushions and frames to embark on acquisitions to acquire the capability to develop entire seating systems on a just-in-time basis. Further, it is doubtful that JCI, Lear and Faurecia would have been able to meet the stringent demands (includes global technical, scheduling and lean practice support) of the automakers without an aggressive acquisitions strategy. The sheer pressure by their automaker clients reverberates across the entire value chain, as first-tier suppliers are now encouraged by automakers to acquire lower-tier suppliers, as they wish to deal with only a few key suppliers (Chapter 4), freeing up time and resources for the higher value-added activities of branding, marketing and next-generational research. Despite the inherent risks involved in acquisitions, they do enable first-tier suppliers to secure some control over the technologies or raw materials that go into making their products; the risks involved are significant particularly if acquisitions are heavily financed by debt (Lear's case in Chapter 4). It is this very same desire for control that compels some tyre companies (e.g., Bridgestone and Michelin) to acquire and maintain rubber plantations despite the considerable costs involved (Chapter 3).

In the global CVJs subsector, GKN surpassed industry pioneer, NTN through a series of acquisitions cloaked under the guise of joint ventures[3] (hereafter 'JVs'); this strategy proved highly effective in penetrating foreign markets and eventually acquiring controlling stakes in opportune circumstances (e.g., a relaxation of the regulations limiting foreign ownership). Further, it would be more judicious for firms to acquire JV partners (or even their suppliers), as they tend to be more familiar with their operations, culture, financials and management. The key firms in the global tyres and brakes subsectors have also deployed this strategy of using JVs as a springboard to acquisition albeit to a limited extent. Despite its effectiveness at circumventing regulatory scrutiny, this strategy does not provide eager companies with the desired control within a relatively short time frame. However, it could be argued that this strategy gives firms more time to examine their partners before deciding whether to further commit themselves to a costly takeover; the costs of unravelling a failed merger are considerably higher.

As evidenced in Chapter 5, to alleviate ever-increasing demands for scale economies and bolster their respective international presence, even bitter rivals such as GKN and NTN have been compelled to work together; both companies have significant stakes in Unidrive Pty Ltd (hereafter 'Unidrive'), an Australian CVJs maker (Unidrive, 2010). Further evidence of such 'unusual' cooperation between fierce rivals (e.g., STM and Freescale) in an industry marked by even greater competition, increasingly untenable R&D costs and a virtually insatiable demand for economies of scale and scope could be found in the automotive semiconductor subsector (see Chapter 7).

Like the automotive seats subsector, the three key firms (i.e., Continental, Bosch and TRW Automotive (hereafter 'TRW')) in the global brakes subsector basically derived their kick-start through acquisitions. For instance, Continental became more than a tyre maker through its US$1.93 billion acquisition of the automotive brake and chassis operations of ITT Industries in 1998 (Klier and Rubenstein, 2008). Similarly, Bosch entered the brakes subsector through its US$1.5 billion acquisition of the brake systems division of Allied Signal in 1996 (WardsAuto, 1996). In 1999, TRW (a leading maker of automobile airbags along with steering and suspension parts in the 1980s-1990s) staged the most ambitious acquisition in the brakes subsector for that period by acquiring LucasVarity (then the world's second-largest maker of automotive brakes, after Bosch) for US$6.6 billion (Bloomberg News, 1999). With this acquisition, TRW quickly positioned itself as one of the key firms in the global braking systems subsector. However by 2015, TRW was also acquired by ZF (a maker of transmission equipment) in the ruthless consolidation wave sweeping across the industry; in one fell swoop, ZF became the third largest player in the global braking systems subsector (ZF, 2015b).

In the global automotive semiconductor industry, the leading firms (i.e., Renesas, Infineon, STM and Freescale) are not only the products of relentless consolidation but are now 'trapped' in an escalating arms race to develop the latest technologies, needed to ensure their survival and competitive advantage. However, the case of Renesas (Chapter 7) shows that an acquisitions strategy may not be sufficient to resolve a firm's problems in this subsector. Renesas' key shareholders (i.e., Hitachi Ltd and Mitsubishi Electric Corp) had merged its semiconductor operations with NEC Corp but Renesas continued to be plagued by escalating scale economy demands and lack of profitability. These mounting problems combined with the untold devastation wrought on the firm's production facilities by the 2011 Fukushima earthquake ultimately led to its acquisition by the Japanese government-backed investment firm, the Innovation Network Corporation of Japan (hereafter 'INCJ') and a consortium of Japanese firms in 2012 (Schlesinger and Frischkorn, 2012).

Renesas' case is hardly unusual, as this book reveals that many of these components suppliers, despite their growing market power, are not necessarily profitable and are in fact beset by ever-increasing demands for economies of scale and scope, burgeoning R&D costs and pressure from their automaker customers. To deal with this increasingly demanding operating environment, subsystems integrators such as Renesas have also turned to cooperating with their suppliers (e.g., TSMC) in next-generational R&D efforts.

The manifold corporate tussles precipitated by the massive consolidation forces reshaping the automotive industry indicate that an acquirer could be better served, purchasing specific target assets (e.g., plants, intellectual property) instead of entire divisions or companies; this is evidenced by Infineon's acquisition of Qimonda's manufacturing assets as seen in Chapter 7. This surgical strategy not only ensures greater cost-effectiveness (the acquirer is only procuring what it needs) but also limits any potential obligations; once an acquirer secures full or majority control of a target firm, it also assumes full responsibility of its legal and financial obligations, which may be buried deep within the legalese of its financial statements.

Moreover, the significant emphasis on acquisitions does not imply that the companies covered in this book have neglected organic growth. On the contrary, the subsequent chapters reveal that some of these firms (e.g., Goodyear, Michelin, Faurecia, and GKN) have over the years increased their internal production capacities in key markets such as the US and China. Nonetheless this approach is often complemented by a judicious acquisitions strategy. Strategic alliances[4] have also been used with varying degrees of success by firms (e.g., Goodyear-Sumitomo, Renesas-TSMC) to gain much-needed access to emerging technologies, markets and networks but they do not grant firms the level of control they desire. However, they are less financially risky and far easier to unravel. It is evidenced that many of these firms would not have been able to achieve their current market standing (or even have met the initial standards required to secure business from the automakers) without the earlier boost provided by an aggressive acquisitions strategy.

Throughout this book, it is evident that financiers (e.g., Kohlberg Kravis Roberts & Co. L.P. (hereafter 'KKR'), The Carlyle Group (hereafter 'Carlyle'), The Blackstone Group L.P. (hereafter: 'Blackstone') have become a powerful force in the rapacious consolidation trend that has swept across the automotive industry over the past three decades. They are known by various colourful epithets such as corporate raiders, the 'barbarians at the gate' and more recently (and blandly) as private equity. These private equity firms tend to target struggling and/or underperforming companies. In the case of publicly held firms, it would be those firms whose market values have fallen far below the value of their assets. Once they have acquired control of these targets, these financiers would proceed to fix the troubled portions of the firm (e.g., infusing more capital or in most cases, simply divesting them to the next available buyer). The acquired firm could also be used as a vehicle to acquire the other players in the industry, further expediting the consolidation wave. Given their modus operandi, it is evident that private equity players are not in it for the long haul, and could be expected to 'flip' their port-folio firms after a three- to five-year horizon, to reap the rewards of their initial investments. It could also be argued that they already have an 'exit strategy' well in place, the moment they acquire control of their targets.

2. Case study approach

This book is fundamentally case study oriented as it involves in-depth analyses of the strategies of today's leading automotive components companies. It is driven by the premise that 'an intensity of information around a few observations' could be more relevant than a large dataset that comprises largely superficial historical financial data (Morck and Yeung, 2011: 54). The case study approach is particu-larly relevant in this context, as it facilitates the analysis of a particular phenome-non (i.e., rising industrial consolidation in the automotive components industry) within its real-life context. Further, case studies enable the researcher to retain comprehensive and significant characteristics of real-life events (e.g., organisa-tional and managerial processes, the maturation of industries). It is also use-ful when various sources of evidence are used (Yin, 1981a, 1981b, 1984). The strength of the case study approach in ascertaining the determinants of industry structure is also supported by Morck and Yeung (2011); the authors assert that the rich tapestry of data, afforded by a thorough documentation of the strate-gic decision-making process (via case studies), reveals that companies' strategies should be the ultimate arbiter of their structures (not the converse).

This book makes use of primary data whenever possible. Some of the primary data was obtained through interviews and email exchanges with mid-level/senior executives of global tyre and seats companies.[5] They also provided insight-ful views on their competitors and the overall direction of the industry. This is a highly competitive industry and it proved extremely difficult to obtain per-sonal interviews on such a commercially sensitive topic with senior executives within the automotive components industry. The remaining primary data was obtained from company annual reports. Fortunately, many of the firms covered in this book are public companies and a considerable amount of information on them is available in their respective annual reports, websites and analyst reports. The author was able to secure considerable access to personnel at upper middle management levels in Goodyear's US office, thus gaining a rare insight into the industry's development over the coming decade. As for one of the leading seats suppliers, the interviewee was a mid-ranked technical manager with considerable managerial experience in its Detroit office who provided insights on its acquisi-tion and vertical integration strategy. The book also draws heavily on the author's professional experience, as he not only worked at Goodyear in the early part of his career but also invested seven exciting years as an automotive analyst across several major consultancies; the role of an analyst today could sometimes seem rather Sisyphean given the sheer transformative forces relentlessly buffeting the industry's landscape. Further information was gleaned from academic journals, trade organisations, news agencies, and trade journals. The use of both primary and secondary data provides a more balanced analysis of the subject and is not biased towards a particular point of view.

3. Era of the mega suppliers

Ultimately, this book endeavours to shed light on the workings of the automotive components mega suppliers, which undoubtedly play an increasingly critical role in our lives yet are strangely taken for granted. The massive outsourcing, triggered by the powerful forces of the cascade effect, has led to the creation of these mega suppliers who now control the critical electrical and mechanical engineering expertise ('the building blocks') of the automotive industry and thus possibly the destiny of the automotive industry going forward. In a sense, the automakers are themselves responsible for the creation of the mega suppliers, who are breaking free from their once hegemonic control. By the same measure, the once 'insignificant' third-tier suppliers are now merging, and gaining the wherewithal to resist the existing mega suppliers. This is evidenced in the case of the natural rubber suppliers (Chapter 3), where the various players are starting to merge, in order to resist the oligopolistic pressure exerted on them by the leading tyre makers. In the case of the automotive semiconductor industry (Chapter 7), the so-called third-tier suppliers (i.e., Taiwan Semiconductor Manufacturing Company Limited (hereafter 'TSMC'), United Microelectronics Corporation (hereafter 'UMC'), GLOBALFOUNDRIES Inc. (hereafter 'GLOBALFOUND-RIES')) have through successful M&A become multinationals themselves with revenues and profitability rivalling and even exceeding that of the mega suppliers (i.e., NXP, Infineon, Renesas and STM). These increasingly gargantuan mega suppliers are now also the key players at the forefront of a technological revolution transforming the very fabric of our economic and social landscape. The cutting-edge technologies (e.g., smart tyres capable of reading road conditions, intelligent car seats with biometric sensors, high-tech braking systems, driverless car systems powered by sophisticated microchips) emerging from their R&D efforts could potentially eliminate the countless meaningless deaths emanating from road accidents worldwide. They would also lead to unprecedented levels of connectivity (and hopefully, productivity), as once humdrum everyday vehicles become inextricably intertwined with our homes and offices through this powerful technological nexus.

However cutting-edge technology such as driverless car systems also brings a whole host of problems and uncertainty; for instance, in the event of an accident, the issue of liability becomes somewhat murky (i.e., should the manufacturer or the vehicle owner be held accountable?), as the vehicle occupant is technically not the driver. In addition, the advent of autonomous vehicle technology could eliminate the need for human bus and taxi drivers, displacing significant numbers of public transportation workers worldwide. Needless to say, its impact on the once vaunted job security of the legions of truck drivers employed in the global logistics industry would also be nothing sort of devastating.[6] Moreover the overreliance on these emerging technologies could have tragic ramifications on vehicle occupants, as evidenced by the unfortunate death of a driver in a Tesla Model S (set in self-driving mode) in 2016; such incidents are less likely to occur in future with technological refinements over the coming years but devotees of these increasingly intelligent automated systems are well-advised to avoid complacency.

This steady robotisation of one of the critical means of our daily commute also exposes society to exponentially raised chances of hacking by terrorists with potentially deadly consequences. Further, the deluge of unemployment that could be unleashed by this disruptive artificial intelligence driven technology would widen the painful fissures in increasingly fractured societies, already besieged by the resurgent spectres of populism and spiralling income inequality. Contrary to the beliefs of certain mainstream thinkers, the jobs created, in the wake of this technology-induced unemployment carnage, would scarcely offset the devastation it wrought; if anything, the bulk of the largesse generated by this technological revolution (or disruption) would accrue only to a privileged stratum that possesses the requisite specialised skills and/or command ownership of these rarified technologies. While not discounting its tremendous life-saving potential, the advent of autonomous driving and its accompanying technologies would invariably play a critical role in introducing a false dawn of technological haves and have-nots, with its chasm-like societal divisions. These portentous scenarios reveal the significant price societal stakeholders must bear, in the automakers' and now their mega suppliers' relentless quest to create market dominating intelligent driving systems.

Notes

1 Foxconn is a Taiwanese company that assembles Apple's famous iPhone. It also assembles personal computers for major companies such as Acer, Dell, and Hewlett Packard. It has become synonymous with low value-added assembly work.
2 Lean involves creating an organisational culture with employees across all levels focused on eradicating waste, creating value for customers and continuous improvement (Womack and Jones, 1996).
3 A JV is a business arrangement in which two or more parties agree to share their resources with a view towards accomplishing a specific task and mutual profit. Under this arrangement, each partner is responsible for profits, losses and costs associated with it. Typically, JVs involve establishing an entity, separate from the partners' other commercial interests. JVs are commonly used by firms to penetrate foreign markets; foreign companies in a JV typically bring new technologies and processes, while the domestic companies provide the local knowledge and network (Investopedia, 2013; Legal Information Institute, 2013).
4 Strategic alliances involve two companies pooling resources to carry out a commercial undertaking (e.g., sharing production platforms, distribution channels and

technology). However strategic alliances are typically less formal than JVs and do not involve establishing a separate business entity (Investopedia, 2012; Gluckman and Kurczewski, 2009).

5 The names of some interviewees have been withheld, as they were only willing to speak on the basis of anonymity.

6 In the US alone, there were 1,797.700 truck drivers in 2014. This figure is expected to grow by 5 percent in the 2014–2024 period (U.S. Bureau of Labour Statistics, 2015).

References

Bloomberg News (1999) TRW, Outbidding Federal-Mogul, to Buy Lucas Varity of Britain, Bloomberg News [internet] Available at: http://www.nytimes.com/1999/01/29/business/trw-outbidding-federal-mogul-to-buy-lucas-varity-of-britain.html [Accessed on 23 December, 2016].

Bosch (2015) *Bosch Annual Report 2015*, Stuttgart: Bosch.

Bratzel, S. (2011) Volkswagen, BMW Feel Pinch as Suppliers Struggle to Keep Pace, Bloomberg.com [internet] Available at: http://www.bloomberg.com/news/2011-01-26/volkswagen-bmw-feel-pinch-as-suppliers-struggle-to-keep-pace.html [Accessed on 11 March, 2011].

DaimlerChrysler (2005) *Challenges, Measures and Opportunities*, Stuttgart: DaimlerChrysler.

First Research (2015) *Automobile Auto Dealers Industry Profile*, Austin: First Research.

Foy, H. (2014) Age of mega supplier heralds danger for carmakers, *ft.com* [internet] Available at: www.ft.com/cms/s/0/50c272c4-dce9-11e3-ba13-00144feabdc0.html#slide0 [Accessed on 18 August, 2016].

Gluckman, D. and Kurczewski, N. (2009) Fiat and Chrysler announce strategic alliance, *Car And Driver* [internet] Available at: www.caranddriver.com/news/fiat-and-chrysler-announce-strategic-alliance-car-news [Accessed on 2 August, 2013].

Groupe Renault (2015) *2015 Annual Report*, Boulogne-Billancourt Cedex: Groupe Renault.

International Organization of Motor Vehicle Manufacturers (2015) World ranking of manufacturers: year 2015, *OICA.net* [internet] Available at: http://www.oica.net/wp-content/uploads//ranking2015.pdf [Accessed on 12 February 2017].

Investopedia (2012) Definition of 'Strategic Alliance', *Investopedia* [internet] Available at: www.investopedia.com/terms/s/strategicalliance.asp [Accessed on 7 July, 2012].

Investopedia (2013) Definition of 'Joint Venture – JV', *Investopedia* [internet] Available at: www.investopedia.com/terms/j/jointventure.asp [Accessed on 1 August, 2013].

Klier, T.H. and Rubenstein, J.M. (2008) *Who Really Made Your Car? Restructuring and Geographic Change in the Auto Industry*, Kalamazoo, Michigan: W.E. Upjohn Institute for Employment Research.

Legal Information Institute (2013) *Joint Ventures: An Overview*, Cornell University Law School [internet] Available at: www.law.cornell.edu/wex/joint_venture [Accessed on 1 August, 2013].

McGee, P. (2016) Germany's carmakers gear up for tech challenge, *ft.com* [internet] Available at: www.ft.com/cms/s/0/27d9ead0-dfd1-11e5-b072-006d8d362ba3.html#axzz4HgrKn9Rs [Accessed on 19 August, 2016].

Mitchell, M.L. and Mulherin, H.J. (1996) The impact of industry shocks on takeover and restructuring activity, *Journal of Financial Economics*, 41: 193–229.

Morck, R. and Yeung, B. (2011) Economics, history and causation, *Business History Review*, 85(1): 39–63.

Motavalli, J. (2010) The dozens of computers that make modern cars go (and stop), *nytimes.com* [internet] Available at: www.nytimes.com/2010/02/05/technology/05electronics.html?_r=0 [Accessed on 6 August, 2012].

Nolan, P. (2008) Capitalism and Freedom, the Contradictory Character of Globalisation, London: Anthem Press.

Nolan, P., Zhang, J. and Liu, C. (2008) The global business revolution the cascade effect, and the challenge for firms from developing countries, *Cambridge Journal of Economics*, 32(1): 29–47.

Pagliery, J. (2014) Your car is a giant computer – and it can be hacked, *CNNMoney* [internet] Available at: http://money.cnn.com/2014/06/01/technology/security/car-hack/ [Accessed on 30 July, 2016].

PwC (2015) Driving Value: 2015 Automotive M&A Insights, New York: PwC.

PwC Autofacts (2015) *Q3 Data Release*, New York: PwC Autofacts.

Rajan, R., Volpin, P. and Zingales, L. (2000) The eclipse of the U.S. tire industry, in Kaplan, S.N. (ed.), Mergers and Productivity, Chicago: University of Chicago Press.

Reuters (2009) FACTBOX: Why does the auto industry matter? *Reuters* [internet] Available at: www.reuters.com/article/us-autos-factbox-idUSTRE54P2HU20090526 [Accessed on 18 August, 2016].

Schlesinger, J.M. and Frischkorn, B. (2012) Japan govt-backed fund mulls bid for renesas to counter KKR offer – source, *wsj.com* [internet] Available at: http://online.wsj.com/article/BT-CO-20120922-700853.html [Accessed on 28 October, 2012].

Unidrive Pty Ltd (2010) About Unidrive Pty Ltd: Our history, *Unidrive* [internet] Available at: www.unidrive.com/about-us.html [Accessed on 28 November, 2011].

U.S. Bureau of Labour Statistics (2015), Occupational outlook handbook: Heavy and tractor-trailer truck drivers, *U.S. Bureau of Labour Statistics* [internet] Available at: www.bls.gov/ooh/transportation-and-material-moving/heavy-and-tractor-trailer-truck-drivers.htm [Accessed on 21 February, 2017].

WardsAuto (1996) AlliedSignal brakes put Bosch in systems business, *WardsAuto* [internet] Available at: http://wardsauto.com/news-amp-analysis/alliedsignal-brakes-put-bosch-systems-business [Accessed on 20 March, 2012].

Womack, J.P. and Jones, D.T. (1996) *Lean Thinking: Banish Waste and Create Wealth in Your Corporation*, New York: Simon & Schuster.

Yin, R.K. (1981a) The case study as a serious research strategy, *Knowledge: Creation, Diffusion, Utilization*, 3 (September): 97–114.

Yin, R.K. (1981b) The case study crisis: Some answers, *Administrative Science Quarterly*, 26 (March): 58–65.

Yin, R.K. (1984) *Case Study Research: Design and Methods*, Beverly Hills, CA: Sage Publications, Inc.

ZF Friedrichshafen AG (2015a) *Annual Report 2015*, Friedrichshafen: ZF Friedrichshafen AG.

ZF Friedrichshafen AG (2015b) ZF completes acquisition of TRW automotive, *ZF* [internet] Available at: www.zf.com/corporate/en_de/press/press_releases/press_release.jsp?newsId=22096936 [Accessed on 23 July, 2016].

2 The global automobile industry

1. Highly concentrated industry with persisting consolidation

The global automobile industry is highly concentrated at the automaker level, with around ten to 12 companies dominating the global automotive industry (International Organization of Motor Vehicle Manufacturers, 2015). These automakers were the first firms to make the three-pronged investments 'in manufacturing, marketing, and management essential to exploit fully the economies of scale and scope' thus facilitating their swift dominance of the automobile industry. They (i.e., Toyota, Volkswagen, GM and Ford) have continued to dominate the industry for decades. Latecomers in this industry have to construct plants of similar size while the first movers have long since eliminated the inefficiencies in the production process, and maximised the economies of scale and scope. Further, these latecomers must forge distribution and retailing channels to gain footholds in markets where first movers have already firmly established themselves. Moreover, these latecomers have to hire requisite managerial expertise vital in competing with increasingly entrenched players well-versed in existing production, marketing, distribution and R&D practices (Chandler, 1992a; Chandler, 1992b); in an increasingly technologically exacting automotive industry buffeted by ever-rising demands for economies of scale and scope, cutting-edge R&D has become an increasingly critical arbiter of industry dominance. These exigent factors make it tremendously difficult for latecomers to challenge the established automakers, with their extensive global production, distribution and marketing networks, which are buttressed by their significantly greater financial resources.

Nonetheless, latecomers such as Tata Motors (hereafter 'Tata') and Geely Automobile (hereafter 'Geely') have been able to mount credible challenges recently, backed by significant war chests and strategic acquisitions of premium Western automakers such as Jaguar Land Rover and Volvo. Through these ambitious acquisitions, Tata and Geely were able to gain control of established carmakers with significant billion-dollar R&D spend; for instance, Jaguar Land Rover recorded average R&D expenditures of US$1.89 billion for the 2011–2015 period (Jaguar Land Rover, 2013–2016). As evidenced in Table 2.1, the top ten automakers in the world controlled 70–80 percent of

Table 2.1 Top ten automakers in terms of global production: 1998 (in units)

1998 Rank	Automakers	Country of Origin	1998 Global Production	Share of Global Production (%)
1	GM	US	7,582,000	14.3
2	Ford	US	6,556,000	12.4
3	Toyota	Japan	5,210,000	9.8
4	Volkswagen	Germany	4,809,000	9.1
5	DaimlerChrysler	Germany/US	4,512,000	8.5
6	Fiat	Italy	2,696,000	5.1
7	Nissan	Japan	2,620,000	4.9
8	Honda	Japan	2,328,000	4.4
9	Renault	France	2,283,000	4.3
10	PSA*	France	2,247,000	4.2
	Top Ten Automakers' Production		**40,843,000**	77.1
	Global Total Production		**52,987,000**	

PSA*- PSA Peugeot Citroën

Source: International Organization of Motor Vehicle Manufacturers

global production in 1998; the top five players accounting for over 50 percent of total production (International Organization of Motor Vehicle Manufacturers, 1998). The top ten automakers were all from the advanced economies of the US, Japan, Italy, France and Germany, with the Japanese firms (i.e., Toyota, Nissan and Honda) occupying nearly a third of the positions in the hotly-contested global top ten positions.

The ensuing Table 2.2 indicates that by 2015, the status quo remained basically unaltered, despite a near doubling of global production. In this market, ten carmakers still accounted for over three quarters of world vehicle production, with the top five responsible for over 50 percent of overall production (International Organization of Motor Vehicle Manufacturers, 2015; Schmitt, 2016). By 2015, the leading automakers, Toyota, Volkswagen, and GM, which in 1998 ranked within the top five global automobile manufacturers, were still in this elite band, with Toyota and GM retaining their hotly contested status within the global top three automakers. However, Ford has not only lost its position as a marquee top three automaker but has also been edged out of the global top five places by aggressive players such as Renault-Nissan and Hyundai. The meteoric rise of Renault-Nissan and Hyundai over the 1998–2015 period is attributable to strategies comprising a series of ambitious overseas expansion and bold acquisitions under opportune circumstances. South Korea's Hyundai, which did not feature within the global top ten automakers in the earlier 1998 rankings (Table 2.1), has fought its way into the coveted top five ranks.

This steadily intensifying oligopolistic industry structure is unlikely to change much, as the extreme industrial concentration generates high barriers to entry and limits the upgrading prospects of smaller firms; if anything, the smaller firms

Table 2.2 Top ten automakers in terms of global production: 2015 (in units)

2015 Rank	Automakers	Country of Origin	2015 Global Production	Share of Global Production (%)
1	Toyota	Japan	10,083,831	11.2
2	Volkswagen	Germany	9,872,424	11.0
3	GM*	US	9,800,000	10.9
4	Renault-Nissan Alliance	France/Japan	8,202,726	9.1
5	Hyundai	Korea	7,988,479	8.9
6	Ford	US	6,396,369	7.1
7	Fiat Chrysler Automobiles	Italy/US	4,865,233	5.4
8	Honda	Japan	4,543,838	5.0
9	Suzuki	Japan	3,034,081	3.4
10	PSA	France	2,982,035	3.3
	Top Ten Automakers' Production		67,769,016	75.2
	Global Total Production		90,086,346	

GM*- estimated production figures

Source: International Organization of Motor Vehicle Manufacturers, Forbes

are likely to become the acquisition targets of the major players. For most carmakers, a new vehicle design usually requires more than 30,000 engineering hours, takes three to five years to complete and necessitates several billion dollars of up-front investment. Moreover, concentration at the top of the value chain enables each carmaker to create its own standards and specifications, driving up transaction costs for suppliers and making investment in information technology and production equipment highly customer-specific. Resultantly, it creates a top-heavy structure of innovation that makes it extremely difficult for smaller upstarts to seek new customers or develop their own unique products and technologies (Sturgeon and Van Biesebroeck, 2009). The industry has undergone considerable consolidation over the past few decades. For instance, Volkswagen (in an attempt to secure new product lines) acquired significant interests in Seat and Skoda, in 1986 and 1991 respectively (Jurgens, 1995). In GM's case, it acquired a 34.2 percent stake in Isuzu in 1971, which it increased to 49 percent in 1989 (Shuchman and White, 1998). Similarly, in 1981, GM bought a 5 percent stake in Suzuki which it later raised to 20 percent in 2000. GM also forged JVs with the two Japanese carmakers in efforts to strengthen its capabilities in small car production; in 1982, the company formed a JV with Isuzu (known as 'Isuzu Motors Overseas Distribution Corporation') to market Isuzu vehicles in Southeast Asia, the Middle East, Latin America and Africa (Reuters, 1982). Moreover, in 1986, GM formed a 50–50 JV (Cami Automotive Inc) with Suzuki to make small cars for sale in North American markets. Besides Isuzu and Suzuki, GM also formed a JV ('New United Motor Manufacturing Inc.', also known as 'NUMMI') with Toyota to make front-wheel-drive Nova cars at a formerly shuttered GM plant in Fremont, California (Suzuki, 2016; Greimel, 2009; Scherer, 1996). Further, GM in an effort to acquire capabilities in high-performance cars, acquired a controlling 59.7 percent stake in Lotus with a US$20 million investment in 1986 (The New York Times, 1986).

GM's smaller rival, Chrysler, was equally aggressive in its acquisitions. For instance, Chrysler acquired control of American Motors in 1987, by purchasing Renault's 46.1 percent stake in the firm for a considerable US$1.5 billion. Renault had acquired control of an ill-performing American Motors in 1980. However Renault's investment in American Motors failed to reverse its declining fortunes and the latter haemorrhaged a stupendous US$858.6 million over the 1980–1987 period; this invariably led to Renault offloading its stake in 1987 (Holusha, 1987; Brown, 1987). Over the ensuing two decades, Chrysler would itself become the target of acquirers from Europe (i.e., Daimler and Fiat). By the end of 1998, Daimler completed its 100 percent acquisition of Chrysler through a US$92 billion share swap between the two firms, which resulted in the formation of the new entity, DaimlerChrysler (Schmid, 1998; Vlasic and Stertz, 2001; Blaško, Netter and Sinkey, 2000). The former shrewdly leveraged on the high value of its shares to acquire the relatively less valuable shares of the latter; in fiscal year 1997, Daimler and Chrysler posted price/earnings multiples of 24.4 and 9.9 respectively (a higher price/earnings multiple suggests investors' expectations of greater earnings growth in the future) (U.S. Securities and Exchange Commission, 2001; Sudarsanam; 2010).

However, with the failed materialisation of the promised synergies and the constant clashes between the American and German management of the merged DaimlerChrysler, Daimler eventually sold the bulk of its stake (80.1 percent) to private equity firm, Cerberus Capital (hereafter 'Cerberus') in 2007 for US$7.4 billion. In 2009, Daimler divested its remaining 19.9 percent stake in Chrysler to Cerberus; the divestment required Daimler to pay US$600 million into Chrysler's pension plan over three years and the writing off of loans it made to Chrysler earlier in 2007 (Bunkley, 2009). In June 2009, Fiat started targeting Chrysler by acquiring an initial 20 percent stake which was subsequently raised to full ownership in a US$4.35 billion deal in January 2014. Fiat's methodical acquisition of Chrysler over the 2009–2014 period is an illustration of how ambitious companies could vault ahead by acquiring their less successful peers, particularly ones which have been enfeebled by macroeconomic shocks such as the 2008 global financial crisis (Krisher, 2011; Castonguay, 2012; Ebhardt and Clothier, 2014). Through this surgically executed acquisition, Fiat was not only able to strengthen its presence in the US market but also secured the much-needed economies of scale essential in keeping its dreams of competing with the marquee automakers alive; in 2008 (just prior to its acquisition of Chrysler), Fiat placed tenth in terms of global production but bolstered by this merger, it became the seventh largest automaker in the world by 2013 (International Organization of Motor Vehicle Manufacturers, 2008; International Organization of Motor Vehicle Manufacturers, 2013).

In the case of GM and Chrysler, government intervention was also required at critical junctures in their history over the past three decades. For instance,

Chrysler, in 1979, lobbied the US government for loan guaranties that it needed to stave off a bankruptcy filing; Chrysler's financial woes was largely the outcome of focusing on building gas-guzzling cars in the 1970s, an era plagued by two major oil crises which eviscerated demand for such vehicles. This resulted in the Chrysler Corporation Loan Guarantee Act of 1979 which enabled the company to secure US$1.5 billion in federally backed private loans (NPR, 2008; Lawniczak, 2010). During the 2008 global financial crisis, GM and Chrysler received loans from the US government, amounting to US$49.5 billion and US$12.5 billion respectively. Through these loans, the US government secured significant stakes in GM and Chrysler which amounted to 61 percent and 9 percent respectively; in the case of GM, the stake was so large that it could be argued that the government had effectively nationalised the firm. As of December 2013, the US government has liquidated its stake in both companies but not without suffering substantial losses; for GM and Chrysler, the government's losses amounted to US$10.5 billion and US$1.5 billion respectively (Colias, 2013; Whoriskey, 2011). The above bailouts reflect a relatively high degree of state intervention in what it is supposedly the world's freest market economy. However, it could be argued that government intervention was necessary in such extenuating situations, as the automotive industry (inclusive of suppliers) was directly and indirectly responsible for the livelihood of millions.

The other key American carmaker, Ford, embarked on an even more ambitious acquisition campaign, as indicated by the sheer size and scale of its acquisitions over the 1989–2000 period. In 1989, Ford paid US$2.5 billion to acquire Jaguar. The company global ambitions extended even further, as it acquired Volvo for US$6.5 billion in 1999, which was soon followed by its US$2.9 billion acquisition of Land Rover in 2000 (IHS Markit, 2007; Kinnander and Naughton, 2010; CNN Money, 2000). However, these multi-billion-dollar acquisitions involving outsized premiums failed to deliver on the desired synergies, as indicated in the following section 2.

Given the sheer relentlessness of this consolidation wave, it was inevitable that the leading Japanese automakers were soon drawn into this ruthless contest for scale economies and market share via means of acquisition. In Toyota's case, it assumed virtual control of Daihatsu Motor Co. by raising its 34.5 percent stake to a controlling 51.2 percent, making Daihatsu its subsidiary in 1998. Moreover, Toyota had owned part of Daihatsu (around 16.8 percent) since 1967 and had been steadily tightening its grip on Daihatsu over the decades; Toyota's acquisition of Daihatsu was driven by its confidence in the growth potential of the small car market and it wanted to cement its hold over this then growing market (Pollack, 1995; The Japan Times, 1998).

Soon after this acquisition, Toyota also secured control of Hino (a maker of trucks and buses) by increasing its stake to above 50 percent in 2001, converting it to subsidiary status; Hino has had a business partnership with Toyota since 1966 (Hino, 2011; Toyota, 2010). Renault secured control of Nissan in 1999. The Renault-Nissan alliance is only an alliance in name, as Renault has considerable control over Nissan through a sizeable 43.4 percent stake in the company.

Through a cross-shareholding arrangement, Nissan also has a 15 percent stake in Renault but this stake has no voting rights (Nissan, 2016; Chow and Kubota, 2015). Currently, the French government has a 19.74 percent stake in Renault, which indicates the considerable presence of industrial planning in shaping Renault's strategic direction. The French government exercised this power in 2015 by introducing legislation which increased the power of long-term investors (i.e., itself) in the firm (Renault, 2015; Ruddick, 2015). This demonstration of state power was soon witnessed again in April 2016 when the French government exercising its right as a key shareholder voted against the €7.3 million pay package of Renault's CEO, Mr Carlos Ghosh; Renault eventually capitulated in July 2016 by agreeing to reduce the variable component of Mr Ghosh's salary by a fifth and limit it to no more than 180 percent of his fixed salary (Stothard, 2016; Landauro, 2016).

Despite Renault's recent travails, the Renault-Nissan alliance has, on the whole, generated considerable economies of scale and scope for both companies. Through this alliance, both firms could enter new markets faster and with lower costs as they do not have to build new plants; Renault makes cars in Nissan's Mexican plants while Nissan leverages on Renault's Brazil plant and distribution networks. Further, both companies are collaborating on building common platforms, components and engines. Moreover, each partner excels in complementary aspects of engine design (i.e., Renault has strengths in diesel engines while Nissan leads in gasoline). Together, the partners have augmented purchasing power (with its accompanying expanded bargaining leverage) because they buy components for a considerably larger number of cars (Smith, 2004).

The Renault-Nissan alliance, in its declared mission to join the marquee ranks of the top three global automakers, has stepped up its acquisitive efforts in recent years. In October 2016, Nissan secured a significant 34 percent stake in its troubled smaller rival Mitsubishi for US$2.3 billion. Earlier in May 2016, Mitsubishi, in a mea culpa, confessed to overstating the fuel economy of four of its small car models retailing in Japan and the firm was expected to provide restitution approximating US$1 billion to its affected customers. This incident eradicated a significant 42 percent (about US$3 billion) of Mitsubishi's market capitalisation and provided the circumstances favourable for ravenous rivals to stage an acquisition.

Notwithstanding Mitsubishi's fuel economy scandal and the financial devastation it wrought, it would have been extremely difficult for a relatively small-scale automaker such as Mitsubishi to compete internationally or even maintain its independence in a sea of colossal rivals. In 2015, Mitsubishi produced only a little over 1.2 million vehicles annually, which rendered it highly uncompetitive in an industry with an insatiable appetite for economies of scale and scope; virtually all its other domestic rivals, with the exception of Mazda, produce well over three million vehicles annually. After establishing a foothold in Mitsubishi, the Renault-Nissan alliance in a bid to cement its already considerable grip over the firm, swiftly appointed Nissan's Chief Executive (also Chairman) and Chief Performance Officer, Carlos Ghosn and Trevor Mann to the positions of Mitsubishi's

Chairman and Chief Operating Officer respectively. This aggressive acquisition is expected to give the newly forged trinity of Renault, Nissan and Mitsubishi an annual production volume of approximately 10 million vehicles, placing it in a league traditionally reserved for industry titans, Toyota, and Volkswagen. This emerging leviathan would also be able to strengthen its technological expertise (particularly in the cutting-edge areas of autonomous vehicles and hybrid systems) and slash nearly US$600 million off its cost base by 2018 through joint raw material sourcing efforts (Mclain, 2016; Tajitsu, 2016; International Organization of Motor Vehicle Manufacturers, 2015; Krok, 2016).

Amidst this raging torrent of consolidation sweeping across the industry, the Korean automakers, long viewed as the poor cousin of their American and Japanese rivals, also spied a golden opportunity to ascend the ranks of the marquee automakers. Throughout most of the 1980s and 1990s, the leading automaker, Hyundai, had enjoyed steady, moderate success. On the back of conservative organic growth strategies, Hyundai exported its first batch of cars to the lucrative US market in 1988 and fostered the capability to develop its proprietary diesel engine and transmission system by the beginning of the 1990s. By 1996, the company also opened its first plant in India; this was a milestone, as it was Hyundai's first overseas plant in an emerging market (Chung, 2015). However, this steady rate of growth did not suffice for the emerging Korean automaker which harboured outsized global ambitions. Capitalising on the economic havoc wreaked by the 1998 Asian financial crisis, Hyundai seized the chance to acquire its then debt-laden insolvent rival, Kia for US$886 million in October 1998; Kia, then Korea's eighth largest automaker, experienced a precipitous collapse (and was swiftly placed under bankruptcy protection) in July 1997 under a staggering mountain of debt amounting to US$10.7 billion. Hyundai emerged victorious following an intense bidding war with rivals, Ford, Daewoo and Samsung Motors. Through this decisive victory, Hyundai was able to push its already considerable domestic market share of approximately 45–50 percent to an overwhelming 61 percent in one fell swoop (Pollack, 1997; Drake, 1998; Thornton, 1998). This acquisition also proved instrumental in propelling Hyundai to ninth place globally (in terms of production) by 2001, as it enabled the two firms to share design knowledge, R&D costs over a broad range of models, and in the process achieving unprecedented economies of scale (International Organization of Motor Vehicle Manufacturers, 2001).

To stave off cannibalisation and cover a broad spectrum of the market, Hyundai and Kia deliberately maintained distinctly different branding strategies; this ability to cover an extensive product range was only made possible through Hyundai's acquisition of Kia. Hyundai generally projected a more upmarket image vis-à-vis Kia, as it also makes luxury models such as the Equus and Genesis. Conversely, Kia, with its then emphasis on a youthful and sporty image, targeted the lower end of the market with models such as the Cadenza and Soul (Henry, 2013). This strategy was virtually unchanged until 2010–2011, when Kia started producing the relatively more upscale third-generation Optima; this strategised deviation is possibly due to efforts to spur internal competition in an increasingly powerful automobile group, which could prove vulnerable to the accompanying hubris and stasis prevalent in industrial juggernauts (Kia, 2016; Schmidt, 2016).

2. Emerging market automakers: the savvy dealmakers?

With increasing consolidation at the top-tier levels of their industry, leading automakers from the triad countries are starting to turn their attention at the lower-tier automakers, often as a means of penetrating or augmenting their market share in the emerging markets where these firms are based. For instance, Suzuki acquired a majority stake (54.2 percent) in its Indian joint-venture partner, Maruti Udyog Ltd in May 2002 before changing its name to Maruti Suzuki India Limited by September 2007 (Suzuki, 2002; Suzuki, 2007; Suzuki, 2011). However, some cash rich lower-tier automakers from the emerging markets may buck the trend of leading automakers from triad regions acquiring their less prestigious counterparts. For instance, India's Tata acquired Jaguar and Land Rover from Ford in 2008 for US$2.3 billion, significantly less than the US$5.4 billion which Ford paid for the acquisition of both companies (Koenig and Krishnamoorthy, 2008). Additionally, China's Geely completed a 100 percent acquisition of Volvo from Ford in August 2010, in a deal valued at US$1.5 billion (it comprised US$1.3 billion in cash and a US$200 million loan note), markedly less than the US$6.5 billion which Ford originally paid for the Swedish firm (Kinnander and Naughton, 2010). As in the case of the Jaguar and Land Rover sale, Ford divested Volvo at a significant discount. The fact that Ford was offloading these marquee brands at a fraction of what it originally paid provides strong evidence that the company had failed in assimilating the brands it acquired during its aggressive 1989–2000 acquisition campaign. Moreover, Ford was undergoing a painful restructuring at that time, which further strengthened the case to carry out these divestitures.

The acquisition of these marquee brands has not only given companies such as Tata and Geely access to new technologies, distribution channels and markets but also facilitated their entry into the premium luxury segment. On their own, it would have taken these companies decades and far greater financial investment to develop and build these luxury brands from scratch; industry analysts assert that Geely's acquisition of Volvo enabled it to bypass at least a decade of R&D investment. Nonetheless such acquisitions by emerging country automakers remain rare and they are generally still not in a position to challenge the hegemony of leading triad country automakers.

3. The hegemony of the marquee players

The overwhelming market dominance of the top three automotive makers (i.e., Toyota, Volkswagen and GM) is evident in their global sales. In 2015, these three players sold approximately 10 million vehicles each. By contrast, Geely and its subsidiary, Volvo recorded sales of only around 500,000 vehicles each; even the smaller European automakers, BMW and Daimler had 2015 sales of around

2 million each (Sodempalm and Shanley, 2016). With such a relatively low sales volume, it is extremely difficult for Geely to generate the economies of scale and scope needed to compete with the leading global automakers, which on average sell twenty times as many cars. Further, the fear of diluting Volvo's quality and brand image has also hampered a deeper integration of their production platforms and operations. Thus Geely has not been able to derive the maximum possible economies of scale and scope from its acquisition of Volvo (Milne and Shepherd, 2016a; Milne and Shepherd, 2016b). Geely's integration of Volvo is clearly not a straightforward process. As in any acquisition, the acquirer requires a relatively lengthy period to assimilate legacy systems and cultures, and derive the expected synergies of the merger; this is a positive assumption, as many acquisitions fail to achieve their desired synergies and ultimately unravel (Rosenzweig, 2006).

Where R&D investment is concerned, the three marquee brands (i.e., Toyota, Volkswagen, and GM) also outpaced their emerging country counterparts (e.g., Shanghai Automotive Industry Corporation (hereafter 'SAIC'), Chongqing Changan Automobile Company (hereafter 'Changan'), Dongfeng Motor Group Company (hereafter 'Dongfeng'), Geely, Tata) by a significant margin (see Table 2.3). As evidenced in Table 2.3, Volkswagen records the highest industry R&D expenditure, and its US$15.1 billion commitment to R&D was nearly twice that of second ranked, Toyota's. Moreover, for any given year in the 2011–2015 period, GM's R&D expenditure is considerably more than that of the emerging market players' combined (Volkswagen, 2011–2015; Toyota, 2012–2016; GM, 2013–2015; SAIC, 2012–2015; Dongfeng, 2012–2015; Tata, 2012–2016; Changan, 2012–2015; Geely, 2012–2015).

There were also other acquisitions/partial acquisitions by emerging market players (in a bid to augment their technical and marketing capabilities, and penetrate new markets) of less marquee brands in developed countries. For instance, in 2002, China's SAIC paid US$59.7 million for a 10 percent stake in Daewoo

Table 2.3 Comparison of leading automakers' R&D expenditure against emerging market players' (US$ million)*

Automakers' R&D Expenditure	Country of Origin	2011	2012	2013	2014	2015
Volkswagen	Germany	10,026	12,232	15,596	17,434	15,104
Toyota	Japan	9,488	8,585	8,847	8,359	9,368
GM	US	8,100	7,400	7,200	7,400	7,500
SAIC	China	939.7	916.8	862.5	1,116.5	1,289.1
Dongfeng	China	549.0	96.8	266.6	397.5	445.7
Tata	India	307.6	323.4	351.7	352.5	331.6
Changan	China	255.7	269.8	265.4	328.8	394.7
Geely	China	16.8	32.8	45.2	34.6	39.9

*Leading Automakers refer to Volkswagen, Toyota and GM.

Source: Volkswagen, Toyota, GM, SAIC, Dongfeng, Tata, Changan and Geely Annual Reports

Motor. Further, SAIC grew increasingly ambitious, as it acquired 48.9 percent of SsangYong Motor (hereafter 'SsangYong'), a South Korean maker of SUVs and RVs for US$500 million in July 2004; this was the first major acquisition of a foreign automaker by a Chinese company and expectations were significantly buoyed by national pride (China Daily, 2004). Additionally, China's Nanjing Auto acquired Britain's MG Rover for a reported US$87 million after a protracted acquisition campaign against SAIC and some private equity firms in 2005 (China Daily, 2005). However, in line with mainstream academic research (research suggests 60–75 percent of acquisitions fail), not all of these acquisitions were successful (Rosenzweig, 2006). In SAIC's case, it encountered significant problems after investing heavily in SsangYong. The South Korean managers of SsangYong resisted the technology transfers that SAIC demanded, while SAIC grossly mismanaged tense Korean labour relations. SAIC subsequently withdrew its financial support from SsangYong in 2009, compelling the firm to file for bankruptcy. SAIC then shortsightedly pared its stake in SsangYong to less than 10 percent, thus missing out on the opportunity to maximise its initial investment, as SsangYong later rebounded strongly in a recovering Korean market (EIU, 2011). This incident reveals that failed acquisitions not only involve significant financial risks but also considerable reputational risks, as acquirers (i.e., SAIC) could be viewed as myopic, greedy investors out to milk target companies of their intellectual properties (Zeng and Williamson, 2007).

4. 'Lieutenants' to the automakers

Buffeted by the relentless forces of the cascade effect, these increasingly large automakers, with growing international operations, are also demanding greater support from their suppliers in global technical (includes process improvement), R&D and supply chain support (i.e., suppliers who are able to assemble large complex modules such as entire seating and braking systems for multiple platforms, meet exacting lean practice requirements and participate in next-generation research) as it means that they could spend less resources on managing suppliers, and focus more on higher value-added activities such as marketing, raising finance for developing next-generation technologies and other acquisitions; Automakers that do not commit sufficient resources to these higher value-added activities would not be able to compete effectively in an increasingly oligopolistic market plagued by rising costs (includes R&D, branding, marketing and international expansion costs) and ever-increasing demands for economies of scale and scope.

Further investigation into automotive components companies reveals that automakers such as GM actually encourage their first-tier suppliers to embark on acquisitions to build vertically integrated companies with the capabilities to develop entire vehicle modules. Most automakers want to deal with only a few key suppliers, who act as their lieutenants in managing this increasingly complex global value chain. This rising automaker pressure on their suppliers (resulting from the cascade effect) is evidenced in the following chapters. However, this outsourcing strategy has its limitations. In the current state of affairs, the first-tier mega suppliers acting as lieutenants to their carmaker clients also have their immediate and preferred suppliers, and this arrangement could extend further down the global value chain. There could be at least three to four degrees of separation between the carmaker and the lowest rung supplier. Very often, the actions of the lowest rung supplier could have considerable ramifications for the carmaker. If a rubber supplier from the emerging markets were to supply inferior quality natural rubber to a tyre maker, which in turn uses it for the manufacture of tyres used by its carmaker clients, the consequences would invariably be disastrous. In addition, it may not be possible for the carmaker to immediately isolate the cause of any unfortunate incident, as the root cause may have arisen from a rubber tapper in Indonesia and/or the supervisor of the rubber processing factory who failed to ensure that the quality of the raw material was up to mark; foreign material (e.g., the 'remains' of a Rolex watch) have been known to be found in the natural rubber (procured from Hat Yai, Thailand) slated for the tyre processing plants of Europe.

Moreover, this outsourcing strategy causes critical knowledge and skills to atrophy. In an age where automobiles are increasingly becoming mobile super-computers powered by sophisticated microchips, carmakers have become reliant on a few increasingly oligopolistic semiconductor suppliers (see Chapter 7), and they have become the ones with intimate knowledge of the workings of the vehicles' 'brains'. Even at a less sophisticated level, carmakers may have lost vital mechanical engineering knowledge of how vehicle seats and interiors are put together. Automakers would do well to take heed of this increasing trend, which could mean ceding the future of the automotive industry to their increasingly powerful immediate lieutenants. As evidenced in the coming chapters, many of these so-called lieutenants have become industrial titans in their own right, with the potential to turn the tables on their once dominant clients. Across the five automotive components industries covered in this book, the top two-four players in each field have become market-dominating oligopolists and even duopolists (i.e., CVJs), with significant market shares ranging from approximately two-fifths to over three-quarters of their respective domains. This unprecedented concentration of market power in the hands of a few components suppliers far outstrips the already considerable might wielded by their automaker clients; the top three automakers (i.e., Toyota, Volkswagen, GM) control at best a little more than a third of the vehicular market (Kubota, 2016).

References

Blaško, M., Netter. J.M. and Sinkey Jr., J.F. (2000) The DaimlerChrysler merger, short-term gains, long-run wealth destruction, *Issues in International Corporate Control and Governance*, 15: 299–329.

Brown, W. (1987) Chrysler plans to buy Amc Renault would sell its share, *Morning Call* [internet] Available at: http://articles.mcall.com/1987-03-10/news/2560 460_1_amc-shares-amc-stockholders-amc-officials [Accessed on 18 August, 2016].

Bunkley, N. (2009) Daimler reaches deal to unload Chrysler stake, *nytimes.com* [internet] Available at: www.nytimes.com/2009/04/28/business/28chrysler. html [Accessed on 18 August, 2016].

Castonguay, G. (2012) Fiat to raise stake in Chrysler, *wsj.com* [internet] Available at: http://online.wsj.com/article/SB100014240527023042997045775041336456 30116.html [Accessed on 23 December, 2012].

Chandler, A.D. (1992b) What is a firm? A historical perspective, *European Economic Review*, 36: 483–492.

Chandler, A.D. (1992a) Organizational capabilities and the economic history of the industrial enterprise, *The Journal of Economic Perspectives*, 6(3): 79–100.

China Daily (2004) SAIC takes on Ssangyong motors, *China.org* [internet] Available at: www.china.org.cn/english/2004/Oct/110682.htm [Accessed on 12 February, 2012].

China Daily (2005) Nanjing auto buys collapsed British MG Rover, *China.com.cn* [internet] Available at: www.chinadaily.com.cn/english/doc/2005-07/23/con tent_462703.htm [Accessed on 12 February, 2012].

Chongqing Changan Automobile Company Limited (2012) *2012 Annual Report*, Chongqing: Chongqing Changan Automobile Company Limited.

Chongqing Changan Automobile Company Limited (2014) *2014 Annual Report*, Chongqing: Chongqing Changan Automobile Company Limited.

Chongqing Changan Automobile Company Limited (2015) *2015 Annual Report*, Chongqing: Chongqing Changan Automobile Company Limited.

Chow, J. and Kubota, Y. (2015) French government, Renault agree on double-voting rights, *wsj.com* [internet] Available at: www.wsj.com/articles/french-government-renault-agree-on-double-voting-rights-1449851048 [Accessed on 14 August, 2016].

Chung, M-K (2015) A retrospective of entrepreneurship in the global financial crisis, in Yu, T.F-L. and Yan, H-D. (eds), *Handbook of East Asian entrepreneurship*, Routledge: New York.

CNN Money (2000) Ford buys Land Rover, *CNN Money* [internet] Available at: http://money.cnn.com/2000/03/17/europe/ford/ [Accessed on 14 August, 2016].

Colias, M. (2013) U.S. sells last of GM shares, ending 'Government Motors' era, *Autonews* [internet] Available at: www.autonews.com/article/20131209/OEM/ 131209866/u.s.-sells-last-of-gm-shares-ending-government-motors-era [Accessed on 17 August, 2016].

Dongfeng Motor Group Company Limited (2012) *2012 Annual Report*, Wuhan: Dongfeng Motor Group Company Limited.

Dongfeng Motor Group Company Limited (2013) *2013 Annual Report*, Wuhan: Dongfeng Motor Group Company Limited.

Dongfeng Motor Group Company Limited (2014) *2014 Annual Report*, Wuhan: Dongfeng Motor Group Company Limited.

Dongfeng Motor Group Company Limited (2015) *2015 Annual Report*, Wuhan: Dongfeng Motor Group Company Limited.

Drake, N. (1998) Thermoplastics and Thermoplastics Composites in the Automotive Industry 1997–2000, Shawbury: Rapra Technology Limited.

Ebhardt, T. and Clothier, M. (2014) Fiat gains full control of Chrysler in $4.35 billion deal, *Bloomberg* [internet] Available at: www.bloomberg.com/news/

articles/2014-01-01/fiat-agrees-to-buy-rest-of-chrysler-in-4-35-billion-deal [Accessed on 15 August, 2016].

Economist Intelligence Unit (2011) China cars: Key player – SAIC, *EIU* [internet] Available at: http://viewswire.eiu.com/index.asp?layout=ib3Article&article_id= 718266656&pubtypeid=1112462496&country_id=1800000180&fs=true [Accessed on 11 February, 2012].

Geely Automobile Holdings Limited (2012) *Annual Report 2012*, Hangzhou: Geely Automobile Holdings Limited.

Geely Automobile Holdings Limited (2013) *Annual Report 2013*, Hangzhou: Geely Automobile Holdings Limited.

Geely Automobile Holdings Limited (2014) *Annual Report 2014*, Hangzhou: Geely Automobile Holdings Limited.

Geely Automobile Holdings Limited (2015) *Annual Report 2015*, Hangzhou: Geely Automobile Holdings Limited.

Greimel, H. (2009) GM buys Suzuki's stake in CAMI joint-venture, *Automotive News* [internet] Available at: www.autonews.com/article/20091204/ OEM01/912049998/gm-buys-suzukis-stake-in-cami-joint-venture [Accessed on 14 August, 2014].

Groupe Renault (2015) *2015 Annual Report*, Boulogne-Billancourt Cedex: Groupe Renault.

Henry, J. (2013) Balancing Act: Hyundai and Kia share products under the skin, but must not blur identities, *Forbes* [internet] Available at: www.forbes.com/sites/jim henry/2013/05/31/balancing-act-hyundai-and-kia-share-products-under-the-skin-but-must-avoid-blurring-identities/#1cca3e3b7cc8 [Accessed on 7 January, 2017].

Hino Motors Ltd (2011) Milestones after establishment, *Hino* [internet] Available at: www.hino-global.com/about_us/organization/milestones.html [Accessed on 16 November, 2011).

Holusha, H. (1987) Chrysler is buying American Motors; cost is US$1.5 billion, *nytimes.com* [internet] Available at: www.nytimes.com/1987/03/10/business/ chrysler-is-buying-american-motors-cost-is-1.5-billion.html [Accessed on 14 August, 2016].

IHS Markit (2007) Reports Say Tata will buy Jaguar and Land Rover, but when? *IHS Markit* [internet] Available at: www.ihs.com/country-industry-forecasting. html?ID=106597312 [Accessed on 14 August, 2016].

International Organization of Motor Vehicle Manufacturers (1998) 1998 World motor vehicle production by manufacturer: World ranking, *OICA.net* [internet] Available at: www.oica.net/wp-content/uploads/2007/06/cl98cons2.pdf [Accessed on 12 August, 2016].

International Organization of Motor Vehicle Manufacturers (2001) World motor vehicle production by manufacturer: World ranking 2001, *OICA.net* [internet] Available at: www.oica.net/wp-content/uploads/2007/06/worldranking2001. pdf [Accessed on 7 January, 2017].

International Organization of Motor Vehicle Manufacturers (2008) World motor vehicle production: World ranking of manufacturers- year 2008, *OICA.net* [internet] Available at: http://oica.net/wp-content/uploads/world-ranking-2008.pdf [Accessed on 7 January, 2017].

International Organization of Motor Vehicle Manufacturers (2015) World motor vehicle production: World ranking of manufacturers- year 2015, *OICA.net* [internet]

Available at: www.oica.net/wp-content/uploads//ranking2015.pdf [Accessed on 25 December, 2016].

Jaguar Land Rover Automatic Plc (2014) *Annual Report 2013–14*, Coventry: Jaguar Land Rover Automatic Plc.

Jaguar Land Rover Automatic Plc (2015) *Annual Report 2014–15*, Coventry: Jaguar Land Rover Automatic Plc.

Jaguar Land Rover Automatic Plc (2016) *Annual Report 2015–16*, Coventry: Jaguar Land Rover Automatic Plc.

Jurgens, U. (1995) VW at a turning point- success and crisis of a German production concept, Working Paper, *Actes Du GERPISA* N°10.

Kia Motors Corporation (2016) High-class cabin and cutting-edge technology for stylish all new Kia Optima, *Kia Motors Corporation* [internet] Available at: https://press.kia.com/eu/products/optima/optima%202016/ [Accessed on 7 January, 2017].

Kinnander, O. and Naughton, K. (2010) Geely seals takeover of Volvo from Ford; Jacoby Named CEO, *Bloomberg* [internet] Available at: www.bloomberg.com/news/2010-08-02/geely-said-to-announce-completion-of-volvo-cars-purchase-from-ford-today.html [Accessed on 18 March, 2012].

Koenig, B. and Krishnamoorthy, A. (2008) Ford motor sells Land Rover, Jaguar to India's Tata (Update5), *Bloomberg.com* [internet] Available at: www.bloomberg.com/apps/news?pid=newsarchive&sid=aYOSbXIDi3g4 [Accessed on 15 March, 2012].

Krisher, T. (2011) Fiat stake in Chrysler rises to 30%, aiming for 51%, *Associated Press* [internet] Available at: http://usatoday30.usatoday.com/money/autos/2011-04-12-fiat-chrysler-stake.htm [Accessed on 18 February, 2012].

Krok, A. (2016) Nissan finalizes Mitsubishi deal, let the cost-cutting begin, *CNET* [internet] Available at: www.cnet.com/roadshow/news/nissan-acquires-34-per cent-controlling-stake-in-mitsubishi/ [Accessed on 27 December, 2016].

Kubota, Y. (2016) Toyota again No. 1 in global car sales, *MarketWatch* [internet] Available at: www.marketwatch.com/story/toyota-again-no-1-in-global-car-sales-2016-01-26 [Accessed on 6 January, 2017].

Landauro, I. (2016) Renault board cuts CEO's 2016 pay after spat with shareholders, *wsj.com* [internet] Available at: www.wsj.com/articles/renault-board-cuts-ceos-2016-pay-after-spat-with-shareholders-1469656763 [Accessed on 27 August, 2016].

Lawniczak, J.M. (2010) When the business of government is business: The U.S. auto industry and the future of government bailouts, *TMA* [internet] Available at: the Turnaround Management Association website: www.turnaround.org/Publications/Articles.aspx?objectID=12653 [Accessed on 16 February, 2014].

Mclain, S. (2016) Nissan formally takes controlling stake in Mitsubishi motors, *wsj.com* [internet] Available at: www.wsj.com/articles/nissan-formally-takes-controlling-stake-in-mitsubishi-motors-1476965004 [Accessed on 27 December, 2016].

Milne, R. and Shepherd, C. (2016a) Volvo and Geely aim to deepen ties, *FT.com* [internet] Available at: www.ft.com/cms/s/0/f12a0a52-3489-11e6-bda0-04585c31b153.html#axzz4H7F0PzZd [Accessed on 12 August, 2016].

Milne, R. and Shepherd, C. (2016b) Volvo: Remaking the marque, *FT.com* [internet] Available at: www.ft.com/cms/s/0/bfed4c32-339f-11e6-bda0-04585c31b153.html#axzz4H7F0PzZd [Accessed on 12 August, 2016].

Nissan Motor Corporation (2016) *Alliance Facts and Figures 2016*, Yokohama: Nissan Motor Corporation.

NPR (2008) Examining Chrysler's 1979 rescue, *NPR* [internet] Available at: NPR website: www.npr.org/templates/story/story.php?storyId=96922222 [Accessed on 16 February, 2016].

Pollack, A. (1995) International business; Toyota doubles its holdings in Daihatsu motor of Japan, *nytimes.com* [internet] Available at: www.nytimes.com/1995/09/21/business/international-business-toyota-doubles-its-holdings-in-daihatsu-motor-of-japan.html [Accessed on 10 March, 2012].

Pollack, A. (1997) Koreans place Kia Motors under bankruptcy shield, *nytimes.com* [internet] Available at: www.nytimes.com/1997/07/16/business/koreans-place-kia-motors-under-bankruptcy-shield.html [Accessed on 7 January, 2017].

Reuters (1982) Isuzu-G.M. pact, *nytimes.com* [internet] Available at: www.nytimes.com/1982/07/05/business/isuzu-gm-pact.html [Accessed on 23 February, 2014].

Rosenzweig, P. (2006) Learn to stay on track for transaction success, *FT.com* [internet] Available at: www.ft.com/cms/s/2/369523ca-4e34-11db-bcbc-0000779e2340.html#axzz1MB1kZTNK [Accessed on 12 May, 2011].

Ruddick, G. (2015) Renault-Nissan agree truce after French government vows to limit its interference, *The Guardian* [internet] Available at: www.theguardian.com/business/2015/dec/11/renault-nissan-agree-truce-after-french-government-vows-to-limit-its-interference [Accessed on 15 August, 2016].

SAIC Motor Corporation Limited (2012) *Annual Report 2012*, Shanghai: SAIC Motor Corporation Limited.

SAIC Motor Corporation Limited (2013) *Annual Report 2013*, Shanghai: SAIC Motor Corporation Limited.

SAIC Motor Corporation Limited (2014) *Annual Report 2014*, Shanghai: SAIC Motor Corporation Limited.

SAIC Motor Corporation Limited (2015) *Annual Report 2015*, Shanghai: SAIC Motor Corporation Limited.

Scherer, F.M. (1996) *Industry Structure, Strategy and Public Policy*, New York: HarperCollins College Publishers.

Schmid, J. (1998) Daimler-Benz takes over Chrysler as VW acquires Rolls-Royce: Fast lane for German firms, *nytimes.com* [internet] Available at: www.nytimes.com/1998/05/08/news/08iht-daimler.t_0.html [Accessed on 14 August, 2016].

Schmidt, D. (2016) Kia's next-gen 2017 Cadenza capably competes with anyone's full-sized sedan, *AutoWritersInk* [internet] Available at: www.theoaklandpress.com/lifestyle/20161221/kias-next-gen-2017-cadenza-capably-competes-with-anyones-full-sized-sedan [Accessed on7 January, 2017].

Schmitt, B. (2016) Nice Try VW: Toyota again world's largest automaker, *Forbes* [internet] Available at: www.forbes.com/sites/bertelschmitt/2016/01/27/nice-try-vw-toyota-again-worlds-largest-automaker/#31f3c4642b65 [Accessed on 26 December, 2016].

Shuchman, L. and White, J.B. (1998) Auto consolidation heats up as GM increases Isuzu stake, *wsj.com* [internet] Available at: www.wsj.com/articles/SB913969967044744500 [Accessed on 14 August, 2016].

Smith, N.D. (2004) Nissan-Renault alliance faces down a few challenges, *MIT News* [internet] Available at: http://web.mit.edu/newsoffice/2004/ghosn.html [Accessed on 12 November, 2011].

Soderpalm, H. and Shanley, M. (2016) China's Geely cars think big with Volvo makeover, *Reuters* [internet] Available at: www.reuters.com/article/us-autos-geely-design-idUSKCN0Y81C3 [Accessed on 12 August, 2016].

Stothard, M. (2016) French government warns Renault to change Ghosn pay deal, *ft.com* [internet] Available at: www.ft.com/cms/s/0/7d633ec8-113d-11e6-91da-096d89bd2173.html?siteedition=intl#axzz4IVwALvOb [Accessed on 27 August, 2016].

Sturgeon T.J. and Van Biesebroeck, J. (2009) Crisis and protection in the automotive industry: A global value chain perspective, *Poverty Reduction and Economic Management Network*, Policy Research Working Paper, 5060, Washington DC: The World Bank, International Trade Department.

Sudarsanam, S. (2010) *Creating Value From Mergers and Acquisitions: The Challenges*, Second Edition, Essex: Pearson Education Limited.

Suzuki Motor Corporation (2002) Suzuki gains majority stake in Maruti Udyog Limited, India, *Globalsuzuki.com* [internet] Available at: www.globalsuzuki.com/globalnews/2002/0516.html [Accessed on 10 May, 2012].

Suzuki Motor Corporation (2007) Suzuki Indian subsidiary changing name to Maruti Suzuki India Limited, *Globalsuzuki.com* [internet] Available at: www.globalsuzuki.com/globalnews/2007/0726.html [Accessed on 10 May, 2012].

Suzuki Motor Corporation (2011) Maruti Suzuki India's production reaches 10 million units, *Globalsuzuki.com* [internet] Available at: www.globalsuzuki.com/globalnews/2011/0315.html [Accessed on 10 May, 2012].

Suzuki Motor Corporation (2016) *History*, Suzuki [internet] Available at: www.globalsuzuki.com/corporate/history/1980.html [Accessed on 14 August, 2016]

Tajitsu, N. (2016) Mitsubishi Motors says has cash to ride out widening mileage affair, *Reuters* [internet] Available at: www.reuters.com/article/us-mitsubishimotors-scandal-briefing-idUSKCN0Y20G0 [Accessed on 8 January, 2017].

Tata Motors (2013) *68th Annual Report 2012–2013*, Mumbai: Tata Motors.

Tata Motors (2014) *69th Annual Report 2013–2014*, Mumbai: Tata Motors.

Tata Motors (2015) *70th Annual Report 2014–2015*, Mumbai: Tata Motors.

Tata Motors (2016) *71st Annual Report 2015–2016*, Mumbai: Tata Motors.

The Japan Times (1998) Toyota to take over Daihatsu Motor. The Japan Times [online] Available at: http://search.japantimes.co.jp/cgi-bin/nn19980828a4.html [Accessed on 27 February, 2010].

The New York Times (1986) G.M. acquires 59.7% of Lotus, nytimes.com [internet] Available at: www.nytimes.com/1986/01/23/business/gm-acquires-59.7-of-lotus.html [Accessed on 23 December, 2012].

Thornton, E. (1998) Hyundai Kia: Car deal or car crash? *Bloomberg* [internet] Available at: www.bloomberg.com/news/articles/1998-11-08/hyundai-kia-car-deal-or-car-crash-intl-edition [Accessed on 8 January, 2017].

Toyota Motor Corporation (2010) *Annual Report 2010: Year Ended March 31 2010*, Nagoya: Toyota Motor Corporation.

Toyota Motor Corporation (2012) *Form 20-F*, Nagoya: Toyota Motor Corporation.

Toyota Motor Corporation (2013) *Form 20-F*, Nagoya: Toyota Motor Corporation.

Toyota Motor Corporation (2014) *Form 20-F*, Nagoya: Toyota Motor Corporation.

Toyota Motor Corporation (2015) *Form 20-F*, Nagoya: Toyota Motor Corporation.

Toyota Motor Corporation (2016) *Form 20-F*, Nagoya: Toyota Motor Corporation.

U.S. Securities and Exchange Commission (2001) In re DaimlerChrysler securities litigation, *U.S. Securities and Exchange Commission* [internet] Available at: www.sec.gov/Archives/edgar/data/1067318/000091205701509243/a2044963zex-99_3.txt [Accessed on 28 December, 2016].

Vlasic, B. and Stertz, B.A. (2001) *Taken for a Ride: How Daimler-Benz Drove Off With Chrysler*, New York: HarperCollins Publishers Inc.

Whoriskey, P. (2011) GM and Chrysler, owned by the government, lobby the government, *washingtonpost.com* [internet] Available at: www.washingtonpost.com/wp-dyn/content/article/2011/01/13/AR2011011306544.html [Accessed on 17 August, 2016].

Zeng, M. and Williamson P.J. (2007) Dragons at Your Door: How Chinese Cost Innovation Is Disrupting the Rules of Global Competition, Boston, MA: Harvard Business School Press.

3   The global tyres sector

1. Introduction

Despite its relatively staid image, the global tyre market totalled an estimated US$187.2 billion in 2015, with light-vehicle tyres and truck tyres accounting for 60 percent and 30 percent of tyre sales respectively. Currently, three out of four tyres are sold in the replacement market (TireBusiness.com, 2015b).[1] It is in this supposedly traditional global tyre industry that one sees the real impact of the 'centralisation of capital' (i.e., M&A) wrought by the cascade effect (Marx, 1961). In fact, the US tyre industry was probably the most affected by the wave of M&A that transpired in the 1980s. For instance, 75 percent of the companies in the US tyre industry (accounting for 90 percent of the value) experienced a takeover bid or were forced to restructure during the 1982–89 period (Mitchell and Mulherin, 1996). Consequently, control changed hands in over half the companies in this industry. In most cases, control was transferred to foreign owners. By the end of the decade, traditional American firms like Firestone, Uniroyal, Goodrich, Armstrong, and General Tire belonged to foreign companies. Resultantly, large US-owned tyre manufacturers, which accounted for 59 percent of global tyre production in 1971, represented only 17 percent by 1991.

During this period, the number of US-owned tyre manufacturers in the global top five positions (by production) also fell from four to only one (Rajan, Volpin and Zingales, 2000). Conversely, most of the European and Japanese tyre companies were relatively difficult to acquire. Michelin, the leading French tyre maker has historically been fully controlled by a limited partnership, a legal structure that provides virtually unassailable fortification against potential hostile acquisitions (Betts, 2010). Back in the 1980s, where consolidation was rife in the global tyres market, it was Francois Michelin (Michelin's unlimited partner), rather than the majority of Michelin shareholders, that determined Michelin's corporate future. Similarly, in the case of Continental, its convoluted web of shareholdings prevented Pirelli from acquiring it in 1990. As for Japanese tyre companies (e.g., Bridgestone), they enjoy even greater protection from takeovers due to their significantly more complicated cross-shareholdings system (Rajan, Volpin and Zingales, 2000). On the other hand, US companies such as Goodyear were forbidden by antitrust regulations to buy their domestic competitors (e.g., Firestone) (Mercer, 1990). This situation gave the leading European and Japanese tyre makers a distinctly unfair advantage, as they aggressively acquired US tyre makers in the 1980s, culminating in their eventual market dominance (Bridgestone and Michelin are now the world's top two tyre makers).

By 2015, Bridgestone and Michelin recorded global market shares (by revenues) of 16.8 percent (US$31.4 billion) and 12.6 percent (US$23.6 billion) respectively, with once dominant tyre maker, Goodyear possessing 8.8 percent (US$16.4 billion) in third place (Bridgestone, 2015; Michelin, 2015b; Goodyear, 2015). These three companies had secured their approximate 40 percent global market share through a series of M&A since the 1980s. They also position themselves as marquee brands and claim not to compete with low-end brands (e.g., Doublestar, GITI, Hangzhou Zhongce from China). This is partially evidenced by a statement from Keith Price, Goodyear's Director of Director National Media Relations and Business Communications who stated: 'The stuff coming in from China is primarily low end. We got out of that market years ago' (Price, 2012). Other key tyre companies (the so-called 'second-tiers') include Continental, Pirelli, Cooper Tire & Rubber Company (hereafter 'Cooper'), Maxxis International (hereafter 'Maxxis'), Hankook Tire Co., Ltd. (hereafter 'Hankook'), Toyo Tire & Rubber Co (hereafter 'Toyo'), Kumho Tires Co., Inc. (hereafter 'Kumho') and the Yokohama Rubber Co., Ltd (hereafter 'Yokohama').

2. The cascade effect's impact on tyre makers

The current state of the global tyres industry has been largely shaped by the tremendous industrial consolidation that has transpired at the automaker level. The significant consolidation among the automakers has greatly impacted the industry structure of the automotive industry through the cascade effect. This cascade effect has resulted in automakers (with their cutting-edge technologies and global marketing capabilities) actively selecting their most competent suppliers (in this case, tyre manufacturers), in a form of 'industrial planning'. These automakers typically pick 'aligned suppliers' who can work with them globally while concurrently providing them with products that are competitively priced.[2] This cascade effect also generates intense pressures for first-tier suppliers such as the global tyre companies to themselves merge and acquire, and develop leading global positions (Nolan, 2008). These suppliers, in turn, pass on this intense pressure to their own supplier networks (i.e., the natural rubber suppliers). This consolidation of the global tyre industry has granted these oligopolists unprecedented market power, which they have ruthlessly used to lower procurement costs.

The automakers have long practised the strategy of pitting tyre manufacturers against one another, in an attempt to extract the best possible bargain. This strategy has enabled them to avoid the costly investment of building their own tyre factories, with the exception of Ford, which briefly did so in 1938. Despite the fact that tyre manufacturers draw most of their revenues from the replacement market, the automaker market has historically been important because it provides large orders (along with the scale) as well as the prospect of future replacement sales (car owners usually replace tyres with the same original brand) (Rajan, Volpin and Zingales, 2000). However, with the increasing size of the leading tyre manufacturers, there could be a shift in this 'balance of power' as these tyre manufacturers have become industry titans themselves, and gained considerably more latitude in the pricing process.

As a consequence of the cascade effect, leading automakers (intending to focus on their core value-added activities such as marketing, raising finance, next-generation R&D and building a global brand) place considerable pressure on their first-tier suppliers (i.e., the major tyre companies) to attain the technical progress critical in the provision of high-quality inputs, the mainstay in addressing the demands of end customers (Nolan, 2008). In short, the tyre companies are expected to be technological innovators. By the mid-1980s, the R&D expenses of the key tyre companies had reached astronomical levels ranging from a few hundred million to over a billion dollars (e.g., Goodyear's annual R&D expenses reached as high as US$1 billion in 1986), compelling these companies to consolidate (via means of mergers) so as to secure greater economies of scale and scope (Krueger, 1991).

Further, automakers have leveraged their immense procurement budgets to maximise the efficiency of their supply chain, by requiring that major tyre companies meet their just-in-time requirements worldwide; GM's existing procurement budget is estimated to be around US$80 billion (Nolan, 2014). According to Raghuram Rajan of the University of Chicago, these tyre manufacturers 'must have a distribution set-up capable of giving Detroit what it wants, where it's wanted – and on time' (Rajan, Volpin and Zingales, 2000). Thus it is no surprise in Japan, Bridgestone, the world's largest tyre manufacturer, has a key plant in the Tochigi prefecture with rapid access to leading automaker customers such as Toyota and Honda which are located in the same area; independent supplier plants (known as 'dokuritsu kaisha') such as Bridgestone are usually about 87 miles away (at most a few hours' drive) from automakers such as Toyota (Bridgestone, 2012). However the Japanese earthquake in March 2011 exposed the vulnerability of the 'just-in-time' system and the price Japanese automakers have paid for their cult-like devotion to this practice; Bridgestone's plant in Tochigi and surrounding areas, along with that of their automaker clients (e.g., Honda and Toyota) were all crippled by the earthquake (Wassener and Nicholson, 2011).

3. The leading tyre makers

The powerful forces generated by the cascade effect have had a transformative effect on the industry structure of the leading tyre companies, who play the role of first-tier suppliers (i.e., subsystems integrators) to the automakers. Through 'the centralisation of capital' triggered by the cascade effect, firms such as Bridgestone, Michelin and Goodyear have emerged to dominate the tyre industry. As mentioned earlier, these three firms accounted for about 40 percent of global tyre market sales and had combined revenues of around US$71.4 billion in 2015. Today, the top three market positions in the global tyres industry are typically occupied by these three players, with all three seemingly taking turns to occupy the position of industry leader in this high-stakes game of 'musical chairs'.

However, unlike their automaker clients, these tyre companies enjoy considerably more market power over their natural rubber suppliers and are able to use their massive procurement budgets and economies of scale to compel them to grant significant discounts. Compared to the oligopolistic tyre manufacturers, rubber suppliers could be described as being in a purely competitive industry (relatively speaking), as their industry is defined by hallmarks of pure competition which are numerous sellers, homogenous products and relative ease of entry.

Currently, scores of rubber suppliers of varying sizes across Thailand, Indonesia and Malaysia (these three countries account for 75 percent of the global rubber production) supply rubber to these titans who control over half the world's tyre production (Rubberbands, 2010). In such situations, companies such as Goodyear, Bridgestone and Michelin are able to lower their procurement costs (to some extent) by asking for price reductions from this army of rubber suppliers with limited bargaining power; if a rubber supplier does not acquiesce when a discount is 'requested', it could lose its business to a more compliant competitor eager to gain business from leading tyre makers such as Goodyear; even the world's largest vertically integrated natural rubber supplier, Thailand's Von Bundit (the company has over 6,000 employees with annual processing capacity of 1.842 million metric tons in 2015) has revenues of approximately US\$1.71 billion (5.18 percent of global natural rubber sales) in 2015, a relatively 'paltry' sum compared to Goodyear's 2015 revenues which was nearly tenfold at US\$16.4 billion and Goodyear is the smallest among the top three tyre makers (Von Bundit, 2016; Goodyear, 2015).[3] These suppliers (as indicated in a discussion with a Goodyear Purchasing Manager) would then defend their positions by claiming rubber supply has been limited by conditions such as inclement weather (in the 2003–2011 period, strong demand from China has been cited as a reason too), thus making it harder for them to meet the price demands of these tyre manufacturers (Goodyear, 2001; Goodyear, 2011b).

Nonetheless, Goodyear's market power (along with that of Bridgestone and Michelin) could be undermined if their rubber suppliers started to consolidate and merge among themselves (moving towards a more oligopolistic market structure), thus augmenting their bargaining position and altering the balance of power in the process. This would be an extension of the cascade effect, which affects even the suppliers of the first-tier suppliers/subsystems integrators (i.e., the tyre manufacturers). However, these natural rubber suppliers are still a long way from matching the sheer market power wielded by the three key tyre companies (i.e., Bridgestone, Michelin and Goodyear), which is derived from their significant economies of scale and scope.

These gargantuan tyre producers have achieved their dominant oligopolistic positions through a relentless series of M&A (over the past few decades) triggered by the cascade effect; interviews with Goodyear's management suggest that the tyres industry has consolidated at the marquee brand level (i.e., Goodyear, Bridgestone and Michelin) but is still expected to consolidate at the second/third-tier level (i.e., second and third-tier tyre companies such as Kumho and Hangzhou Zhongce are still expected to consolidate over the coming years in their bid to improve quality, secure greater economies of scale and scope and possibly compete with the marquee brands). The following sections examine the M&A that these companies have undergone, since the 1980s, when merger activities were most intense. The 1980s was a decisive period for the major tyre companies, as industry power was fast being consolidated in the hands of three oligopolists, with America's leading tyre makers, Firestone and Uniroyal Goodrich being at the centre of this struggle for market dominance.

Bridgestone: profile

Despite the vicissitudes enveloping the industry, Bridgestone began 2016 as the world's largest tyre company.[4] In 2015, it posted annual revenues of US$31.4 billion, giving it a reigning 16.8 percent global market share; it was by far the most profitable among the top three tyre makers with a net income of US$2.357 billion. At the end of 2015, Bridgestone also recorded over 180 manufacturing plants and R&D facilities located in 25 countries worldwide, with total staff strength of 144,303 employees (Bridgestone, 2015). For 2015, Bridgestone derived 84 percent (about US$26.4 billion) of its revenues from its tyres business (Figure 3.1). Moreover, for that year, Bridgestone earned approximately 51 percent (about US$16 billion) of its revenues from the Americas, an outcome of its acquisition of Firestone in 1988 (see following section). Other significant countries/regions include Japan and Europe which accounted for 17 percent (approximately US$5.3 billion) and 11 percent (around US$3.5 billion) of its 2015 revenues respectively (Figure 3.2).

Bridgestone, like its key competitors (i.e., Michelin, Goodyear) obtains at least 75 percent of its sales from the replacement markets (Balboni et al., 2010; Michelin, 2015a). Major tyre makers such as Bridgestone prefer selling to replacement markets rather than automakers as these gargantuan carmakers tend to insist on significant discounts. Further the automaker market tends to be more cyclical, as people may postpone car purchases in an economic downturn, resulting in poorer sales for tyre makers. Conversely, while people may postpone purchases of new cars, they would still need to replace their tyres, thus making the replacement market a more attractive and stable revenue stream (Hicks, 1990). However, this does not mean that Bridgestone and other major tyre makers would ditch selling directly to automakers entirely. This is because the more motorists purchase an automaker's vehicles, with Bridgestone's tyres (or its competitor's) as original equipment (hereafter 'OE'), the more these motorists would look to replace those tyres later by buying the same brands for retail prices. Thus the replacement market is evidently the tyre industry's 'cash cow' and servicing automakers is, for tyre manufacturers, ultimately necessary for garnering retail sales (Yamanouchi, 2001). Further, Bridgestone views its relationship with automakers as a means of developing relevant next-generation technologies. This is evidenced in the following statement (on its relationship with automakers) from Mike Martini, original-equipment tyre sales chief for the U.S. and Canada Consumer Tyre Sales

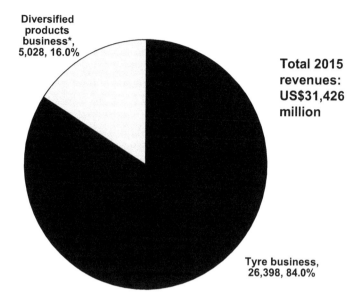

Diversified
products
business*,
5,028, 16.0%

Total 2015
revenues:
US$31,426
million

Tyre business,
26,398, 84.0%

Figure 3.1 Bridgestone's 2015 annual revenues (US$ million)

Diversified Products Business*- Chemical and Industrial Products, Sporting Goods, Bicycles and Other

Source: 2015 Bridgestone Annual Report

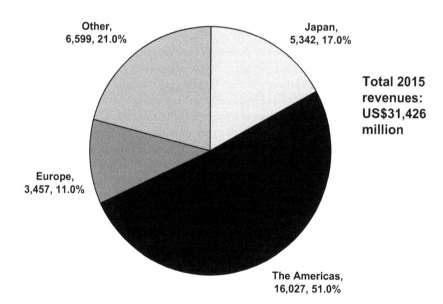

Other,
6,599, 21.0%

Japan,
5,342, 17.0%

Total 2015
revenues:
US$31,426
million

Europe,
3,457, 11.0%

The Americas,
16,027, 51.0%

Figure 3.2 Bridgestone's 2015 revenues by region (US$ million)

Source: 2015 Bridgestone Annual Report

Division of Bridgestone Americas Tyre Operations: 'We're really in lock step with them' and he also added: 'Our team is with them every single day. That's how you develop the appropriate technology' (quoted in Meyer, 2011).

In 2015, Bridgestone recorded procurement expenses of US$4.6 billion (Bridgestone, 2015). This sizeable procurement budget gives Bridgestone significant power over its rubber suppliers and positions it well to play one against another, easily extracting discounts on purchases. Even the world's largest natural rubber supplier, Von Bundit has revenues (about US$1.8 billion in 2015) that is barely 6 percent of Bridgestone's overall revenues; in truth, Bridgestone's 2015 purchasing spend (US$4.6 billion) alone eclipses Von Bundit's revenues for that year. The next biggest suppliers, Sri Trang recorded 2015 revenues of approximately US$1.7 billion (Sri Trang, 2015); these are relatively miniscule figures compared to the revenues of the top three tyre makers that are independently well in excess of US$10 billion.

To mitigate its dependence on these disparate rubber suppliers, Bridgestone has acquired nearly 24,000 hectares of rubber (the largest internal reserve among the major tyre producers) spread across two sizeable plantations in Indonesia; the plants are respectively the P. T. Bridgestone Sumatra Rubber Estate and P. T. Bridgestone Kalimantan Plantation (Bridgestone, 2010). Although these plantations are still not able to meet all of Bridgestone's raw material needs, they nonetheless augment Bridgestone's bargaining position in price negotiations with its suppliers.

Bridgestone's acquisitions since the 1980s

By the time Bridgestone celebrated its 50th anniversary in March 1981, it had the strategic intent of becoming one of the top three global tyre and rubber companies, by consolidating its domestic market and ramping up its overseas expansion strategy. As part of this growth strategy, it first acquired a tyre plant in Tennessee from Firestone (then America's third largest tyre manufacturer) in 1983 for US$52 million. This factory was Firestone's La Vergne factory and it represented Bridgestone's first North American manufacturing facility; the US was becoming increasingly important for Bridgestone at that time, as it represented 45 percent of global tyre sales. Further, Bridgestone commenced production of truck and bus radial tyres at the La Vergne plant in that same year. This acquisition also greatly bolstered Bridgestone's distribution system in North America (Bridgestone, 2012; Hicks, 1988). In March 1988, Bridgestone consolidated its acquisition strategy by purchasing the rest of Firestone for US$2.6 billion in cash (a premium of 160 percent) and the payment of this outsized premium is indicative of the escalating competition between Bridgestone and its rivals in their tussle to secure control of the tyre industry (Rajan, Volpin and Zingales, 2000); Firestone at the point of its acquisition held 15 percent of the US tyre market and 8 percent of the global market (Brooks, 1988; Hicks, 1988). Bridgestone had gained control of Firestone by trumping a competing offer of US$1.86 billion from Pirelli; the Firestone bid offered Pirelli an opportunity to become a key player in a rapidly globalising industry. Pirelli had also hoped to gain a larger foothold in the highly profitable US market and concurrently disrupt the internationalisation strategy of Bridgestone, which was already a formidable competitor of the firm in Europe (Hicks, 1988).

To ensure its successful acquisition of Firestone, Bridgestone had to more than double its original bid of US$1.25 billion (made in February 1988) for a 75 percent stake in the firm, trumping Pirelli's bid by around 40 percent (Brooks, 1988; Hicks, 1988); Bridgestone decided to acquire all of Firestone in March 1988 instead of the 75 percent stake it had earlier sought, as it did not want Pirelli to secure control of Firestone's assets and significant market share (Mackinnon, 2008).[5]

The fierce bidding war for Firestone reflects the drive towards an increasingly oligopolistic structure in the global tyres industry, an outcome of the powerful forces cascading across the global automotive supply chain compelling the suppliers (i.e., the tyre makers) to the automakers to themselves consolidate and build dominant global positions (Nolan, 2009). Bridgestone's acquisition of Firestone not only represented the single largest investment made by Corporate Japan in an American manufacturing citadel but also enabled the former (then the world's third largest tyre and rubber company) to challenge its key rivals Goodyear and Michelin for industry supremacy (Hicks, 1988). This acquisition gave Bridgestone a large number of production sites in North America, Central and South America, Europe, and other locations; the deal involved four factories in the United States and 11 overseas, along with 30,000 employees worldwide (mostly in the US). Moreover, this acquisition gave Bridgestone control of Firestone's domestic network of 1,500 automobile service centres, where its tyres are sold; prior to its acquisition of Firestone, Bridgestone sold its tyres in the US through independent dealers and at stores of Montgomery Ward & Company, and the automobile components stores owned by the Pep Boys chain (Hicks, 1988). Bridgestone also began operations in Turkey under a joint management agreement in 1988. In a move to reflect the company's enhanced corporate identity, Bridgestone Tire Co., Ltd. was subsequently renamed Bridgestone Corporation in 1984 (Hicks, 1988; Bridgestone, 2012). By 1992, Firestone was fully integrated into Bridgestone's operations and Bridgestone/Firestone's corporate headquarters was moved from Akron, Ohio to Nashville Tennessee (Bridgestone Americas, 2012).

Since then, Bridgestone has been relatively more circumspect in its acquisition attempts. Bridgestone did not make any high-profile acquisitions until March 2003, when it acquired an 18.9 percent interest in Finnish tyre manufacturer, Nokian Tyres PLC for €78.3 million to boost its European operations; Nokian was the largest tyre producer in the Nordic region with sales of €479 million in 2002. The aim of this acquisition was to penetrate the Nordic markets and acquire Nokian's technical expertise in winter tyres (FundingUniverse.com, 2012; Bridgestone, 2012).

Bridgestone also has a vertical integration strategy. For instance, it acquired 100 percent of the shares in one of its main suppliers, Mecamold SA in June 2004;

at that point, Mecamold was producing moulds for the tyre industry with its main production site in Herstal (Belgium), and had been a key supplier to Bridgestone Europe for 35 years (Bridgestone Europe, 2004). This strategy[6] enabled Bridgestone to negate the significant bargaining power wielded by some suppliers, thus alleviating cost pressures. Moreover, this strategy was executed to ensure the timely and uninterrupted delivery of critical materials/services needed by Bridgestone (a supply disruption could disrupt a Bridgestone plant's utilisation levels and may even force it to shut down, resulting in significant losses).

Further, Bridgestone is using M&A strategies to control the full range of products and services available in the tyres industry. For instance, in 2006, Bridgestone acquired Bandag (a leading manufacturer of tyre retreading materials and equipment) for US$1.05 billion in cash. At the point of its acquisition, Bandag (based in Muscatine, Iowa) had a global network of more than 900 franchised dealers that produced and marketed retread tyres and provided tyre management services. Additionally, Bandag owned and operated Tyre Distribution Systems, Inc. (TDS), a commercial retail operation that retails and services new and retread tyres,[7] and it possessed an 87.5 percent stake in Speedco, Inc., a provider of on-highway truck lubrication and routine tyre services to commercial truck owner-operators and fleets. In 2005 Bandag had global sales of US$921 million. After its acquisition by Bridgestone, Bandag became a wholly owned subsidiary of Bridgestone Americas Holding, Inc. Thus through this single acquisition, Bridgestone acquired the ability to provide a total tyre offering which encompasses addressing customers' needs throughout the product's life cycle (Bandag, 2006). Due to the increasingly oligopolistic nature of the tyres industry, it is apparent there is a shift 'from price competition to non-price competition' (Chandler and Hikino, 1999). For instance, Bridgestone by acquiring Bandag is able to differentiate its product offerings beyond that of a 'mere' tyre maker, and has in fact progressed into becoming a more highly valued solutions provider (by offering a comprehensive tyre management system).

In October 2015, Bridgestone also acquired TireConnect Systems, which makes online tyre sales tool connecting retailers to wholesalers and is equipped with consumer ecommerce capabilities. Through this deal, Bridgestone would be able to give its dealers the capacity to secure credit for online tyre sales, while retaining full visibility of their inventory, labour/installation and pricing expenditures. Moreover this acquisition would augment the tyre buying experience between Bridgestone's customers and their preferred local dealers, as the acquired TireConnect technology is equipped with research and purchasing experience ecommerce capabilities (Bridgestone Americas, 2015; TireBusiness.com, 2015a). In May 2016, Bridgestone also embarked on the acquisition of Speedy France, a car service retail company with significant tyre networks in France; the acquisition is expected to increase Bridgestone's retail outlets in France to over 800 stores (Bridgestone, 2016). There is a blurring of lines between manufacturing and services in this case. In an increasingly competitive, oligopolistic market, seemingly traditional manufacturers such as Bridgestone are behaving more like service firms as a means of product differentiation.

Bridgestone's rapid expansion in the US by means of acquisition was not without problems. Soon after its acquisition by Bridgestone, Firestone lost a contract to supply tyres to GM and its US plants were also affected by a strike launched by the United Rubber Workers (Mackinnon, 2008). Further in 1991, Bridgestone had to inject US$1.4 billion into salvaging the debt-ridden Bridgestone/Firestone. The newly merged Bridgestone/Firestone had accumulated considerable debt as it had to modernise Firestone's relatively obsolete manufacturing facilities (Reuters, 1991). Later, in the summer of 2000, Firestone also underwent the worst reputational crisis in its history when it was compelled to recall 6.5 million tyres linked to fatal accidents, mostly on Ford Explorers (Aeppel, 2003). However, the company was able to quickly overcome this recall crisis, due to the unwavering support of Firestone's loyal dealers. An industry analyst, asserted that: 'The ongoing loyalty of Bridgestone/Firestone's 8,000-strong independent tyre dealer network is one of the untold stories in the Firestone-recall saga of the past year' and he also commented that 'Firestone dealers, for the most part, have rallied around their tyre supplier and continue to support the brand' (TireBusiness.com, 2001). This unwavering loyalty from Bridgestone/Firestone's dealers is largely attributable to the firm's favourable treatment of its dealers over the years. This is indicated in the following statement from an industry analyst: 'in an era where large manufacturers cut out small retailers, Firestone has stuck by them. It's easier to be loyal to a company that has been loyal to you' (Abrams, 2000). In fact, the bulk of Bridgestone/Firestone's tyres are sold through its 'Family Channel' which comprises mostly independent dealers who are able to sell some of the company's best-priced tyres. Further, Bridgestone/Firestone was willing to provide much needed financial support for cash-strapped independent dealers who were affected by the tyre recall; for instance, many of these dealers who typically had 90 days to pay for their tyres received easier credit terms (Abrams, 2000; Farrell, 2000).

Today, Bridgestone/Firestone has survived and prospered, with the merged entity now the world's largest tyre company. This merger was in many ways unavoidable due to the powerful forces (generated by the cascade effect) compelling consolidation in an increasingly mature industry, subjected to rising pricing and other pressures (i.e., delivery and technical progress demands) from powerful automakers. Bridgestone's success, thus far, validates the massive debt and risks it assumed in its then seemingly over-ambitious acquisition of Firestone in 1988.

Key drivers of Bridgestone's market dominance: technical progress and lean

Bridgestone has been able to dominate the global tyre market due to its ability to achieve and deliver significant technical progress over the decades. The company asserts that it assiduously conducts cutting edge R&D in order to deliver products and services (under increasingly quick time to market conditions) of value to its customers (Bridgestone, 2012). Over the past decade, Bridgestone's technical progress has been particularly significant. For instance, during this period,

Bridgestone has made considerable progress in computer-aided design, which it has developed into its 'Grand Unified Tyre design Technology' (GUTT). This pioneering automatic tyre simulation and design method has altered modern tyre construction conventions and straightened out a once convoluted process. With regard to on-road tyres, this technology has been applied to create Bridgestone's latest 'Driver Oriented New Ultimate Tyre Science' (DONUTS) tyres for passenger cars, commercial trucks and buses. Bridgestone asserts that its DONUTS tyres, even when worn, display superior durability, grip, handling and manoeuvrability in adverse wet conditions; owing to these superlative qualities, Bridgestone has continued to dominate Formula-1 motor sports racing (Bridgestone, 2011).

As for off-the-road tyres, GUTT has also contributed significantly to the development and production of extremely durable tyres, along with reducing the time to market for new tyres (Bridgestone, 2007; Bridgestone, 2012). In 2011, Bridgestone also declared that it had developed revolutionary technology that provides drivers with critical real-time information on road surface conditions via the tyres and this new technology is based on a concept called 'Contact Area Information Sensing' (CAIS). CAIS is capable of analysing road surface condition information and also has the capacity to detect sudden vibration and digitise this alteration in road surfaces via an in-vehicle analysis equipment. It then proceeds to categorize road conditions and transmits this critical information to the motorist via an in-car display. This revolutionary new technology augments drivers' ability to deal with unexpected changes in driving conditions brought about by the sudden onset of ice, rain and snow. Further, it includes the capability to apprise other motorists on the same road of these changes (Bridgestone, 2011). Owing to the significant breakthroughs in road safety rendered by its CAIS technology. Bridgestone won the '2012 Tyre Technology of the Year Award'. Industry analysts have attested to Bridgestone's superior technical progress (via CAIS) as evidenced in the following statements: 'this technology from Bridgestone really impressed us' and 'it's an ultra high-technology development which can potentially make a genuine contribution to road safety' (Bridgestone, 2012). The immense computing power needed to power sophisticated systems such as CAIS invariably creates a demand for equally (if not more) advanced microchips. It is this increasing digitisation of automotive components suppliers that has contributed to the microchip's relentlessly breath-taking rise over the past decade as the lynchpin of an industry once synonymous with a benighted industrial age.

In an ambitious move to bring cutting-edge tyre technology into the mainstream, Bridgestone launched its DriveGuard run-flat tyre in January 2016. The unique design of Bridgestone's DriveGuard tyre allows it to be fitted to any passenger vehicle regardless of origin, in the process facilitating widespread adoption. Further, the tyre's advanced proprietary cooling fin design coupled with its robust, reinforced sidewalls gives drivers the ability to continue driving safely in relative comfort for 80 kilometres (at speeds up to 80 kilometres per hour) in the event of a puncture. Moreover, the tyre's revolutionary material (i.e., the unique polyester used in its carcass body ply) also grants exceptional resistance to heat generation, significantly enhancing its overall durability. In addition, Bridgestone asserts that its DriveGuard tyre offers superior best-in-class grip even under the most adverse wet conditions, coupled with the ability to deliver remarkably short stopping distance when needed (Bridgestone Europe, 2016).

Evidently, the tyre industry has advanced greatly ahead of its vulcanised rubber roots and Bridgestone has been able to dominate this industry through its superior innovation. Bridgestone's superior innovation is partially driven by its significant investment in R&D. The company's recorded R&D investment of US$787.5 million in 2015, nearly double its 2000 R&D investment of US$463 million; Bridgestone's R&D was also the highest among the top three tyre makers (Bridgestone, 2015; Bridgestone, 2001). The company is cognisant that R&D ultimately has to deliver technologies that address customer needs, buttressed by a thorough understanding of the differing nature and requirements of global markets (successful R&D is not just about increasing its budget); for instance, customers in developing countries demand more resilient tyres due to rougher road conditions, while those living in wintry climates need tyres with tighter grip to prevent skids. To meet the different needs of customers worldwide, Bridgestone has established Technical Centres for its tyre products in Japan (Tokyo), the US (Akron, Ohio), Italy (Rome), and China (Wuxi) (Bridgestone, 2012). Further, Bridgestone's judicious acquisition strategy has enabled it to control the various technologies that go into tyre making. Bridgestone's drive for superior innovation (includes not just product but also process and service innovation) as a differentiation factor in a tightly contested oligopolistic market has also compounded the impact of the cascade effect over the past two-three decades; it has compelled them to acquire other firms globally in an attempt to acquire new technologies and capabilities (i.e., Bridgestone's acquisition of Bandag in 2006 to acquire capabilities in tyre management systems) (Bandag, 2006).

Although lean is not the primary factor for Bridgestone's dominance of the global tyres market, it has played a critical role in ensuring that the company maintains its lead over its closest rivals (i.e., Michelin and Goodyear) over the past decade. In fact, lean appears to be playing a greater role in Bridgestone's operations after its disastrous tyre recall in 2000; Bridgestone Firestone recalled 6.5 million tyres and spent US$440 million on recall-related costs (excluding the legal expenses) (The Associated Press, 2005). Bridgestone introduced lean in its key market, the Americas (accounted for more than two-fifths of its market in 2011) relatively late. For instance, in 2000, Bridgestone introduced lean in its Aiken County, South Carolina Bridgestone/Firestone plant (produces passenger and light truck tyres). From 2000 to 2002, the plant recorded a reduction in hazardous and solid waste generation of 53 percent and a decline in material scrap of 38 percent. Further, it achieved a 39 percent reduction in cost per thousand pounds of rubber (United States Environmental Protection Agency, 2003). For this achievement, the plant won the Shingo Prize for Excellence in Manufacturing (known as the 'Nobel Prize of Manufacturing') in April 2002 (Shingo Institute, 2017). Although Bridgestone had practised certain lean concepts such as kaizen and just-in-time for some time, it did not have a centralised lean system that incorporated all the various lean concepts until around 2009; there is a possibility that if a centralised lean system had been introduced and actively practised across Bridgestone before the year 2000, it could have avoided or at least mitigated the disastrous consequences of its tyre recall.

The introduction of a centralised lean system was critical in enabling lean to permeate Bridgestone's organisational culture; the development of a lean culture (one with employees across all levels focused on eradicating waste, creating value for customers and continuous improvement) goes far beyond that of just introducing just-in-time; many firms are actually still practising antiquated mass production systems with one or two lean practices such as just-in-time in place which possibly explains why very few firms have successfully replicated Toyota's success (Toyota was the first true practitioner of lean) in lean thinking (Bozdogan et al., 2000; Womack and Jones, 1996). Bridgestone's introduction of a centralised lean system could be considered a major advance in its process innovation.

In 2009, Bridgestone launched a centralised 'lean and strategic' management system that attempted to apply lean concepts effectively across the entire organisation. With the introduction of this comprehensive lean system, Bridgestone has already witnessed the benefits of this approach; total asset turnover in the company has increased from 0.93 in 2009 to 1.12 in 2011 (and was expected to exceed 1.2 in 2012); an increase in total asset turnover indicates that Bridgestone's assets are being used more effectively (Bridgestone, 2012). As mentioned earlier, lean involves letting customer pull value from the firm, which is giving customers what they want and not wasting resources in trying to convince them that the product is what they require (Womack and Jones, 2005). Bridgestone has deftly deployed this lean strategy by closing unprofitable plants such as Bridgestone Australia Ltd's Adelaide Plant and Bridgestone New Zealand Ltd's Christchurch Plant and focusing resources on product areas where growth in demand is expected (i.e., giving customers what they want). Further, Bridgestone assessed that demand for ultra large off-the-road radial tyres for construction and mining vehicles was expected to remain strong thus it increased production capacity for these tyres (by at least 30 percent) by the second half of 2012 compared with 2009 levels (Bridgestone, 2006; Bridgestone, 2009; Bridgestone, 2012). However, with deteriorating global demand for off-the-road tyres (wrought by an anaemic global mining industry) in 2015, Bridgestone reacted with characteristic dexterity by swiftly cutting production in this segment.

In an added display of lean-driven organisational agility, Bridgestone soon focused its efforts on the production of higher-end passenger car tyres (e.g., run-flat tyres) to address rising consumer concerns on road safety; in June 2016, Bridgestone implemented its five-year US$164 million plan which involves production of such tyres at its Wilson facility in North Carolina, US. Sensing a sustained increase in demand for high-quality passenger car tyres (e.g., its DriveGuard run-flat tyres), Bridgestone initiated plans to invest another US$180 million in this plant in January 2017, in the process installing the capacity to raise daily tyre production at this plant from its existing 32,000 to an estimated 35,000 units by 2018 (Ohnesorge, 2016; Ohnesorge, 2017; Tire

Review, 2017). As evidenced, a lean-driven strategy is not simply about addressing customer needs but one that involves the active deployment or redeployment of valuable organisational resources under constantly mutating business or economic conditions.

Michelin: profile

Notwithstanding the contentious forces transforming its industrial landscape, Michelin stood steadfast as the world's second largest tyre company at the dawn of 2016; it began the year with a global market share of 12.6 percent (based on 2015 revenues). This renowned industry innovator has an illustrious history dating back to 1889 (it was known back then as Michelin & Co). By introducing the radial tyre in 1948, Michelin essentially revolutionised the tyre market, by displacing the earlier bias-ply tyres. Michelin's invention, the radial tyre found worldwide customer acceptance (includes automakers and replacement market customers) over the coming decades, as it resulted in significantly greater fuel economy, superior starting and stopping traction and augmented handling and cornering; owing to the cascade effect, the leading automakers also placed intense pressure on all their supplier firms to develop/adapt this revolutionary new technology. However, the radial tyre also led to the costliest changeover in pneumatic tyre history and possibly resulted in the closure of more than 50 tyre plants globally; the radial tyre was clearly a 'disruptive technology' that brought about 'the perennial gale of creative destruction' (Michelin, 2015b; Christensen, 1997; Schumpeter, 1943). Since Michelin's introduction of the radial tyre in 1948, many tyre makers have spent millions of dollars globally retooling their former bias-ply plants for radial production; In the US, the cost of industry wide conversion to radials was estimated (in 1971) to be around US$400-US$500 million (ITEC, 2012).[8] It is possible that Michelin's introduction of radial tyre technology played a part in spurring the industry consolidation in the ensuing decades, as tyre makers sought greater economies of scale and scope as a means of alleviating rising cost pressures brought about by radial conversion.

In 2015, Michelin recorded revenues and net income of approximately €21.2 billion (US$23.6 billion) and €1.163 billion (US$1.292 billion) respectively. By 2015, Michelin also had 111,700 employees and 68 production facilities across 17 countries (supported by marketing and sales operations spread across more than 170 countries and regions) (Michelin, 2015b). Like its key competitors, Bridgestone and Goodyear, Michelin derives the bulk (75 percent or €15.9 billion in 2015) of its revenues from the replacement market (Figure 3.3). Despite drawing only 25 percent (€5.3 billion in 2015) of its revenues from the OE market, Michelin continues to maintain active communication with automakers as a means of ascertaining industry trends and technological requirements. For instance, Michelin has discovered through discussions with automakers that there is an increase in corporate average fuel economy requirements and thus an increasing demand for more fuel-efficient low-rolling-resistance tyres, and it has moved swiftly to capture this increasing demand (Meyer, 2011).

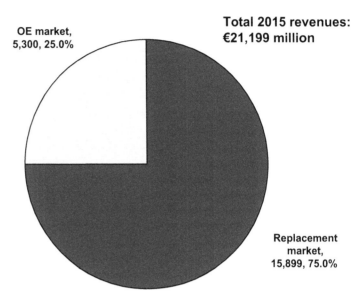

Figure 3.3 Michelin's 2015 annual revenues (€ million)

Source: Michelin, 2015a, Morningstar

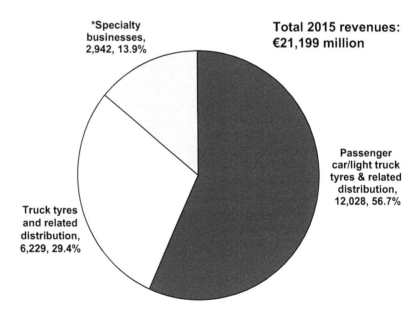

Figure 3.4 Michelin's 2015 annual revenues (€ million)

*Specialty Businesses include earthmover, agricultural, two-wheel and aircraft tyres

Source: Michelin, 2015a; Michelin, 2015b

As indicated in Figure 3.4, Michelin in 2015 was also heavily dependent on the passenger car and light truck tyres market, with 56.7 percent (approximately €12.03 billion) of its sales coming from this segment alone. Despite its aggressive expansion plans (e.g., by acquiring Uniroyal Goodrich and Oliver Rubber Company) in the US, it is still a predominantly European-based firm, with 38.7 percent (€8.2 billion) of its revenues coming from Europe in 2015; France alone accounted for 9.3 percent of overall revenues (Figure 3.5).

Michelin is stepping up its international growth strategy, possibly due to the relatively poor economic growth prospects in Europe in years, following the events of the 2008 global financial crisis. For instance, in 2012 it rolled out plans to build a new Earthmover tyre manufacturing plant in Anderson County, South Carolina. Further, Michelin expanded its other already operational Earthmover tyre facility in the state. These investments cost Michelin around US$750 million and created an additional 500 jobs in South Carolina (Selko, 2012). Unfortunately, by 2015, Michelin was compelled to suspend operations at its earthmover tyre facility in South Carolina due to anaemic global demand for these tyres. The suspension of Michelin's earthmover plant in South Carolina does not just reveal the relatively weak state of the global economy but also the sheer intensity of competition in the global tyres market. Nonetheless, Michelin still has nine plants in South Carolina and 21 manufacturing facilities across North America. In 2016, Michelin is building a new US$510 million plant in Leon, Guanajuato (Central Mexico) to produce passenger cars and light truck tyres This new facility, expected to be completed in 2018, would initially supply four to five million tyres annually to Mexico-based automakers and the North American consumer

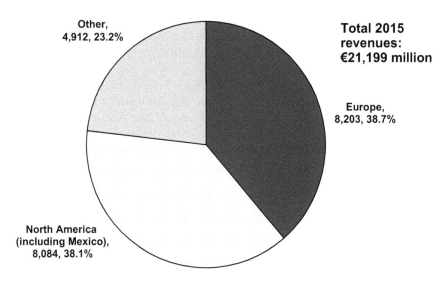

Figure 3.5 Michelin's 2015 revenues by region (€ million)

Source: Michelin 2015a; Michelin, 2015b

tyres market. Michelin also stated that the decision to locate its new facility in Leon was partly due to its short three-hour drive to 18 automakers in the region. The company stated the new plant's Leon location would not only enable it to reduce its transportation costs but also improve its carbon footprint (Bell, 2016). However, with the looming prospect of a hefty tariff on imports entering the US (under the Trump administration), Michelin (or its competitors) could be compelled to shift part of its production efforts in Mexico back to the US.

In 2015, Michelin's procurement spend was approximately €4.382 billion (US$4.868 billion), with about €1.148 billion (US$1.275 billion) allocated for natural rubber purchases (Michelin, 2015b). The company's purchasing expenses was the highest among the leading marquee tyre producers; Michelin alone consumes 10 percent of the natural rubber produced in Indonesia, the world's second largest supplier of natural rubber (Hapsari and Teguh, 2011). As in the case of Bridgestone, this significant budget grants Michelin considerable market power over its numerous raw material (i.e., mainly natural rubber) suppliers. Nonetheless, to mitigate its dependence on its rubber suppliers, Michelin has cultivated about 21,000 hectares of Hevea plantations in Brazil and Nigeria, which meet 12 percent of its natural rubber requirements (Michelin, 2011). Although this reserve of natural rubber meets only a small percentage of Michelin's raw material requirements, it nonetheless increases Michelin's bargaining power in price negotiations with its suppliers. Further, this involvement in rubber cultivation (a vertical integration strategy) enables Michelin to develop technical expertise and experiment with innovative agricultural practices. This practice has not only led to the spread of sustainable rubber cultivation but also enabled Michelin (in conjunction with CIRAD, the French Agricultural Research Centre for International Development) to develop scientific expertise in combating the Microcyclus uleï, a fungus that could deleteriously impact the leaves of South American rubber trees; further complicating matters was the potential of it spreading to Asian and African plantations (Michelin, 2010); Michelin benefits from such collaborations, as it would not only gain greater, uninterrupted access to higher quality rubber but such joint efforts also serve to alleviate the rising cost of conducting cutting-edge biotech research.

Despite the above apparent benefits, Michelin's vertical integration (i.e., backward integration) strategy of operating its own rubber plantations comes at significant reputational risk (on top of the considerable operational costs), as it has to deal with accusations of worker exploitation and wreaking untold environmental damage in countries such as Nigeria; for instance, in December 2007, Michelin was accused of bulldozing 3,500 hectares of forests as well as the people's farmlands in Iguobazuwa, Nigeria without prior seeking the consent of the community or conducting a formal Environmental Impact Assessment (WRM, 2009).

Michelin's acquisitions since the 1980s

Michelin, like its keen competitor, Bridgestone, was not spared from the powerful forces cascading through the entire value chain in the 1980s. Like Bridgestone, it too was compelled to use acquisitions as a means of securing greater economies of scale and scope, and expanding its market share in international markets. In Michelin's case, it tried to supplant Goodyear as the industry leader by acquiring Uniroyal Goodrich Tire Co. for US$1.5 billion in September 1989 (Associated Press, 1989). Michelin essentially paid US$690 million in cash and assumed the $810 million in debt that Uniroyal Goodrich incurred when it was taken private in 1987 by its owner, Clayton & Dubilier Inc, a New York investment firm.

Prior to its acquisition by Michelin, a number of tyre companies had been keen in acquiring Uniroyal Goodrich over the last few years, but they lacked the financial muscle and found its debt levels too daunting. The considerable interest in Uniroyal Goodrich (and Firestone) and the significant financial risk Michelin was willing to assume also highlights the rapid consolidation and the intense desire for market dominance in an increasingly oligopolistic industry; in some respects, Michelin's daring acquisition of Uniroyal Goodrich was driven by necessity, as it was then being outpaced by Goodyear and particularly, the fast-rising Bridgestone which had acquired Firestone earlier in 1988 (Hicks, 1989).

At the time of the acquisition, Michelin was already the world's second-largest tyre maker, after Akron-based Goodyear. Uniroyal Goodrich, also based in Akron, was the second-largest American producer, after Goodyear. Further, it was still a largely US-based firm with six out of its nine production plants in the US; in 1988, Uniroyal Goodrich recorded sales of US$2.2 billion, considerably lower than the US$8.7 billion posted by its acquirer, Michelin in that same year (Associated Press, 1989; Engel, 1989). As evidenced by the earlier case of Bridgestone (that acquired Firestone in 1988) and Michelin's acquisition of Uniroyal Goodrich, the industry structure of the global tyres industry was becoming increasingly oligopolistic with the major players moving aggressively to acquire their smaller competitors (Hicks, 1988a).

Through its acquisition of Uniroyal Goodrich, Michelin also augmented its expanding sales and marketing network in the US and strengthened its competitive position in an increasingly international industry. Further, Michelin gained greater access to the private-label market (where a manufacturer's products are sold under another name), as Uniroyal Goodrich was particularly strong in the private-label market, supplying tyres to retail chains. Thus, Michelin, which was already selling to Sears, Roebuck & Company earlier, was able to fulfil its long desire of securing a significant market presence in the US private-label market through its Uniroyal Goodrich acquisition (Brooks, 1989; Hicks, 1989). An industry analyst asserted that control over Uniroyal Goodrich's private-label business has given Michelin greater pricing flexibility (a distinct competitive advantage in an oligopolistic market where price cutting is anathema and subject to retaliation from competitors). This is evidenced by the following statements from the analyst on Michelin's acquisition of Uniroyal Goodrich: 'It's like the perfume market. They don't ever cut prices, they just give you a purse with it'. He also added: 'Michelin never wanted to cut prices on its premium line so now they have something they can cut prices on' (Brooks, 1989).

Michelin, by acquiring Uniroyal Goodrich, had also effectively secured control of two respected tyre brands (i.e., Uniroyal and B.F. Goodrich). This is because Uniroyal

Goodrich comprised the former B. F. Goodrich Company (which made the first tyre for passenger automobiles in 1896) and the former Uniroyal Inc. Further, the B. F. Goodrich brand had acquired a superb reputation for high-performance tyres. Moreover, Uniroyal, prior to its integration with B.F. Goodrich, was the largest supplier to GM. The tyre operations of Uniroyal were acquired by Clayton & Dubilier in 1985. Those operations were merged with the tyre business of B. F. Goodrich in 1986 when Goodrich formed a 50–50 partnership with Clayton & Dubilier. However, Clayton & Dubilier subsequently bought Goodrich's 50 percent stake in 1987 for about US$250 million (Hicks, 1989). Shortly after in 1989, Michelin acquired Clayton & Dubilier's stake in Uniroyal Goodrich, illustrating the ruthless centralisation of capital in an increasingly oligopolistic industry (Brooks, 1989).

Following its successful acquisition of Uniroyal Goodrich, Michelin continued to deploy acquisition strategies as a means of breaking into new markets (e.g., retreading market), regions (e.g., Central Europe and Asia) and securing control of new technologies, and distribution networks. For instance, in 1995, in an attempt to bolster its presence in Central Europe Michelin acquired a 51.2 percent stake in Polish tyre manufacturer Stomil Olsztyn for US$105 million (Warsaw Business Journal, 2004). By May 2000, Michelin had increased its stake in Stomil to 58.4 percent and officially changed its name to Michelin Polska (Warsaw Business Journal, 2000); within three years, Michelin effectively owned the whole company by raising its stake to 98.99 percent (Michelin, 2003). Further, in September 1996, in a concerted effort to dominate the Central European market, Michelin acquired a 90 percent stake in Taurus Rt, a Hungarian agricultural tyre maker (also Hungary's largest tyre maker), by paying US$66 million in cash and debt assumption. Additionally, the company agreed to invest another US$60 million to upgrade Taurus' facilities. There were about 18 firms that expressed interest in acquiring Taurus and three made actual bids (two of them strong). Michelin's competitors, Bridgestone, Continental and Goodyear, were known to have been interested in acquiring Taurus (Europolitics, 1996; Davis, 1996). In an attempt to strengthen its presence in the steel wheel business and control all technologies needed in tyre making, Michelin also acquired 51 percent of German steel wheel maker, Mannesmann Kronprinz AG (mefro wheels, 2012; Ajami et al., 2006).

In 2003, Michelin through a US$20.1 million investment acquired a 2.5 percent stake in South Korea's, Hankook (as part of a strategic alliance), with the option of eventually increasing its stake to a sizeable 10 percent. Michelin steadily increased its stake to 6.3 percent in 2006 and eventually to 9.98 percent. The aim of the partnership between Michelin and Hankook was to jointly develop distribution, R&D and manufacturing capabilities in Asia. However, by 2011, Michelin decided the partnership was not yielding the desired synergies and decided to sell its 9.98 percent in Hankook for US$555.7 million (Park, 2011; tyrepress.com, 2011). Despite selling its entire Hankook stake at a 12 percent discount, Michelin still managed to secure a US$255 million profit on its initial investment in 2003; Michelin subsequently used this largesse to finance its international expansion (either through acquisitions or organic growth) (Park, 2011; Warburton, 2011).

In 2003, Michelin also acquired the European tyre distribution assets of specialist Danish group Viborg for US$307 million; Viborg was mainly engaged in tyre distribution via its network of 465 sales outlets, largely located in Germany and Denmark. This acquisition greatly augmented Michelin's European distribution network, particularly in Germany, which is Europe's largest tyre replacement market. Viborg's also added €313 million to Michelin's 2003 revenues (Michelin, 2003). Further, in October 2007, Michelin acquired Oliver Rubber Company from Cooper for US$89 million; Oliver which made tread rubber and retreading equipment became a subsidiary of Michelin North America, Inc. Michelin basically acquired Oliver to augment its tread manufacturing capacity and leverage on Oliver's dealer network to extend its reach across North America's growing retreading market (Michelin, 2007). In June 2014, Michelin acquired Sascar, a Brazilian fleet management firm for US$602 million, with the aim of incorporating the firm's telematics technology into enhancing its smart tyre solutions capabilities; the acquisition of Sascar along with its advanced fleet management technology also augmented the capabilities of Michelin's truck tyre business in Brazil (Michelin, 2014). This strategy of moving into the retreading and smart tyres market is similar to Bridgestone's earlier acquisition of Bandag in 2006. This similarity in strategy is best described by Alfred Chandler and Takashi Hikino, who argue that oligopolies (driven by the shift from price competition to nonprice competition) tend to move 'more quickly into expanding markets' (i.e., retreading and smart tyres solutions) in their search for product/service differentiation. Like all oligopolistic players, Michelin is trying to differentiate itself in a hotly contested market by offering 'total tyre solutions' rather than just simply providing products (Chandler and Hikino, 1999; Truck News, 2007). This drive towards becoming a 'total tyre solutions' provider inevitably accelerates the consolidation process, as firms strive to acquire more capabilities (thus covering more product segments) by means of acquisition.

Michelin's JVs: springboard to acquisition and market expansion

Michelin has also used JVs as a means towards acquisition and expanding its market share in overseas markets. In 1996, it had established its first JV in Shenyang, China with ShenYang Tyres General Factory to make radial tyres for the Chinese market. Michelin quickly invested in three more JVs in Shenyang, in the process doubling its car tyre production capacity (in China) to 1.2 million units annually; these JVs were in effect Michelin's subsidiaries, as it held a controlling stake in all four JVs (in 1997, Michelin's shareholding ranged from around 65.4 percent to 84.1 percent) (Michelin, 1997). It swiftly negotiated a 70 percent controlling stake in another JV with Shanghai Tyre and Rubber, the largest domestic tyre producer in China. Having established a controlling interest in all these JVs, it then merged them into a single entity (rapidly securing greater economies of scale and scope) in which it held a dominant 85 percent stake (Ajami et al., 2006). Having validated the effectiveness of using JVs as a strategy for eventual acquisition and market dominance, Michelin formed another Chinese JV in

September 2011 to produce and market 'Warrior' brand passenger car and light truck tyres in China; this JV is known as the Double Coin Group (Anhui) Warrior Tires Co, with Michelin investing €87 million for a 40 percent stake while the remaining 60 percent is held by its Chinese partners (Double Coin Holdings Ltd. and Shanghai Huayi (Group) Company) (Michelin, 2011).

Technical progress and the Michelin manufacturing way: key to Michelin's success

Backed by significant investments in R&D, Michelin has delivered innovations that have placed it consistently among the global top three tyre makers over the last two-three decades; Michelin's R&D investment has grown consistently from €589.4 million (US$592.1 million) in 1999 to €689 million (US$765.5 million) in 2015 (Michelin, 2000; Michelin, 2015). Michelin's steady commitment to R&D is driven by its recognition that tyres are sophisticated products with a significant role in road safety; resultantly, tyre technology must be constantly in sync with evolving vehicle behaviour (Michelin, 2000). Currently, to support its global R&D efforts, Michelin has more than 6,000 Michelin employees spread across four major test centres in France (Ladoux), Spain (Almeria), the US (Laurens), and Japan (Jari) (Michelin, 2012); to further spur innovation and shorten the time-to-market of its tyres, Michelin, in 2012, invested more than €100 million to upgrade its key R&D centre in Ladoux (this centre alone has 19 test tracks and houses 3,600 research staff, which is more than half of its global research staff strength) (Michelin, 2011; Michelin, 2012).

As mentioned earlier, Michelin was the first to introduce the then revolutionary radial tyre for passenger cars in 1949. Over the subsequent four decades, Michelin's radial tyre technology found widespread usage across a remarkable spectrum of vehicles such as trucks, earthmovers, tractors, aircrafts, and motorcycles. Not one to rest on its laurels, Michelin continued to make significant strides in tyre making technology in its quest for market supremacy. By the mid-1990s, Michelin launched its pilot MXM4 tyres which at that time, delivered sui generis vehicle handling, comfort and ride experience (i.e., reduced vehicular noise and vibration). These features made the pilot MXM4 tyre a tremendous success with luxury automakers; even today, the tyre may still come pre-fitted as OE on the BMW 7-series (a testament to the tyre's long standing engineering superiority). Bolstered by the exceptional success of this tyre, Michelin, over the ensuing 15 years, developed superior variants which were collectively known as the Primacy range. One of the most renowned tyres in the Primacy range is the Primacy MXM4, which not only surpasses its predecessor in the core areas of handling and comfort but also possesses best-in-class stopping power; the Primacy MXM4 which was a virtual shoo-in for OE status with luxury car models such as the Mercedes-Benz E-Class, Infiniti Q70 and the Buick LaCrosse, also found considerable popularity in the aftermarket with drivers of mainstream makes (e.g., Ford, Honda), as suggested by Michelin's collated customer feedback (Evans, 2010; Michelin, 2016).

Michelin's success is also based on its superlative ability to address the needs and expectations of the broader passenger car market. The company's all-season standard passenger car tyre, the Defender with its 90,000-mile warranty (a whopping 21,000 miles more than most comparable competitors), launched in 2012 is widely regarded by industry analysts and customers as the industry's best-in-class. The Defender range was conceived as a replacement to Michelin's successful Harmony and HydroEdge ranges, which were the stalwarts of its mainstream passenger car segment for nearly two decades (Michelin, 2016; Modern Tire Dealer, 2012).

Over the 2011–2012 period, Michelin, ever the aggressive innovator, also released a series of high-tech tyres with enhanced safety features. For instance, Michelin's new studded tyre for 4WD vehicles and SUV (designed mainly for Nordic winters) reduces braking distances on ice and snow by 6 percent owing to its Durastud System while its Full Active Tread feature increases traction in snow by 15 percent. Further, Michelin's passenger car tyre (suitable for city cars, compacts and sedans), the 'ENERGY XM2' tyre, is billed as 'a damage-resistant tyre' suitable for roads of uneven quality in developing countries. Moreover, Michelin continued to build on the earlier success of its Primacy range, by launching its Primacy 3 tyre (OE on the Audi A6, BMW 5 & 7 series and Mercedes S-class) in European replacement markets in February 2012. The Primacy 3 was shown to have superior grip on both dry and wet surfaces (Michelin, 2011). Michelin swiftly sought to surpass the superior performance of its Primacy tyres, by launching its Premier A/S tyres in 2014; this range of tyres based on Michelin's 'Ever-Grip' technology, outperformed its Primacy counterpart in terms of stopping distance and grip under all road conditions (Petersen, 2014).

Michelin's exceptional track record in technical achievement has always been its unhesitating willingness to break with established conventions, starting with the launch of its revolutionary radial tyre nearly seven decades ago. However, the following case proved to be an aberration in its distinguished history of cutting-edge innovation. In the 1990s, Michelin's engineers were developing its revolutionary Tweel technology, which is essentially an airless tyre. Like the earlier game-changing radial tyre, an airless tyre, unencumbered by the prospect of punctures, should have naturally upended the entire industry, with its formal introduction in 2005. However, it only found success in the less lucrative agricultural, construction, contracting, landscaping and refuse/recycling industries but not the far-more profitable passenger car segment. The Tweel tyre's lack of mainstream success is largely owing to the considerable (still on-going) deliberation behind the technology's introduction into the larger passenger car market. Michelin asserts the relatively hesitant introduction of its Tweel tyres into the broader market, is owing to the nascent development (despite a near twenty year development phase) of the technology and the still general superiority of its radial air-filled tyres (Bell, 2014; Michelin, 2014). From a commercial standpoint, it is perfectly understandable why incumbents in possession of this technology would be hesitant in ensuring its general release; a virtually maintenance free 'indestructible' tyre would scarcely require replacement and its widespread adoption would spell the eradication of existing profitable product lines. Moreover, in an era of quarterly financial report where short-termism is the order of the day, it would be difficult to find the corporate management with the gumption and tenacity needed to weather the potential 'creative destruction' wrought by the mass adoption of Tweel technology (if it fulfils its technical potential); the disruptive nature of Tweel could even surpass that of its antecedent, the radial tyre (Schumpeter, 1943).

Since 2004–2005, Michelin has adopted some aspects of lean (e.g., continuous improvement) but it does not appear to be as comprehensive as Bridgestone's. The Michelin approach is known as the 'Michelin Manufacturing Way' (MMW), which is used 'to identify, standardise and systematically implement the best practices after their effectiveness has been demonstrated, whether they be methods or processes'. The MMW's key objectives are 'improving safety, ergonomics, quality and industrial productivity'. By the end of 2006, 75 percent of Michelin's industrial sites had implemented this system (Michelin, 2006). Further by the end of 2006, the implementation of this lean system had resulted in significant operational improvements across Michelin's North American plants; in the case of machine downtime, there was a 40 percent reduction in rubber preparation, followed by a 38 percent reduction in tyre curing, and a 20 percent reduction in tyre classification; as for the cost of scrap, there was a 14 percent reduction in rubber preparation and a 35 percent reduction in tyre building; as for first pass yield and output, there was a 20 percent increase in the first pass yield rate and a 10 percent rise in total output (Tefen, 2009). The cost savings generated through these lean process improvements could be subsequently channelled into next-generational R&D (augmenting technical progress) or even be used to bolster Michelin's war chest for further acquisitions.

Goodyear: profile

Goodyear long associated with American prowess in premium tyre manufacturing, is placed third worldwide amongst the world's tyre makers. In 2015, it recorded a global market share of 8.8 percent. The company was incorporated in August 1898 (with a capital stock of US$100,000) by Frank A. Seiberling. At the end of the 2015 financial year, Goodyear recorded revenues and net income of US$16.4 billion and US$376 million respectively; the company also employed about 66,000 full-time and temporary personnel throughout the world, including approximately 37,000 people covered under collective bargaining agreements. In 2015, the company operated 49 plants in 22 countries, with marketing operations in almost every country worldwide (Goodyear, 2015). Besides its trademark Goodyear tyres, the company also owns several brands such as the Dunlop, Kelly, Debica, Sava and Fulda brands. As evidenced in Figure 3.6, Goodyear derived the bulk (87 percent or about US$14.3 billion) of its revenues from the replacement market in 2015. This reliance on the replacement market is to avoid the cyclicality of the OE market. However, Goodyear continues to work closely with automakers to develop cutting-edge technology. This is evidenced in the following statement from Goodyear: 'starting at the early stages of new vehicle model creation, Goodyear works together with car manufacturers

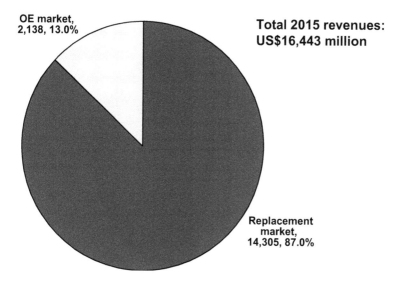

OE market,
2,138, 13.0%

**Total 2015 revenues:
US$16,443 million**

Replacement
market,
14,305, 87.0%

Figure 3.6 Goodyear's 2015 annual revenues (US$ million)
Source: 2015 Goodyear Annual Report

(e.g., BMW, Nissan and Toyota) to drive technology and innovation' (quoted in Southern Africa Treads, 2010).

The following Figure 3.7 indicates that Goodyear in 2015, derived nearly 50 percent (around US$7.8 billion) of its revenues from its North American tyre segment, followed by its Europe, Middle East and Africa tyre segment which accounted for a considerable 31.1 percent (US$5.1 billion). Both segments outweighed the other two remaining segments (i.e., the Latin American and Asia Pacific segments) by a significant margin. However, the Asia Pacific segment is expected to play an increasingly crucial role in the company's future, due to the burgeoning automobile markets in China and India (Goodyear, 2010). The fact that Goodyear has invested US$700 million in its Pulandian plant (this investment costs US$200 million more than the original figure announced in 2008) in China underscores the company's growing commitment to the Chinese market; the Pulandian facility has a maximum capacity of 10 million consumer tyres. In March 2015, Goodyear added a development centre to its Pulandian plant to foster advances in high value-added tyre development for China-based automakers (Tire Review, 2011; Goodyear, 2015).

Goodyear's 2015 procurement expenses of US$2.464 billion (2015 natural rubber purchases amounted to around US$838 million) was still substantial despite being markedly smaller than those of its key competitors, Bridgestone and Michelin, which posted purchasing expenditure approximating US$5 billion each (Goodyear, 2015; Moore, 2015). Further, Goodyear believes in leveraging its considerable purchasing power to extract concessions (e.g., discounts,

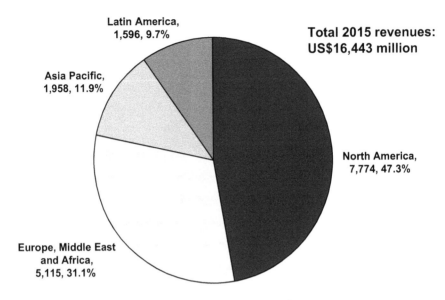

Figure 3.7 Goodyear's annual revenues by region (US$ million)

Source: 2015 Goodyear Annual Report

higher-quality rubber at discounted rates) from the numerous, unconsolidated suppliers across Thailand, Indonesia and Malaysia; a senior Goodyear manager asserted in a meeting that Goodyear could exert its 'financial muscle' to extract discounts of up to 20 percent from its suppliers (Goodyear, 2001; Goodyear, 2015). Moreover, Goodyear's case illustrates that not all leading subsystems integrators are able to deliver a consistent track record of profitability despite their considerable market power; the underlying theme is that leading subsystems integrators are under incredible pressure to secure ever-increasing economies of scale and scope to alleviate rising R&D and operational costs. As indicated in Table 3.1, Goodyear registered a net loss in seven out of 15 years (2001–2015).

Goodyear's acquisitions strategy (1980s-1990s) and subsequent reversal

Goodyear underwent an active consolidation period in the 1980s and 1990s, making several bold acquisitions in its attempts to becoming a vertically integrated company. For instance, in 1986, Goodyear acquired Long Mile Rubber Company, the largest full line tread rubber producer in the US. Soon after this acquisition, Goodyear also launched its own retreading system and developed a large network of Goodyear retread shops that posed a serious challenge to Bandag's dealer network (a leading manufacturer of tyre retreading materials and equipment that was later acquired by Bridgestone in 2006). Consequently,

Table 3.1 Goodyear's net income (loss)
2001–2015 (US$ million)

Year	Net Income (Loss)
2001	(255)
2002	(1247)
2003	(807)
2004	115
2005	211
2006	(348)
2007	583
2008	(77)
2009	(375)
2010	(216)
2011	343
2012	212
2013	629
2014	2452
2015	307

Source: Goodyear Annual Reports

Goodyear became the largest single retreader in the US (Bandag, 2006; Fisher, 2008). In 1986, Goodyear also acquired Min Tire Equipment Inc., a premier supplier of rubber extruder equipment and industrial machinery. Like its key competitors, Bridgestone and Michelin, Goodyear was developing expertise in several areas of the tyre industry and was not restricting itself to being just a tyre maker; this strategy is a version of non-price competition that characterises oligopolies (Chandler and Hikino, 1999). Goodyear, itself, became a takeover target in 1986, and was forced to buy back its own shares from the corporate raider, Sir James Goldsmith who had accumulated a significant stake in Goodyear; the company then spent more than US$2.6 billion buying back its shares from Sir James Goldsmith and other investors (Mercer, 1990). In 1987, Goodyear was also compelled to sell its profitable aerospace business (Goodyear Aerospace) to Loral Corporation for US$640 million to repay the debt incurred in repurchasing its shares from Sir James Goldsmith (as indicated by Goodyear's Communications Director, Keith Price in an interview for this book).

According to Keith Price, Goodyear was later compelled to sell its 1,233-mile oil pipeline business (the All American Pipeline System) in 1998 to Plains Resources Inc for US$420 million to service its still considerable debt position; Goodyear's oil pipeline was meant to take the cyclicality out of Goodyear's business (i.e., an alternative means of revenue during periods of weaker tyre sales). This oil pipeline was earlier acquired by a Goodyear subsidiary, Celeron Corporation, an oil and gas company which owned and managed more than 2,700 miles of natural gas pipelines and three natural gas processing facilities. Goodyear had acquired Celeron in 1983 for US$825 million in stock and was the company's first major diversification in twenty years. This acquisition was significant for Goodyear as it represented nearly 8 percent of Goodyear's 1983 revenues, 11 percent of operating income and 12 percent of assets (Teichner, 1991). To service the massive debt incurred in fending off Goldsmith's acquisition attempt, Goodyear sold Celeron for US$650 million to Exxon Corporation in 1987 (Hicks, 1987).

It is possible that Goodyear had made itself vulnerable to corporate raiders such as Goldsmith through its over-diversification, particularly into unrelated businesses such as its oil pipeline. Management theorists such as Peter Drucker and Michael Porter constantly urge companies to 'stick to the knitting' (their core businesses) instead of acquiring a series of unrelated businesses as a means of spurring growth (Drucker, 2007; Porter, 1985). Further, Goodyear's management had grown complacent and the firm was regarded by Merrill Lynch, which had worked with Goldsmith in its attempted acquisition as being highly inefficient. Denis Kelly, the head of M&A at Merrill Lynch described Goodyear as 'horribly inefficient and fat and happy – they had I don't know how many vice presidents and golf memberships' (quoted in Warner, 2011). He was also dismissive of Goodyear's attempts at diversifying into the oil business through Celeron due to its lack of relevant industry experience. Kelly's argument is similar to that of Michael Jensen's (Professor at Harvard Business School) who argued that managers in industries with significant cash flows where poor performance necessitates retrenchment, tend to engage in low-return or even value-destroying mergers; Jensen asserts that diversification strategies also tend to fall into this category (Warner 2011; Jensen, 1988).The 'stick to the knitting' argument does not apply in Goodyear's case, as the businesses which it diversified into were actually profitable (i.e., Goodyear Aerospace) or potentially very lucrative (i.e., Celeron, its oil and gas company and the oil pipeline it manages; given the upward spike in oil prices from the 1980s to around June 2014,[9] Celeron would have proven very profitable for nearly three decades) (The Economist, 2014). The fact that Goodyear had to divest these profitable businesses to stave off Goldsmith's raid undermined its long-term interests.

Mainstream thinkers (e.g., James Flanigan (LA Times) and Michael Jensen) often argue that corporate raiders such as James Goldsmith tend to discourage companies (like Goodyear) from embarking on wasteful diversification and focus on their core business (tyres in Goodyear's case). Flanigan even compares Goldsmith to Charles Jule Pilliod Jr., Goodyear's CEO from 1973–1982, who focused entirely on organic growth and made Goodyear the dominant industry player. However, this view may not be accurate, as Goldsmith had spent his entire career buying 'distressed companies', breaking them up and selling off the various assets to investors for quick, hefty profits. Thus, it is very unlikely that Goldsmith would change his modus operandi in Goodyear's case (Flanigan, 1986).

Despite these setbacks, Goodyear was still relatively active in M&A during the mid-1990s. In 1996 alone, Goodyear purchased a 50 percent stake in Sweden's Dackia, a tyre retailer (Goodyear purchased the remaining 50 percent in 2004) along with acquiring the tyre assets of Sime Darby Pilipinas in the Philippines; Goodyear eventually divested Dackia to Procuritas Capital Investors IV, a private equity firm in mid-2009, which in turn sold the firm to Goodyear's rising competitor, Pirelli for about US$87.2 million (this highlights Pirelli's determination to catch up with the 'Big Three' tyre makers through M&A) (Argentum, 2011; Masoni, 2012). That same year, it purchased a 60 percent stake in Contred, a South African tyre company and acquired the assets of Belt Concepts of America, a lightweight conveyor belt maker, in Spring Hope, North Carolina. Later in 1999, Goodyear forged an alliance with Japan's Sumitomo Rubber Industries Ltd., becoming again the world's top tyre maker for the first time in more than a decade. Through this deal, Goodyear was able to secure 22.6 percent of the US$75 billion tyres market in 1999. Prior to this alliance, Goodyear had 16.6 percent of the global tyre market while Sumitomo had around 5 percent (Marketwatch, 1999; The Economist, 1999; Michelin, 1999). It was erroneous for Goodyear's management to believe this strategic alliance would quickly enable Goodyear to surpass both Bridgestone and Michelin (Michelin and Bridgestone at that time, had 19.2 percent and 18.8 percent of the global tyre market respectively) (Michelin, 1999). Despite the larger combined market share brought about by their strategic alliance, Goodyear and Sumitomo were still relatively autonomous companies with diametrically opposed cultures unlike Bridgestone and Michelin who were single, integrated companies that still had larger market shares than Goodyear or Sumitomo independently. Given the lack of integration between Goodyear and Sumitomo, it is questionable whether Goodyear was able to reap the necessary gains in economies of scale and scope.

Under the alliance, Goodyear paid US$936 million to Sumitomo, in the process, acquiring 10 percent of the company and becoming Sumitomo's second largest shareholder (The Japan Times, 2003). The alliance enabled Goodyear to secure control of Sumitomo's non-Japanese assets (i.e., Sumitomo's Dunlop brand). Together, Goodyear and Sumitomo also formed six JVs around the world. Further, Sumitomo, which controlled the Dunlop tyre brand in major world markets, would secure a minor 1.4 percent shareholding in Goodyear in a stock swap valued at US$88 million. The deal, like many initially promising strategic alliances/mergers, was greeted with considerable enthusiasm on both sides (Marketwatch, 1999). This alliance was to some extent, also driven by the intense pressure (generated by the cascade effect) on tyre suppliers to establish global networks to meet the demands of increasingly globalised automakers (Nolan, 2008).

However, like many poorly integrated strategic alliances/mergers, the Goodyear/Sumitomo alliance soon unravelled. By 2003, Goodyear had sold at a loss (approximately US$17.6 million) the bulk (around 80 percent) of its 10 percent Sumitomo stake back to Sumitomo Rubber Industries, Ltd. The proceeds were supposedly meant to be used as operating funds while Goodyear underwent restructuring in the then weak North American market which was still recovering from the ravages of the earlier dot-com bubble burst (2000) and the September 11 terrorist incident (2001); an overreliance on the North American market has been Goodyear's perennial weakness (The Japan Times, 2003). Some industry analysts also assert that Goodyear may have overpaid for a 10 percent stake in Sumitomo,[10] as many of Sumitomo's non-Japanese assets were obsolete and required significant investment to modernise (Aeppel, 2003). With the unravelling of its investment in Sumitomo, Goodyear had once again ceded its number one title. The argument that Goodyear had overpaid for its stake in Sumitomo matches, to some extent, Michael Jensen's assertion that hubristic managers in their imperialistic quest for market dominance have a tendency to overpay for acquisitions (Jensen, 1988).

In discussions with Goodyear staff, some of the longer-serving ones in Goodyear's Singapore office had commented that the only beneficiary from the strategic alliance was Sumitomo, as it had used Goodyear's sizeable investment of US$936 million to modernise (i.e., robotise) its originally outmoded plants in Japan, greatly bolstering the company's technical capabilities and competitive advantage (Goodyear, 2001). In hindsight, the sale of the bulk of its 10 percent stake in Sumitomo back in 2003 proved rash, as the investment was simply too brief for Goodyear to extract the full benefits of the dominant global market share secured through the alliance; Goodyear's 10 percent stake in Sumitomo would be worth a lot today, as Sumitomo's market capitalisation has grown from US$1 billion in 1999 to approximately US$3.5 billion in July 2016 (Deutsch, 1999; Yahoo Finance, 2016). To reap the full benefits of strategic alliances, firms such as Goodyear need to be resilient and look beyond short-term financial pain. Nonetheless, the cooperation between Goodyear and Sumitomo continued through four JV operating companies across North America, Europe and Japan. Even then, these JVs between Goodyear and Sumitomo were formally dissolved in October 2015. Through the dissolution agreement, Sumitomo acquired Goodyear's 75 percent interest in Goodyear Dunlop Tires North America, Ltd. which includes 100 percent ownership of the JV's tyre plant in Tonawanda, New York. In Europe, Goodyear acquired Sumitomo's 25 percent stake in Goodyear Dunlop Tires Europe B.V. With regard to their Asian JVs, Goodyear acquired Sumitomo's 75 percent interest in Nippon Goodyear Ltd. (supplies the Japanese replacement market with Goodyear tyres) while Sumitomo acquired Goodyear's 25 percent interest in Dunlop Goodyear Tires Ltd. (supplies the OE market in Japan with Goodyear and Dunlop brand tyres). By December 31, 2015, Goodyear sold its remaining 3.4 million shares in Sumitomo for US$47 million (Goodyear, 2015).

Over the past decade, Goodyear has slowed down considerably with regard to its M&A strategy. Goodyear's Keith Price asserted that Goodyear was in 'reverse mode' and is in the process of divesting non-core assets, preferring to focus on organic growth (Price, 2011). For instance, in 2001, Goodyear sold its specialty chemicals business to private equity firm, Littlejohn & Company. Later, in 2007, Goodyear's Global tyre fabric operations were sold to South Korea's Hyosung Corporation for US$80 million. That same year, Goodyear also sold its Engineered Products division to another private equity firm, Carlyle for US$1.475 billion. Nonetheless, Goodyear has made some attempts to consolidate its industry position by increasing its holdings in firms it had earlier invested in. For instance, Goodyear made Sava Tyres a wholly owned subsidiary by 2004 (earlier in 2002, Goodyear already had a substantial 80 percent stake in Sava). It also completed its acquisition of South Pacific Tyres, by purchasing the remaining 50 percent from Ansell for US$40 million (Goodyear, 2011a).

However, in December 2010, Goodyear sold its European and Latin American farm tyre operations to Titan Tire Corporation, a subsidiary of Titan International Inc for about US$130 million; the deal included a licensing agreement that allows Titan to manufacture and sell Goodyear-brand farm tyres in Europe, Africa, Eastern Europe, Russia, Latin America and North America. This sale was apparently driven by Goodyear's desire to focus on its core consumer and commercial tyre business but in reality, it was probably done to raise cash to service its growing liabilities. In 2010, Goodyear's total current liabilities and total liabilities amounted to a considerable US$5.3 billion and US$14.1 billion respectively. Goodyear's 2010 total current liabilities were higher than its 2004 levels (the high debt obligations then may have compelled Goodyear to sell its Sumatra plantation to Bridgestone in 2005 (for about US$62 million) to service its debt obligations) (Goodyear, 2010).

Further Keith Price confirmed that Goodyear no longer owns any rubber plantations. This situation exposes Goodyear to the volatility in the natural rubber market; natural rubber which cost around US$2 a kilogram in 2007 has doubled to around US$4 a kilogram in 2011 (Australia Network, 2008; tyrepress, 2011). Unlike Michelin and Bridgestone who have their own rubber plantations, Goodyear has little or no buffer stocks to fall back on. Nonetheless, Price insists that Goodyear has little to worry about, as it enjoys good relations with its rubber suppliers. However, relationships (particularly tenuous ones driven strictly by financial interests) could vary over time, and Goodyear could find itself at the mercy of its suppliers, if they were to merge and gain increasing market power (a trend that is emerging, as evidenced in section 5 of this chapter).

It could be argued that even if Goodyear had kept all its rubber plantations, the company still would not be enough to meet all of its rubber requirements (Price, 2011). Some managers may not subscribe to this view, as the ownership of rubber plantations, in their opinion, is not to meet all of Goodyear's rubber requirements, but rather to act as a signalling device to its suppliers that it is not entirely vulnerable and has some buffer when it comes to price negotiations; for instance, the US' Strategic Petroleum Reserves is not enough to meet all of the country's energy requirements but it is fundamentally a critical safeguard and signalling device. Thus, the lack of ownership of any rubber plantations remains Goodyear's 'Achilles' heel', particularly if its chief rivals Michelin and Bridgestone still own significant rubber plantations.

Increasing focus on organic growth strategy

In a move to underscore its commitment to organic growth, Goodyear had invested about US$700 million in its Pulandian factory in China by around 2013; Goodyear's Pulandian plant is its only manufacturing facility in China. This new Chinese factory was fully operational by 2013 and had significant capacity (produced about 30,000 consumer tyres and 7,400 truck tyres daily). In 2015, Goodyear also announced plans to invest about US$135 million through 2017 to increase capacity at its Pulandian facility for the production of an additional two million or more car tyres annually. Goodyear's expansion plans would also include capacity for 48,000 run-flat tyres a year and the 1.25 million-square-feet plant would have a capacity of 10.5 million tyres. This increasing investment in China is also intended to reduce Goodyear's exposure to the North American markets. The tyres produced by Goodyear's Pulandian Factory and its other operations in China are meant exclusively for the Chinese market; Goodyear operates on the principle of having a short supply chain, which means that products are made in the region in which they are sold, thus minimising time-to-market, logistical costs and foreign exchange exposure (McNulty, 2015; Price, 2011). The research in this book indicates that the global tyres market has fundamentally consolidated at the marquee brand level (i.e., Goodyear, Bridgestone and Michelin). However, further consolidation is currently happening at the lower-end of the market involving brands such as Taiwan's Maxxis and Korea's Kumho (Goodyear, 2011b).

Technical progress and lean: Goodyear's competitive advantage

Goodyear relies heavily on R&D to secure the technical progress needed to compete in an increasingly sophisticated tyre market. Nonetheless Goodyear's R&D investment (its 2015 R&D expenditure was US$382 million) is eclipsed by the significantly larger R&D investments of Bridgestone and Michelin, which are easily twice that of Goodyear's (Goodyear, 2015). Goodyear's Keith Price asserts that despite Goodyear's relatively small R&D expenditure, its R&D is more focused nowadays with greater emphasis on working closely with the company's suppliers, universities (e.g., University of Akron) and US government bodies.

Goodyear has a long-standing relationship with the University of Akron, a neighbouring university; it is known as a benefactor of the university and funded the development of the Goodyear Polymer Centre which houses the university's Department of Polymer Science and Institute of Polymer Science (University of Akron, 2012). The university also played a role in the development of Goodyear's run-flat tyres by running a parametric study of inflation pressure and stresses in tyres (ALGOR, 2011); Goodyear's run-flat tyres are based on its 'RunOnFlat' technology, which enables vehicles to keep going for up to 80 kilometres after a puncture or blowout; this technology is fundamentally similar to its competitors, Bridgestone and Michelin, which suggests that any cutting-edge development (with commercialisation potential) in this technological 'arms race' would quickly find widespread adoption by incumbents (Goodyear, 2011c). Further, Goodyear has developed an airless tyre in conjunction with the NASA Glenn Research Centre in Cleveland, Ohio (Goodyear, 2009). In 2011, Goodyear also secured a US$1.5 million grant from the US government's Department of Energy (DOE) to develop a potentially game-changing self-inflating tyre for commercial trucks (Schoenberger, 2011). This self-inflating tyre technology by Goodyear, which is still undergoing development and testing, is known as 'air maintenance technology' (AMT). This technology enables tyres to remain inflated at the optimum pressure without the need for any external pumps or electronics and all components of the AMT system, including the miniaturised pump would be entirely contained within the tyre; underinflated tyres increase a vehicle's resistance, invariably causing added strain on its engines and concurrently raising its fuel consumption (Shea, 2015).

Goodyear's cutting-edge technology has won industry accolades. For instance, Goodyear's still-in-development AMT was chosen by 'Car and Driver' magazine as one of the top ten upcoming technologies with propitious prospects in its 2012 Ten Best edition. This AMT technology, if successfully developed and commercialised, has the potential to be the new 'industry standard' and enable it to leapfrog its existing competitors. Nonetheless, some industry analysts have long questioned whether it is worthwhile for companies to invest hundreds of millions (even billions) on R&D, as advances in the tyre industry are easily reversed engineered and it would be well-nigh impossible to sustain a significant competitive advantage over the long term; this argument actually applies across all industries and sectors (Car and Driver, 2011; Tire Review, 2011; Aeppel, 2003). Through collaborations with universities and government bodies, Goodyear has been able to alleviate rising research costs and secure high value-added technologies that could give it an edge in an increasingly competitive tyres market. By extension, it could also be argued that government assistance in the form of R&D support is a manifestation of a country's industrial policy in sustaining the competitiveness of its domestic industries.

To further spur organic growth (via superior technology), Goodyear is increasing production of high-tech green tyres (meant to improve fuel efficiency) and run-flat tyres in key markets such as China (Goodyear, 2011b; Mcnulty, 2015). Goodyear's superior tyre technology could also give it a significant competitive advantage in fast-growing Asian markets, as its tyres are tougher, and more suitable for roads across developing markets (e.g., China) where roads could be considerably rougher than those of Europe and commercial vehicles (e.g., trucks) are more prone to overloading (Asian Development Bank, 2013).

In this all-out clash for market dominance between industry leviathans, Goodyear continues to relentlessly pursue the next breakthrough in tyre technology, which would restore what it believes to be its rightful place as industry leader. For instance, in March 2016, the company unveiled its concept Eagle-360 tyre which was conceived with the intention of complementing the capabilities of autonomous vehicles; the artificial intelligence on board driverless cars can fully optimise the multi-directional capabilities of the Eagle-360, a feat which is impossible with human drivers. The Eagle-360's unique spherical shape and multi-directional capabilities offer unprecedented manoeuvrability, road grip and safety standards. At the heart of this revolutionary tyre is its magnetic levitation technology, which suspends the tyre from the vehicle, in a manner akin to today's magnetic levitation trains, in the process, significantly bolstering the driving experience (due to noise reduction and increased passenger comfort).

Like Bridgestone's CAIS system, the sophisticated sensors in the Eagle-360 can assess road conditions while simultaneously communicating this to the driver and more remarkably to other vehicles; the ability to network with other vehicles to enhance safety standards may not be present in Bridgestone's CAIS system. Further, the Eagle-360, through its cutting-edge tread wear and pressure monitoring system, can ascertain and even regulate tyre conditions with the aim of extending mileage. There is also a distinct possibility of customising the Eagle-360, using 3-D printing technology, to suit the distinctive road conditions of different regions (Moseman, 2016; Goodyear, 2016). It is important to recognise that the Eagle-360 (at least currently) remains a concept but even if a fraction of its capabilities were to diffuse into the mainstream, it would significantly enhance overall safety standards.

Like its key competitors (i.e., Bridgestone and Michelin), Goodyear has adopted lean over the past decade (around 2004/2005) to bolster its competitive advantage but it has been relatively slow in promoting lean across the entire organisation. Nonetheless, it is now reaping the benefits of lean, as evidenced in the case of its Fayetteville plant in North Carolina. Up until 2010, the plant was still struggling to survive, producing 31,200 tyres daily below its expected daily output of 36,000–38,000 tyres. Nonetheless, with the introduction of lean in June 2010, Goodyear was able to increase daily production at the Fayetteville plant to 38,000 tyres, without having to increase the number of employees or make a significant investment in equipment. In 2009, the plant was making a little over 30,000 tyres on 14,400 hours daily. However, by 2011, it was making over 38,000 tyres on about 13,000 hours daily and the cost of production had declined by US$2.27 per tyre (Goodyear, 2012a). Goodyear's case demonstrates again the value of lean in facilitating process improvements that lower costs and strengthen a company's bottom line. The resultant cost savings also creates a virtuous cycle where more resources are extricated for next-generational R&D, further bolstering technical progress.

4. Industry consolidation beyond the big three tyre makers (1980s-present)

The big three tyre manufacturers (Bridgestone, Michelin and Goodyear) were not the only subsystems integrators affected by the disruptive forces cascading through the global supply chain. The so-called second-tier tyre manufacturers such as Pirelli, Continental and Cooper were also impacted by this cascade effect, compelling them to embark on acquisition campaigns to seek greater economies of scale and scope. As mentioned earlier, Pirelli was unsuccessful in the aggressive bidding war for Firestone, as its competitor, Bridgestone had a larger financial war chest. However, it was more successful in its second attempt in penetrating the US tyre market, as it managed to secure control of Armstrong Tire Company from Armtek Corporation for US$190 million in April 1988 (a month after its failed bid for Firestone). An industry analyst asserted that the acquisition of Armstrong granted Pirelli the American presence it wanted albeit of a smaller scale than it had originally desired (Hicks, 1988). The other European tyre manufacturer, Continental proved more successful in its initial attempts in penetrating the US market as it managed to acquire General Tire, the third largest US tyre maker, from Gencorp for US$650 million (in cash) in June 1987 (Reuters, 1987). Nonetheless, it is apparent that the most highly desired targets (i.e., Firestone and Uniroyal Goodrich) in the highly lucrative US market were all acquired by the companies with the greatest financial muscle (i.e., Bridgestone and Michelin), leaving the second-tier players (i.e., Pirelli and Continental) to contend themselves with the smaller and less desirable American targets.

Continental was relatively more successful in Europe. The company entered the 1980s, on the back of its successful acquisition of the European assets of Uniroyal in 1979 – a deal that brought plants in Belgium, the UK, France, and Germany into its fold. In 1985, Continental started its acquisition campaign by purchasing Semperit, an Austrian tyre producer for DM47 million, in the process gaining plants in Austria and Ireland (Sturgeon and Lester, 2003; Reference for Business, 2012). Further, Continental persisted with its acquisition drive, by acquiring the Czech tyre maker, Barum, a former leading East European brand in 1993, in the process strengthening its market position in Eastern Europe (Continental, 2012). Continental also had some success in penetrating the rapidly growing Mexican market, as it acquired the tyre business of Mexican industrial group, Grupo Carso (Mexico's then largest tyre maker with 1997 sales of US$328 million); Continental secured control of Grupo Carso's tyre business (which comprised two tyre factories and a conveyor-belt plant) by giving it a 19.4 percent stake in its US division, Continental General Tire along with US$18.9 million in cash (Bloomberg, 1998a).

Despite these successes, Continental still could not achieve the sheer economies of scale and scope, and market share achieved by its larger rivals, Bridgestone and Michelin. This is attributable to the fact that Bridgestone and Michelin were able to acquire and integrate the top American players (i.e., Firestone and Uniroyal Goodrich), in the process gaining dominant scale economies and market share in the US, the world's largest tyre market by the 1990s. Even in the ensuing years, Continental continued to seek further acquisitions. For instance, in 2007, Continental acquired a controlling 51 percent stake in Slovak Republic-based tyre maker Matador Rubber (2006 revenues: US$584 million) for a reported US$201 million, before purchasing the remaining shares in 2009 (Hetzner, 2007; Matador, 2012).

Continental's acquisition of Matador Rubber bolstered its presence in the low-budget brand segment (hitherto it only had the Barum brand), where it faces intense competition from low-price Chinese imports; Continental mainly competes in the premium and standard segments with its Continental, Semperit and Uniroyal brands (Europa, 2007). Further, Continental's acquisition of Matador Rubber expands its Central and Eastern European presence. The fact that Continental had a long-standing successful JV with Matador for the production of truck tyres in Puchov, Slovakia (since 1998) also greatly facilitated this acquisition; this proves the value of JVs as a means of understanding partners and markets before deciding on an acquisition (Continental, 2007). To augment its presence in India's expanding tyres market, Continental acquired 100 percent shareholding of Modi Tyres Company Limited (MTCL), a subsidiary of Modi

Rubber Ltd for US$26.5 million. Through this acquisition, MTCL became a fully owned subsidiary of Continental and was renamed Continental Tyres India Private Limited. This new subsidiary not only focused on local production and distribution of radial passenger car tyres but also the bias and radial truck and bus tyres market for the subcontinent. This was not a random acquisition for Continental, as it was well-acquainted with MTCL's previous owner (i.e., Modi Rubber), having established a technical collaboration agreement with Continental in 1974 to launch a plant in Meerut; the tyres produced by the Meerut plant were marketed under the name Modi-Continental (Continental, 2011; Business Standard, 2011).

As mentioned earlier, Pirelli also tried to acquire a controlling interest in Continental in 1990 but was ultimately unsuccessful in its acquisition attempt. Pirelli had hoped to combine the respective strengths of the two companies; Continental dominated the German and northern European markets while Pirelli had greater market presence in Italy and southern Europe (in the US, Continental and Pirelli also controlled General Tire and Armstrong respectively). This merger strategy would have created a combined company strong enough to challenge the triumvirate of Bridgestone, Michelin and Goodyear (Hicks, 1990). Unfortunately, Pirelli was unable to move beyond a 5 percent stake it had accumulated in Continental due to strong resistance from Continental's management, which did not see any synergistic gains. In hindsight, it would have been advisable for the two firms to merge, as neither held more than 8 percent of the global tyre market, and their merger would have enabled them to augment/complement each other's strengths in Europe and the US. Further, a merger would have given the combined Continental/Pirelli significantly greater economies of scale and scope, perhaps even enabling the firm to supplant Goodyear as the world's third largest tyre maker today (Hicks, 1990).

Cooper, one of the smallest of the American tyre makers (in 1996, Cooper had sales of US$1.6 billion compared to Goodyear's US$13.2 billion), also attempted to consolidate its market position by means of acquisition. Unfortunately, its financial resources were even more limited than those of Pirelli and Continental thus it could only target the relatively smaller third-tier tyre manufacturers. For instance, Cooper acquired the UK's Avon Rubber p.l.c. (a leading supplier of sports racing tyres) for US$110.4 million in March 1997. This acquisition gave Cooper a plant in England, a distribution network that spanned France, Germany, and Switzerland, and footholds in several Asian markets. Further, it contributed an additional US$169 million to Cooper's revenues (Business Wire, 1997; fundinguniverse, 2012; CNNMoney, 2012). However, compared to the multi-billion acquisitions made by Bridgestone and Michelin, such acquisitions could hardly give Cooper the significant boost in economies of scale and scope needed to compete in an increasingly capital-intensive and internationalised tyre market. Consequently, Cooper has not been able to penetrate the top seven positions in Tire Business' annual ranking of the world's largest tyre makers and has in fact fallen to tenth place in 2011; even tyre companies that did not rank in the top ten in the 1990s have overtaken it in terms of overall revenue. For instance, Taiwan's Maxxis (also known as Cheng Sin Rubber Industry Co.

Ltd) has overtaken Cooper to become the ninth largest tyre company globally in 2011 with revenues of US$4.27 billion, as opposed to Cooper's 2011 revenues of US$3.93 billion; in 1999, Maxxis was ranked fourteenth worldwide. Hankook which ranked eleventh worldwide in 1999, has also overtaken Cooper and was ranked the eighth largest tyre company globally in 2011 with revenues of US$5.74 billion (TireBusiness.com, 2012).

In May 2013, Cooper found itself the takeover target of Apollo, an Indian tyre maker, which sought to acquire Cooper for US$2.5 billion. However, Apollo's bid fell through in December 2013, undone by Apollo's attempt to cut its original US$35 a share bid; Apollo's attempt to reduce its original bid was driven by the fact that Cooper, at that time, was plagued by union problems in the United States and troubles with its Chinese JV partner (Gelles, 2013; Hoffman, 2013). Not long after this failed merger attempt, Cooper's China JV partner, Chengshan Group Co also acquired Cooper's 65 percent stake in their JV, Cooper Chengshan (Shandong) Tire Co for US$284.5 million in October 2014; this acquisition undoubtedly hampered Cooper's plan to expand its operations and market share in China, the world's largest automotive market (Murphy, 2014). In a bid to gain much needed scale economies in an industry constantly buffeted by the forces of consolidation, Cooper acquired a majority 65 percent stake in China-based Qingdao Ge Rui Da Rubber Co., Ltd. (GRT) for US$93 million in 2016. Following this acquisition, the new merged entity was renamed Cooper Qingdao Tire Co (hereafter 'CQT'), which would serve as a global source of truck and bus radial tyre production for Cooper (including the Roadmaster brand tyres) for the North American and international markets; CQT is Cooper's eighth plant globally. Further, Cooper's passenger car radial tires are also expected to be manufactured at CQT's plant in future. CQT is estimated to have the capacity to produce about 2.5 million to 3 million truck and bus radial tyres annually. Moreover, this facility is also expected to have the capability to produce approximately the same number of passenger car tyres, with room to expand capacity (Cooper, 2016; Davis, 2016).

As evidenced earlier in this chapter, the pace of consolidation seems to have slowed at the top-tier level (the marquee brands of Bridgestone, Michelin and Goodyear), with the second/third-tier brands still experiencing considerable consolidation, as they struggle to secure greater economies of scale and scope to survive/grow in an increasingly oligopolistic industry. For instance, Pirelli has been targeting smaller players in Russia such as Sibur Russian Tyre and Amtel Povolzhye Tire Complex J.S.C. (in Kirov). In November 2010, Pirelli acquired a 10 percent stake in Sibur as a means of securing its own production plants in the Russian Federation and possibly also as a springboard to a larger stake in that company. As for Amtel Povolzhye Tire Complex J.S.C., Pirelli acquired all its assets in November 2011; the 68-year-old Kirov plant has listed annual capacity of 7 million car and light truck tyres. Further, through its wide-ranging JV agreements with Russian Technologies State Corp. and Sibur Holding, Pirelli would gain control of production assets with the capacity to generate annual revenues of US$715 million by 2014 (Davis, 2011a). Pirelli was planning to use these arrangements (if they work out) to consolidate its market presence, secure greater economies of scale and scope, and maybe even contest for a place in the top three global rankings. In this scramble for market power, it is not surprising that Pirelli itself became an acquisition target of a Chinese state-owned enterprise, China National Chemical Corp (hereafter 'CNCC'). In March 2015, CNCC acquired a 26.2 percent stake in Pirelli for US$7.7 billion, which was followed by a mandatory takeover bid for the rest of Pirelli. CNCC's acquisition of Pirelli gave it access to premium tyre making technology which would not only enable it to command higher margins in an increasingly competitive tyre market but also position it as a viable challenger to the marquee brands (i.e., Bridgestone, Michelin, and Goodyear) (Arosio and Masoni, 2015).

Japan's fourth-largest tyre maker, Toyo, acquired Malaysia's second-largest tyre manufacturer, Silverstone Bhd, for US$148 million in October 2010, in an attempt to bolster its presence in Southeast Asia. Further, Toyo acquired a 75 percent stake in Shandong Silverstone Luhe Rubber & Tyre Co. Ltd. in July 2011 for US$21.5 million and changed the unit's name to Toyo Tire (Zhucheng) Co. Ltd. These two acquisitions could have added US$250 million to Toyo's annual revenues (Toyo, 2010; Patrascu, 2010). Additionally, Titan International Inc., an agricultural tyre specialist, acquired Goodyear's Latin American farm tyre business for approximately US$98.6 million in April 2011 (Modern Tire Dealer, 2011; Titan, 2011).

This flurry of deals indicates that there is still considerable consolidation occurring in the global tyres industry, despite the fact that the top three tyre companies now control around 40 percent of the global tyre market. The competition is probably more intense than what it was in the 1980s, with the major second-tier players (e.g., Pirelli, Continental, Cooper) scrambling to acquire the remaining smaller tyre companies, to better position themselves in their fight against the top three tyre makers. Despite their best efforts, it is questionable whether it would pay off, as even the smallest of the big three tyre makers (i.e., Goodyear) has revenues that are still considerably larger than that of the larger second-tier firms, Continental and Pirelli; in 2015, Goodyear recorded revenues of US$16.4 billion while Continental and Pirelli recorded significantly smaller revenues of US$11.3 billion and US$6.9 billion respectively (given this situation, the others such as Cooper, Maxxis, Hankook, Toyo, Kumho and Yokohama would scarcely stand a chance) (Continental, 2015; Pirelli, 2015).

5. Emergence of consolidation among natural rubber suppliers

The 'captive' natural rubber suppliers

The natural rubber industry is a US$33 billion industry, making it the world's second largest tropical agriculture crop after palm oil. The natural rubber industry is highly dependent on China, with the country alone accounting for 39.1 percent of global consumption. Currently, this industry is still largely made up of small players, with the largest supplier (by revenues), Von Bundit, accounting for only 5.18 percent (US$1.71 billion) of the overall market (Von Bundit, 2016;

Research In China, 2015; Philippine Rural Development Program, 2015). Trailing Von Bundit by only a whisker, the next largest player, Sri Trang, with 2015 revenues of about US$1.704 billion, controls about 5.16 percent of the global natural rubber market (Von Bundit, 2016). Not resigned to living in the shadow of the two industry leaders, Sinochem International's (hereafter 'Sinochem') rubber division (with revenues of US$600 million in 2014) would vault to pole position in the natural rubber market after it completes its integration of acquired firm, Halcyon Agri Corporation Limited (hereafter 'Halcyon'); the merged entity would have revenues of approximately US$2.3 billion. Even after its assimilation of Halcyon, Sinochem would account for no more than 7 percent of the market. The remaining market share is spread across a disparate pool of smaller suppliers, illustrating the considerable room for consolidation (see Figure 3.8).

In this industry, approximately 80 percent of the plantations are small-scale operations of only a few hectares, run mostly by small independent farmers. However, this industry provides employment for nearly 6 million people directly and some 20 million indirectly across the world. Tyre makers account for 70 percent of global natural rubber consumption and this gives them significant market power in price negotiations with disparate rubber producers scattered across Thailand, Indonesia, Malaysia, China and India. As tyre makers are the major customers in this industry, they have no qualms in leveraging on their market power to extract sizeable discounts (sometimes up to 20 percent); Natural rubber

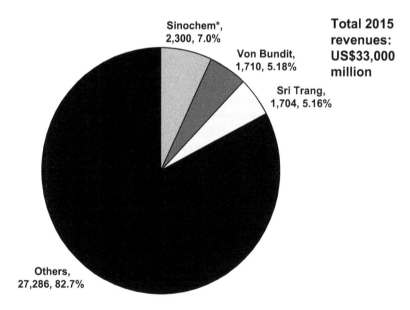

Figure 3.8 Natural rubber suppliers by 2015 revenues (US$ million)

Source: 2015 Sri Trang Annual Report, Von Bundit Website, Reuters

*Sinochem after incorporating Halcyon would have an estimated US$2.3 billion in revenues

purchases could account for as much as 15 percent of a tyre maker's revenues, thus it is in their interest to flex their financial muscle to lower their purchasing costs (Corre, 2012; Goodyear, 2001).

In a bid to augment their bargaining power in price negotiations with their considerably larger tyre producer customers, some natural rubber suppliers have also turned to M&A strategies over the past decade. Von Bundit, the existing market leader is the least acquisitive of the pack. It made its major acquisition in 1994, where it acquired a factory (based in Punpin district, Suratthani Province) from Euro Siam Co. Ltd, a Thai-French rubber company. The company has since expanded the factory site by 18 times and significantly raised its production output from 2,000 metric tons (mt) to 40,800 mt per month. Following this acquisition, Von Bundit has since relied on organic growth; in 2012, the company established three more factories in Chumphon, Trang and Phuket. However, in view of the growing competition from its rivals and mounting pressure from its tyre maker clients, Von Bundit has decided to adopt a more acquisitive approach, by acquiring Trang Latex in 2012 (Von Bundit, 2016; Phuket Gazatte, 2014).

In December 2006, the world's then largest natural rubber supplier by revenues (now second place), Sri Trang, bolstered its economies of scale and scope, by investing an estimated US$32 million to raise its equity stake in seven Thai subsidiaries (Table 3.2) to 99.9 percent.

That same year, it also tightened its control over its Indonesian subsidiary, PT Sri Trang Linga Indonesia through a US$2.5 million investment which increased its considerable 80 percent stake to 90 percent. Further, through its 100 percent owned subsidiary, Shi Dong Investment, Sri Trang acquired a 99 percent stake in PT Star Rubber, an Indonesian company (with a monthly rubber processing capacity of 2,000–2,500 tons) for US$8 million in 2009 (Sri Trang, 2006; Sri Trang, 2009). Another example of consolidation among natural rubber suppliers would be that of China's Sinochem International acquiring Malaysia-based natural rubber producer Euroma Rubber Industries (with annual rubber processing capacity of 30,000 tons) in September 2007; this represented Sinochem's first overseas acquisition with regard to its natural rubber business, following its acquisition of three domestic natural rubber plants (i.e., Hainan Enlian, Yunnan Xiangdong and Hainan Chengxin) earlier in 2007. In its overseas expansion

Table 3.2 Sri Trang increased investment in seven subsidiaries (December 2006)

Sri Trang Subsidiaries	Investment (US$ million)
Anvar Parawood Company Limited	0.7
Rubberland Products Company Limited	17.0
Numhua Rubber Company Limited	6.5
Sadao P.S. Rubber Company Limited	1.3
Startex Rubber Company Limited	0.8
Premier System Engineering Company Limited	3.9
Starlight Express Transport Company Limited	1.8

Source: Sri Trang Agro-Industry Public Company Limited

drive, Sinochem quickly followed up with the acquisition of a controlling 51 percent stake in Singapore-headquartered GMG Global Ltd (a rubber plantation
group with significant operations in Central Africa, West Africa and Indonesia)
for an estimated US$198 million in 2008. In 2007, GMG recorded revenues
of approximately US$134.1 million and had total annual production of above
50,000 mt (GMG, 2007).

At the time of Sinochem's investment, GMG had a 90 percent stake in
Cameroon-based Hevecam, which operates a rubber plantation with an annual
processing capacity of over 50,000 mt on a land concession of 40,000 hectares
since December 1996. Further in the Ivory Coast, GMG had a 51.2 percent stake
in Tropical Rubber Cote d'Ivoire (listed as a GMG subsidiary), which owns a
processing facility with annual capacity of 30,000 mt and a rubber plantation on
a land concession of 1,511 hectares (Anguededou Plantation) since 1995 (GMG,
2007). Additionally, GMG had a 51 percent subsidiary (since April 2007), PT
Bumi Jaya in South Kalimantan, Indonesia, which owned a rubber processing
facility with an annual capacity of 30,000 mt. Moreover, GMG accounted for
approximately 60 percent and 12 percent of Cameroon's and Ivory Coast's annual
rubber exports, respectively (in Ivory Coast, it was the second largest buyer of
smallholders' rubber) (GMG, 2007). Further, in late 2009, GMG expanded into
Pontianak, West Kalimantan by acquiring a 75 percent stake in a JV, PT GMG
Sentosa (deal was completed by January 2010) that has an annual production
capability of 25,000 mt (GMG, 2009). In its aggressive overseas expansion bid,
GMG soon acquired a 80 percent stake in Cameroon-based JV company, Sud-
Cameroun Hevea (hereafter 'SCH'), for the development of a 45,000 hectares
land concession for natural rubber plantings (GMG, 2011).

Further, GMG formally acquired Thailand's Teck Bee Hang Co., Ltd (hereafter 'TBH') in December 2010; through this acquisition, GMG gave its parent company, Sinochem effective control of TBH's five rubber processing plants
across Thailand (Surat Thani, Thung Song, Pattani, Yala and Narathiwat) and
significantly increased its natural rubber processing capacity from 300,000 mt to
500,000 mt, in the process also making Sinochem the third largest natural rubber supplier globally (Sinochem, 2010; GMG, 2012). The fact that GMG's controlling shareholder, Sinochem has a deep understanding of TBH's operations
through a long-standing relationship (they had jointly established a company
known as Dehua Rubber Company in the 1980s) greatly facilitated this acquisition (Sinochem, 2011).

In December 2011, GMG acquired a dominant 60 percent stake in ITCA, an
existing processing factory in Dabou, Cote d'Ivoire which has a rubber processing capacity of 20,000 tons. In that same period, GMG also acquired a controlling 60 percent in another JV, based in Aboisso, Cote d'Ivoire, with a potential
rubber processing capacity of 30,000 mt (GMG, 2011). Not letting up on this
burst of acquisition, GMG soon acquired a 35 percent stake in SIAT SA, a Bel-
gian-incorporated producer of natural rubber for an estimated €192.56 million
in July 2012; SIAT had plantation operations in Nigeria, Ghana, Gabon, Cote
d'Ivoire, Belgium and Cambodia thus GMG's partial acquisition of SIAT greatly

bolstered its international presence (following this transaction, SIAT was listed as an associate company of GMG's, which meant GMG exercised a high degree of control over its operations) (SIAT, 2012; GMG, 2012).

Over the past seven years, smaller emerging players such as Singapore-based Halcyon (founded in 2010) are also turning to M&A to consolidate their market power and gain swift access to additional marketing and distribution capabilities. In February 2011, Halcyon acquired two crumb rubber factories in Palembang, Indonesia. Drawing on its considerable war chest following its successful 2013 Initial Public Offering in Singapore, Halcyon also embarked and completed its acquisition of two Standard Malaysian Rubber factories and 10,000 hectares of 99-year leasehold Sultanate land in the Malaysian State of Kelantan by the first quarter of 2014 for approximately US$360 million. By August 2014, Halcyon also acquired control of Anson Company (Private) Limited, the Indonesian arm of the Lee Rubber Group of Companies for about US$362 million. Anson comprised four Indonesian legal entities, namely PT Hok Tong, PT Rubber Hock Lie, PT Sunan Rubber and PT Remco along with nine crumb rubber factories, largely spread across Sumatra. This acquisition also boosted Halcyon's production capacity by over 300,000 mt annually (Halcyon, 2014).

In August 2014, Halcyon also acquired New Continent Enterprises, a rubber distributor and dealer for approximately US$30 million; the deal was executed to further strengthen Halcyon's marketing and distribution capabilities (Chan, 2014). Not resting on its laurels, Halcyon continued its relentless acquisition campaign by acquiring the CentroTrade Rubber Group in June 2015 for approximately US$9.7 million. This acquisition augmented Halcyon's already strong global distribution capabilities (its distribution capacity was about one million tonnes annually), as CentroTrade had logistical assets across seven countries. In addition, this deal gave Halcyon added capabilities in dry natural rubber and latex products (Halcyon, 2015). Through these acquisitions, Halcyon has acquired capabilities across the natural rubber value chain, enabling the firm to give its customers the grades of rubber they require with consistent quality standards and in accordance to their specifications (Moore, 2015). Without an aggressive acquisitions strategy, it would not have been possible for Halcyon (founded in 2010) to more than double its revenues from US$231.4 million in December 2011 to US$479.2 million by December 2014 (Halcyon, 2012; Halcyon, 2014).

The entry of non-traditional players (i.e., private equity firms and billionaire investors) into the traditional rubber industry also bolstered Halcyon's buoyant fortunes and acquisition war chest. For instance, in 2013, private equity firm Credence Partners invested approximately US$24 million for a 13 percent stake in Halcyon. In August 2014, a Singapore billionaire investor, Sam Goi also acquired 25 million Halcyon shares (a 5.94 percent stake in the firm) for approximately US$15 million (Soh, 2015).

By 2016, the 'hunter soon became the hunted', with Halcyon itself becoming the acquisition target of Sinochem, in a potential deal valued at approximately US$300 million (Venkat, 2016). The deal is expected to create the world's largest natural rubber supply chain manager which controls 153,000 ha of land spanning Africa and South-east Asia. Further the combined entity would have 35 processing facilities across Africa, China, Indonesia, Malaysia and Thailand with an expected total annual processing capacity of approximately 1.5 million tonnes. Moreover it would have revenues exceeding US$2.3 billion (Aravindan, 2016; Cheok, 2016). By August 2016, Sinochem secured a controlling 65.73 percent stake in Halcyon. As its coup de grâce, Sinochem, through its use of Halcyon as a buyout vehicle, also successfully acquired 100 percent control of GMG by November 2016; even prior to its acquisition of Halcyon, Sinochem already held a significant 51.12 percent shareholding in GMG and simply used Halcyon to scoop up the remaining shares it did not own by the end of 2016. This series of acquisitions invariably paved the way for Sinochem's ascension to the status of the world's top natural rubber supply chain manager (Halcyon, 2016a; Halcyon, 2016b; GMG, 2015). This consolidation trend indicates the sheer resolve of rubber suppliers to gain the market power needed to engage tyre makers on a level playing field with regard to price negotiations.

Although these natural rubber suppliers are still too small to challenge the market power of the tyre makers (Bridgestone, Michelin and Goodyear account for at least 60 percent of global natural rubber purchasing), it is conceivable that given time (and after considerable industry consolidation), the balance of power could change in their favour (Takada, Suwannakij and Song, 2012; Wong, 2013). Like their customers (i.e., the tyre makers) and the automobile industry nearly a century earlier, the natural rubber suppliers are starting to understand and more importantly apply the Chandlerian principles of economies of scale and scope, which are subsequently coupled with judicious acquisition strategies aimed at securing greater scale economies, market access and industry power. These natural rubber suppliers are trying to control the various aspects of their value chain (from production to marketing and distribution), in the hope of securing an edge with regard to price negotiations with their significantly larger tyre maker clients.

'Tug of war' between tyre makers and their rubber suppliers

The tyre makers are cognisant of their dependence on their natural rubber suppliers and have been investing millions in developing their synthetic rubber technologies (e.g., from 1997 to 2003, Goodyear spent an estimated US$600 million in synthetic rubber research) (ICB, 1997). Synthetic rubber is not necessarily a cheaper alternative as its key building block, oil is subject to considerable market volatility. This dependency on oil in turn has over the past decade compelled tyre majors such as Goodyear to work with companies such as DuPont Industrial Biosciences (collaboration was formed in 2008) to develop BioIsoprene, a potential bio-based alternative to petroleum-derived isoprene which is used to make synthetic rubber (Goodyear, 2012b). Nonetheless synthetic rubber properties are still a long way from matching the heat-resistance and flexibility ('less build-up of heat from flexing and greater resistance to tearing when hot') of their natural counterparts; this inherently superior quality of natural rubber virtually ensures the tyre producers' continued reliance on their rubber suppliers over the long term (Columbia University Press, 2009). The stranglehold wielded by the inimitable properties of natural rubber on the tyres industry reflects mankind's inextricable dependence on the natural environment despite the dazzling technological progress it has attained over the millennia.

6. Conclusion

Since the 1980s, the global tyres market, driven by the cascade effect, has evolved into a highly oligopolistic market with the top three companies (i.e., Bridgestone, Michelin and Goodyear) accounting for around 40 percent of global market share by 2015 (Bridgestone, 2015; Michelin, 2015; Goodyear, 2015). If the market shares of Continental and Pirelli (the fourth and fifth largest tyre makers) were to be included, their global market share would be over 50 percent of 2015 global tyre sales (Continental, 2015; Pirelli, 2015). It is arguable that, if these companies had not embarked on massive acquisition campaigns in the 1980s (with the US being the key battle ground), it is highly possible that some of them (the ones that are not in the top five positions) would either have gone out of business or assimilated into a larger and more successful company.

This is especially so, in an era, where tyre companies face rising R&D, volatile raw material costs and an increasing need to expand their international operations to match the growth strategies of their increasingly multinational automaker clients, along with their exacting demands for supplier support in just-in-time operations worldwide; due to the demands of just-in-time, even second-tier players such as Kumho do not keep more than one to two days' supplies (tyrepress, 2011; Bridgestone, 2010; Kumho, 2004). Tyre companies that do not have the requisite economies of scale and scope would have difficulty expanding (or even surviving) in this increasingly competitive and costly environment where corporate agendas leveraging on technological superiority to achieve market dominance are now in the ascendant; the escalating costs plaguing this technological 'arms race' may be a necessary evil to these incumbents but they would undoubtedly prove beneficial to their customers, owing to the transformative improvements in safety standards and driving experience. Currently, the global tyre industry seems to be highly consolidated at the marquee brand level and most consolidation, according to industry players, is now happening at the lower-tier levels. Further, the major second-tier firms such as Pirelli and Toyo have been attempting to acquire a sizeable number of smaller firms as a means of quickly strengthening its economies of scale and scope, with the hope of challenging the top three players for market dominance.

However, their ambitions and resources have been outmatched by the entry of gargantuan state-owned enterprises such as CNCC, which is trying to penetrate the marquee ranks by acquiring Pirelli itself; CNCC's acquisition of Pirelli would give it access to new markets and technologies, positioning it as a possible contender for a place in the top three ranks. Nonetheless, M&A do not always result in the desired synergies (as evidenced in the case of Goodyear and Sumitomo), as the acquirer has to assimilate different legacy systems along with varied corporate cultures. Moreover, with the emergence of a consolidation trend among their natural supplier suppliers over the past decade, it is questionable whether the major tyre producers would be able to enjoy the considerable leverage they have over these suppliers over the long term. The larger firms amongst the natural rubber suppliers are now transforming themselves through aggressive acquisition strategies into multinational natural rubber supply chain companies with extensive rubber resources and processing facilities across the Asian and African regions. Given time, the balance of power between the tyre makers and their natural rubber suppliers could change. With this emerging trend, it is doubtful these increasingly powerful natural rubber suppliers would cede price and make other concessions as readily as they currently do.

Notes

1 The tyre industry was made possible by Charles Goodyear's disputed discovery of vulcanisation (this process made rubber sufficiently durable and resilient for industrial use) in 1839. Despite this remarkable discovery and the use of his name (by what was to become one of the largest global tyre manufacturers), Charles Goodyear did not reap any financial benefits. This discovery also benefitted from the bicycle boom of the 1890s and the subsequent arrival of the automobile soon after (Goodyear, 2011a; Goodyear, 2012; MIT, 1999).

2 The trend of squeezing tyre makers for lower prices is evidenced in the following statement by William O' Neil, Sr., the founder of General Tire: 'Detroit wants tyres that are round, black, and cheap and it don't care whether they are round and black' (Tedlow, 1991).

3 Vertical integration is a strategy through which companies expand by acquisition of suppliers and retailers to develop and augment control over raw materials and retail capabilities respectively; in the process, firms are able to reduce transaction costs (Chandler, 1992; Chandler, 2004). Backward integration is driven by a firm's belief that it could produce some of its material requirements more economically that it could purchase them in the open market. Firms intending to embark on backward integration, should not only consider the estimated cost savings, but they should also consider the 'opportunity cost of resources' deployed in integrating their former suppliers. Forward integration is driven by the desire for better control of the product sold; it facilitates greater advertising, a more effective sales team and prudent management of product design that could ensure greater customer satisfaction (Galbraith, 1972; Penrose, 1995).

4 The first Bridgestone tyre was produced on 9 April 1930, by the Japan 'Tabi' socks Tyre Division. A year later, the founder, Shojiro Ishibashi, made the Japan 'Tabi' socks Tyre Division independent and established the Bridgestone Tire Co., Ltd. in the city of Kurume, Fukuoka Prefecture (Bridgestone, 2012a).

5 Even Goodyear's former CEO Robert Mercer has considered acquiring Firestone but said it would have been impossible given US antitrust laws which made it extremely difficult (possibly illegal) for major US companies to acquire their domestic competitors (Mercer, 1990).

6 This is a backward integration strategy, as it involves the acquisition of one's suppliers, with the aim of reducing costs (Penrose, 1995).

7 Retreading enables customers to maximise the value of a new tyre through the constant reuse of its casing. This process has become a critical component of an efficacious total tyre management system (Bandag, 2006).

8 US tyre maker, Gates Rubber Co. exited the tyre business in 1973, due to the overly capital-intensive nature of manufacturing the increasingly global standard of radial tyres. Other small firms such as Mansfield Tire & Rubber Co. also went

out of business due to its inability to compete in the increasingly capital-intensive business of manufacturing radials. There were others such as Armstrong Rubber Co. in the US, that decided to compete as niche players (it became the second largest maker of tyres for farm machinery in the US) rather than joust in the intensifying competitive mainstream business of making radials; this strategy may have been ill-advised, as niche players were especially vulnerable to takeovers by their larger mass-market counterparts with their significantly greater economies of scale and scope (Hicks, 1988; ITEC, 2012).

9 Oil prices began their precipitous decline by end June 2014. However, there was still the distinct possibility that Goodyear could have derived significant profitability by retaining ownership of Celeron for a longer period instead of divesting the company early on in 1987 (The Economist, 2014; Hicks, 1987).

10 Goodyear acquiring 10 percent of Sumitomo may not be an outright acquisition but the deal still made Goodyear the second largest shareholder in Sumitomo (The Japan Times, 2003).

References

Abrams, R. (2000) When the Rubber meets the road: Lessons from a brand in crisis, *Inc.com* [internet] Available at: www.inc.com/articles/2000/11/21212.html [Accessed on 24 September, 2012].

Aeppel, T. (2003), Goodyear misses opportunity to capitalize on Rival's Woes, *wsj.com* [internet] Available at: http://online.wsj.com/article_print/0,,SB1045608 649276547023,00.html [Accessed on 4 February, 2012].

AG Continental (1998) Continental buys 'Brake and Chassis' Unit from ITT Industries, *Continental AG* [online] Available at: www.conti-online.com/generator/www/com/en/continental/portal/themes/ir/news_adhoc/archive/ad_hoc/ad_hoc_1998_07_27_1_en,version=10.html [Accessed on 6 February, 2012].

AG Continental (2007a) Continental to acquire 51 percent of Matador Rubber Group, *Continental AG* [online] Available at: www.conti-online.com/generator/www/de/en/continental/automobile/themes/news/archive/2007/goto_pr_2007_04_11_matador_en.html [Accessed on 20 July, 2012].

AG Continental (2007b) Continental Harnesses forces as purchase of Siemens VDO ushers in New Era, *Continental AG* [online] Available at: www.continental-corporation.com/www/portal_com_en/themes/ir/news_adhoc/archive/news/071205_day_one_en.html [Accessed on 20 July, 2012].

AG Continental (2011) *Annual Report 2011*, Hanover: Continental AG.

AG Continental (2012a) Continental acquires joint-venture shares from RICO auto, *Continental AG* [online] Available at: www.conti-online.com/generator/www/in/in/continental/pressportal/themes/press_releases/3_automotive_group/chassis_safety/goto_pr_2012_03_09_indien_jv_rico_en.html [Accessed on 12 April, 2012].

AG Continental (2012b) Corporate history, *Continental AG* [online] Available at: www.conti-online.com/generator/www/us/en/continental/pressportal/themes/basic_information/140_years_continental/hidden/goto_geschichte_en.html [Accessed on 12 April, 2012].

AG Continental (2015) *Annual Report 2015*, Hanover: Continental AG.

Ajami, R., Cool, K., Goddard, J. and Khambata, D. (2006) *International Business: Theory and Practice*, Second Edition, New York: M.E. Sharpe, Inc.

ALGOR (2011) ALGOR FEA Chosen to Verify Wheel Design for Goodyear "Runflat" Tires, ALGOR [internet] Available at: http://www.algor.com/news_pub/cust_app/goodyear/ [Accessed on 12 April, 2012].

Aravindan, A. (2016) Sinochem International, Halcyon Agri to create biggest natural rubber supply chain manager, *Reuters* [internet] Available at: www.reuters.com/ article/us-hac-m-a-sinochem-intl-idUSKCN0WU04D [Accessed on 2 July, 2016].

Argentum (2011) Procuritas acquires Sweden's leading tire service chain, Argentum [internet] Available at: http://www.argentum.no/en/Market-Database/Details/ ?type=deal&objId=794909 [Accessed on 3 August, 2012].

Arosio, P. and Masoni, D. (2015) ChemChina to buy into Italian tire maker Pirelli in \$7.7 billion deal, *Reuters* [internet] Available at: www.reuters.com/article/us-pirelli-chemchina-idUSKBN0MI0PQ20150323 [Accessed on 7 July, 2015].

Asian Development Bank (2013) *2013 Annual Evaluation Review: Issues in Road Maintenance*, Mandaluyong: Asian Development Bank.

Associated Press (1989) Michelin will buy Uniroyal Goodrich in \$1.5-billion deal, *Associated Press* [internet] Available at: http://articles.latimes.com/1989-09-22/ business/fi-891_1_uniroyal-goodrich [Accessed on 29 February, 2012].

Australia Network (2008) Asia's rubber growers to reduce production, Australia Network [internet] Available at: http://www.abc.net.au/australianetwork/news/sto ries_to/2406550.htm [Accessed on 28 November, 2011].

Balboni, A., Law, A., Duthoit, A., Alary, H., and Marty, L. (2010) World tyre manufacturers, market analysis – 2010–2015 trends – corporate strategies, *Global Markets and Competition* [internet] Available at: http://edu.u-bordeaux4.fr/courses/ ANAFI/document/Travaux_dirig%E9s/2012/autres_documents_li%E9s_au_ td03/01_Xerfi_%E9tude_sectorielle.pdf?cidReq=ANAFI [Accessed on 1 September, 2012].

Bandag (2006) Bridgestone Americas to acquire Bandag for \$1.05 billion in cash merger, *Bandag* [internet] Available at: www.bandag.com/pdfdisplay.aspx?id=87 [Accessed on 2 July, 2012].

Bell, R. (2014) Michelin executive: Tweel not ready for passenger car market, *GreenvilleOnline* [internet] Available at: www.greenvilleonline.com/story/ news/local/2014/11/20/michelin-executive-tweel-ready-passenger-car-mar ket/70026218/ [Accessed on 23 January, 2017].

Bell, R. (2016) Michelin says Mexico plant won't affect its SC operations, Greenville-Online [internet] Available at: http://www.greenvilleonline.com/story/money/ business/2016/07/05/michelin-says-mexico-plant-wont-affect-its-sc-opera tions/86721548/ [Accessed on 23 January, 2017].

Betts, P. (2010) Group clear about the road ahead, *FT.com* [internet] Available at: www.ft.com/intl/cms/s/0/69c21d66-cb26-11df-95c0-00144feab49a. html#axzz2NFBuHpYB [Accessed on 12 February, 2012].

Bloomberg (1998a) Continental buys Mexican Tire Business, *Los Angeles Times* [internet] Available at: http://articles.latimes.com/1998/nov/12/business/ fi-41892 [Accessed on 19 July, 2012].

Bloomberg (1998b) Goodyear to sell oil pipeline unit to plains for \$420 million, *Los Angeles Times* [internet] Available at: http://articles.latimes.com/1998/mar/24/ business/fi-32013 [Accessed on 3 December, 2011].

Bozdogan, K, Milauskas, R., Mize, J., Nightingale, D., Taneja, A., and Tonaszuck, D. (2000) Transitioning to A Lean Enterprise: A Guide for Leaders Volume III Roadmap Explorations, Massachusetts Institute of Technology, 1-147.

Bridgestone Americas Inc. (2012) Who we are: About Bridgestone Americas, Inc., *Bridgestone Americas* [internet] Available at: www.bridgestone-firestone.com/cor porate/whoweare/index.html [Accessed on 12 February, 2012].

Bridgestone Corporation (2001) *2001 Annual Report*, Tokyo: Bridgestone Corporation.

Bridgestone Corporation (2006) Bridgestone to build plant in Kitakyushu for large and Ultralarge Radial Tires for mining and construction equipment: First new tire plant in Japan since Hofu facility built in 1976, *Bridgestone Corporation* [internet] Available at: www.bridgestone-earthmover.com.au/Kitakyushu.htm [Accessed on 10 October, 2012].

Bridgestone Corporation (2007) Annual report 2007, Tokyo: Bridgestone Corporation.

Bridgestone Corporation (2009) *Annual Report 2009: Operational Review*, Tokyo: Bridgestone Corporation.

Bridgestone Corporation (2010) *Annual Report 2010: Operational Review*, Tokyo: Bridgestone Corporation.

Bridgestone Corporation (2011) Bridgestone Announces New Tire Technology for Determining Road Surface Conditions based on the concept of "CAIS", Bridgestone Corporation [internet] Available at: https://www.bridgestone.com.sg/b/wp-content/uploads/2013/09/110913-136-E.pdf [Accessed on 10 October, 2012].

Bridgestone Corporation (2012a) *Bridgestone: The European Story*, Tokyo: Bridgestone Corporation.

Bridgestone Corporation (2012b) Bridgestone Europe buys shares of Nokian Tyres, *Bridgestone Corporation* [internet] Available at: www.bridgestone.eu/bfe/v/index.jsp?vgnextoid=SZIT00000000000000043_7_70950articleRCRD&vgnextchannel=SZIT000000000000000000000000000004191RCRD [Accessed on 14 July, 2012].

Bridgestone Corporation (2012c) Bridgestone to increase production capacity of large and ultralarge off-the-road tires for construction and mining vehicles in Kitakyushu plant, *Bridgestone Corporation* [internet] Available at: www.bridgestone.com.sg/news/120216-18-E-Kitakyushu.pdf [Accessed on 10 October, 2012].

Bridgestone Corporation (2012d) *Financial Results for Fiscal 2011*, Tokyo: Bridgestone Corporation.

Bridgestone Corporation (2015) *Annual Report 2015: Operational Review*, Tokyo: Bridgestone Corporation.

Bridgestone Corporation (2016) Bridgestone to acquire Speedy, Bridgestone Corporation [internet] Available at: http://www.bridgestone.eu/corporate/press-releases/2016/05/bridgestone-to-acquire-speedy/ [Accessed on 10 October, 2016].

Bridgestone Europe (2004) Bridgestone Europe purchases Belgian mould manufacturer Mecamold, *Bridgestone Europe* [internet] Available at: www.bridgestone.eu/bfe/v/index.jsp?vgnextoid=00000000000000000001_2_52117articleRCRD&vgnextchannel=b80daab44eeaf110VgnVCM100000cc65a10aRCRD [Accessed on 14 July, 2012].

Bridgestone Europe (2016) Bridgestone Driveguard revolutionises the tyre industry, bringing additional benefits and safety for all consumers, Bridgestone Europe [internet] Available at: http://www.bridgestone.eu/corporate/press-releases/2016/01/bridgestone-driveguard/ [Accessed on 12 November, 2016].

Brooks, N.R. (1988) Firestone agrees to sell to Japan's Bridgestone for $2.6 billion cash, *Los Angeles Times* [internet] Available at: http://articles.latimes.com/1988-03-18/business/fi-1643_1_firestone-tire-rubber [Accessed on 3 April, 2012].

Brooks, N.R. (1989) Michelin Group to buy Uniroyal Goodrich in a deal worth $1.5 billion, *Los Angeles Times* [internet] Available at: http://articles.latimes.com/1989-09-23/business/fi-571_1_uniroyal-goodrich-tire-co [Accessed on 3 April, 2012].

Business Standard (2011) Continental to take over Modi Tyre Company, *Business Standard* [internet] Available at: www.business-standard.com/article/companies/continental-to-take-over-modi-tyre-company-111041900055_1.html [Accessed on 2 July, 2016].

Business Wire (1997) Cooper Tire & Rubber Company to acquire world tire operations of U.K.'s Avon Rubber p.l.c., *Business Wire* [internet] Available at: www.the-freelibrary.com/Cooper+Tire+%26+Rubber+Company+to+acquire+world+tire+operations+of . . . -a019133122 [Accessed on 23 February, 2012].

Car and Driver (2011) 2012 10Best: 10 most promising future technologies, *Car and Driver* [internet] Available at: www.caranddriver.com/features/2012-10best-10-most-promising-future-technologies-feature [Accessed on 3 March, 2012].

Chan, F. (2014) Halcyon Agri agrees to buy Singapore-based rubber distributor, *The Straits Times* [internet] Available at: www.straitstimes.com/business/com panies-markets/halcyon-agri-agrees-to-buy-singapore-based-rubber-distributor [Accessed on 7 July, 2016].

Chandler, A.D. (1992) What is a firm? A historical perspective, *European Economic Review*, 36: 483–492.

Chandler, A.D. (2004) *Scale and Scope: The Dynamics of Industrial Capitalism*, Seventh Printing, Cambridge, MA: Harvard University Press.

Chandler, A.D. and Hikino, T. (1999) The large industrial enterprise and the dynamics of modern economic growth, in Chandler, A., Amatori, F. and Hikino, T. (eds), Big Business and The Wealth of Nations, Cambridge: Cambridge University Press.

Cheok, J. (2016) Halcyon, Sinochem to merge natural rubber businesses, *The Business Times* [internet] Available at: www.businesstimes.com.sg/companies-markets/hal cyon-sinochem-to-merge-natural-rubber-businesses [Accessed on 12 July, 2016].

Christensen, C.M. (1997) The Innovator's Dilemma: When New Technologies Cause Great Firms to Fail, Boston, Mass: Harvard Business School.

CNN Money (2012) Fortune 500: Goodyear Tire & Rubber 1996 rank: 88, *CNN Money* [internet] Available at: http://money.cnn.com/magazines/fortune/for tune500_archive/snapshots/1996/1363.html [Accessed on 6 February, 2012].

Columbia University Press (2009) Rubber, *Columbia University Press* [internet] Available at: http://education.yahoo.com/reference/encyclopedia/entry/rubber [Accessed on 12 September, 2012].

Cooper Tire & Rubber Company (2016) Cooper Tire to acquire majority interest in China joint venture for truck and bus radial (TBR) tire production, *Cooper Tire & Rubber Company* [internet] Available at: http://coopertire.com/News/Corporate-News-Releases/Cooper-Tire-to-Acquire-Majority-Interest-in-China.aspx [Accessed on 5 July, 2016].

Corre, E.L. (2012) Michelin: a commodity-based industry, *INFO Magazine*, November/December, London: French Chamber of Commerce in Great Britain.

Davis, B. (1996) Push Eastwards alters European Tire Outlook, *RubberNews.com* [internet] Available at: www.rubbernews.com/article/19961118/ISSUE/3111 89971/push-easward-alters-european-tire-outlook [Accessed on 12 January, 2011).

Davis, B. (2011a) Pirelli set to take leading role in Russian tire market, *TireBusiness.com* [internet] Available at: www.tirebusiness.com/article/20110909/NEWS/309099991/0/SEARCH [Accessed on 15 July, 2012].

Davis, B. (2011b) Pirelli to take over Kirov, Russia, tire plant, *TireBusiness.com* [internet] Available at: www.tirebusiness.com/article/20110725/NEWS/307259988 [Accessed on 15 July, 2012].

Davis, B. (2011c) Tire market up 20% in 2010; Bridgestone No. 1 again, *TireBusiness.com* [internet] Available at: www.tirebusiness.com/article/20110830/NEWS/308309992 [Accessed on 15 July, 2012].

Davis, B. (2016) Cooper buying into China TBR plant (updated) *Tire Business* [internet] Available at: www.tirebusiness.com/article/20160106/NEWS/160109967 [Accessed on 6 July, 2016].

Deutsche, C.H. (1999) Deal reached by Goodyear and sumitomo, *The New York Times* [internet] Available at: www.nytimes.com/1999/02/04/business/deal-reached-by-goodyear-and-sumitomo.html?src=pm [Accessed on 3 February, 2011].

Drucker, P.F. (2007) *Management Challenges for the 21st Century*, Abingdon, Oxon: Routledge.

Engel, L (1989) Michelin to acquire tire maker, The Milwaukee Sentinel [internet] Available at: http://news.google.com/newspapers?nid=1368&dat=19890923&id=JopQAAAAIBAJ&sjid=7hIEAAAAIBAJ&pg=5441,6872087 [Accessed on 10 January, 2012].

Europa (2007) Mergers: Commission approves proposed acquisition of Matador by Continental, Europa [internet] Available at: http://europa.eu/rapid/press-release_IP-07-787_en.htm [Accessed on 20 February, 2012].

Europolitics (1996) Michelin Buys Hungary Tiremaker Taurus, Europolitics [internet] Available at: http://www.europolitics.info/michelin-buys-hungary-tyre maker-taurus-artr169593-5.html [Accessed on 29 February, 2012].

Evans, S. (2010) Green and Grippy: Michelin's Primacy MXM4 Tire, *Motor Trend* [internet] Available at: www.motortrend.com/news/michelin-primacy-mxm4-tire/ [Accessed on 23 January, 2016].

Farrell, G. (2000) Will dealers stand by Firestone? - Some profess loyalty while others hesitate, USA Today [internet] Available at: http://www.usatoday.com/money/consumer/autos/mauto895.htm [Accessed on 24 September, 2012].

Fisher, P (2008) Memories: TB's 25th anniversary has Peggy looking back at tire industry changes, tirebusiness.com [internet] Available at: http://www.tirebusiness.com/article/20081013/NEWS/310139992/memories-tbs-25th-anniversary-has-peggy-looking-back-at-tire [Accessed on 3 March, 2012].

Flanigan, J. (1986) Goldsmith bid might be good for Goodyear, *Los Angeles Times* [internet] Available at: http://articles.latimes.com/1986-11-07/business/fi-15496_1_goodyear-stock [Accessed on 4 February, 2012].

Funding Universe (2012) Bridgestone Corporation history, *Funding Universe* [internet] Available at: www.fundinguniverse.com/company-histories/bridgestone-corporation-history/ [Accessed on 28 February, 2012].

Galbraith, J.K. (1972) *The New Industrial State, Second Edition Revised*. London: Andre Deutsch Limited.

Gelles, D. (2013) Cooper Tire Abandons Merger, The New York Times [internet] Available at: https://dealbook.nytimes.com/2013/12/30/cooper-tire-abandons-merger/?_r=0 [Accessed on 12 December, 2016].

GMG Global Limited (2007) *Annual Report 2007*, Singapore: GMG Global Limited.

GMG Global Limited (2009) *Memorandum of Understanding*, Singapore: GMG Global Limited.

GMG Global Limited (2011) Our plantations, *GMG* [internet] Available at: www.gmg.sg/our_plantation.html [Accessed on 3 August, 2012],

GMG Global Limited (2012) Corporate Presentation: Financial Year Ended 31 December 2011, February 2012, Singapore: GMG Global Limited.

GMG Global Limited (2015) *Annual Report 2015*, Singapore: GMG Global Limited.

Goodyear (2001) *Discussion With Goodyear Staff*, Meeting at Goodyear's Singapore Office.

Goodyear (2009) 2009 Annual Report, Akron: The Goodyear Tire & Rubber Company.

Goodyear (2010) 2010 Annual Report, Akron: The Goodyear Tire & Rubber Company.

Goodyear (2011a) History by year, Goodyear [internet] Available at: www.good-year.com/corporate/history/history_byyear.html [Accessed on 3 December, 2011].

Goodyear (2011b) *Interview With Keith Price, Director of National Media Relations & Business Communications*, Akron: The Goodyear Tire & Rubber Company.

Goodyear (2011c) RunOnFlat: A revolution in history of run flat tyres, *Goodyear* [internet] Available at: www.goodyear.eu/uk_en/tires/run-flat-tires/index.jsp [Accessed on 29 November, 2011].

Goodyear (2012a) Goodyear Tire & Rubber Co: Fayetteville Living Lean, Akron: The Goodyear Tire & Rubber Company.

Goodyear (2012b) Bio-based Tires Edge Closer to Reality / Collaboration between The Goodyear Tire & Rubber Company and DuPont Industrial Biosciences results in breakthrough technology for tires made with renewable raw materials, Goodyear [internet] Available at: http://www.goodyear.com/cfmx/web/corporate/media/news/story.cfm?a_id=646 [Accessed on 3 August, 2012].

Goodyear (2015) *2015 Annual Report*, Akron: The Goodyear Tire & Rubber Company.

Goodyear (2016) Goodyear unveils Eagle-360, a visionary tire concept for future autonomous vehicles, *Goodyear* [internet] Available at: http://news.goodyear.eu/events/all/innovation–automated-driving–autonomous-vehicles–self-driving-cars–goodyear–future-mobility–co/s/87437154–19d9–4f0d-b7dd-fc6cf1309467 [Accessed on 23 January, 2017].

Halcyon Agri (2012) *Annual Report 2012*, Singapore: Halcyon Agri Corporation Limited.

Halcyon Agri (2014) *Transformation: Annual Report 2014*, Singapore: Halcyon Agri Corporation Limited.

Halcyon Agri (2015) Halcyon Agri completes acquisition of Centrotrade, Singapore: Halcyon Agri Corporation Limited.

Halcyon Agri (2016a) *HAC Transactions Update*, Singapore: Halcyon Agri Corporation Limited.

Halcyon Agri (2016b) *Q3 2016 Financial Results: 14 November 2016*, Singapore: Halcyon Agri Corporation Limited.

Hapsari, R., and Teguh, A. (2011) Michelin Enters Indonesia, Indonesia Finance Today [internet] Available at: http://en.indonesiafinancetoday.com/read/4047/Michelin-Enters-Indonesia# [Accessed on 16 July, 2012].

Hetzner, C. (2007) Continental AG buys 51 pct of Matador Rubber, *Reuters* [internet] Available at: www.reuters.com/article/2007/04/11/idUSL1172834220070411 [Accessed on 20 July, 2012].

Hicks, J.P. (1987) COMPANY NEWS; Exxon Will Buy Celeron, The New York Times [internet] Available at: http://www.nytimes.com/1987/08/11/business/company-news-exxon-will-buy-celeron.html?n=Top%2fReference%2fTimes%20Topics%2fSubjects%2fF%2fFinances [Accessed on 29 February, 2012].

Hicks, J.P. (1988a) Bridgestone in deal for firestone, *The New York Times* [internet] Available at: www.nytimes.com/1988/03/18/business/bridgestone-in-deal-for-firestone.html [Accessed on 29 February, 2012].

Hicks, J.P. (1988b) Bridgestone's new U.S. challenge, *The New York Times* [internet] Available at: www.nytimes.com/1988/02/22/business/bridgestone-s-new-us-challenge.html?pagewanted=all&src=pm [Accessed on 29 February, 2012].

Hicks, J.P. (1989) Michelin to Acquire Uniroyal Goodrich, The New York Times [internet] Available at: http://www.nytimes.com/1989/09/23/business/michelin-to-acquire-uniroyal-goodrich.html [Accessed on 29 February, 2012].

Hicks, J.P. (1990) German tire maker is target of Pirelli bid, *The New York Times* [internet] Available at: www.nytimes.com/1990/09/18/business/company-news-german-tire-maker-is-target-of-pirelli-bid.html [Accessed on 29 February, 2012].

Hoffman, L. (2013) Cooper Tire Ends Merger Pact With Apollo Tyres, wsj.com [internet] Available at: https://www.wsj.com/articles/cooper-tire-terminates-merger-agreement-with-apollo-tyres-1388406103 [Accessed on 12 December, 2016].

ICB (1997) Goodyear spends to reinforce leadership, ICB [internet] Available at: http://www.icis.com/Articles/1997/10/27/50579/goodyear-spends-to-reinforce-leadership.html [Accessed on 20 February, 2012].

ITEC (2012) Radial tire spawned industry revolution, *ITEC* [internet] Available at: http://itec-tireshow.com/history/Radial%20tire%20spawned%20industry%20revolution.pdf [Accessed on 2 February, 2012].Jensen, M. (1988) Takeovers: Their causes and consequences, *The Journal of Economic Perspectives*, 2(1): 21–48.

Krueger, D. (1991) Goodyear Tire & Rubber Company, *BUS329 Readings*, Available at: http://homepages.bw.edu/~dkrueger/BUS329/readings/goodyear.html [Accessed on 18 July, 2012].

Kumho Tires (2004) It's a vision thing- Automated Kumho Tires plant culminates 11 years of R&D, *Kumho* [internet] Available at: www.kumhotire.com/company/pr/pr_press_view.jsp?spage=0&lpage=0&num=38&sYear= [Accessed on 18 September, 2012].

Mackinnon, J. (2008) Bridgestone's buy of Firestone, 20 years later, *Ohio.com* [internet] Available at: www.ohio.com/news/top-stories/bridgestone-s-buy-of-firestone-20-years-later-1.96847 [Accessed on 16 August, 2012].

MarketWatch, Inc. (1999) Goodyear, Sumitomo shake on deal, *CBS.MarketWatch.com* [internet] Available at: www.marketwatch.com/story/goodyear-sumitomo-shake-on-deal [Accessed on 22 May, 2012].

Marx, K. (1961) Capital: A Critical Analysis of Capitalist Production, Volume I, Moscow: Foreign Languages Publishing House.

Masoni, D. (2012) Pirelli buys Swedish tyre distributor, Reuters.com [internet] Available at: http://in.reuters.com/article/2012/06/13/pirelli-sweden-idINL5E8HD8U520120613?type=companyNews [Accessed on 3 August, 2012].

Massachusetts Institute of Technology (1999) Inventor of the week: Charles Goodyear, *MIT* [internet] Available at: http://web.mit.edu/invent/iow/goodyear.html [Accessed on 12 February, 2012].

Matador (2012) Company transition, *Matador* [internet] Available at: www.matador.sk/index.cfm?Module=ActiveWeb&page=WebPage&s=history&a=1 [Accessed on 15 September, 2012].

McNulty, M. (2015) Goodyear expands operations in China, *Rubber & Plastics News* [internet] Available at: www.rubbernews.com/article/20150415/NEWS/304069995 [Accessed on 3 July, 2016].

Mefro Wheels France S.A.S (2012) History, *Mefro Wheels* [internet] Available at: www.mefro-wheels.fr/english/company/history.html [Accessed on 13 September, 2012].

Mercer, R. (1990) The economic consequences of high leverage and stock market pressures on corporate management: A roundtable discussion, in Stern, J.M. and

Chew D.H. Jr. (eds), *The Revolution in Corporate Finance*, Massachusetts: Blackwell Publishers Ltd.

Meyer, B. (2011) Tire makers no longer victims of OE demands, *tirebusiness.com* [internet] Available at: www.tirebusiness.com/article/20110509/ISSUE/3050 99965/0/SEARCH [Accessed on 6 February, 2012].

Michelin (1997) *Annual Report 1997*, Paris: Michelin.

Michelin (1999) *Annual Report 1999*, Paris: Michelin.

Michelin (2000) *Annual Report 2000*, Paris: Michelin.

Michelin (2003) *Annual Report* 2003, Paris: Michelin.

Michelin (2006) Michelin Performance and Responsibility 2005-2006, Paris: Michelin.

Michelin (2007) *2007 Annual Report*, Paris: Michelin.

Michelin (2010) *2010 Annual and Sustainable Development Report*, Paris: Michelin.

Michelin (2011) *2011 Annual and Sustainable Development Report*, Paris: Michelin.

Michelin (2012) *2012 Annual and Sustainable Development Report*, Paris: Michelin.

Michelin (2014) Michelin Tweel technologies expands line up of skid steer airless radials, *Michelin* [internet] Available at: www.michelintweel.com/tweelNews_10-22-14-1.html [Accessed on 23 January, 2017].

Michelin (2015a) 2015 Annual and Sustainable Development Report, Paris: Michelin.

Michelin (2015b) *2015 Registration Document*, Paris: Michelin.

Michelin (2016) Defender®, *Michelin* [internet] Available at: www.michelinman. com/US/en/tires/products/defender.html [Accessed on 24 January, 2017].

Michelin (2016a) Primacy 3, *Michelin* [internet] Available at: www.michelin.com.sg/ SG/en/tires/products/primacy-3.html# [Accessed on 24 January, 2017].

Michelin (2016b) Primacy™ MXM4®, *Michelin* [internet] Available at: www. michelinman.com/US/en/tires/products/primacy-mxm4.html# [Accessed on 24 January, 2017].

Mitchell, M.L. and Mulherin, H.J. (1996) The impact of industry shocks on takeover and restructuring activity, *Journal of Financial Economics*, 41: 193–229.

Modern Tire Dealer (2011) Titan buys Goodyear's Union City, Tenn., plant, Modern Tire Dealer [internet] Available at: www.moderntiredealer.com/channel/ retailing/news/story/2011/11/tian-buys-goodyear-s-union-city-tenn-plant.aspx [Accessed on 16 October, 2012].

Moore, M (2015) 2 ex-Goodyear employees in Singapore charged with fraud (Update), Tire Business [internet] Available at: www.tirebusiness.com/article/20160623/ NEWS/160629960/2-ex-goodyear-employees-in-singapore-charged-with-fraud-update [Accessed on 6 August, 2016].

Moseman, A. (2016) Goodyear made Spherical MagLev Tires that are totally nuts, *Popular Mechanics* [internet] Available at: www.popularmechanics.com/cars/ a19747/goodyear-eagle-360-spherical-tires/ [Accessed on 24 January, 2017].

Murphy, C. (2014) Cooper Tire to Sell Its Stake in China Joint Venture, wsj.com [internet] Available at: https://www.wsj.com/articles/cooper-tire-to-sell-its-stake-in-china-joint-venture-1412759430 [Accessed on 12 December, 2016].

Nolan, P. (2008) Capitalism and Freedom, the Contradictory Character of Globalisation, London: Anthem Press.

Nolan, P. (2009) *Crossroads: The End of Wild Capitalism*, London: Marshall Cavendish Limited.

Nolan, P. (2014) Chinese Firms, Global Firms: Industrial Policy in the Era of Globalization, New York: Routledge.

Ohnesorge, L.K. (2016) Tire giant Bridgestone taps Wilson for expansion, *Triangle Business Journal* [internet] Available at: www.bizjournals.com/triangle/news/2016/01/05/bridgestone-expansion-wilson-nc.html [Accessed on 15 January, 2017].

Ohnesorge, L.K. (2017) Bridgestone makes additional $180M investment in Wilson, *Triangle Business Journal* [internet] Available at: www.bizjournals.com/triangle/news/2017/01/09/bridgestone-makes-additional-180m-investmentin.html [Accessed on 15 January, 2017].

Park, J.M. (2011) Michelin sells Hankook Tire stake at 12 percent discount, Reuters.com [internet] Available at: http://www.reuters.com/article/2011/11/09/us-michelin-hankooktire-idUSTRE7A80A320111109 [Accessed on 3 July, 2012].

Patrascu, D. (2010) Toyo Tire Buys Silverstone Berhad, Autoevolution [internet] Available at: http://www.autoevolution.com/news/toyo-tire-buys-silverstone-berhad-25530.html [Accessed on 1 March, 2012].

Penrose, E. (1995) *The Theory of the Growth of the Firm*, 2nd edn, Oxford: Oxford University Press.

Petersen, G. (2014) A car tire that doesn't give up grip as it wears: Wet or dry, impressive new Michelin Premier A/S retains traction, *Consumer Reports* [internet] Available at: www.consumerreports.org/cro/news/2014/08/tests-reveal-the-michelin-premier-as-tire-that-doesn-t-give-up-grip-as-it-wears/index.htm [Accessed on 23 January, 2017].

Philippine Rural Development Program (2015) *Value Chain Analysis and Competitiveness Strategy: Rubber Sheets-Cotabato*, Cotabato: Department of Agriculture.

Phuket Gazette (2014) Ruler of the rubber world, *Phuket Gazette* [internet] Available at: www.phuketgazette.net/articles/articles/print_detail/32480 [Accessed on 7 July, 2016].

Pirelli (2015) *2015 Annual Report*, Milan: Pirelli.

Porter, M. (1985) Competitive Advantage: Creating and Sustaining Superior Performance, New York: The Free Press.

Price, K. (2011) *Interview on Global Tyres Industry at Goodyear*, Interviewed by Wilson Wong Kia Onn.

Price, K. (2012) Get-Tough policy on Chinese Tires Fall Flat, *wsj.com* [internet] Available at: http://online.wsj.com/article/SB10001424052970204301404577171130489514146.html [Accessed on 2 February, 2012].

Rajan, R., Volpin, P. and Zingales, L. (2000) The eclipse of the U.S. tire industry, in Kaplan, S.N. (ed.), *Mergers and Productivity*, Chicago: University of Chicago Press.

Reference for Business (2012) History of Continental Aktiengesellschaft, Reference for Business [internet] Available at: http://www.referenceforbusiness.com/history2/44/CONTINENTAL-AKTIENGESELLSCHAFT.html [Accessed on 12 September, 2012].

Research In China (2015) Global and China Natural Rubber Industry Report, 2014-2018, Beijing: Research In China.

Reuters (1987) Gencorp Selling Tire Unit for $650 Million, Los Angeles Times [internet] Available at: http://articles.latimes.com/1987-06-30/business/fi-1313_1_gencorp [Accessed on 20 March, 2012].

Reuters (1991) COMPANY NEWS; Japanese Parent to Aid Bridgestone/Firestone, nytimes.com [internet] Available at: http://www.nytimes.com/1991/05/17/business/company-news-japanese-parent-to-aid-bridgestone-firestone.

html?n=Top%2fReference%2fTimes%20Topics%2fSubjects%2fF%2fFinances [Accessed on 6 August, 2012].

Rubberbands (2010) Frequently asked questions: Who are the largest producers? Rubberbands [internet] Available at: www.rubberbands.co.uk/faq/faq.htm [Accessed on 12 August, 2012].

Schoenberger, R. (2011) Goodyear wins grant to develop self-inflating tires, *Cleveland. com* [internet] Available at: www.cleveland.com/business/index.ssf/2011/08/goodyear_wins_grant_to_develop.html [Accessed on 3 March, 2012].

Schumpeter, A. J. (1943) *Capitalism, Socialism and Democracy*, London: Allen & Unwin.

Selko, A. (2012) Michelin's New Plant in South Carolina Makes 9th Facility in the State: $750 million investment creates 500 jobs, IndustryWeek.com [internet] Available at: http://www.industryweek.com/industry-clusters/michelins-new-plant-south-carolina-makes-9th-facility-state [Accessed on 24 September, 2012].

Shea, S. (2015) EERE energy impacts: Self-inflating tires could save you money on gas, improve driving safety, *US Department of Energy* [internet] Available at: www.energy.gov/eere/articles/eere-energy-impacts-self-inflating-tires-could-save-you-money-gas-improve-driving [Accessed on 30 August, 2016].

Shingo Institute (2017) Shingo Prize Recipients: Recipient Archive, 1988-2009, Shingo Institute [internet] Available at: http://www.shingoprize.org./assets/press/Database-Past_Recipients_2009_back.pdf [Accessed on 16 February, 2017].

Siat Group (2012) Siat entered into a partnership with the Singaporean based GMG Global Ltd (GMG), *Siat* [internet] Available at: www.siat.be/index.cfm/page:news/id:siat-entered-into-a-partnership-with-the-singaporean-based-gmg-global-ltd [Accessed on 19 September, 2012].

Sinochem Group (2010) *2010 Annual Report*, Beijing: Sinochem Group.

Sinochem International Corporation (2010) The contract of GMG's acquisition of Teck Bee Hang Trading Co. was formally signed, *Sinochem International Corporation* [internet] Available at: www.sinochemintl.com/en/news/detail.asp?id=1400 [Accessed on 8 August, 2012].

Sinochem International Corporation (2011) Euroma Rubber Industries Sdn. Bhd, *Sinochem International Corporation* [internet] Available at: www.sinochemintl.com/en_rubber/index/detail.asp?id=1026 [Accessed on 28 November, 2011].

Soh, A. (2015) Singapore-listed rubber firms eye rebound in prices and fortunes, *The Business Times* [internet] Available at: www.businesstimes.com.sg/energy-commodities/singapore-listed-rubber-firms-eye-rebound-in-prices-and-fortunes [Accessed on 12 July, 2016].

Southern Africa Treads (2010) Investments make Goodyear first choice for high-end vehicles internationally, satreads [internet] Available at: https://issuu.com/satreads/docs/sa_treads_june_2010 [Accessed on 20 December, 2016].

Sri Trang Agro-Industry Public Company Limited (2006) *Annual Report 2006*, Thailand: Sri Trang Agro-Industry Public Company Limited.

Sri Trang Agro-Industry Public Company Limited (2009) *Annual Report 2009*, Thailand: Sri Trang Agro-Industry Public Company Limited.

Sri Trang Agro-Industry Public Company Limited (2015) Consolidated and Company Financial Statements: 31 December 2015, Thailand: Sri Trang Agro-Industry Public Company Limited.

Takada, A., Suwannakij, S. and Song, Y. (2012) Biggest rubber glut since 2004 offers respite to Bridgestone: Commodities, *Bloomberg.com* [internet] Available at: www.bloomberg.com/news/2012-01-10/biggest-rubber-glut-since-2004-offers-res pite-to-bridgestone-commodities.html [Accessed on 19 November, 2012].

Tedlow, R. (1991) Hitting the skids: Tires and time horizons. *Unpublished manuscript*, Harvard Business School.

Tefen (2009) Lean Training Implementation at Michelin, North America, Tefen Management Consulting [internet] Available at: http://www.tefen.com/nc/TEFEN-Romania/best_of_tefen/details/archive/2009/nov/15/art/lean_train ing_implem.html [Accessed on 18 July, 2012].

Teichner, W. (1991) The All American Pipeline, MA: Harvard Business School.

The Associated Press (2005) Bridgestone and Ford Settle Dispute Over Defective Tires, The Associated Press [internet] Available at: http://www.nytimes.com/2005/10/13/business/13ford.html?_r=1 [Accessed on 23 May, 2012].

The Economist (1999) Tyres: Tread carefully, The Economist [internet] Available at: www.economist.com/node/185280 [Accessed on 3 February, 2012].

The Economist (2014) The Economist explains: Why the oil price is falling, The Economist [internet] Available at: www.economist.com/blogs/economist-explains/2014/12/economist-explains-4 [Accessed on 10 October, 2016].

The Japan Times (2003) Sumitomo Rubber in share buyback, The Japan Times Online [internet] Available at: www.japantimes.co.jp/text/nb20030409a7.html [Accessed on 2 February, 2012].

Tire Review (2011a) Goodyear 'going to continue to win in China', *Tire Review* [internet] Available at: http://autonews.gasgoo.com/china-news/goodyear-going-to-continue-to-win-in-china-110330.shtml [Accessed on 3 March, 2012].

Tire Review (2011b) Goodyear research targets self-filling tires, *Tire Review* [internet] Available at: www.tirereview.com/article/90700/goodyear_research_targets_selffilling_tires.aspx [Accessed on 3 March, 2012].

Tire Review (2011c) Goodyear's technology gets car & driver nod, *Tire Review* [internet] Available at: www.tirereview.com/goodyear-s-technology-gets-car-driver-nod/ [Accessed on 3 March, 2012].

Tire Review (2017) Bridgestone invests another $180 million in Wilson facility, *Tire Review* [internet] Available at: www.tirereview.com/bridgestone-adds-180-million-investment-to-wilson-facility-expansion-plan/ [Accessed on 15 January, 2017].

TireBusiness.com (2001) Dealers rally behind Firestone, *TireBusiness.com* [internet] Available at: www.tirebusiness.com/article/20010604/OPINION/306049981/0/SEARCH [Accessed on 10 May, 2012].

TireBusiness.com (2012) Global Tire Company rankings, *TireBusiness.com* [internet] Available at: www.maxxis.com/Repository/Files/2012GlobalRankings.pdf [Accessed on 8 March, 2013].

TireBusiness.com (2015a) Bridgestone buying TireConnect, online sales tool developer, TireBusiness.com [internet] Available at: http://www.tirebusiness.com/article/20151022/NEWS/151029972/1022 [Accessed on 8 February, 2017].

TireBusiness.com (2015b) Global Tire Report-2015, Akron, Ohio: Tire Business.

Titan International, Inc. (2011) Titan tire closes on Goodyear Latin American, *Titan* [internet] Available at: www.titan-intl.com/news/detail.php?id=24 [Accessed on 16 September, 2012].

Toyo Tires (2010) Toyo Tires to Acquire Silverstone Berhad, Toyo Tires [internet] Available at: http://eu.toyodev.com/news/item/id/6811 [Accessed on 29 February, 2012].

Truck News (2007) Michelin acquires Oliver Rubber Co., Truck News [internet] Available at: http://www.trucknews.com/news/michelin-acquires-oliver-rubber-co/1000216607/ [Accessed on 2 March, 2012].

Tyrepress.com (2011) Rubber prices remain stable, Thai floods make little impact, *tyrepress.com* [internet] Available at: www.tyrepress.com/News/business_area/70/23565.html [Accessed on 28 November, 2011].

United States Environmental Protection Agency (2003) Lean Manufacturing and the Environment: Research on Advanced Manufacturing Systems and the Environment and Recommendations for Leveraging Better Environmental Performance, EPA.gov[internet] Available at: http://www.epa.gov/lean/environment/pdf/leanreport.pdf [Accessed on 15 January, 2012].

University of Akron (2012) Goodyear Polymer Centre, University of Akron [internet] Available at: http://www.uakron.edu/dps/facilities/gpc.dot [Accessed on 20 February, 2012].

Venkat, P.R. (2016) China's Sinochem in talks to buy Halcyon Agri: Valued at $300 million, deal would continue a string of commodities acquisitions by Chinese companies, *wsj.com* [internet] Available at: www.wsj.com/articles/chinas-sinochem-in-talks-to-buy-halcyon-agri-1452659225 [Accessed on 8 June, 2016].

Von Bundit (2016) Company profile, *Von Bundit* [internet] Available at: www.vonbundit.com/en/company_profile.html [Accessed on 7 July, 2016].

Warburton, S. (2011) France: Michelin disposes of Hankook Tire Stake, just-auto.com [internet] Available at: http://www.just-auto.com/news/michelin-disposes-of-hankook-tire-stake_id116697.aspx [Accessed on 8 March, 2012].

Warner, S. (2011) 25 years ago: Driving back the raider at the gates of Goodyear Tire and Rubber Co., Cleveland.com [internet] Available at: http://www.cleveland.com/business/index.ssf/2011/11/25_years_ago_driving_back_the.html [Accessed on 20 March, 2012].

Warsaw Business Journal (2000) Michelin takes steps to steer Stomil off stock exchange, wbj [internet] Available at: http://www.wbj.pl/article-11975-michelin-takes-steps-to-steer-stomil-off-stock-exchange.html [Accessed on 12 January, 2012].

Warsaw Business Journal (2004) Stomil Olsztyn fades into Michelin Polska, wbj [internet] Available at: http://www.wbj.pl/?command=article&id=25163 [Accessed on 12 January, 2012].

Wassener, B. and Nicholson, C.V. (2011) In Quake's aftermath, Japanese companies try to take stock, *nytimes.com* [internet] Available at: www.nytimes.com/2011/03/12/business/global/12yen.html?pagewanted=all&_r=0 [Accessed on 20 November, 2012].

Womack, J.P. and Jones, D.T. (1996) Lean Thinking: Banish Waste and Create Wealth in Your Corporation, New York: Simon & Schuster.

Womack, J.P. and Jones, D.T. (2005) Lean Solutions: How Companies and Customers Can Create Value and Wealth Together, London: Simon & Schuster UK Ltd.

Wong, W. (2013) To what extent and why has the structure of the global automotive components industry changed since the 1980s? An analysis of the global tires, seats, constant velocity joints, brakes and automotive semiconductor sectors, Ph.D., University of Cambridge.

World Rainforest Movement (2009) Nigeria: Michelin's rubber plantations destroyed women's livelihoods, *World Rainforest Movement* [internet] Available at: www. wrm.org.uy/bulletin/140/Nigeria.html [Accessed 14 August, 2012].

Yahoo Finance (2016) SMTUFSumitomo Rubber Industries Ltd., *Yahoo Finance* [internet] Available at: http://finance.yahoo.com/quote/SMTUF/financials [Accessed on 3 July, 2016].

Yamanouchi, K. (2001) Tiremakers rolling out red carpet for Ford, *Chicago Tribune* [internet] Available at: http://articles.chicagotribune.com/2001-05-24/business/0105240190_1_firestone-tires-additional-tires-goodyear [Accessed on 7 July, 2012].

4 The global automotive seats industry

1. Introduction

After extensive M&A spanning the last few decades, three firms (i.e., Adient, Lear and Faurecia) today control more than three quarters (an overwhelming 77.3 percent in 2015) of the global automotive seats market; the global automotive seats market was valued at approximately US$60 billion in 2015. The industry leader, Adient, prior to its 31 October 2016 spinoff, was the seats and interior systems division of JCI (known collectively as its 'Automotive Experience' division). In 2015, JCI, Lear and Faurecia reported estimated market shares of 33.5 percent (US$20.1 billion), 23.5 percent (US$14.1 billion) and 20.4 percent (US$12.2 billion) respectively (JCI, 2016; Lear, 2015; Faurecia, 2015a; Lucintel, 2012). Since the 1980s, JCI, Lear and Faurecia have launched aggressive acquisition campaigns to gain greater economies of scale and scope, consolidate their market shares and become vertically integrated firms. However, their acquisition strategies have produced varying results. For instance, Lear's aggressive acquisition strategy in the 1990s saddled it with massive debt, which left the company particularly vulnerable to the industry downturn precipitated by the global financial crisis of 2008; Lear eventually filed for Chapter 11 bankruptcy protection on 7 July 2009 (Emery, 2009).[1] The fact that Lear had to seek Chapter 11 protection reinforces the argument that not all leading subsystems integrators are profitable and are in fact under incredible pressure to seek (sometimes risky debt-financed) acquisitions as a means of securing greater scale economies.

Conversely, JCI's M&A strategy has made the firm the dominant player in the automotive seats industry; since the 1980s, JCI has grown its automotive seating business considerably through a number of acquisitions that encompassed firms such as Roth Freres, Prince Holding Corp, Becker Group and Ikeda Bussan (Beecham, 2010). The relentless M&A strategies (includes vertical integration strategies) of these two dominant seat makers have placed a considerable amount of technologies (including emerging technologies) that go into making seating systems/automotive interiors in their hands. Thus, there is a steady shift in the balance of power between seat makers and their automaker clients, as seat makers gather increasing responsibility for making entire seating systems, which include seats and the accompanying interior systems; in the calculation of seat makers' market share, this book accounts for the above trend by considering both the seating and interior systems revenues of each firm. In the case of Faurecia (third in terms of market share), its acquisition strategy has taken a different path from its peers. Instead of competing head-on with JCI and Lear, with their larger market shares, it decided in the late 1990s to move into the global automotive emissions control technology business by means of acquisition. This strategy has paid off considerably for Faurecia, as it has become the leading company in the global automotive emissions control business,[2] an industry with higher margins and greater growth potential than the relatively more mature seats business.

One could scarcely imagine the humble car seat as the tip of the spear in altering the balance of power between automakers and suppliers; in the early days of the automobile, it was basically consequential in the vehicular production process. Moreover, on a prima facie basis, the car seat, on its own, appears little changed over the past century, unmarked by the vast technological leaps over this period. In 1903, Henry Ford spent approximately US$16 per vehicle (4 percent of production costs) on seats (Klier and Rubenstein, 2008; Lear, 2006). Today, car seats per se account for about 5 percent of a car's total production cost, marginally higher than its industrial age counterpart. However, this rudimentary cost analysis belies the sea change which the car seat has undergone (and is still undergoing). As indicated earlier, the car seat has now evolved into a far more complex seating system which incorporates its surrounding interiors and the cutting-edge technology of the digital age (e.g., modern car seats have an increasing number of electronic control units (hereafter 'ECUs') embedded in them); in fact, some of the seating systems in cars rolling off today's production lines are virtual high-tech cockpits surrounded by an increasing myriad of electronics such as telematics and head-up-displays (Charette, 2009; Faurecia, 2017). With driving or travelling experience (particularly in the advent of driverless cars) becoming a critical arbiter of automakers' commercial success, automobile seats and interiors are playing an increasingly vital role in enhancing this aspect; the authoritative 2016 J.D. Power Auto Avoider Study states that poor interiors (includes seating) is the second most important reason in a person's decision not to purchase a vehicle (J.D. Power, 2016).

Further, the market structure of the automotive seats industry has evolved considerably since the 1980s. Back in the 1980s, the industry had several big and mid-sized players scrambling for market dominance by M&A. Today, the industry is highly oligopolistic with the big three players in control of more than three-fifths of the market. Despite having JCI, Lear and Faurecia firmly entrenched as the industry oligarchs, the industry is still subject to considerable seismic change. For instance, in July 2015, JCI's decision to spin off its Automotive Experience (includes seats) business as an independent, publicly traded entity was an event of significant magnitude in the automotive seats industry. The spun-off entity known as Adient is expected to retain the revenues, market position and capabilities of its earlier existence and its shares were scheduled to commence trading on the New York Stock Exchange on 31 October 2016 (JCI, 2016). Lear continues to make the critical investments in acquisitions and R&D to forge ahead in the period of uncertainty surrounding JCI's spinoff. Due to the intensifying competition in this industry, Faurecia has divested its automotive exteriors in 2015, to free up more resources to augment its seating and interiors businesses. The second-tier seat makers, Toyota Boshoku and Magna are now struggling more than ever before to compete with their first-tier counterparts. It is doubtful that these players would be able to compete effectively with the first-tier stalwarts in an era which demands increasing levels of sophistication (includes electronic connectivity, safety and luxury massage features) and the exponentially increasing investments they entail.

2. The cascade effect's impact on seat makers

During the 1980s, the manufacture and assembly of car seats was generally carried out by automakers in-house, and they procured only a small portion from external suppliers. This changed dramatically through the tumultuous 1980s-1990s period, when the disruptive forces of the cascade effect compelled automakers to outsource non-core activities such as direct manufacture and components making (e.g., making car seats). GM used to make most of its seats through its Fisher Body division in Detroit, Michigan while Ford endured the same process at its nearby Rouge complex in the same state. The duo's domestic rival, Chrysler also manufactured most of its own seats in the above 'Wolverine State'. To 'unshackle' themselves from onerous seat-making, the aforementioned Detroit three basically had to go through the cumbersome process of acquiring most of the components (needed for seat making) from multiple sources that were awarded contracts on the basis of price (Beecham, 2010; Klier and Rubenstein, 2008). Throughout the 1980s-1990s, they started to focus increasingly on 'coordinating and planning the supply chain'; automakers began channelling their resources instead into higher value-added activities such as international marketing, building a global brand name and developing next-generation technologies needed to dominate an increasingly competitive automotive industry (Nolan, 2009). This race to develop and apply state-of-the-art technologies has intensified significantly in recent years, as automakers (through their proxies, the mega suppliers) compete ferociously to install as many of these emerging technologies as a means of product differentiation; the complexity of today's automobiles has reached stupendous proportions.

Even the seemingly unremarkable car seat in today's average automobile has a number of microprocessor-based ECUs embedded in it along with the remaining 30 or more installed practically everywhere else in the vehicle. This increasing complexity in seat making is also the consequence of an increasing need to meet rising safety regulations and consumer demand for amenities, convenience and comfort. Spurred by the powerful cascade effect, the manufacturing, assembly and inventory holding of car seats was eventually entirely outsourced to the then emerging tier-one automotive seat suppliers (i.e., JCI and Lear) (Beecham, 2010; Charette, 2009).

In contrast to the suppliers of other automotive components (e.g., tyres) which have considerably more experience in supplying the automakers, JCI and Lear had very limited experience in supplying the automotive industry. JCI had entered the automotive parts business only in 1978 while Lear entered the industry earlier in 1964. However, their resulting success was attributable to their ability to respond effectively, and rapidly to the just-in-time and outsourcing requirements of the automakers. It is this very organisational agility that enabled them to make the successful transition from mere suppliers to today's gargantuan subsystems integrators in the global automotive value chain.

To facilitate the automakers' uncompromising just-in-time practices, the seat assembly plants of these suppliers are located extremely close to the automakers' final assembly plants, usually within an hour's drive. Additionally, these seats are delivered to the automakers' final assembly plants on an in-sequence basis, minutes before they are installed in the vehicles, thus minimising inventory storage costs and maximising efficiency for the automakers (Klier and Rubinstein, 2008). Further, the automakers exert considerable influence over their seats suppliers (compared to the tyre suppliers), as seat makers generally derive most if not all their revenue from them. Bolstered by this outsourcing wave, a number of seat makers grew into multi-billion-dollar businesses over the next two decades. Like in the case of the earlier tyre industry, these seat makers themselves began acquiring smaller firms (perhaps even more aggressively) in attempts to secure ever increasing economies of scale and scope (this was critical in what had essentially become an 'arms race' to build increasingly comfortable and safe seats fused with the latest technologies that interact with the rest of the vehicle interior). Unlike their counterparts in the tyres industry, the seats makers (especially JCI and Lear) are relatively more vertically integrated, as they strove to control all the technologies and parts that go into car seats, by acquiring many of their own suppliers (Henry, 2011). These seat makers are trying to bolster their bargaining power with their automaker clients, by controlling most of the technologies and components that span the value chain of seat making. Nonetheless, vertical integration strategies (like other merger strategies) are extremely costly endeavours and the cost of unravelling failed mergers could far outweigh the potential gains.

3. The leading automotive seat makers

Adient: profile

Adient is the world's largest automotive seating systems maker, accounting for a little over a third of the industry's revenue. The firm is the outcome of JCI spinning off its Automotive Experience (includes seats) division on 31 October 2016 and retains all the revenues, leading market share and operational wherewithal of its earlier existence. Given this illustrious origin, Adient started its corporate life with over US$17 billion in revenues (end 2016) and is much more than just a seat-maker, as it also supplies virtually every aspect of the automotive interior which encompasses seating and overhead systems, door systems, floor consoles, instrument panels, cockpits and integrated electronics; these various components are so interlinked today (in a single module) that only multinationals such as Adient possess the economies of scale and scope needed to produce them on a global scale (using just-in-time) required by increasingly internationalised automakers. Currently, the firm provides these systems and related services to over 25 million vehicles world-wide. Supporting this highly intricate global supply chain are 75,000 employees working in 230 manufacturing/assembly plants spread across 33 countries (JCI, 2012; Adient, 2016). Adient's spinoff from JCI also resulted in the firm's legal domicile shifting to Ireland. This controversial move also saw its corporate tax rate declining from approximately 35 percent (prior to any adjustments) to around 10–12 percent, promising tax savings of approximately US$150 million (Adient, 2016).

Adient bursting into the scene as the world's largest automotive seats maker was clearly made possible by the considerable efforts (spanning three decades) of its previous existence as a JCI division. This book traces the rise of this seating and automotive interior systems empire, starting from its days as a JCI division. In 2015, JCI, in its entirety, posted revenues and net income of approximately US$37.2 billion and US$1.563 billion respectively (see Figure 4.1). As of September 2015, the company employed about 139,000 employees, of whom approximately 91,000 were hourly-rated and 48,000 were salaried. Its key competitors include Lear, Faurecia and Magna International Inc (hereafter 'Magna'). By 2015, JCI, alone accounted for 33.5 percent of the global auto-motive seating systems market (JCI, 2016); the calculation of this market share

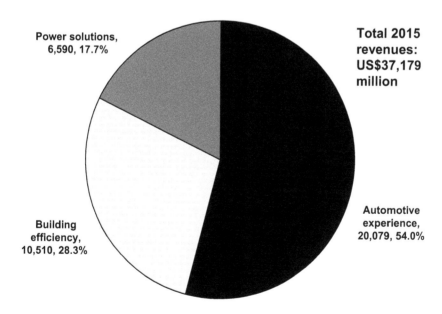

Figure 4.1 JCI's 2015 Annual revenues (US$ million)

The Automotive Experience division makes car seats along with other parts of the vehicle interior

Source: 2015 JCI Annual Report

considers the entire revenues of JCI's Automotive Experience division (includes seats and accompanying interior systems). As indicated in Figure 4.1, JCI's Automotive Experience division accounted for over half (around US$20.08 billion) of its 2015 revenues. The Automotive Experience division, in its own capacity, was unquestionably a leviathan, inevitably paving the way for its spinoff which was aimed at unlocking further value through a more focused business model.

As for JCI's key seating business, it generated about US$16.5 billion in 2015 revenues, which is 82.4 percent of the Automotive Experience division's sales and 44.5 percent of the company's overall revenues (JCI, 2016); the fact that JCI's annual report does not separate its Automotive Experience division revenues into seats and automotive interiors suggests the increasing integration between the two systems, as automakers are now more interested in purchasing entire modules rather than individual parts; industry analysts now classify entire modules as encompassing seats, upholstery, dashboards, door panels, and related components (Donovan, 1999). This division, the forerunner of Adient, produced entire seating modules (includes related interiors) for automakers across 32 countries worldwide. By 2015, JCI was the embodiment of operational efficiency, producing and delivering over 22 million plus seat sets annually, from over 120 just-in-time plants worldwide (JCI, 2016; JCI, 2012). For instance, JCI (now Adient) in Sunderland, UK is required to deliver correct seat variants to its automaker client Nissan in precisely the right order, 170,000 times a year, where errors are not tolerated; to facilitate seamless execution, this plant is located adjacent to Nissan's in Sunderland; Japanese automakers have uncompromisingly stringent just-in-time requirements, requiring seats suppliers to be less than 10 miles from their assembly plants (Dyer, 1994).

In 2015, the Automotive Experience division's largest customers globally were Ford, GM, Chrysler and Volkswagen. JCI's Automotive Experience division draws the bulk (36 percent or US$7.228 billion) of its revenues from North America (Figure 4.2) (JCI, 2016).

For the same year, JCI's procurement spending was approximately US$2.377 billion, spread over 500 suppliers (who carry over 50 different products); the key raw materials include lead, steel, urethane chemicals, copper, sulfuric acid and polypropylene. JCI's 2015 purchasing expenditure was significantly larger than that of its two closest competitors, Lear and Faurecia which recorded markedly smaller purchases of US$946.7 million and US$1.2047 billion respectively. Given the size of its purchasing expenditure, JCI wields considerable influence over these numerous, relatively unconsolidated suppliers (e.g., UK's Harrison Spinks, a 300-employee maker of high-quality mattresses supplies JCI with the technologies needed to make its 'ComfortThin' seats). In a manner reminiscent of their automaker clients, mega suppliers such as JCI are able to extract discounts and other concessions (e.g., higher quality products at discounted rates) from their suppliers by virtue of size and purchasing spend (JCI, 2016).

Adient's/JCI's acquisitions since the 1980s

Prior to its move into the automotive seats industry in the 1980s, JCI was a maker of thermostats, automated building controls and automotive batteries. JCI

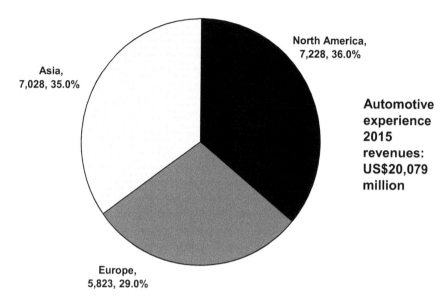

Figure 4.2 JCI's 2015 automotive experience by region (US$ million)

The Automotive Experience division makes car seats along with other parts of the vehicle interior

Source: 2015 JCI Annual Report

made its foray into the automotive seats business by acquiring Michigan-based Hoover Universal for an estimated US$490 million in 1985 (Los Angeles Times, 1985). At the time of its acquisition, Hoover had 57 plants and more than 8,000 employees in North America and abroad. The acquisition of Hoover was fortuitous, as the company was then transitioning from merely supplying seating components to providing fully assembled automotive seating systems. Further, Hoover possessed excellent just-in-time capabilities valued by the automakers, thus immediately providing its acquirer, JCI with ready skills needed to succeed in the seats-making business (Los Angeles Times, 1985; Wood, 2008). JCI's acquisition of Hoover highlights the role of the cascade effect in driving acquisitions that result in significant gains in desired technical and process innovation for the acquirer. In that same year, JCI consolidated its position in the automotive seats industry by acquiring Ferro Manufacturing for US$98.3 million (Funding Universe, 2012). With the successful acquisition of Hoover and Ferro, JCI became the largest supplier of automotive seats to the automakers (JCI, 2012). Further, Hoover and Ferro units (combined 1984 sales of US$360 million) unrelated to JCI's automotive businesses were quickly divested to a division of Citicorp for approximately US$217 million (The New York Times, 1985).

To secure greater economies of scale and scope and consolidate its market position as leading automotive seat-maker, JCI continued to make a number of acquisitions following the 1980s. In November 1995, JCI acquired Roth Freres SA, a French maker of automotive seats and interior components for approximately

US$175-US$200 million. The deal gave JCI a controlling stake of 75 percent in Roth Freres, which recorded 1995 revenues of US$600 million. JCI and Roth Freres had also been JV partners since 1988, thus JCI may have had intimate knowledge of Roth Freres' operations before its acquisition (this knowledge could have greatly facilitated JCI's acquisition of Roth Freres) (The New York Times, 1995).

In 1996, JCI, in an attempt to overtake rising rival, Lear, acquired Holland, Michigan-based Prince Automotive for US$1.35 billion. Prince, which had estimated 1996 sales of approximately US$850 million, was a key supplier of interior systems and components including overhead systems, consoles, door panels, floor consoles, visors and armrests. Further, Prince Automotive had 4,500 employees and eight manufacturing plants – seven in Michigan and one in Mexico City – and was a major supplier to the leading American automakers. The acquisition of Prince was also motivated by the fact that vehicle interiors were increasingly integrated with seats, as suppliers sold entire vehicle interior systems (including seats) to the automakers; this trend was unsurprising, as automakers, impacted by the cascade effect, have been seeking to deal with fewer suppliers in an effort to simplify their components acquisitions operations, reduce costs and focus resources on the higher-value activities of marketing and next-generation R&D (Nolan, 2009). This acquisition drove JCI's revenues to around US$6 billion in 1996, ahead of Lear's earlier US$4.7 billion in 1995. According to an industry analyst, the acquisition of Prince also gave JCI the capacity to develop and retail complete interior systems (PR Newswire, 1996; Greg, 1996; Los Angeles Times, 1996). Shortly after, JCI would acquire the Becker Group (a privately-held vehicle interior supplier) in 1998 for around US$550-US$600 million, in the process becoming the leading supplier of vehicle interiors in Europe and significantly consolidating its capabilities in North America (CNN Money, 1998).

JCI's acquisition attempts did not slow down in the early years of the twenty-first century. For instance, it purchased Ikeda Bussan (a Japanese supplier of automotive seats) in 2000 for US$187 million in cash and debt (JCI paid US$102 million of cash for the stock, and assumed US$85 million of Ikeda Bussan debt). Ikeda Bussan, which recorded consolidated 1999 sales of about 130 billion yen (US$1.2 billion), had five manufacturing plants and about 2,100 employees within Japan (with a similar number overseas). Further Ikeda was the primary seat supplier to Nissan which also owned 38 percent of Ikeda Bussan stock. JCI and Ikeda have been partners since 1986 and were operating two JVs that supplied seats to Nissan in the US and the UK (Lerner, 2000). Further, in 2000, JCI acquired the automotive electronics division of Sagem (a French high-technology group) for US$435 million, to secure technologies needed for complete cockpit and total systems (PR Newswire, 2012a). To bolster its capabilities in automotive interior electronics (e.g., high-end electronic instrument clusters) and strengthen its European presence, JCI also acquired German-based automotive electronics maker, Borg Instruments AG for US$134 million (financed entirely by cash) in July 2003 (The Business Journal, 2003).

As part of its vertical integration strategy (a critical component of its overall M&A strategy), JCI also started to acquire the various suppliers of seat making components (i.e., upholstery, metal seat structures and recliner systems); JCI's vertical integration strategy involves backward integration, which is the acquisition of one's suppliers to mitigate costs (Penrose, 1995). For instance, in December 2010, JCI acquired Michel Thierry (a French supplier of seating upholstery) (JCI, 2010). Additionally, JCI purchased C. Rob. Hammerstein (a German supplier of high-quality metal seat structures, components and mechanisms) in December 2010; the acquisition was executed to secure capabilities needed to bolster JCI's seating components portfolio (PR Newswire, 2010). However, this deal came with the added risk of antitrust issues, as it involved a significant transfer of clients and high-end technological expertise; there is increasing scrutiny from antitrust regulators (e.g., the US Justice Department, the European Commission and their Japanese counterpart) following the numerous acquisitions occurring in the rapidly consolidating global automotive components industry which invariably generated concerns about uncompetitive practices (e.g., collusive behaviour) (Simon, 2011).

Despite increasing scrutiny by antitrust regulators, JCI continued with its vertical integration strategy and purchased the auto-parts business of the Keiper Recaro Group in January 2011 (Keiper makes reclining systems for vehicle seats, metal seat structures and complete seats for commercial vehicles while Recaro makes premium vehicle seats for automakers and aftermarket sales) (Recaro, 2011; Automotive Business Review, 2011). Industry analysts assert that JCI spent US$1.2 billion in its acquisitions of Michel Thierry, C. Rob. Hammerstein and the auto-parts business of the Keiper Recaro Group (Clothier, 2011). It is evident that JCI is now positioning itself as a vertically integrated player in the automotive seats subsector. In short, JCI is trying to augment its negotiating power with its automaker clients by controlling all the technologies that go into seat making. Further, JCI did not rest on its laurels and continued on its relentless acquisition strategy (targets include specialty mechanisms and electric-drive motor suppliers that could be integrated into JCI's portfolio) (Diem, 2010).

However, in July 2015, JCI announced that it would be spinning off its Automotive Experience (includes seats) business and the new entity would be operating as an independent, publicly traded company. In January 2016, JCI stated that the new entity would be known as Adient and would be listed on the New York Stock Exchange in October 2016 (JCI, 2015; JCI, 2016). JCI's management was of the opinion that the spin-off would relieve the company of the cyclicality of the automotive industry and the need to make ever-increasing investments in next-generational technology needed to sustain its market leading position (Wernie, 2016; Molinaroli, 2016). Moreover the margins in JCI's seats business was relatively poor vis-à-vis its building products business; the margins for JCI's seats business was 6.5 percent (its accompanying automotive interiors business was 5.8 percent) while its building products and power business posted far healthier margins of 10 percent and 15.9 percent respectively (Tita, 2015). Further, like in most spin-offs, JCI's management could believe that its seats business was undervalued and aimed to unlock more value through this spin-off. In January 2016, JCI also announced that it had entered into a formal agreement to merge with

Tyco to create a world leader in areas (it perceives to provide greater value-add and are far less cyclical than seats) such as building products and technology, power solutions and energy storage (JCI, 2016).

Technical progress and lean: Key to Adient's/JCI's climb to market dominance

Business historians have traditionally argued that technical progress in firms is fostered through the integration of growth factors such as capital, labour, materials and technological change (Chandler and Hikino, 1999). However, in an era of rapid consolidation across various industries and sectors, acquisitions have become a major catalyst to driving technical progress. The significant economies of scale and scope (along with desired technologies and skills) secured through acquisitions has enabled JCI to generate and sustain the technical progress needed to dominate the seats industry. This was augmented by JCI's significant investment in R&D, which has increased exponentially over the past two decades; JCI's R&D expenditure increased significantly from US$95 million in 1993 to US$733 million in 2015 (JCI, 1995; JCI, 2016); this considerable increase in R&D expenditure further compelled JCI to seek more acquisitions to gain the massive scale economies needed to alleviate what was becoming uncontainable cost pressures. JCI's massive R&D expenditure was not the only factor that led to its market dominance. Although JCI's 2015 R&D expenditure was considerably greater than its immediate rival Lear (2015 R&D: US$194 million), its R&D expenditure was less than its other major competitor, Faurecia (2015 R&D: US$1.007 billion) (Lear, 2015; Faurecia, 2015a).

The advances in automotive seating have been occurring at a far greater pace than may be apparent on the surface. These advances are driven by the following factors: the automakers are insisting on greater differentiation in their seat designs (i.e., greater safety, comfort, flexibility and even cosmetic issues such as colour and design, the covering materials and durability), customers also prefer more luxury features such as cooling and heating capabilities, and even massage features[3] (Beecham, 2009).

JCI forged ahead of its rivals by being at the forefront of this trend of placing increasing emphasis on safety and comfort, without compromising on design and flexibility. It was the first to realise that the car seat had the potential to transcend its bare-bones functionality; JCI was cognisant that automakers would eventually crave and insist on seat designs with distinctive styling, and individual drivers would desire higher degrees of luxury and functionality (JCI quickly put together these desired technologies by means of in-house development and acquisitions) (Beecham, 2010). The company's prescience and ready embrace of these emerging trends coupled with its aggressive M&A strategy has enabled it to control the various technologies that go into making today's increasingly sophisticated car seats and dominate the industry.

To meet increasing automaker demands for sophisticated seating systems, JCI launched its 'Slim Seat' concept in 2011. JCI's new system offers more interior cabin room as its thin seatback requires less space. Further, it provides safety and comfort features, like an active head restraint and lumbar support. JCI also asserts that its revolutionary 'Slim Seat' system has 'new vibration-dampening seat foam' that ensures greater passenger comfort (JCI, 2012). In the ensuing years, JCI successfully developed a next-generation front seat structure which not only met its client, Toyota's uncompromising safety standards but also successfully reduced weight, complexity of components and overall costs. Even as Adient, the firm continues to unremittingly push the boundaries of technical excellence by striving to produce a car seat weighing less than 10 kilograms by 2020; the average car seat today weighs around 10–14 kilograms. Adient wants to achieve this considerable weight reduction without compromising the tensile strength and overall structural integrity of the vehicle seat. If successful in this revolutionary technological endeavour, Adient would not only be able to significantly lower the weight (along with carbon emissions) but concurrently raise the efficiency and performance of vehicles, in the process cementing its already vice-like grip on the market leader's position (JCI, 2015; Leggett, 2015; Adient, 2016).

It is not possible (or at least not financially optimal) to develop all the relevant technologies in-house thus JCI's aggressive acquisition strategy has enabled it to secure needed technologies quickly and effectively; in-house R&D may not always produce the desired results within the targeted budget and time frame. This move to supply automakers with increasingly high-tech seats is also driven by the desire of JCI and other leading seat suppliers to position themselves as suppliers of a sophisticated product instead of a highly-commoditised plain vanilla product vulnerable to eroding profit margins (resulting from the demands for significant discounts by the automakers).

The adoption of 'lean' business practices also played a critical part in JCI's ascent to the position of market leader. JCI basically acquired significant expertise in just-in-time practices (one of the key practices advocated in lean) through its earlier acquisition of Hoover Universal in 1985. Hoover, prior to its acquisition, possessed considerable expertise in just-in-time; this meant that Hoover was able to supply its automaker customers with needed components precisely when they needed them (in the process, minimising or eliminating storage charges). Hoover was in fact the first supplier capable of delivering entire seats on a just-in-time basis for installation in the final assembly line (Klier and Rubenstein, 2008; fundinguniverse, 2012). It is unquestionable that JCI could have acquired significant expertise in just-in-time on its own but the acquisition of Hoover greatly shortened its learning curve, highlighting again the effectiveness of a judicious acquisitions strategy in securing the right skills needed for market leadership.

However lean production extends far beyond just-in-time, as it advocates using less resources vis-à-vis mass production (Womack, Jones and Roos, 2007).[4] JCI started embracing lean in a much bigger way when it became a supplier to Toyota in 1988 (Toyota had decided to make cars in Kentucky in 1988); this also revealed the critical role which automaker pressure played in the widespread implementation of lean. JCI had initially intended to expand its nearby facility, but Toyota asserted that it should not do so, as an expansion would involve a significant investment and erode its profits. Instead, Toyota challenged JCI to produce more seats in an existing building. This seemingly impossible task was eventually achieved with the assistance of Toyota's lean-manufacturing experts; this implementation of lean required JCI to restructure its shop floor, slash inventories and JCI was subsequently able to make seats for Toyota using its existing space.

After this revelatory experience, JCI realised that lean was not just about delivering seats just-in-time but would involve a relentless commitment towards reducing costs and the strengthening of quality; from 1994 to 2004, JCI, through the implementation of lean, was able to significantly reduce defect rates from around 2000 defective parts per million (ppm) to about 100 defective ppm (Hogan, 2005). Through its successful lean implementation experience, JCI's operating philosophy was more aligned with that of its client, Toyota (Liker and Choi, 2005); the relationship became so strong that Toyota refused to consider another supplier when it wanted to develop another range of seats in 2004 (Liker and Choi, 2004).[5] Lean has played a critical part in ensuring JCI's rise to the top of the global automotive seats industry. Over the years, JCI made extensive effort to integrate lean thinking into its 'Johnson Controls Manufacturing System'; this quality management system reflects the consistent manner lean thinking was applied to JCI's manufacturing process and extended from incoming components to the final products assembled into automakers' vehicles, with the entire operations team responsible for eliminating waste (JCI, 2012a).

Even now in its current form as Adient, the firm is still refining its lean strategy as a means of strengthening its competitive advantage; lean is essentially based on the Japanese concept of kaizen and advocates a radical policy of not competing directly with one's competitors but rather with one's own highest possible standards (Womack and Jones, 2003).

Lear: profile

Amidst the escalating consolidation turmoil erupting across the automotive industry, Lear has staunchly defended its hard-fought status as the world's second largest supplier of seating systems to automakers. As 2016 unfolded, it accounted for approximately a quarter of the industry's revenues. The firm, at that point, had manufacturing, engineering and administrative capabilities spread across 36 countries and 240 facilities; of the 240 facilities, 82 were just-in-time facilities. In consonance with the expectations of its automaker clients and the demands of just-in-time production, Lear's just-in-time seat assembly facilities are located near its customers' assembly plants. By the end of 2015, Lear had 136,200 employees worldwide. The company's main competitor is Adient and its other competitors include Faurecia, Toyota Boshoku Corporation (hereafter 'Toyota Boshoku'), TS Tech Co. Ltd (hereafter 'TS Tech') and Magna. In 2015, Lear recorded annual revenues of about US$18.2 billion, with 77.4 percent (US$14.1 billion) of overall revenues coming from its Seating division (Figure 4.3). Further, Lear posted a net income of US$745.5 million for that period.

Its Seating division spans a wide range of technologies that go into the car seat and interior (includes seat systems, seat frames, recliner mechanisms, seat tracks,

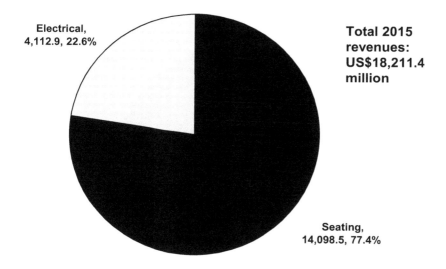

Electrical,
4,112.9, 22.6%

Total 2015
revenues:
US$18,211.4
million

Seating,
14,098.5, 77.4%

Figure 4.3 Lear's 2015 annual revenues (US$ million)

Seating includes seat systems and related parts (seat frames, recliner mechanisms, seat tracks, seat trim covers, headrests and seat foam).

Electrical includes electrical distribution systems, electrical control modules and wireless modules.

Source: 2016 Lear Form 10-K, Lear Corporation Annual Report 2015

seat trim covers, headrests and seat foam). This wide product offering is the result of a relentless acquisition strategy since the 1980s. In 2015, Lear drew the bulk (42.6 percent or about US$7.8 billion) of its revenues from North America (Figure 4.4). Further, its top three customers in 2015 were Ford, GM and BMW which accounted for 23 percent, 20 percent and 10 percent of sales respectively. Lear's other clients include Daimler, Fiat Chrysler, Jaguar Land Rover and Renault-Nissan (Lear, 2015; Lear, 2016).

Lear is constantly under pressure from its leading automaker clients (e.g., GM). In March 2012, Lear was named 'Corporation of the Year' for its considerable contributions to GM's global success in 2011. In 2011, Lear was also recognised as the 'GM Supplier of the Year for Seat Assemblies' marking the eighth consecutive year which it had received the award; this was the fourteenth time that Lear has been named a 'GM Supplier of the Year'[6] (Lear, 2012). As illustrious as this award sounds, it sends a serious message to Lear that it is expected by GM to consistently deliver superior standards (an extremely costly endeavour that could greatly erode profit margins). In an industry plagued by single-digit profit margins, Lear has to fiercely defend its status as a preferred supplier. Owing to its considerable purchasing spend (US$947.6 million in 2015), Lear also wields considerable market power over its suppliers (mainly steel, copper, diesel fuel, chemicals, resins and leather) (Lear, 2016); it is able to extract concessions (e.g., discounts) by playing one against the other.

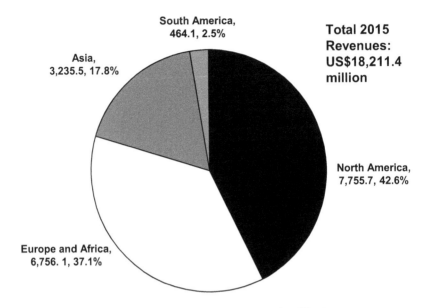

Figure 4.4 Lear's 2015 annual revenues by region (US$ million)

Source: 2016 Lear 10-K Form, Lear Corporation Annual Report 2015

Lear's acquisitions since the 1980s

In an earlier corporate life, Lear was known as American Metal Products Company (AMP), a manufacturer of tubular, welded and stamped steel seat frames. However, by the time of its acquisition by Lear Siegler (a conglomerate that made aerospace electronics, climate control devices and plastics) in 1966, it had developed the capabilities needed to build entire car seats. AMP was subsequently renamed the Automotive Group. By 1983, the Automotive Group's annual sales had reached US$160 million; a year later, the Automotive Group built its first outsourced passenger car seat and established its first just-in-time plant near a GM facility. Lear Siegler (the parent conglomerate of the Automotive Group) itself was later acquired by a private equity firm, Forstmann Little & Co in 1986 for US$2.6 billion.

However, the Automotive Group came into existence by virtue of a US$500 million (more than US$400 million was debt) management buyout led by Kenneth L Way (a corporate vice-president of the Automotive Group) in 1988; the firm was renamed Lear Siegler Seating Corporation and was headquartered in Southfield, Michigan (Funding Universe, 2012). Thus the birth of Lear was in itself, a product of the ruthless 'centralisation of capital' as proposed by Marx (Marx, 1961).

Like the industry leader, JCI, Lear's growth was largely triggered by the powerful cascade effect that reverberated throughout the entire automotive value chain, which compelled the leading automakers to increase outsourcing (to first-tier supplier firms such Lear) and place greater emphasis on just-in-time practices

(Nolan, 2009). In the seat segment, Lear and JCI effectively became competitors for market leadership by the late 1980s. Automakers are cognisant of this intense competition, thus they would often negotiate for better prices, improved features and greater efficiency by pitting Lear against JCI; this pressure from automakers has greatly eroded the profitability of the car seats segment, as evidenced by Matt Simoncini's (Lear's CEO) following comment on the segment's low margins: 'the segment has a "natural margin" of 7 percent to 8 percent of sales'. He also added that 'the pricing environment has always been brutal, and it remains brutal' (Webb, 2011). Moreover, barely two years after its management buyout, Lear Seating's sales had increased nearly eight-fold, from around US$150 million to US$1.24 billion in 1990. In 1990, the company also changed its name to Lear Seating Corporation to distinguish itself from its former parent company (Reference for Business, 2012).

By the beginning of the 1990s, an oligopolistic market was starting to form in the global automotive seats industry, with Lear and JCI spearheading this change. In the 1990s, at the alleged urging of certain automakers (primarily GM), Lear aggressively set out to become a vertically integrated firm capable of designing, sourcing and delivering entire vehicle interiors (including seats). Lear executed this strategy by reportedly making around 17 acquisitions in the 1990s. In 1993, Lear acquired Ford's Favesa, S.A. de C.V automotive seating and seat trim operations (headquartered in Mexico) for US$173.4 million in cash, in the process becoming Ford's preferred seat maker. This acquisition included five Ford plants in Juarez, Mexico, which employed around 6,085 workers; following this deal, Ford was left with one major seat and interior trim plant in the US (The New York Times, 1993; Reference for Business, 2012). Like JCI, Lear also strove to acquire capabilities in entire vehicle interiors (including seating systems). This was evidenced by its earlier acquisition of Saab's Swedish and Finnish interior operations (in 1991) and Volvo's interior business (in 1992).

In 1994, Lear became a publicly listed company, in the process, raising sufficient funds to make further acquisitions. Using these additional funds procured from its listing, Lear soon acquired Automotive Industries Holdings Inc., a supplier of automotive interiors (its products included seatbacks, door panel accessories and inserts, armrests, consoles and headliners) for US$626 million in cash (The New York Times, 1995; Bloomberg, 2012). After its acquisition, Automotive Industries Holdings Inc was renamed as Lear's AI Division. AI was not only Lear's biggest acquisition (at that point) but also added an additional US$300 million to its 1995 revenues. Following this acquisition, Lear became a full-fledged interior systems provider capable of meeting the increasingly complex module requirements of automakers (Lear, 1995; Reference for Business, 2012). In a move that reflected its determination to become a fully-integrated interior systems provider, Lear quickly went on to acquire Masland Corp. (it produced automotive carpeting and luggage compartment trim) for around US$385 million in 1996. That year, in a move to indicate that it was no longer 'just a seats provider', Lear also dropped the word 'seating' from its name and renamed itself Lear Corporation (Reference for Business, 2012).

In addition, Lear consolidated its earlier purchase of Ford's seating assets, with its subsequent acquisition of ITT Industries Inc.'s North American seat subsystems unit, (it made power seat adjusters and power recliners) for around US$40 million in 1997. ITT's seat subsystems unit recorded sales of US$200 million in 1996 and had 1,000 employees across four plants in Michigan and Ontario, Canada. According to Lear, this acquisition not only augmented its technical expertise but also enabled it to mitigate costs by developing the capacity to assemble a seat's frame and relevant components concurrently (Peisner, 1997; Bloomberg, 1997). Lear proved to be relentless in its acquisition drive, as it quickly moved to purchase the automotive seat division of GM's Delphi subsidiary; this acquisition added a significant US$1.2 billion to Lear's then burgeoning market share in seats and automotive interiors (Morris, 1998). An industry analyst asserted that, from 1994 to 1998, Lear spent around US$1.5 billion in its acquisition drive, acquiring companies that run the gamut of seats and interiors development, including ones with capabilities in making armrests, carpets, air conditioning systems and even visors (Donovan, 1999). The company made its most significant purchase with its acquisition of United Technologies Automotive (UTA) in 1999 (topping its earlier acquisition of Automotive Industries Holdings, Inc.), for US$2.3 billion, trumping even an earlier offer of US$2.25 billion from top private equity firm, Blackstone (Reuters, 1999). The acquisition of UTA greatly augmented Lear's vehicle interior capabilities, not only giving the company increased capabilities in instrument panel, headliner and door panel design but also gave it much-needed expertise in electric and electronic distributions systems. Following this acquisition, Lear was soon able to provide full-service modules that combined interior systems and electrical and electronic components and systems (PR Newswires, 2012b).

In 2007, Lear itself became the acquisition target of one of its leading shareholders, Carl Icahn who attempted to buy out the firm for US$2.9 billion; Icahn had earlier in 2006 acquired a 16 percent stake in Lear for around US$200 million (Olson, 2006). Later, with his takeover attempt rejected by Lear's shareholders, Icahn quickly divested two-thirds of his stake in Lear (bringing his stake to just under 5 percent) by 2008 (Dealbook, 2008). Having just survived Icahn's takeover attempt, Lear (in 2008) continued its acquisition drive by purchasing a 75 percent stake in the automotive fabric business of New Trend Group Co. Ltd., a privately held Chinese company. This acquisition gave Lear the ability to make its own automotive seat fabric, rather than relying on a handful of fabric suppliers, such as Milliken & Co, Aunde Group and BMD Textiles Ltd (Murphy, 2008). Lear's acquisition of its own seat fabric supplier was later emulated by JCI which too acquired its fabric supplier, Michel Thierry. The two companies basically had vertical integration (specifically backward integration) strategies that mirrored each other's, in their scramble to control all the components that went into seat making.

However, Lear's aggressive acquisitions strategy (from the 1980s-2008) also saddled it with massive debt, which left the company vulnerable to the industry downturn precipitated by the global financial crisis of 2008; before Lear went into Chapter 11 protection in 2009, it had accumulated over US$3 billion in debt (Treasury & Risk, 2011). The financial crisis had dealt a massive blow to Lear's key automaker clients (i.e., GM, Ford and Chrysler) thus crippling demand for Lear's seats; GM (it alone accounted for 23 percent of Lear's sales in 2008) and Chrysler had to be bailed out by the US government in 2009 and has since landed into the hands of its European rival, Fiat (Kamalakaran et al., 2009; Terlep, 2012; Reed, 2012). Further, Lear had in that period relied too heavily on the light truck and large SUV platforms (light trucks alone accounted for 35 percent of Lear's sales in 2008) of these US automakers, which, according to Lear Vice President and Treasurer Shari Burgess 'were experiencing significant competitive pressures as consumer purchasing patterns shift toward passenger cars, crossover vehicles and other vehicle platforms' (Lear, 2009; Kamalakaran et al., 2009).

Lear eventually filed for Chapter 11 bankruptcy protection on 7 July 2009. However, Lear was able to emerge quickly from Chapter 11 bankruptcy protection (by 9 November 2009) through the reduction of its debt obligations by US$2.8 billion (Emery, 2009). Nonetheless, Lear's experience highlights the risks involved in pursuing an overly-aggressive M&A strategy financed by debt. After emerging from Chapter 11 bankruptcy protection, Lear has continued with its acquisition strategy. In March 2011, Lear increased its stake in an affiliate company, TS Lear Sdn Bhd by 44 percent, bringing its overall shareholding to 90 percent; TS Lear Sdn Bhd is a JV between Lear and Thai Summit, Thailand's leading automotive components maker (Lear, 2011; TS Lear, 2011). In April 2012, Lear also agreed to acquire Guilford Mills (a privately-held portfolio company of Cerberus Capital Management, L.P. which has annual sales of US$400 million) that makes fabrics for the automotive markets; this is in effect a continuation of its earlier vertical integration strategy (The New York Times, 2012). On the back of this relentless acquisition campaign, Lear also gained control of Eagle Ottawa, LLC, the world's leading provider of leather for the automotive industry, through the acquisition of its parent company, Everett Smith Group, Ltd. for about US$844 million in January 2015. Eagle Ottawa was a supplier to Lear (sells US$200 million worth of leather products to Lear) with annual revenues of US$1 billion (Lear, 2016). This was swiftly followed by Lear's acquisition of intellectual property and technology from Autonet Mobile (a developer of wireless communication software and devices for automotive applications) in August 2015. As part of the deal with Autonet Mobile, Lear would also secure employment of critical members of the company's software and product development team; in acquisitions (particularly in high technology industries), human capital could matter a lot more than hardware.

Over this relentless acquisition blitz, Lear also acquired Arada Systems Inc., an automotive technology company (strengths in vehicle-to-vehicle and vehicle-to-infrastructure communications) in November 2015. The procurement of intellectual property and technology from Autonet Mobile and the subsequent acquisition of Arada Systems were executed to equip Lear with added software and hardware capabilities needed to augment connectivity and communication features in vehicles. More importantly, these acquisitions were intended to bolster growth opportunities in the company's electrical segment (Lear 2015; Lear, 2016).

It is also arguable that Lear has no choice but to persist in its pre-Chapter 11 acquisition strategy (despite the sheer costs) as automakers are rapidly increasing their economies of scale and scope by means of acquisitions and strategic alliances (e.g., Fiat-Chrysler, Renault-Nissan-Daimler, GM-PSA). With this augmentation of automaker power, they are also making increasing demands on their seat suppliers such as providing further support in their growth in fast-growing emerging economies and even conducting next-generation R&D. If Lear is deemed as incapable of providing this requisite support, it would not only lose market share to its larger rival, Adient but might also be overtaken by its other major rival, Faurecia. Given that automotive suppliers such as Lear are now responsible for an increasingly greater value of the automobile, it is a matter of time before they embark on similar strategic alliances so as to alleviate rising costs involved in R&D, product development, expanding overseas and breaking into new markets and product lines; even a strategic alliance which involves merging only global purchasing operations, if executed correctly, can yield relatively considerable scale economies in the form of reduced procurement costs (Pollard, 2012).

Technical progress and lean: essential factors in Lear's rise

Lear has achieved its leading market position through a firm commitment to acquisition-driven technical progress and innovation, backed by a R&D expenditure of US$194 million in 2015. Although Lear's R&D investment has increased nearly twelve fold since 1993 (its 1993 R&D expenditure was US$16.2 million), its investment is miniscule compared to JCI and Faurecia, which posted 2015 R&D expenditures of US$733 million and US$1.007 billion respectively (Lear, 2015; Lear 1994; JCI, 2016; Faurecia, 2015a). Over the last two decades, Lear chose instead to actively acquire proven technologies (such as ITT's seat subsystems capabilities) via M&A; in the industry build-up phase of 1993–2000, the company was far more acquisitive than JCI and Faurecia, making a total of 17 strategic acquisitions (Lear, 2007).

By 2015, Lear was conducting cutting-edge research globally across six advanced technology centres and product engineering centres. At these centres, Lear's products are designed 'to comply with applicable safety standards, meet quality and durability standards, respond to environmental conditions and conform to customer and consumer requirements'. The fact that Lear was ranked the highest quality major seat manufacturer in the 2011 J.D. Power and Associates Seat Quality and Satisfaction (it achieved this distinction ten times from 2000 to 2011) underscores Lear's commitment to advancing technical progress (Lear, 2011; Lear, 2015). Lear's commitment to innovation supported by its integration of acquired technologies has yielded significant progress in automotive seating technology. For instance, Lear in 2009/2010 introduced the Dynamic Environmental Comfort System (DECS), its patent-protected, multi-layer advanced seat comfort system that is installed in the 2010 Ford Fusion Hybrid. This seating system provides up to 50 percent weight savings and is far more environmentally-friendly as it reduces volatile organic compounds by up to 70 percent (Lear, 2010). More recently, Lear is expending herculean effort towards the development of commercially viable high-tech next-generational seats which are not only capable of sensing and identifying occupants but also automatically making the requisite adjustments to suit their respective physical specifications and preferences (Wernie, 2016). This ambitious endeavour which necessitates the deployment of cutting-edge software and hardware capabilities has been bolstered by Lear's 2015 procurement of Autonet Mobile's automotive technological applications and its 100 percent acquisition of Arada Systems in the same year.

To bolster its competitiveness in an increasingly oligopolistic market (plagued by rising costs and surging demand for scale economies), Lear implemented a comprehensive lean manufacturing strategy relatively late in 2007; JCI had adopted lean nearly two decades earlier (albeit a far less comprehensive version then) which probably explains its stronger market position. Lear's lean system is known as the Lear Manufacturing System (LMS) which focuses on improving the work environment, overall quality, plant layouts and material flow. It not only focuses on employee participation but also requires their unrelenting commitment to efficient product design (Lear, 2007). Through its LMS, Lear quickly achieved improvements across several facilities. For instance, Lear employees working at one supplier base raised productivity by 33 percent and reduced floor space by 18 percent through the realignment of work stations, adopting one-piece flow and reducing non–value-added work (Katz, 2007).

Lear's LMS also prompted the reduction of corrugated pads deployed in the transportation of certain back panels and this subsequently reduced shipping costs for the panels by more than 30 percent. The implementation of LMS also resulted in the switching from 'expendable' to re-usable containers for certain metal parts, following which Lear derived a first-year package cost reduction of nearly 40 percent (Lear, 2007). However, at that point, Lear did not realise that the effectiveness of lean extends far beyond manufacturing and failed to incorporate it beyond its manufacturing operations. If it had implemented lean across all its operations (e.g., finance, human resource, general administration), it could have reaped greater savings (savings that could have funded next-generational R&D or facilitated more acquisitions, resulting in greater technical progress), productivity gains and overall profitability.

Faurecia: profile

Despite the undulating siege wrought by incessant competition and automaker pressure, Faurecia has managed to retain its stature, as the world's third largest automotive seating systems supplier at the dawn of 2016. Based on 2015 financial year figures, this seats titan accounted for over a fifth of the industry's revenues. More impressively, Faurecia also recorded world leading market share in emissions control technologies, where it accounted for approximately 27 percent (€7.45 billion) of the industry's revenues in the same year. By the end of 2015, Faurecia had 103,000 employees worldwide, along with 330 plants and

30 R&D centres across 34 countries (Faurecia, 2015a; Faurecia, 2016). This significant global manufacturing and R&D presence is largely attributable to relentless automaker pressure for active supplier support in managing their extensive worldwide business network, along with the development of new vehicle models; this considerable automaker pressure is highlighted by Faurecia's CFO, Frank Imbert: 'it's vital to be close to the car production plants. If the OEMs (i.e., automakers) move, we have to move too' (quoted in Arons, 2011). Faurecia's biggest shareholder continued to be PSA which controlled 46.62 percent of the capital stock but 63.22 percent of the voting rights of the company as of 31 December 2015; of the big three seat makers, it is the only non-independent automotive seat maker (it is controlled by an automaker wanting to ensure that there is no disruption to its supply chain). From 2001 to 2015, PSA has steadily diluted its capital stake in Faurecia, from a high of 71.53 percent to 46.62 percent. Despite owning less than 50 percent of Faurecia's capital stock, PSA still has significant leverage over its supplier as it retains majority control of the firm's voting rights (Faurecia, 2001; Faurecia, 2011a; Faurecia, 2015a).

In December 2015, Faurecia's reported revenues and net income were €18.77 billion (US$20.46 billion) and €371.8 million (US$405.26 million) respectively, after making a €1.9215 billion (US$2.0944 billion) adjustment (in accordance with International Financial Reporting Standards) for the firm's Automotive Exteriors business that it was in the process of divesting. Prior to this adjustment, Faurecia's consolidated revenues and net income were €20.69 billion (US$22.55 billion) and €370.1 million (US$403.4 million) respectively; the following segmental analyses are based on Faurecia's pre-adjustment revenues. The following Figure 4.5 indicates Faurecia's core automotive seating revenues accounted for approximately 30 percent (€6.1882 billion or US$6.7451 billion) of its overall revenues, behind its Emission Control Technologies business which generated 36 percent (€7.45 billion) of its overall revenues in 2015 (Faurecia, 2015a). Faurecia's Emission Control Technologies business actually supplanted its seating division as the leading revenue generator in 2010; it was a watershed year for Faurecia as this was the first time in Faurecia's history, that its core seats division was surpassed by a sister division. While it is true that the Emissions Control Technologies division did deliver strong performances from 2005 to 2008, it only took a great leap forward in 2010 with its acquisition of Emcon Technologies in November 2009, which added around €3.4 billion to Faurecia's Total Revenues in 2010.[7] However, if Faurecia's seating and interior systems divisions are considered as one entire seating system division (as in the earlier case of Lear), it would account for over half (€11.2 billion) of the company's 2015 revenues.

The following Figure 4.6 indicates that Faurecia in 2015, derived over half (€11.26 billion) of its revenues from Europe, outdistancing all other regions. Over the past seven years, Faurecia has been trying to reduce its dependence on Europe; as inferred from Figure 4.6, Faurecia secured 45.6 percent of its revenues from outside Europe which was nearly double that of the 23.8 percent it declared in 2009 (Faurecia, 2009; Faurecia, 2015a; Pearson, 2011). The strong performance of its key customer, Volkswagen, and other luxury customers such as BMW in China, has greatly bolstered Faurecia's confidence in Asian markets.

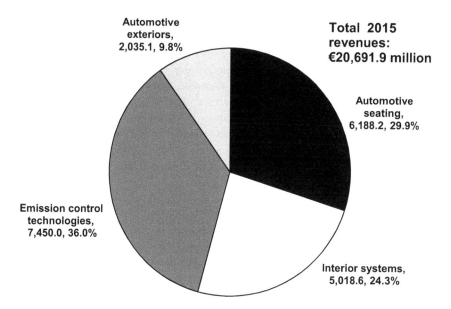

Figure 4.5 Faurecia's 2015 annual revenues (€ million)

Source: 2015 Faurecia Annual Report

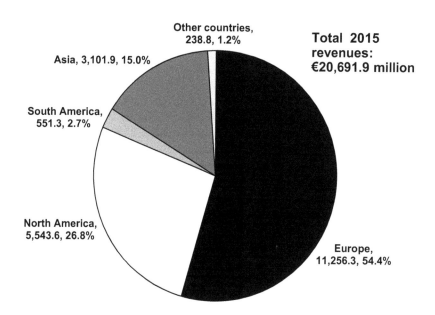

Figure 4.6 Faurecia's 2015 revenues by region (€ million)

Source: 2015 Faurecia Annual Report

Moreover, by 2015, Faurecia derived about €3.1 billion in revenues from Asia (see Figure 4.6), with an estimated €2.5 billion coming from China alone. China's growing contribution to Faurecia's Asian and overall revenues is quite remarkable, considering that just a little over a decade earlier, its Chinese revenues were essentially negligible (Faurecia, 2015a; Pearson, 2011). This buoyant performance from Faurecia's Asian segment (particularly China) is attributable to rising car ownership in Asia precipitated by their growing economies (Reuters, 2011). Further, countries such as China who wish to expect to increase their automotive exports to Europe, with its considerably more stringent emission policy, would need to install the relatively more sophisticated exhaust systems provided by Faurecia, the largest provider of such systems today.

Volkswagen was Faurecia's biggest client in 2015, as it accounted for 22.7 percent of its product sales (approximately €3.1 billion). It is followed by Ford, PSA Peugeot Citroen (Faurecia's biggest shareholder), and Renault Nissan which accounted for 15.9 percent (about €2.5 billion), 13.3 percent (about €2.1 billion) and 12.7 percent (about €2.0 billion) of Faurecia's product sales respectively (Faurecia, 2015a). Faurecia's customers (e.g., Volkswagen, and others such as Renault Nissan and BMW) have benefitted from the recovery in North America and fast-growing emerging markets such as China (where demand for luxury brands such as BMW is growing), thus bolstering demand for Faurecia's products, particularly in emission control technologies and automotive exteriors; this demand indicates an increasing preference for stylish products that are perceived to be green, fuel-efficient, aerodynamic and safe, which would subsequently allow automakers to charge a premium for their cars (Reuters, 2011). Further, Faurecia asserts that premium automakers such as BMW have exceedingly high standards and a number of these luxury brands now define the global touchstone for high-quality and arguably impeccable multifunction seats, instrument panels and front-end assemblies. The company also added it is expected to develop, produce and deliver these superlative systems required by their uncompromising luxury automaker clients (Faurecia, 2011b). Faurecia is also able to exert considerable pressure on its raw material suppliers due to the size of its purchasing spend; its 2015 purchasing expenditure was €1.1052 billion (US$1.2047 billion), even larger than Lear's US$946.7 million in the same year (Faurecia, 2015a). Faurecia, according to Jean-Michel Vallin, President of Faurecia China, tries to keep its procurement expenses in check by purchasing 80–85 percent of its raw materials locally (using 'local cost competitiveness') (Yang, 2011); many of Faurecia's suppliers in developing countries such as China are considerably smaller than their counterparts in the developed countries, thus rendering them even more vulnerable to demands from major subsystems integrators such as Faurecia (e.g., China's Wuhan Park Rubber & Plastic Co., Ltd which supplies automotive rubber and plastic parts to Faurecia, has only about 200 employees and barely US$7.8 million in assets) (Wuhan Park, 2012).

From 2005–2015, Faurecia's Automotive Seating division registered relatively lacklustre growth, merely advancing from €4.7944 billion to €6.1882 billion (CAGR: 2.6 percent). This anaemic growth is largely attributable to the growing commoditisation of the seats industry. The deleterious impact of this commoditi-sation current coupled with rising pressure from automakers have steadily eroded Faurecia's Automotive Seating revenues and subsequent profit margins. In this 'corrosive' environment, seat makers such as Faurecia face increasing difficulty in charging their automaker customers the higher prices needed to cover ris-ing operational and R&D costs. Faurecia's Interior Systems division also expe-rienced similarly moderate growth over the 2005–2015 period, increasing from €3.4827 billion to €5.0186 billion (CAGR: 3.7 percent) (Faurecia, 2006; Faure-cia, 2015a); nowadays, the interior systems and seats divisions of major seats pro-viders are inextricably intertwined as they are often produced together as entire modules; thus the downward pressure on the pricing of automotive seats (due to commoditisation) could exert similar pressure on interior systems. Like its Automotive Seating division (in Faurecia, both Automotive Seating and Interior Systems are classified together as Interior Modules), Faurecia's Interior Systems division has been subjected to equally brutal pricing pressure (Faurecia, 2011a). According to industry analysts, most interior systems generate margins of around 4–5 percent, which are even lower than the 7–8 percent earned on seats (Roland Berger and Lazard, 2011).[8]

Faurecia's acquisitions since the 1980s

Faurecia, in its present form is the product of a relentless series of M&A stretch-ing over two centuries. Faurecia's origin dates as far back as 1810 when the brothers Jean-Pierre and Frederic Peugeot partnered with Jacques Maillard-Salins to establish a steel foundry. However the formation of Faurecia only began to take shape, when the two firms AOP (Aciers & Outillages Peugeot, Peugeot Steels and Tools) and Cycles Peugeot (the two were sister companies owned by Peugeot) were merged to form Ecia in 1987; this merger was driven by the desire of both firms to gain the scale economies and capabilities needed to compete in a rapidly growing global automotive seats, interiors and exhaust systems industry, which was the product of increasing outsourcing by automakers (the automakers had turned to outsourcing non-core activities to focus resources on building their respective global market shares and brands and developing next-generational technologies (Funding Universe, 2012).

Ecia supplied exhaust systems, seats, vehicle interior parts and front ends to Volkswagen, Daimler-Benz, Renault, Opel, Honda and Mitsubishi. Concur-rently, Ecia made a number of acquisitions which included exhaust suppliers: Leistritz Abgastechnik in Germany and PCG Silenciadores in Spain, making Ecia the European market leader for exhaust systems. Ecia subsequently acquired Rentrop in Germany, in the process establishing itself as the leading car-seat com-pany and related components company in Europe. Later in 1997, Ecia acquired Bertrand Faure in a friendly takeover (increasing its direct and indirect share-holding in the firm to 99 percent), resulting in the formation of Faurecia in its current form. Prior to its acquisition, Bertrand Faure was starting to focus largely on its automotive equipment business while divesting its beds (Epeda and Merinos), luggage (Delsey) and aeronautics (Ratier-Figeac) businesses; by 1998, the merged firm was focused largely on automotive seats. The merger also greatly strengthened Ecia's international presence, especially in Germany, where Bertrand Faure had earlier established firm ties with leading automakers such as BMW and Volkswagen (Faurecia, 2011a; Funding Universe, 2012a).

Faced with increasing pressure from automakers to assume greater outsourcing responsibilities and furnish corrosive pricing discounts, Faurecia has continued with its acquisitions strategy to secure greater economies of scale and scope; this unrelenting pressure from automakers has greatly eroded industry margins. For instance, in October 2000, Faurecia acquired the auto-parts business of fellow French supplier Sommer Allibert for approximately €1.053 billion (Faurecia, 2001). The target, Sommer Allibert's leading positions in the European instrument panel, door trim panel and floor systems markets, complemented Faurecia's strong position in the seat assembly, seat adjuster and seat recliner markets; the acquisition greatly bolstered Faurecia's strengths in vehicle cockpits and interiors (just-auto, 2000); for instance, Faurecia was soon able to produce BMW's order for entire seats, cockpits and vehicle front-end components all under one roof in its Leipzig plant. The acquisition of Sommer Allibert also gave Faurecia near total control over SAI Automotive AG, another European maker of dashboards, cockpits and instrument panels (27.48 percent held directly and 69.34 percent indirectly, through Sommer Allibert) (Faurecia, 2001).

In 2007, Faurecia acquired a 50 percent stake in Euro Auto Plastics System (Euro APS) for €9.4 million from Portuguese supplier Simoldes Plasticos, in the process strengthening its presence in Eastern Europe, as Euro APS made instrument panels, door panels, bumper systems, headliners, carpeting and acoustic trims for the Dacia plant in Pitesti (Romania), which produces the Logan[9] (Supplier Business, 2010b). This move validates the effectiveness of acquisitions in securing market share in new growth markets. In its bid to transcend the role of mere seat making (with its eroding profit margins) and become the preferred supplier of entire vehicle cockpits to the automakers, Faurecia acquired the German and Spanish operations of Plastal (a first-tier supplier of vehicle exterior parts) for €49.9 million in March 2010 and September 2010 respectively. These acquisitions not only added nearly €387 million to Faurecia's consolidated sales in 2010 but also established it as one of the world's largest automotive exteriors manufacturer; at the time, Faurecia wanted to use automotive exteriors as a means of product differentiation in its business model which was hampered by increasingly squeezed profit margins in highly competitive automotive seats and interiors markets (Faurecia, 2010a; Faurecia, 2015).

Further, Faurecia aggressively pursued an acquisitions strategy to build a vertically integrated firm (i.e., one with significant backward integration) with regard to its automotive seating business. In December 2010, Faurecia completed its acquisition of the seat comfort division of Germany's Hoerbiger in a deal valued at €7 million. This acquisition would give Faurecia control over a series of high value-added seat technologies such as massage, shoulder, lumbar and lateral and side supports. Additionally, the acquisition of Hoerbiger strengthened Faurecia's presence in the premium seats segment (i.e., seats used in luxury vehicles such as Audi, BMW and Mercedes Benz; these automakers were also Hoerbiger's clients); thus acquisitions are also useful in opening/strengthening new market segments (Faurecia, 2010b). Traditionally, Faurecia was dependent on external suppliers such as Hoerbiger for these technologies (Henry, 2011).

This backward integration strategy is similar to that of JCI and Lear which have acquired other lower-tier suppliers such as Michel Thierry, C. Rob. Hammerstein and Guilford Mills. Through this strategy, JCI, Lear and Faurecia are trying to control the various technologies that go into automotive seats. Industry analysts assert that this trend is driven by the automakers' insistence that their suppliers develop an increasingly vertically integrated structure; this would mean that these automakers would have to deal directly with fewer suppliers, thus freeing up more resources for higher value-added activities such as marketing and conducting cutting-edge R&D (Henry, 2011). These events suggest that first-tier suppliers such as Faurecia have under increasing automaker pressure embarked on acquisitions to develop vertically integrated organisations. This vertical integration approach may not be tenable over the long-term as it involves significant costs and an ineffective vertically integrated organisation is extremely painful to unravel.

Faurecia has also intensified its acquisition strategy in China, the world's largest and fastest-growing automotive market. In June 2010, Faurecia expanded its presence in China by taking a 18.75 percent stake in the Xuyang Group, a leading Chinese automotive components supplier which counts China's first car manufacturer, the FAW Group (First Auto Works), and its international affiliate, FAW-VW (Audi and Volkswagen) as its clients; this move is expected to bolster Faurecia's presence in the world's fastest-growing and largest automotive market, along with reducing its dependence on an increasingly mature European market. In June 2011, Faurecia also cemented its relationship with the Changchun Xuyang Group by forging a new agreement which included the following:

- Seating and Interior Systems Technical Centre in Changchun: Faurecia would jointly invest and develop a Technical Centre in Changchun, as proposed by the Changchun Xuyang Group;
- New JV in Foshan (Guangdong, China): To support the future production of new FAW-VW models in Foshan, Faurecia would establish a new JV with Changchun Xuyang Group in Foshan. This new JV would result in the establishment of three new plants:
  - Faurecia would hold 60 percent of the seating and interior plants while the remaining 40 percent would be held by the Changchun Xuyang Group;
  - The Changchun Xuyang Group would hold 60 percent of the soft trim plant while the remaining 40 percent would be in Faurecia's possession (Faurecia, 2011d).

Not resting on its laurels, Faurecia soon acquired Ford/ACH, an interior components plant in Saline, Michigan (US) in May 2012. This plant, with annual sales of US$1.1 billion, was responsible for the provision of cockpit modules, central consoles, door panels and instrument panels for twelve automotive programmes (i.e., Escape, Edge/MKX, Explorer, Econoline, Expedition/Navigator, F150, Focus, MKS, Mustang, Taurus, Flex/MKT, Transit) spread across eight North American Ford plants. The acquisition was carried out to augment Faurecia's market position in automotive interiors and also position itself as a key supplier to the Ford F 150, Ford's and also North America's best-selling vehicle (Faurecia, 2015a; Faurecia, 2012a). In August 2012, Faurecia pressed on with its relentless acquisition campaign by acquiring Plastal France (Plastal SAS), a first-tier supplier of plastic exterior parts for Daimler's Smart brand of vehicles; the acquisition also gave Faurecia a new manufacturing plant in Hambach, France (Faurecia, 2012b; Faurecia, 2015a; Plastics News, 2012).

However, in December 2015, Faurecia signed a Memorandum of Understanding to sell its Automotive Exteriors business to Compagnie Plastic Omnium. Faurecia's management deemed the Automotive Exteriors business, which was the smallest of its four divisions (it accounted for 9.8 percent of Faurecia's revenues) too capital intensive for its size and wanted to divert the proceeds of the sale to augment its remaining seats, emissions control technologies and interior systems. Moreover, Faurecia wanted to invest the proceeds in more high value-added technologies such as composite materials; composite materials are lighter yet significantly stronger than most metals, making them choice materials in manufacturing premium seats that could lower the weight of vehicles (resulting in greater fuel efficiency and increased performance). Further, the proceeds from the sale of its Automotive Exteriors division would also enable Faurecia to almost completely eliminate its net debt (Faurecia, 2015b; Jansen, 2015).

Faurecia's organic growth strategy

Faurecia is concurrently using organic growth as a means of driving the company forward and is not slavishly committed to an acquisitions strategy. For instance, it is steadily strengthening its industrial resources and R&D capabilities in China. By the end of 2010, Faurecia employed 5,000 employees at 23 plants and two R&D centres in China. It had also opened seven new manufacturing sites in the country by the end of 2011, along with two fully retrofitted R&D centres. Earlier in 2010, Faurecia also signed a major strategic partnership agreement with Chinese automaker, Geely which acquired Volvo Cars, for whom it is already a preferred supplier in Europe. This agreement would allow Faurecia to develop and manufacture interiors for many of Geely's product lines (Faurecia, 2010e). Underscoring Faurecia's commitment to organic growth, its CEO Yann Delabriere asserted that the company planned to build 60 new plants or carry out major expansions of existing plants worldwide through 2015. He added that Faurecia was already in the process of executing 42 such projects and was planning to spend €2.3 billion through 2015 to facilitate their implementation (Sedgwick and Child, 2012).

Further, in April 2007, Faurecia established a JV with the Shinsung Delta Tech Co, Ltd, a South Korean company, for the production of instrument panels, door panels and centre consoles in South Korea. The creation of this JV, for which Faurecia was the majority stakeholder, was also a critical aspect of Faurecia's Asia-Pacific strategy (South Korea is Faurecia's second most important market in Asia after China). The new JV, 61 percent owned by Faurecia, was named the Faurecia Shinsung Co, Ltd. Its head office and production facilities were instituted in Masan City from where it supplied components to the nearby Renault Samsung plant in Busan; production was believed to have started in early 2009. In the ensuing years, Faurecia forged a series of JVs at a blistering pace worldwide. In May 2012, Faurecia launched a JV with Rush Group Ltd; the JV known as Detroit Manufacturing Systems assumed the role of assembling and sequencing interior parts at a new Detroit plant. Additionally, in April 2013, Faurecia inked another JV pact with Thailand's Summit Auto Seats to supply Ford in its Southeast Asian (particularly Thailand) expansion strategy. Concurrently, Faurecia also rolled out another JV with one of China's leading automobile companies, Chang'an Automobile Group, further augmenting its already considerable market position in China. Moreover, in November 2013, Faurecia sealed another JV agreement with Magneti Marelli to cooperate in the development of cutting-edge Human-Machine Interface products for vehicle interiors; the JV is developing solutions that facilitate the integration of mobile devices (i.e., smartphones and tablets) into a vehicle's centre console, instrument panel and docking station (Faurecia 2013; Faurecia, 2015a; Stanley, 2014).

In rapid succession, Faurecia soon forged another JV with Japan's Howa in January 2014; the resultant JV known as Faurecia Howa Interiors, which supplies interior systems for Renault-Nissan in Mexico. This JV also bolstered Faurecia's prospects with Nissan in Brazil, Spain, South Africa and Thailand. Capping off its JV drive in 2014, Faurecia launched a 50:50 JV with a seemingly unlikely partner, Interval (a leading French agricultural cooperative); the JV known as 'Automotive Performance Materials' would develop environmentally friendly biosourced raw materials capable of reducing vehicle weight, in the process reducing fuel consumption and carbon emissions. More recently in 2015, Faurecia added three more JVs in China. In May 2015, Faurecia unveiled two JVs with Dongfeng Hongtai, which are known as 'Dongfeng Faurecia Automotive Interior Co., Ltd.' and 'Dongfeng Faurecia Automotive Exterior Co., Ltd.' respectively; these JVs are meant to consolidate Faurecia's market position in the Chinese automotive interior and exterior parts market. Soon after in September 2015, Faurecia and Beijing WKW Automotive Parts Co., Ltd formed a 50:50 JV to cooperate in the development of aluminium interior decorative parts for light vehicles; initial customers would include Nissan and Volvo (Faurecia 2013; Faurecia, 2014; Faurecia, 2015a; ET Auto, 2015).

The above JVs gives credence to Drucker's assertion that partnerships such as JVs could become the predominant driver of growth rather than 'outright ownership and command-and-control' (Drucker and Maciariello, 2004). Drucker, however, may have failed to note that even in JVs, there in invariably a stronger partner (even in 50:50 JVs) with access to greater economies of scale and scope, finances, distribution channels and technology. Further, the stronger partner (e.g., Faurecia) could buy out the weaker partner, if the opportunity presented itself (e.g., relaxation of legislation), thus reverting to acquisitions as a growth strategy; in this regard, JVs give companies such as Faurecia a higher degree of flexibility in its growth strategy vis-à-vis outright acquisitions.

Technical progress and lean: Faurecia's competitive advantage

Backed by a significant R&D budget and technologies harnessed through numerous acquisitions, Faurecia has been able to obtain the technical progress needed to secure a place among the top three automotive seats producers. Faurecia's R&D investment has been increasing at a CAGR of 2.9 percent (from 2000 to 2015), rising from €599.3 million (US$644.07 million) in the earlier period to €924.3 million (US$1.007 billion) in 2015 (Faurecia, 2015a, Faurecia, 2001); it is also this steadily increasing R&D expenditure that compels Faurecia to seek increasing economies of scale and scope (to alleviate this cost pressure) via acquisition. In fact, Faurecia recorded the highest 2015 R&D expenditure among the top three automotive seats makers. Through its 30 R&D centres, Faurecia has been able to achieve breakthrough innovations in seating comfort, safety and spaciousness. Faurecia's expertise in postural comfort is evident in the driver's seat of the Renault Scenic, as it is equipped with adjustment mechanisms that enable drivers to determine the ideal position, and the seat could be raised by around 70 mm (the highest value in the market). Further, for the Renault Scenic, Faurecia has provided wrap-around headrests that ensure support, comfort and safety. To attain the highest possible postural comfort in increasingly smart vehicle interiors (under varying road conditions), Faurecia's R&D experts also conducted experiments using sophisticated simulations with avatars illustrating the various human morphologies of occupants in 2D or 3D.

Further examples of Faurecia's industry-leading innovations over the past decade would include its 'RALF' (Reinforced Airbag Lid in Foam). This innovation has been incorporated into the instrument panels of vehicles such as the Renault Laguna III, Opel Insignia and even the Mercedes S Class; its value proposition comes from the ability to optimise the effective deployment of airbags in the event of accidents. Moreover, Faurecia designs the safest possible seats in cars such as the Volkswagen Polo by combining the top of the backrest with headrests to ensure the best protection if the car is struck from behind. Additionally, Faurecia has ensured that head/chest airbags are installed into the side of the front seats' backrests to provide protection against side impacts. Faurecia has also installed ISOFIX attachment points on the rear seat to help secure child safety seats. This comprehensive and methodical approach to seat design has helped its automaker clients (e.g., Renault) to achieve superior standards in international safety assessments; through the use of Faurecia seats, the Renault Laguna II was the first vehicle to score five stars (the highest rating) in the Euro NCAP crash tests (a key global benchmark for vehicle safety) (Faurecia, 2011b; Faurecia, 2011c; Euro NCAP, 2012). Cognisant of an impending future dominated by highly-networked, possibly autonomous vehicles, Renault continues to surpass preceding industry standards by developing an Active Wellness seat (currently version 2.0). This revolutionary seating system, while still an evolving concept, has the capacity to monitor an occupant's physical (e.g., heart rate, facial expressions) and mental state (e.g., stress level), and optimise seating positions for individuals' physical specifications (greatly augmenting the driving experience). More remarkably, this system goes far beyond actively monitoring motion sickness and drowsiness, as it is able to analyse the collated occupant data and deploy optimal remedies which could include adjusting the seat position, ventilation, ambient lighting and audio environment or provide an automated massage (Faurecia, 2017).

Like its peers, Faurecia has turned to lean concepts to bolster its competitiveness. Over the past decade, it has incorporated the various lean practices (e.g., just-in-time and continuous improvement) to form its own system known as the Faurecia Excellence System (FES) in early 2009; among the top three automotive seat makers, Faurecia was the slowest in developing a comprehensive lean system but has since proven to be a quick study. The FES is aimed at attaining excellence with regard to costs, quality and lead times. This system involved implementing 114 core procedures and it has permeated all of Faurecia's businesses and functional areas (encompasses R&D, production and corporate functions and sales). In short, it is far more extensive than Lear's LMS which covers only manufacturing operations. Faurecia asserts that under the FES, 'work is organised among autonomous teams, partnerships are forged with suppliers, customers' expectations are defined, and quality products are consistently delivered on time'. This system for achieving operational excellence is supposedly practised by Faurecia's 102,869 employees worldwide. Additionally, Faurecia has incorporated an ongoing feedback scheme to strengthen working conditions and manufacturing procedures (Faurecia, 2009; Faurecia, 2015a).

4. Beyond the top three seat makers

By the 21st century, the global automotive seats market is even more oligopolistic than the tyre industry; the top three seats makers (i.e., Adient, Lear and Faurecia) today control over three quarters of the global seats market, higher than the approximate 40 percent controlled by their counterparts in the tyre industry. However, like the tyre industry, the second-tier players in the global automotive seats market are now scrambling to secure control of the remaining smaller, independent firms. The second-tier firms, Toyota Boshoku and Magna, are respectively the world's fourth and fifth largest seat makers; Toyota Boshoku has an estimated 8.0 percent market share while Magna has around 7.5 percent (Toyota Boshoku, 2015; Magna, 2015). However, the disparity between them and the big three seat makers is still relatively large. Beyond these top five firms (i.e., Adient, Lear, Faurecia, Toyota Boshoku and Magna), the bulk of the remaining 7.3 percent (estimated) of the global automotive seats market is held by the Japanese firms TS Tech, Tachi-S, with emerging Chinese seat makers such as Shanghai Vehicle Awning and Cushioned Seat Factory and Wuhe Hean Auto Seat Co accounting for a morsel of the remainder (Marukawa, 2005).

Like their considerably larger big three counterparts, Toyota Boshoku and Magna also use acquisitions to achieve greater economies of scale and scope. Toyota Boshoku is a sister company of Toyota which owns a controlling

54 percent of the seat maker (McCombs and Horie, 2015). In 2011, Toyota Boshoku generated around 97 percent of its revenues from Toyota alone (Toyota Boshoku, 2011; Daily Auto News, 2011). Toyota Boshoku became a major supplier of car seats to Toyota's US assembly plants in 2004 when it acquired a Toyota keiretsu,[10] Araco Corporation, which had a stake in Trim Masters, a JV Araco started with JCI with 1987 to provide seats to Toyota's US-based assembly facilities (Klier and Rubenstein, 2008; Bloomberg, 2012). Toyota Boshoku subsequently acquired Trim Masters in late 2011, to consolidate its market share in an increasingly oligopolistic automotive seats market (The Kentucky Standard, 2011). The acquisition of Trim Masters greatly augmented Toyota Boshoku's automotive seat making capabilities, as it possessed not only seat production facilities but also facilities to make seat covering (strengthening Toyota Boshoku's vertically integrated capabilities); even second tier suppliers such as Toyota Boshoku are under mounting automaker pressure to acquire (often via acquisitions) vertically integrated capabilities in seat making. This acquisition also bolstered Toyota Boshoku's strength in automotive interiors, as Trim Masters had considerable capabilities in injection moulding and vacuum forming for door trims (Klier and Rubenstein, 2008).

Earlier, in June 2011, Toyota Boshoku had also acquired the vehicle interior business of Polytec Holding, an Austrian automotive components maker; Polytec's interior division provided door trims and ceilings to leading German automobile manufacturers such as BMW, Daimler, Opel and Volkswagen (Business Wire, 2011). The acquisition of Polytec greatly broadened Toyota Boshoku's client base, as prior to this acquisition, the company only had two customers, namely Toyota and GM (Toyota Boshoku supplied seats for the Cadillac SRX and Saab 9–4x SUVs made by GM in Mexico) (Greimel, 2011). Toyota Boshoku's acquisition of Polytec also indicates a desire to be less reliant on its key customer, Toyota and grow its seats business more aggressively. In a bid to bolster its market position, Toyota Boshoku also acquired the mechanical seat frame component divisions of Aisin Seiki and Shiroki Corporation in December 2014. The acquisition was executed to acquire technology needed to augment Toyota Boshoku's engineering capabilities in the area of seat frames manufacturing (Toyota Boshoku, 2014).

Further, it is questionable whether Toyota Boshoku would ever be able to challenge the top three seat makers for industry leadership, as its existence seems largely to ensure that its major customer and biggest shareholder, Toyota, has uninterrupted access to seating systems, vehicle interiors and related components, and not be subject to the 'mercy' of increasingly powerful oligopolists (i.e., JCI, Lear and Faurecia). Toyota Boshoku's attempt to reduce its dependence on Toyota soon faced a major setback; Polytec, the automotive interiors firm which Toyota Boshoku acquired in June 2011, consistently posted losses and was eventually sold to Austria's Megatech Industries in June 2016 (Higgs, 2016).

Magna, a Canadian firm, became a major seats maker in the 1990s, with its acquisition of Douglas & Lomason Company (a Michigan-based supplier of seating systems, frames, covers, foam and mechanisms) in August 1996 for around

US$135 million in cash; this acquisition made Magna a key seats supplier outside the big three (The New York Times, 1996; Klier and Rubenstein, 2008). Magna has since continued to expand its presence in seating systems albeit not as aggressively as the big three. For instance, in 2010, Magna acquired a Brazilian seat supplier named Resil Minas, the largest supplier of seat frames and stampings in South America. Resil Minas recorded sales of US$174 million in 2009 and counted Fiat, Ford, General Motors, Volkswagen, IVECO and PSA among its clients (thus this acquisition also deepened Magna's relationship with these automakers in South America). The acquisition of Resil Minas also included three manufacturing facilities and around 1,400 employees throughout South America, thus augmenting Magna's capabilities in South America (Magna, 2010). Further, in January 2011, Magna acquired automotive seat supplier Buenos Aires based Pabsa S.A.; Pabsa was previously part of the L'Equipe Monteur Group and was a vertically integrated supplier of complete seats, foam products, trim covers and seat structures (in 2010, Pabsa posted revenues of around US$110 million). The acquisition of Pabsa gave Magna two production facilities in Buenos Aires and one in Cordoba, Argentina (with an additional 960 employees), thus strengthening Magna Seating's global footprint, and positioning it as a leading seating systems supplier in South America (Magna, 2011).

In 2012, Magna acquired Vogelsitze GmbH, a German seat maker for buses and light trains (it counts Mercedes-Benz, Volvo, Bombardier Inc. among its customers). The fact that Magna has to buy a maker of seats for public transportation suggests a lack of buying opportunities in an increasingly oligopolistic car seats market. In a remarkable display of rising supplier power, Magna was nearly successful in its bid for Opel in 2010, an ailing European car maker that is a subsidiary of GM. However, GM eventually chose to keep Opel and is attempting to turn it around (Warburton, 2012). Despite Magna's unsuccessful bid, this example clearly illustrates that there is indeed a shift in the balance of power in automaker-supplier relations. Nonetheless Magna's prospects in the automotive seats industry are relatively limited, as unlike the big three players (i.e., Adient, Lear and Faurecia), it does not have an accompanying interiors division; Magna sold its interiors business to Spanish interiors supplier, Grupo Antolin for US$525 million in April 2015 (Magna, 2015).

Toyota Boshoku's biggest domestic rival in Japan is TS Tech (was known as Tokyo Seat Co. Ltd before October 1997) and it is the key supplier of seats and interiors to Honda Motor Co Ltd; Honda has a 22.6 percent equity stake in TS Tech and more than 60 percent of Honda's products (cars and motorcycles) are fitted with TS Tech products (TS Tech, 2015; TS Tech, 2017). Like Toyota Boshoku, it seems to be extremely dependent on its main customer, Honda and is essentially an affiliate company established to ensure that the automaker has ready access to essential seating and interior systems. Nonetheless, TS Tech does have other customers, although they are still limited to Japanese automakers (e.g., Suzuki Motor Corporation, Yamaha Motor Co., Ltd and Isuzu Motors Limited). Further, it appears to be even less aggressive in M&A than Tokyo Boshoku and in fact has no recent history of M&A. Instead, TS Tech has chosen to rely on the formation of JVs in Thailand, Brazil, India, Indonesia and China since the 1990s, as a means of growing its business; however, JVs could also prove to a useful springboard to acquisition if the opportunity arises (e.g., relaxation of regulatory environment) (TS Tech, 2011). It is also possible, that if not for the complex cross-shareholding system in corporate Japan (that 'protects' companies from takeovers), companies such as TS Tech and Toyota Boshoku would long have been acquired by their larger competitors in the consolidation wave that has swept the industry since the 1980s.

Another smaller Japanese competitor of Toyota Boshoku is Tachi-S, a former subsidiary of Nissan. In the early 1970s, Nissan became the single largest shareholder in Tachi-S by acquiring a 20 percent stake in the firm. This move was to ensure uninterrupted access to car seats as this seamlessness is a critical aspect of just-in-time operations. By the late 1990s, Tachi-S derived 30 percent of its approximately US$1 billion revenues from Nissan. The firm subsequently broke away from Nissan in 1999 by buying back its shares, as it could no longer tolerate the incessant demands for discounts (Nissan had demanded annual discounts of 10 percent just about every year) (Bremner et al., 1999). Due to historical ties, Nissan remains one of Tachi-S' key customers. Tachi-S today has been relegated to third-tier supplier status, as it has now become a supplier to its domestic competitors, TS Tech and Fuji Seat. However, it remains a supplier to Adient, which through its earlier form as a JCI division, acquired a 5 percent stake in the firm in 2010; this investment made JCI the single largest shareholder in the firm. However it is questionable whether Adient is able to enlarge its stake in Tachi-S due to the convoluted ownership structure of Japanese firms (just-auto.com, 2010).

5. Conclusion

The global automotive seats market has grown and consolidated at a remarkable pace over the past three decades. As mentioned earlier, seat making was largely an in-house activity carried out by the automakers themselves. However, impacted by the cascade effect, it became a primarily outsourced activity carried out by a few large first-tier suppliers, as automakers chose to focus on marketing, next generation R&D and building a global brand. The most remarkable feature of this industry is the rate at which it consolidated. Back in the 1980s, the global automotive seats industry was in a manner of speaking, 'non-existent', and seat making, if it was carried out by a supplier, was an inconsequential and unprofitable activity (e.g., Faurecia in its current form did not even exist then). However, with the advent of outsourcing by the automakers (precipitated by the cascade effect), it quickly grew into the US$60 billion-plus global industry it is today, with the big three seat makers being particularly aggressive at acquiring their smaller competitors and even their own suppliers (to control the entire value chain of seat making).

The big three seat makers were the first-movers who successfully leveraged on this outsourcing wave by the automakers, and quickly captured more than 70 percent of the emerging automotive seats market by the end of the 1990s through their aggressive acquisition strategy. The fact that these top three seat makers were subjected to considerable pressure from their automaker clients also compelled them to use acquisitions as a means of securing greater economies of scale and scope (in the process, alleviating this incessant automaker pressure and gaining a stronger bargaining position in price negotiations). However, the more passive players in this consolidation wave, Toyota Boshoku, Magna and TS Tech were left with relatively insignificant market shares and it is unlikely that they would ever catch up, as they are now overshadowed by the big three seat makers in terms of economies of scale and scope and R&D expenditure; for instance, even second-placed Lear posted 2015 R&D expenditure of US$194 million (the lowest R&D expenditure among the 'big three'), more than ten times that of Toyota Boshoku's 2015 R&D expenditure of US$14.8 million (Lear, 2015; Toyota Boshoku, 2015).

Today, the industry is still experiencing consolidation, with the second-tier players (e.g., Toyota Boshoku and Magna) moving to acquire what is left in this highly-consolidated industry (e.g., small and mid-size seat makers in South America and other emerging economies). The price for this relentless consolidation is increased scrutiny by antitrust regulators. Further, the automotive seats industry may have reached a high point (in terms of industrial concentration) as early as 1999 with two dominant players, JCI and Lear, compelling the weaker third player (i.e., Faurecia) to make the decision to move into the higher-margin emissions control technology industry. Faurecia's decision seems vindicated as it is now the leading player in the more lucrative emissions control technology business.

Despite the immense market power wielded by Adient and Lear, they are still plagued by paltry single-digit profit margins, eroded by constant automaker pressure, and the culminating insatiable demands for scale economies and R&D. It is this relative lack of profitability that drove JCI to spin off its seats operations as the new entity, Adient in October 2016 and focus freed-up resources on businesses that deliver the double digit returns it craves. However, with the increasing importance of vehicle interiors (including seats) as an arbiter of consumer vehicle purchases in this increasingly digitised era and the industry oligopolists controlling the 'nuts and bolts' of the industry (through vertical integration), the tide could shift in favour of the mega suppliers over the coming years. These mega suppliers, like their counterparts in other industries, typically need significant time periods to integrate their acquisitions (due to differing systems and cultures), and those who persist in their integration efforts would stand to reap the benefits of their steadfastness (i.e., increased pricing power which translates into stronger profit margins). The key obstacle to the achievement of success is ironically not relentless automaker pressure but rather the short-termism that pervades the management of today's automotive seat makers.

Notes

1 Under Chapter 11, a debtor proposes a plan of reorganisation to keep its business alive and pay creditors over time (US Courts, 2011).

2 The significant growth potential of emissions control technology is due to the emergence of increasingly stringent global regulatory standards on vehicle emissions such as Euro 5 and 6 (the Euro 5 was applied to the registration and sale of new vehicles in January 2011, while Euro 6 is expected to apply to new vehicles in January 2015) and rising consumer demand for vehicles equipped with these clean technologies (Europa, 2010).

3 Massage features are due to ergonomists developing a greater understanding of what the human frame needs for health/safety and they are getting vociferous on this matter, as people spend increasingly more time in their cars (Beecham, 2009).

4 James Womack, Daniel Jones and Daniel Roos assert that although lean involves significantly less inventory, it delivers higher production levels. Further, the application of lean results in greater product variation with fewer defects. Womack and Jones also argue that lean extends far beyond mere production (and transcends the business landscape to include service organisations). They also assert that lean targets a firm's entire value chain extending from raw materials to finished products, the placement of orders to eventual delivery and the initiation of concepts to subsequent launch (Womack, Jones and Roos, 2007; Womack and Jones, 2003).

5 The fact that Toyota has awarded JCI a spate of awards (e.g., '2007 Award for Outstanding Performance', 'Global Contribution Awards' in 2000, 2004 and 2008, and '2010 Toyota Supplier Diversity Award') is affirmation of this strong relationship; Toyota is indirectly pressuring JCI, as these awards mean that JCI has to consistently meet/even exceed its expectations or risk falling from favour.

6 The GM Supplier of the Year award is awarded based on the provision of superlative quality, pioneering technology, premium launch support, crisis management and compelling business cost management competencies (Lear, 2012).

7 The 100 percent acquisition of EMCON's shares was paid via a 20.9 million new Faurecia shares issue, with no significant impact on Faurecia's cash and debt situation (Faurecia, 2009). Faurecia claims that the acquisition of EMCON Technologies has made it the world's leading brand in emissions control technologies (both in terms of revenues and technological capabilities); one in four vehicles worldwide has a Faurecia exhaust system (Sedgwick and Child, 2012).

8 The vehicle interior segment has been described by Faurecia's CEO, Yann Delabriere, as 'still very fragmented, with a number of mid-sized players whose future is uncertain. I don't know what form it will take, but consolidation will happen. It's a global trend' (quoted in Sedgwick and Child, 2012).

9 Dacia is a Romanian car maker acquired by Renault in 1999 and its leading brand is the Logan (Renault, 2013).

10 Keiretsu is the Japanese name for a corporate structure in which various organisations (usually bound by client-supplier ties) cement their relationships, by assuming minor stakes in one another (Hindle, 2009).

References

Adient plc (2016) *About us*, Available at: www.adient.com/about-us [Accessed on 18 January, 2017].

Adient plc (2016) *Form 10-K*, Dublin 1 Ireland: Adient plc.

Arons, S (2011) CFO interview: Faurecia's Frank Imbert- "We have been a consolidator", *CFO Insight* [internet] Available at: www.cfo-insight.com/career-people/interviews/we-have-been-a-consolidator/ [Accessed on 5 June, 2012].

Automotive Business Review (2011) Johnson Controls to acquire Keiper, Recaro, Automotive Business Review [internet] Available at: http://www.

automotive-business-review.com/news/johnson-controls-to-acquire-keiper-recaro-030111 [Accessed on 10 December, 2012].

Beecham, M. (2009) Research analysis: Review of seating technology, *just-auto.com* [internet] Available at: www.just-auto.com/analysis/review-of-seating-technol ogy_id99383.aspx [Accessed on 12 May, 2012].

Beecham, M. (2010) Research analysis: Review of vehicle technology, *just-auto.com* [internet] Available at: www.just-auto.com/analysis/review-of-vehicle-seating_ id103029.aspx [Accessed on 15 May, 2012].

Bloomberg (1997) Lear to Buy ITT Industries Seating Unit, Los Angeles Times [internet] Available at: http://articles.latimes.com/1997/aug/05/business/ fi-19561 [Accessed on 19 July, 2012].

Bloomberg (2012) Auto components: Company overview of Automotive Industries Holdings, Inc., *Bloomberg.com* [internet] Available at: http://investing.business week.com/research/stocks/private/snapshot.asp?privcapId=25297 [Accessed on 13 August, 2012].

Bremner, B., Thornton, E., Kunii, I.M. and Tanikawa, M. (1999) A new Japan? (int'l edition), *Bloomberg.com* [internet] Available at: www.businessweek.com/ 1999/99_43/b3652010.htm [Accessed on 12 June, 2012].

Business Wire (2011) Toyota Boshoku acquires automotive interior business of Poly-tec Group, *Business Wire* [internet] Available at: www.businesswire.com/news/ home/20110609006412/en/Toyota-Boshoku-Acquires-Automotive-Interior-Business-Polytec [Accessed on 13 July, 2016].

Chandler, A.D. and Hikino, T. (1999) The large industrial enterprise and the dynam-ics of modern economic growth, in Chandler, A., Amatori, F. and Hikino, T. (eds), *Big Business and the Wealth of Nations*, Cambridge: Cambridge University Press.

Charette, R.N. (2009) This car runs on code, *IEEE Spectrum* [internet] Available at: http://spectrum.ieee.org/green-tech/advanced-cars/this-car-runs-on-code [Accessed on 19 October, 2010].

Clothier, M. (2011) Magna, Lear may lead global consolidation of automotive-interior suppliers, *Bloomberg.com* [internet] Available at: www.bloomberg.com/ news/2011-08-11/magna-joins-jci-in-global-consolidation-of-car-interiors-mak ers.html [Accessed on 6 February, 2012].

CNN Money (1998) Johnson buys competitor: Johnson Controls to pay up to $600 mil-lion for Becker Group, plus debt, CNN Money [internet] Available at: http://money. cnn.com/1998/04/27/deals/johnson/ [Accessed on 6 February, 2012].

Daily Auto News (2011) The BMW will put seats from a Toyota, *Daily Auto News* [internet] Available at: www.daily-autonews.com/latest-news/2011/08/20/the-bmw-will-put-seats-from-a-toyota.html [Accessed on 15 June, 2012].

Dealbook (2008) Icahn Shears stake in Lear, *The New York Times Company* [internet] Available at: http://dealbook.nytimes.com/2008/11/04/icahn-shears-stake-in-lear/ [Accessed on 16 July, 2012].

Diem, W. (2010) JCI countering OEM trend to vertical integration with strategic acquisitions, *WardsAuto* [internet] Available at: http://wardsauto.com/ar/jci_ strategic_acquisitions_101210 [Accessed on 13 March, 2012].

Donovan, D. (1999) The dawn of the mega-supplier, MA: Bain & Company, Inc.

Drucker, P.F. and Mariariello, J.A. (2004) The Daily Drucker: 366 Days of Insight and Motivation for Getting the Right Things Done, New York: HarperCollins Publishers.

Dyer, J.H. (1994) Dedicated assets: Japan's manufacturing edge, *Harvard Business Review*, November–December: 174–178.

Emery, C. (2009) Car parts maker Lear emerges from bankruptcy, *Reuters.com* [internet] Available at: www.reuters.com/article/2009/11/09/retire-us-lear-idUS TRE5A839420091109 [Accessed on 20 August, 2012].

ET Auto (2015) Faurecia signs 50:50 JV agreement with Beijing WKW Automotive Parts, *ET Auto* [internet] Available at: http://auto.economictimes.indiatimes. com/news/auto-components/faurecia-signs-5050-jv-agreement-with-beijing-wkw-automotive-parts/49415599 [Accessed on 7 July, 2016].

Euro NCAP (2012) History: And finally a new Rating Scheme, *Euro NCAP* [internet] Available at: www.euroncap.com/Content-Web-Page/ee0e0c41-f8e8-4cdc-90fe-414ae5883db6/history.aspx [Accessed on 20 September, 2012].

Europa (2010) Euro 5 and Euro 6 standards: reduction of pollutant emissions from light vehicles, Europa [internet] Available at: http://europa.eu/legislation_sum maries/environment/air_pollution/l28186_en.htm [Accessed on 19 October, 2011].

Faurecia (2001) *2001 Annual Report*, Nanterre Cedex: Faurecia.

Faurecia (2006) *2006 Annual Report*, Nanterre Cedex: Faurecia.

Faurecia (2009) Registration document 2009, Nanterre Cedex: Faurecia.

Faurecia (2010a) Faurecia to acquire Plastal Spain, *Faurecia* [internet] Available at: www.faurecia.com/pressroom/all-press-releases/Pages/Faurecia-to-acquire-Plas tal-Spain.aspx [Accessed on 27 November, 2011].

Faurecia (2010b) Faurecia to acquire seat comfort technology activity from Hoerbiger Automotive Komfortsysteme GmbH, *Faurecia* [internet] Available at: www. faurecia.com/pressroom/all-press-releases/financial-press-releases/faurecia_ pr261010en.pdf [Accessed on 29 November, 2011].

Faurecia (2010c) Faurecia shareholders' meeting confirms the acquisition of EMCON Technologies, *Faurecia* [internet] Available at: www.faurecia.com/pressroom/ news/Pages/acquisition-EMCON-technologies.aspx [Accessed on 27 November, 2011].

Faurecia (2010d) Faurecia takes 18.75% stake in Xuyang Group, China (Changchun, Jilin province), *Faurecia* [internet] Available at: www.faurecia.com/sharehold ers-investors/financial-press-releases/Pages/signing-of-an-agreement-with-the-Municipality-of-Changchun.aspx [Accessed on 29 November, 2011].

Faurecia (2010e) *Annual Results 2010*, Nanterre Cedex: Faurecia.

Faurecia (2011a) *Annual Results 2011*, Nanterre Cedex: Faurecia.

Faurecia (2011b) Technology Highlights: 2011 Frankfurt Motor Show, Nanterre Cedex: Faurecia.

Faurecia (2011c) Vehicles by Faurecia: 2011 Frankfurt Motor Show, Nanterre Cedex: Faurecia.

Faurecia (2012a) Acquisition of ACH Saline business, Nanterre Cedex: Faurecia

Faurecia (2012b) Registration document 2012, Nanterre Cedex: Faurecia.

Faurecia (2013) Faurecia and Magneti Marelli sign cooperation agreement, Faurecia [internet] Available at: http://www.faurecia.com/en/faurecia-and-magneti-marelli-sign-cooperation-agreement [Accessed on 17 February, 2016].

Faurecia (2014) 2014 Registration document, Nanterre Cedex: Faurecia.

Faurecia (2015a) *2015 Annual Report*, Nanterre Cedex: Faurecia.

Faurecia (2015b) Faurecia to divest its automotive exteriors business to plastic omnium, *Faurecia* [internet] Available at: www.faurecia.com/files/corporate/ news/file/faurecia_body_141215_financial_presentation_final.pdf [Accessed on 12 July, 2015].

Faurecia (2016) *Investor Day, April 2016*, Nanterre Cedex: Faurecia.

Faurecia (2017a) Active wellness 2.0 seat – concept, *Faurecia* [internet] Available at: www.faurecia.com/en/innovation/discover-our-innovations/active-wellness [Accessed on 25 January, 2017].

Faurecia (2017b) Automotive seating, *Faurecia* [internet] Available at: www.faurecia.com/en/about-us/automotive-seating [Accessed on 25 January, 2017].

Funding Universe (2012a) Faurecia S.A., *Funding Universe* [internet] Available at: www.fundinguniverse.com/company-histories/Faurecia-SA-company-History.html [Accessed on 6 June, 2012].

Funding Universe (2012b) Johnson Controls, Inc., *Funding Universe* [internet] Available at: www.fundinguniverse.com/company-histories/Johnson-Controls-Inc-Company-History.html [Accessed on 26 February, 2012].

Funding Universe (2012c) Lear Corporation history, *Funding Universe* [internet] Available at: www.fundinguniverse.com/company-histories/lear-corporation-history/ [Accessed on 6 June, 2012].

Greg, G (1996) JCI buys itself a prince, *WardsAuto* [internet] Available at: http://wardsauto.com/news-amp-analysis/jci-buys-itself-prince [Accessed on 20 March, 2012].

Greimel, H. (2011) Toyota loses 670,000 units to quake, plans big October ramp up, *Automotive News* [internet] Available at: www.autonews.com/apps/pbcs.dll/article?AID=/20110610/OEM/306109913/1289 [Accessed on 5 August, 2011].

Henry, I. (2011) Vertical integration- the new acquisition driver, *AutomotiveWorld.com* [internet] Available at: www.automotiveworld.com/news/suppliers/85453-vertical-integration-the-new-acquisition-driver [Accessed on 27 November, 2011].

Higgs, R. (2016) Austria's Megatech acquires loss making Toyota Boshoku auto interiors plants, *Plastics News* [internet] Available at: www.plasticsnews.com/article/20160621/PNE/160629964/austrias-megatech-acquires-loss-making-toyota-boshoku-auto-interiors-plants [Accessed on 8 July, 2016].

Hindle, T. (2009) Keiretsu: Translated literally, it means headless combine, *The Economist* [internet] Available at: www.economist.com/node/14299720 [Accessed on 29 February, 2012].

Hogan, L.M. (2005) Johnson Controls Inc., Global Lean Manufacturing System: The Design & Implementation of a Systematic Performance Improvement Process to Reduce Costs and Improve Quality, ispi.org [internet] Available at: http://www.ispi.org/archives/gotResults/2005/GlobalLeanManufacturingSystemrev4Jan25.pdf [Accessed on 14 May, 2012].

Jansen, K. (2015) Plastic omnium agrees to buy Faurecia's auto exteriors parts unit for $732 million, *Plastics News* [internet] Available at: www.autonews.com/article/20151214/OEM10/151219947/plastic-omnium-agrees-to-buy-faurecias-auto-exteriors-parts-unit-for [Accessed on 10 July, 2016].

J.D. Power (2016) Perceptions of vehicle reliability increasingly influence new-vehicle shopping decisions, J.D. Power 2016 U.S. auto avoider study finds, *J.D. Power* [internet] Available at: www.jdpower.com/press-releases/2016-us-auto-avoider-study [Accessed on 12 July, 2016].

Johnson Controls Inc (1995) *Form 10-K*, Milwaukee: Johnson Controls Inc.

Johnson Controls Inc (2010a) *Form 10-K*, Milwaukee: Johnson Controls Inc.

Johnson Controls Inc (2010b) Johnson Controls announces completion and approval of the acquisition of the Michel Thierry Group, *Johnson Controls* [internet]

Available at: www.johnsoncontrols.co.uk/content/gb/en/news.html?newsitem=
http%3A%2F%2Fuk.johnsoncontrols.mediaroom.com%2Findex.php%3Fs%3D
1281%26item%3D2433 [Accessed on 6 May, 2012].

Johnson Controls Inc (2011a) *Form 10-K*, Milwaukee: Johnson Controls Inc.

Johnson Controls Inc (2011b) Strategic review and 2012 outlook (October 12,
2011), *Johnson Controls* [internet] Available at: www.johnsoncontrols.co.uk/con
tent/dam/WWW/jci/corporate/investors/2011/Johnson_Controls_2011_Ana
lyst_Day.pdf [Accessed on 6 May, 2012].

Johnson Controls Inc (2012a) Manufacturing operations: We invest in business
practices that are as innovative as the products we manufacture, *Johnson Controls*
[internet] Available at: www.johnsoncontrols.com/content/us/en/products/
automotive_experience/our-approach/best-business-practices/manufacturing-
operations.html [Accessed on 15 May, 2012].

Johnson Controls Inc (2012b) Slim seat, *Johnson Controls* [internet] Available at:
www.johnsoncontrols.co.uk/publish/gb/en/products/automotive_experience/
featured-stories/concept-cars/highlights/seating.html [Accessed on 15 May, 2012].

Johnson Controls Inc (2015) Johnson controls is honored for promoting the Toyota new
global architecture, *Johnson Controls* [internet] Available at: www.johnsoncontrols.
com/media-center/news/press-releases/2015/03/04/johnson-controls-is-hon
ored-for-promoting-the-toyota-new-global-architecture [Accessed on 18 January, 2017].

Johnson Controls Inc (2016a) *Form 8-K*, Wisconsin: Johnson Controls Inc.

Johnson Controls Inc (2016b) Johnson Controls Automotive, January 12, 2016,
Johnson Controls [internet] Available at: http://investors.johnsoncontrols.com/~/
media/Files/J/Johnson-Controls-IR/reports-and-presentations/2016/John
son%20Controls%202016%20DB-Detroit%20Auto%20Show.pdf [Accessed on
9 July, 2016].

Johnson Controls Inc (2016c) Johnson Controls board of directors approves separation of Adient, *Johnson Controls* [internet] Available at: www.johnsoncontrols.
com/media-center/news/press-releases/2016/09/08/johnson-controls-board-
of-directors-approves-separation-of-adient [Accessed on 5 October, 2016].

Just-auto.com (2000) FRANCE: Sommer-Allibert to sell?, Just-auto.com [internet]
Available at: http://www.just-auto.com/news/sommer-allibert-to-sell_id77736.
aspx [Accessed on 15 August, 2010].

Just-auto.com (2010) Johnson Controls acquires stake in Tachi S, *Just-auto.com*
[internet] Available at: www.just-auto.com/news/johnson-controls-acquires-
stake-in-tachi-s_id104215.aspx [Accessed on 15 August, 2010].

Kamalakaran, A., Selvi, H., Emery, C. and Kim, S. (2009) Auto parts maker Lear
Corp files for bankruptcy, *Reuters.com* [internet] Available at: www.reuters.com/
article/2009/07/07/us-lear-idUSTRE56616220090707 [Accessed on 12 May,
2012].

Katz, J. (2007) Lean takes the driver's seat at Lear: "Total lean behavior" has helped
auto supplier stay competitive in a struggling market, *Industry Week* [internet]
Available at: www.industryweek.com/industryweek-us-500/lean-takes-drivers-
seat-lear [Accessed on 12 August, 2012].

Klier, T.H. and Rubenstein, J.M. (2008) *Who Really Made Your Car? Restructuring
and Geographic Change in the Auto Industry*, Kalamazoo, MI: W.E. Upjohn Institute for Employment Research.

Lear Corporation (1995) Form 10-Q, Michigan: Lear Corporation.

Lear Corporation (2004) *2004 Annual Report*, Michigan: Lear Corporation.

Lear Corporation (2006) *Form 10-K: For the Fiscal Year Ended December 31, 2006*, Michigan: Lear Corporation.

Lear Corporation (2007) Lear Corporation's lean manufacturing system hikes productivity and reduces costs, *Lear Corporation* [internet] Available at: www.lear.com/InTheNews/1132/1/Lear-Corporation-s-Lean-Manufacturing-System-Hikes-Productiv.aspx [Accessed on 12 July, 2012].

Lear Corporation (2009) Auto parts maker Lear Corp files for bankruptcy, *Reuters.com* [internet] Available at: www.reuters.com/article/2009/07/07/us-lear-idUS TRE56616220090707 [Accessed on 12 May, 2012].

Lear Corporation (2010a) *Annual Report 2010*, Michigan: Lear Corporation.

Lear Corporation (2010b) Lear expands its use of SoyFoam seating technology on the new ford explorer, *Lear Corporation* [internet] Available at: www.lear.com/InTheNews/1044/1/Lear-Expands-Its-Use-of-SoyFoamand8482;-Seating-Technology-o.aspx [Accessed on 26 June, 2012].

Lear Corporation (2011a) *Annual Report 2011*, Michigan: Lear Corporation.

Lear Corporation (2011b) *Form 10-K*, Michigan: Lear Corporation.

Lear Corporation (2012) Lear honored by General Motors as "Corporation of the Year", *Lear Corporation* [internet] Available at: www.lear.com/InTheNews/1516/careers/diversity.aspx [Accessed on 26 June, 2012].

Lear Corporation (2015) *Annual Report 2015*, Michigan: Lear Corporation.

Lear Corporation (2016) *Form 10-K*, Michigan: Lear Corporation.

Lear Seating Corporation (1994) *Form 10-K*, Michigan: Lear Seating Corporation.

Leggett, D. (2015) Frankfurt: Johnson Controls eyes further seat weight savings, *just-auto* [internet] Available at: www.just-auto.com/news/johnson-controls-eyes-further-seat-weight-savings_id163041.aspx [Accessed on 18 January, 2017].

Lerner, S. (2000) Johnson Controls to buy Ikeda Bussan, MarketWatch.com [internet] Available at: http://www.marketwatch.com/story/johnson-controls-to-buy-japanese-auto-seat-maker-200079111400 [Accessed on 11 August, 2012].

Liker, J.K, and Choi, T.Y. (2004) Building Deep Supplier Relationships, Harvard Business Review, 82(12): 104-113.

Liker, J.K. and Choi, T.Y. (2005) What Westerners Don't Know About Keiretsu, Harvard Business School [internet] Available at: http://hbswk.hbs.edu/archive/4791.html [Accessed on 13 May, 2012].

Los Angeles Times (1985) Johnson Controls agreed to buy Hoover Universal, *Los Angeles Times* [internet] Available at: http://articles.latimes.com/1985-03-05/business/fi-12600_1_johnson-controls [Accessed on 16 June, 2012].

Los Angeles Times (1996) Automotive Products., Los Angeles Times [internet] Available at: http://articles.latimes.com/1996-07-19/business/fi-25635_1_prince-automotive [Accessed on 16 June, 2012].

Lucintel (2012) Lucintel Forecasts Good Growth Opportunities for Global Automotive Seat Industry Players during 2012-17, Lucintel [internet] Available at: http://www.prweb.com/releases/2012/5/prweb9518378.htm [Accessed on 12 December, 2012].

Magna International Inc (2010) 2010 Annual Report, Ontario: Magna International Inc.

Magna International Inc. (2011) Magna News – Magna seating continues expansion in South America with acquisition of Pabsa, *Magna* [internet] Available at: www.magna.com/media/press-releases-news/news-page/2011/01/12/magna-news–magna-seating-continues-expansion-in-south-america-with-acquisition-of-pabsa [Accessed on 16 August, 2012].

Magna International Inc (2015) *2015 Annual Report*, Ontario: Magna International Inc.

Marukawa, T. (2005) The supplier network in China's automobile industry from a geographic perspective, *Modern Asian Studies Review*, 1(1): 77–102.

Marx, K. (1961) Capital: A Critical Analysis of Capitalist Production, Volume I, Moscow: Foreign Languages Publishing House.

McCombs, D. and Horie, M. (2015) Toyota Boshoku drops on charge, forecast reversal to loss, *Bloomberg* [internet] Available at: www.bloomberg.com/news/articles/2015-02-03/toyota-boshoku-drops-as-impairment-charge-prompts-loss-forecast [Accessed on 30 August, 2016].

Molinaroli, A. (2015) Interview with Automotive News, *Automotive News* [internet] Available at: www.autonews.com/article/20160112/OEM10/160119849/john son-controls-to-name-seating-and-interiors-spinoff-company-adient [Accessed on 13 July, 2016].

Molinaroli, A. (2016) Johnson Controls to name seating and interiors spinoff company Adient, Automotive News [internet] Available at: http://www.autonews. com/article/20160112/OEM10/160119849/johnson-controls-to-name-seat ing-and-interiors-spinoff-company-adient [Accessed on 20 November, 2016].

Morris, S. (1998) Lear Corp.: Firm Acquires Automobile-seat Unit Of Gm's Delphi Subsidiary, Chicago Tribune [internet] Available at: http://articles.chicagotrib une.com/1998-02-25/business/9802250287_1_lear-auto-analyst-automakers [Accessed on 6 August, 2012].

Murphy, T. (2008) Lear buys 75% of Chinese fabric maker, WardsAuto [internet] Available at: http://wardsauto.com/news-amp-analysis/lear-buys-75-chinese-fab ric-maker [Accessed on 6 August, 2012].

Nolan, P. (2009) *Crossroads: The End of Wild Capitalism*, London: Marshall Cavendish Limited.

Olson, P. (2006) Does Icahn want to be king of Lear? *Forbes.com* [internet] Available at: www.forbes.com/2006/10/17/icahn-lear-ross-face-cx_po_1017autofacescan01. html [Accessed on 12 July, 2012].

Pearson, S. (2011) Car parts makers: Vehicle-buying surge in Brazil fuels component sector, *FT.com* [internet] Available at: www.ft.com/cms/s/0/9d208e58-d968-11e0-b52f-00144feabdc0.html#axzz1lB994YZi [Accessed on 1 February, 2012].

Peisner (1997) Lear to buy ITT industries seating unit, *Los Angeles Times* [internet] Available at: http://articles.latimes.com/1997/aug/05/business/fi-19561 [Accessed on 19 July, 2012].

Penrose, E. (1995) *The Theory of the Growth of the Firm*, Second Edition, Oxford: Oxford University Press.

Plastics News (2012) Faurecia SA acquires Plastal, *Plastics News* [internet] Available at: www.plasticsnews.com/article/20120924/NEWS/309249957/faurecia-sa-acquires-plastal [Accessed on 13 July, 2016].

Pollard, T. (2012) GM and PSA sign a global strategic alliance (2012), *Car* [internet] Available at: www.carmagazine.co.uk/News/Search-Results/Industry-News/GM-and-PSA-sign-a-global-strategic-alliance-2012/ [Accessed on 13 August, 2012].

PR Newswire (1996) Johnson Controls to acquire Prince Automotive, *PR Newswire* [internet] Available at: www.thefreelibrary.com/JOHNSON+CONTROLS+TO+ ACQUIRE+PRINCE+AUTOMOTIVE-a018485868 [Accessed on 1 August, 2011].

PR Newswire (2010) Johnson Controls signs purchase agreement to acquire C. Rob. Hammerstein Group (CRH), *PR Newswire* [internet] Available at: www.

prnewswire.com/news-releases/johnson-controls-signs-purchase-agreement-to-acquire-c-rob-hammerstein-group-crh-111152119.html [Accessed on 1 August, 2011].

PR Newswire (2012a) Johnson Controls to acquire Sagem automotive electronics business, *PR Newswire* [internet] Available at: www.prnewswire.co.uk/news-releases/johnson-controls-to-acquire-sagem-automotive-electronics-business-154449815.html [Accessed on 12 August, 2012].

PR Newswire (2012b) Lear Corporation acquires United Technologies Automotive, *PR Newswire* [internet] Available at: www.prnewswire.co.uk/cgi/news/release?id=57509 [Accessed on 12 August, 2012].

Recaro Automotive Seating (2011) Johnson Controls acquires Keiper and Recaro Automotive, Recaro Automotive Seating [internet] Available at: https://www.recaro-automotive.com/us/press/news/news-view/article/johnson-controls-acquires-keiper-and-recaro-automotive-3.html [Accessed on 10 December, 2012].

Reed, J. (2012) GM and Peugeot Confirm Alliance, ft.com [internet] Available at: http://www.ft.com/cms/s/0/ac3aa4ca-62f0-11e1-9245-00144feabdc0.html#axzz1nmJJyaXH [Accessed on 2 March, 2012].

Reference for Business (2012) Lear Corporation, *Reference for Business* [internet] Available at: www.referenceforbusiness.com/history/Ja-Lo/Lear-Corporation.html [Accessed on 12 September, 2012].

Renault Group (2013) Dacia, *Renault* [internet] Available at: www.renault.com/en/groupe/marques-du-groupe/pages/dacia.aspx [Accessed on 18 March, 2013].

Reuters (1999) Lear to buy UT Automotive for $2.3 billion, *Reuters.com* [internet] Available at: http://articles.latimes.com/1999/mar/17/business/fi-18093 [Accessed on 6 August, 2012].

Reuters (2011) UPDATE 2-Faurecia banks on Asia to boost sales, *Reuters.com* [internet] Available at: www.reuters.com/article/2011/11/07/faurecia-id USL6E7M70TT20111107 [Accessed on 6 August, 2012].

Roland Berger and Lazard (2011) *Global Automotive Supplier Study: Short Version*, Germany: Roland Berger Strategy Consultants GmbH.

Sedgwick, D. and Child, C. (2012) Faurecia thrives as Germans expand in North America, *Plastic News* [internet] Available at: www.plasticsnews.com/article/20120123/NEWS/301239979/faurecia-thrives-as-germans-expand-in-north-america [Accessed on 12 August, 2012].

Simon, B. (2011) Car parts makers face antitrust scrutiny, *ft.com* [internet] Available at: www.ft.com/intl/cms/s/0/1592b926-af00-11e0-bb89-00144feabdc0.html#axzz2NhHsOvgE [Accessed on 18 July, 2012].

Stanley, J. (2014) Faurecia, Magneti Marelli to tackle the HMI future, *Automotive News Europe* [internet] Available at: www.plasticsnews.com/article/20140116/NEWS/140119952/faurecia-magneti-marelli-to-tackle-the-hmi-future [Accessed on 8 July, 2016].

Supplier Business (2010a) *Faurecia-Europe Exhaust Systems*, Supplier Business.

Supplier Business (2010b) The seating systems report, *Supplier Business* [internet] Available at: www.gupta-verlag.com/general-cn/news/literature/9009/the-seating-systems-report/pdf [Accessed on 17 July, 2012].

Terlep, S. (2012) GM, Peugeot will share car designs, purchasing, *wsj.com* [internet] Available at: http://online.wsj.com/article/SB10001424052970203753704577253303659076864.html [Accessed on 2 March, 2012].

The Business Journal (2003) Johnson Controls buys Borg for $134 million, The Business Journal [internet] Available at: www.bizjournals.com/milwaukee/stories/2003/07/21/daily20.html [Accessed on 1 August, 2011].

The Business Journal (2011) Johnson Controls completes Keiper/Recaro acquisition, The Business Journal [internet] Available at: www.bizjournals.com/milwaukee/news/2011/06/20/johnson-controls-completes.html [Accessed on 1 August, 2011].

The Kentucky Standard (2011) Trim Masters bought out by Toyota Boshoku, The Kentucky Standard [internet] Available at: http://www.kystandard.com/content/trim-masters-bought-out-toyota-boshoku [Accessed on 15 September, 2012].

The New York Times (1985) Johnson Controls in sale of assets, nytimes.com [internet] Available at: www.nytimes.com/1985/08/28/business/johnson-controls-in-sale-of-assets.html [Accessed on 26 May, 2012].

The New York Times (1993) Lear buys Ford unit, nytimes.com [internet] Available at: www.nytimes.com/1993/11/02/business/lear-buys-ford-unit.html [Accessed on 26 May, 2012].

The New York Times (1995a) Company News; Johnson Controls agrees to buy Roth Freres, nytimes.com [internet] Available at: www.nytimes.com/1995/10/31/business/company-news-johnson-controls-agrees-to-buy-roth-freres.html [Accessed on 26 May, 2012].

The New York Times (1995b) Company News; Lear seating to buy Automotive Industries, nytimes.com [internet] Available at: www.nytimes.com/1995/07/18/business/company-news-lear-seating-to-buy-automotive-industries.html [Accessed on 26 May, 2012].

The New York Times (1996) Magna International to buy Douglas & Lomason, nytimes.com [internet] Available at: www.nytimes.com/1996/08/30/business/magna-international-to-buy-douglas-lomason.html [Accessed on 26 May, 2012].

The New York Times (2012) Lear Signs Agreement to Acquire Guilford Mills, A Global Leader in Automotive and Specialty Fabrics, from Cerberus, nytimes.com [internet] Available at: http://markets.on.nytimes.com/research/stocks/news/press_release.asp?docTag=201204111628PR_NEWS_USPRX____DE86055&feedID=600&press_symbol=21569071 [Accessed on 12 May, 2012].

Tita, B. (2015) Johnson controls to spin off automotive business: Milwaukee Company reports quarterly earnings in line with expectations, wsj.com [internet] Available at: www.wsj.com/articles/johnson-controls-to-spin-off-automotive-business-1437742476 [Accessed on 13 July, 2016].

Toyota Boshoku America (2012) Toyota Boshoku America supplier day 2012, Toyota Boshoku America [internet] Available at: http://qdocs.tbamerica.com/tbatermsandconditions/6-21-12%204th%20Supplier%20Day%20Presentation%20for%20Supplier.pdf [Accessed on 29 October, 2012].

Toyota Boshoku Corporation (2011) *Toyota Boshoku Report 2011, 2010.4.1–2011.3.31*, Aichi: Toyota Boshoku Corporation.

Toyota Boshoku Corporation (2014) Toyota Boshoku to Acquire Mechanical Seat Frame Component Business from Aisin Seiki and Shiroki, Toyota Boshoku Corporation [internet] Available at: http://www.toyota-boshoku.com/us/news/141219e.html [Accessed on 10 September, 2016].

Toyota Boshoku Corporation (2015) *Toyota Boshoku Report 2015, 2014.4.1–2015.3.31*, Aichi: Toyota Boshoku Corporation.

Treasury & Risk (2011) Finance on the Fast Track: Sixteen acquisitions later, Lear Treasurer Shari Burgess steers through a decade of challenges, Treasury & Risk [internet] Available at: http://www.treasuryandrisk.com/2011/04/27/finance-on-the-fast-track [Accessed on 29 October, 2012].

TS Lear Automotive (Malaysia) Sdn Bhd (2011) Company Information, Jobstreet. com [internet] Available at: http://www.jobstreet.com.my/jobs/2011/4/default/10/1304849.htm?fr=R [Accessed on 12 March, 2012].

TS Tech Co., Ltd (2010) Products and technology, *TS Tech* [internet] Available at: www.tstech.co.jp/english/product/introduction.html [Accessed on 15 August, 2012].

TS Tech Co., Ltd (2011) Fact sheet 2011, *TS Tech* [internet] Available at: www.tstech. co.jp/english/ir/uploads/iro20110628e.pdf [Accessed on 15 August, 2012].

TS Tech Co., Ltd (2015) *TS Tech Report 2015*, Saitama: TS Tech Co., Ltd.

TS Tech Co., Ltd (2017) A Quick Guide to TS Tech, TS Tech [internet] Available at: http://www.tstech.co.jp/english/ir/individual/understanding.html [Accessed on 22 January, 2017].

U.S. Courts (2011) Chapter 11: Reorganization under the bankruptcy code, *U.S. Courts* [internet] Available at: www.uscourts.gov/FederalCourts/Bankruptcy/BankruptcyBasics/Chapter11.aspx [Accessed on 12 July, 2012].

Warburton, S. (2012) Magna won't bid again for Opel, just-auto.com [internet] Available at: http://www.just-auto.com/news/magna-wont-bid-again-for-opel_id121187.aspx [Accessed on 2 August, 2012].

Webb, A. (2011) Lear: Car seat margins unlikely to improve, because it's hard to raise prices, *Bloomberg News* [internet] Available at: www.crainsdetroit.com/article/20111208/FREE/111209915/lear-car-seat-margins-unlikely-to-improve-because-its-hard-to [Accessed on 10 July, 2016].

Wernie, B. (2016) Johnson Controls to name seating and interiors spinoff company Adient, *Automotive News* [internet] Available at: www.autonews.com/article/20160112/OEM10/160119849/johnson-controls-to-name-seating-and-interiors-spinoff-company-adient [Accessed on 13 July, 2016].

Womack, J.P. and Jones, D.T. (2003) *Lean Thinking: Banish Waste and Create Wealth in Your Corporation*, London: Simon & Schuster UK Ltd.

Womack, J.P., Jones, D.T. and Roos, D. (2007) *The Machine that Changed the World: How Lean Production Changed the World*, London: Simon and Schuster UK Ltd.

Wood, R. (2008) Into The Value Zone: Gaining and Sustaining Competitive Advantage, Plymouth: United Press of America, Inc.

Wuhan Park Rubber & Plastic Co., Ltd (2012) Company profile, *whpark.com* [internet] Available at: www.whpark.com/english/ [Accessed on 10 June, 2012].

Yang, C. (2011) Faurecia: International Auto parts Leader with Strong Localization in China, Gasgoo.com [internet] Available at: http://autonews.gasgoo.com/executive-interview/faurecia-international-auto-parts-leader-with-str-110804.shtml [Accessed on 10 June, 2012].

5   The global CVJs industry

1. Introduction

The CVJ is not exactly an automotive component that springs to mind. This little known but yet widely used component is critical in ensuring that the rotational speed of a vehicle's output shaft matches that of the input shaft regardless of the operating angle of the joint, resulting in the more effective transfer of torque (i.e., power) from the engines to the front wheels (GKN, 2011; NTN, 2006). It has proven to be a revolutionary component in the automotive industry by facilitating the arrival of a new generation of front-wheel-drive cars such as the Mini (as the CVJ enabled front-wheel drive, it reduced both cost and space in vehicles). The Suez Crisis of 1956 triggered off a strong demand for low-consumption small cars like the Mini, which in turn increased demand for CVJs. The subsequent oil price shocks of 1973–74 and 1979 also bolstered this trend (Lorenz, 2009). Moreover, the increasing fashionableness of four-wheel-drive vehicles in the US (then the world's largest automotive market) over the coming decades bolstered demand for CVJs (The Economist, 2000). Currently, the CVJ is used in over 80 percent of light vehicles worldwide (GKN, 2012).

Today, GKN is the world's single largest producer of CVJs, possessing a remarkable 42 percent of the global market which was valued at approximately £5.069 billion (US$7.756 billion) in 2015. GKN is followed by Japan's NTN, which possesses a 23 percent market share, giving both firms near two-thirds control of this subsector (GKN, 2015a; GKN, 2016; NTN, 2016). With the sheer power wielded by these two titans, it appears that the CVJs market has effectively become a duopoly. Delphi and Visteon were also known to make CVJs in the 1980s to the early twenty-first century but their respective market shares were insignificant compared to GKN and NTN; they have since exited the CVJs business (Lorenz, 2009). There are even smaller players such as Japan's NKN and some Chinese manufacturers (e.g., Wanxiang) but their technologies and market share are simply too inadequate to challenge the reigning duopolists, GKN and NTN, who have secured overwhelming economies of scale and scope through servicing the major automakers over the past few decades. Further, NKN and Chinese manufacturers such as Wanxiang lack the financial muscle and technological capabilities of Delphi and Visteon, who were more than capable of catching up with GKN/NTN if they wanted to but have instead chosen to focus on higher value-added segments such as automotive electronics, fuel cells and hybrid/electric vehicle systems (the payoff for these technologies is nonetheless more uncertain).

From an industry that was highly fragmented in the 1960s, the global CVJs industry quickly became relatively oligopolistic by the 1980s, with GKN and NTN in the leading positions. However, it was in the 1980s that the gap between GKN and the other players really widened, as the company embarked on an acquisition strategy often via JVs. The following sections indicate that GKN would often acquire the equity stake of its JV partner whenever the opportunity arose (e.g., loosening of regulatory restrictions curbing foreign ownership) (Lees, 1992; Lorenz, 2009). It was essentially this aggressive acquisition strategy (via JVs) that gave GKN over 40 percent of the global CVJs market by the beginning of the first decade of the 21st Century, positioning the firm along with NTN as the duopolists in this subsector. The fact that it has been able to achieve this market share without drawing significant attention from antitrust authorities is quite remarkable. However, it may be relatively harder for GKN or NTN to embark on aggressive acquisitions nowadays, given the increasing scrutiny by antitrust authorities on the automotive components industry in recent years. GKN's fortuitousness in avoiding antitrust scrutiny over the past two decades is possibly attributable to its extensive use of JVs as a springboard to eventual acquisition as opposed to the outright acquisition strategies practised by its counterparts in the tyre and automotive seats industries. As evidenced later in this chapter, this approach essentially became the key driver of GKN's rapid expansion in the 1980s-1990s period.

Beyond the reigning duopolists, there is still a relatively large pool of second and third-tier suppliers. However, their market shares (particularly the third-tier suppliers') are insignificant. Further, rapid consolidation is expected to happen among these lower-tier suppliers, possibly with the second-tier suppliers acquiring their third-tier smaller counterparts. If these firms do not merge, they would not be able to garner the economies of scale and scope needed to withstand the onslaught of the industry leaders, and thus run the risk of being put out of business. These lower-tier suppliers could even find themselves becoming the acquisition targets of the industry leaders.

2. The cascade effect's impact on CVJs makers

Back in the 1980s, leading automakers such as GM and Ford used to have in-house operations that made the CVJs they required. Today, due to the powerful impact of the cascade effect, there are hardly any automakers that make their own CVJs, as they prefer to focus on more high value-added activities (i.e., marketing, growing their global operations, increasing customer satisfaction) and outsourced non-core components manufacturing (i.e., making CVJs) (Nolan, 2008). Indeed, this cascade effect created tremendous opportunities for firms such as GKN. GKN like its counterparts in the seats industry (i.e., JCI and Lear), were initially not major players in the automotive industry but managed to make the transition by seizing the outsourcing opportunities triggered by the cascade effect. Ravaged by the massive decline in the British steel industry in the early 1960s, GKN, a former steel maker, boldly diversified into the automotive industry (i.e., CVJs) with its acquisition of the Birfield automotive components group in 1966.

In a move that signified its departure from the steel industry, GKN, in 1986, formally changed its name from the original Guest, Keen and Nettlefolds (that represented its steel origins) to the existing GKN (GKN, 2011; Lorenz, 1997). Birfield's key business was propshafts, but it also owned two companies that made CVJs: Hardy Spicer in the UK, and Uni-Cardan (a key supplier to Volkswagen and other leading European automakers), based in West Germany which also had operations in France and Italy. The acquisition of Birfield thus enabled GKN to secure control of Hardy Spicer and Birfield's 39.5 percent stake in Uni-Cardan (along with some critical patents on CVJs). The control of Hardy Spicer and Uni-Cardan enabled GKN to benefit immensely from the increasing popularity of front-wheel vehicles. Hardy Spicer being the sole supplier of CVJs to the Mini (the first front-wheel-drive mass-production automobile) enabled GKN to secure critical market share. As for Uni-Cardan, it not only gave GKN CVJ technology but also greater access to leading automakers such as Volkswagen (GKN, 2011; Lorenz, 2009). The increasing popularity of CVJs resulted in GKN's automotive business emerging for the first time as a driving force in the company, generating about one-third of its sales by the end of the 1960s. Like all supplier firms impacted by the cascade effect, GKN continued to acquire other firms in the industry (in its case, mostly JV partners) to gain greater economies of scale and scope. The acquisition of these additional scale economies not only enabled GKN to alleviate intensifying pressures emanating from the incessant demands (both financial and operational) of automakers but also gain increased leverage in price negotiations with these exigent clients. As GKN now controls more than two-fifths of the CVJs market and its automaker clients have generally outsourced their in-house CVJ production facilities, there is a strong possibility that the balance of power may have tilted in favour of suppliers like GKN. Even GKN's key competitor, NTN which used to rely largely on organic growth is now increasingly relying on acquisitions as a driver of growth, and quickly securing the increasingly vital scale economies needed to compete against GKN.

3. The leading CVJs makers

GKN: profile

Over the past few decades, GKN has successfully defended its exalted status as the world's largest producer of CVJs. In 2015, it accounted for over two-fifths of the industry's revenues; the company also recorded CVJ manufacturing facilities in 23 countries, offering the largest global footprint in this subsector. For that year, GKN posted, on a statutory basis, revenues and net income of £7.231 billion and £202 million. These consolidated figures were derived after deducting equity accounted investments of £458 million from management sales of £7.689 billion; equity accounted investments refer to JVs which GKN has voting rights of 50 percent or less, along with associate entities where GKN has limited influence.

The following segmental and geographic analysis provided in Figures 5.1, 5.2 and 5.3 were however based on the management sales of £7.689 billion. In 2015, GKN also had 56,100 employees (spread across 34 countries) with 26,300 in its Driveline division alone (GKN's automotive business). GKN manufactures CVJs through its Driveline division which accounted for nearly half (£3.548 billion) of its overall revenues in 2015 (Figure 5.1). The following Figure 5.2 indicates that in 2015, GKN's CVJs business generated revenues of £2.129 billion which was 60 percent of its Driveline division's sales and 27.7 percent of the company's overall revenues (GKN, 2015a; GKN, 2016). GKN's CVJs remain the mainstay of the group despite its diversification attempts over the past two decades. This is due to widespread recognition of the technical superiority of GKN's CVJs that despite their relatively smaller and lighter configurations, did not compromise on structural integrity. Further, these CVJs were able to meet increasing automaker demands for products that improved vehicle fuel efficiency and reduced noise, heat and vibration (Lorenz, 2009). This technological superiority in a seemingly 'low-tech' product is made possible by the considerable

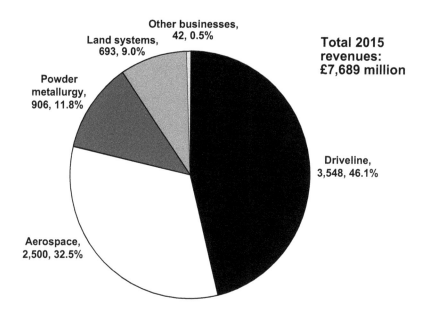

Figure 5.1 GKN's 2015 annual revenues (£ million)

Source: 2015 GKN Annual Report

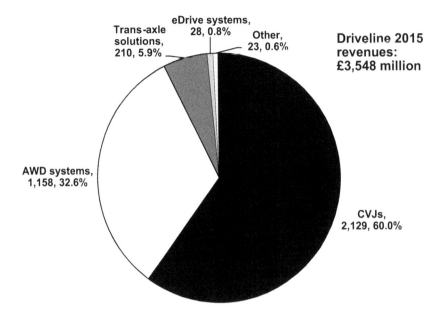

Figure 5.2 GKN's 2015 driveline revenues (£ million)
Source: 2015 GKN Annual Report

economies of scale and scope (along with emerging technologies) derived from GKN's active acquisitions strategy.

Despite GKN's aggressive expansion, it is still very much a European-based firm with nearly half of its revenues (about £3.7 billion) coming from Europe and the UK, followed by the Americas which accounted for 38.2 percent (about £2.9 billion) of the group's revenues in 2015 (Figure 5.3). Within the European region, the UK (2015 revenues: £956 million) was the single biggest contributor and it alone accounted for 12.4 percent of overall group revenues. However, the US (2015 revenues: £2.517 billion) remained GKN's largest single market in 2015, accounting for 32.7 percent of its total revenues. Even at the Driveline divisional level, Europe (2015 revenues: £1.279 billion) accounted for a considerable 36 percent of GKN's driveline revenues in 2015, outpacing the following North American region which accounted for 33.7 percent of divisional revenues (£1.195 million) (GKN, 2015a).

GKN also recorded R&D expenditures of £157 million in 2015, marking a more than doubling of R&D expenses since 2000 (GKN's R&D expenditure in 2000 was £77 million) (GKN, 2001; GKN, 2015). As a consequence of this sizeable R&D investment (and partly due to rising customer expectations), the development of CVJs today extends far beyond metal bashing; according to GKN, its latest countertrack CVJ technology has led to driveshafts of exceptional quality for varying vehicle platform and powertrain

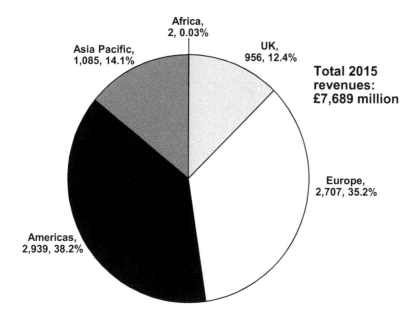

Figure 5.3 GKN's 2015 revenues by region (£ million)

Source: 2015 GKN Annual Report

configurations, with significant breakthroughs in dimensional, weight and particularly component effectiveness (GKN, 2009). The cost of developing these new technologies invariably strengthens the need to secure greater economies of scale and scope to alleviate this rising cost pressure; the deployment of acquisitions is possibly the quickest, though not necessarily the most efficacious way of procuring added scale economies and access to the latest technologies, owing to the considerable cost and uncertainty surrounding this growth strategy.

GKN's top four customers (i.e., Fiat Chrysler, Volkswagen, Ford and GM) accounted for 49 percent of its total sales in 2015 (Table 5.1) (GKN, 2015a). The fact that GKN's top two customers are European automakers (or have parent companies of European origins) also highlights its dependence on the European market. In fact, four out of GKN's top nine clients are European automakers.

In the CVJs industry, GKN has industry-leading annual procurement spend; for 2015, GKN's procurement expenditure reached a sizeable £1.170 billion (US$1.7901 billion), more than its nearest competitor NTN's US$1.483 billion. This significant purchasing spend invariably imbues GKN with considerable market power over its suppliers, enabling it to not only extract discounts (and other concessions) from suppliers but also compel them to meet international quality management standards such as ISO/TS 16949:2002 ('the quality management

Table 5.1 GKN's 2015 sales by customer

Automakers	% of Overall Driveline Revenues
Fiat Chrysler	14
Volkswagen	13
Ford	11
GM	11
Renault-Nissan	10
Toyota	7
Tata	5
BMW	5
Mitsubishi	3
Others	21

Source: 2015 GKN Annual Report

system requirements for the design and development, production and, when relevant, installation and service of automotive-related products') (GKN, 2015a; ISO, 2011).

GKN itself was formed in the early twentieth century through the relentless consolidation of several leading British companies (i.e., Dowlais Iron Company, Patent Nut and Bolt Company and Nettlefolds Ltd) (GKN, 2011). However, it was in the 1980s that GKN stepped up its acquisition strategy, by buying out its partners and competitors in an aggressive drive to become the world's dominant CVJ maker. The company has proven to be a survivor in an era marked by a seemingly precipitous decline in British manufacturing and engineering. GKN's resilience (and uncanny ability to prosper) is driven by its exemplary prowess in anticipating the paradigm shifts of each era, for instance, the shift in the importance of the steel industry in the nineteenth-century to the automotive industry (i.e., CVJs) in the twentieth-century; in the twenty-first century, GKN has developed ultra-lightweight CVJs (using cutting-edge materials) that deliver unprecedented fuel efficiency (without compromising torque) and lower carbon emissions, the twin technical preoccupations of the automotive industry in this era.

One could argue that GKN had been extremely lucky in its then seemingly hasty decision to move into CVJs, and the Group could have gone belly up, if external events had gone the other way. However, if GKN had been resistant to disruptive change and clung stubbornly on to its 'steel roots', the Group may not have survived (or found itself assimilated into a larger, more successful company). In view of this preternatural agility, GKN could be described as a savvy market player that despite lacking a record in pioneering innovation, has demonstrated considerable finesse in discerning and monetising innovative technological trends (Lorenz, 2009). This observation is supported by the fact that GKN did not invent its much-vaunted CVJ but secured control of this technology through its acquisition of the Birfield automotive components group in 1966. Moreover, this successful acquisition supports the argument that it is better to let others do the initial investment and work out the kinks in new technologies, before securing control of these technologies through M&A. By the 1980s, GKN had diversi-fied into other areas of the automotive industry such as powder metallurgy and torque management systems.[1] These acquisitions were meant to reduce GKN's dependence on an increasingly mature CVJs market, strengthen its control over a critical raw material (i.e., powder metal) and extend its overall product offerings. The following sections examine GKN's CVJ and non-CVJ (automotive-related) acquisitions over the past three decades.

GKN's acquisitions since the 1980s

Since the 1980s, GKN has made a series of acquisitions to consolidate its lead-ing position in CVJs while broadening its automotive business. GKN's acquisi-tions strategy was to first start a JV before subsequently increasing its stake to a controlling one or making an outright acquisition. The nature of this strategy is succinctly captured in the following statements from former GKN CEO, Kevin Smith who asserted: 'A one-third share was not a GKN business' and he also added: 'We always had a view that, if we could make the business work, we could eventually acquire the whole company' (Lorenz, 2009: 339–340). According to GKN's former chairman, Sir David Lees, GKN used this approach more exten-sively than any other firm in the automotive components industry in the 1980s (Lees, 1992). This acquisition strategy is different from the tyres and seats sectors mentioned earlier in this book, as it mainly involves acquiring one's JV partners instead of competitors. By the time GKN was ready to acquire its JV partner, it had also gained sufficient knowledge of the local market in which the JV was based, and the local partner had become redundant. In fact, JVs carry with them certain risks, as GKN is in a way, creating its own competition by sharing its tech-nical knowledge with local companies, who could in turn share it with others.

Throughout the 1980s, GKN either established JVs or acquired sizeable stakes in various companies with the ultimate intention of converting them into sub-sidiaries. In 1983, GKN established a JV in Taiwan (Hsin Chu) with an initial 20 percent stake to manufacture CVJs. Around 1987, GKN acquired a 30 percent stake in Australian CVJs maker, Unidrive and doubled its stake in a Spanish JV to 40 percent. Concurrently, it cemented its grip over its subsidiary, Uni-Cardan, by increasing its stake to 96.7 percent (GKN had bought another 10.2 percent for around £38 million). Further, in 1988, GKN launched a JV in India, named Invel Transmissions, in which it held a 40 percent shareholding. By 1989, JVs easily accounted for more than 20 percent of GKN's profits (Lees, 1992).

GKN continued to consolidate its position in CVJs in the 1990s and the first decade of the twenty-first century by acquiring the remaining stakes of JVs it did not already own (the second phase of its acquisition strategy). In 1994, GKN through a £50 million investment, secured a controlling 85 percent stake in the in-house CVJ operations of Fiat, which employed more than 700 people at Flor-ence, Italy (in the process also adding another £100 million to GKN's revenues); Fiat impacted by the cascade effect was outsourcing its non-core CVJ operations to focus on its core activities of designing, developing and assembling vehicles

(Hotten, 1994). By 1996, GKN also acquired Fiat's in-house CVJ operations in Tarwdogora, Poland (PMR, 2005).

Further, in a bid to strengthen its Asian presence, GKN invested about £10 million to acquire a 49 percent stake in a JV with South Korea's Hanwha in 1996; by 1998, in keeping with its acquisitive style, it acquired the remaining equity it did not own in Hanwha-GKN Driveshafts for £1.36 million and renamed it GKN Driveshafts (Korea); the fact that GKN was able to procure the remaining 51 percent for just £1.36 million gives some indication that Hanwha-GKN Driveshafts was probably not doing well in the first place. Moreover, in 1997, it established a JV with the Sikor Group in Thailand known as GKN Driveshafts (Thailand); GKN started with a controlling 51 percent but by 1998, it acquired the remaining 49 percent equity stake of GKN Driveshafts (Thailand) for £750,000 (Birmingham Post & Mail Ltd, 1998). Further, in a move to consolidate its hold on the European CVJs market, GKN also acquired Opel's driveshaft factory (it produced 1,000,000 CVJ systems annually and had assets worth £16 million) at Kaiserslautern, Germany in December 1999 (adding another £60 million to GKN's revenues); this acquisition deepened GKN's relationship with Opel's US parent company, GM, as it became the CVJ supplier for Opel's Astra and Vectra models. GKN's strategic objective in making this acquisition was to strengthen its relationship with GM (Foley, 1999).

In May 2000, GKN also increased its stake in Australia's Unidrive from 30 percent to a controlling 60 percent by securing additional shares from Invensys[2] (GKN, 2000). Further, in September 2000, GKN acquired the remaining 35 percent stake that Dana Albarus S.A., held in Albarus Transmissões Homocinéticas Ltda (hereafter 'ATH'), a Brazilian JV between the two firms. The deal was part of a larger, strategic agreement between GKN's Driveline Division and Dana Corporation that was implemented in January 2000. Through this deal, GKN sold its European medium and heavy propeller (hereafter 'MHP') shaft business to Dana. Further, under the terms of their agreement, GKN secured Dana's shareholding in ATH and its US CVJs operations. The Commission of the European Communities asserted that Dana had effectively traded its CVJ wheelshafts division in exchange for GKN's MHP shaft unit (Europa, 1999). Further, in 2001, GKN made a public offer to acquire another 34.91 percent stake in its Invel Transmissions JV (now known as GKN Driveshafts (India) Ltd) at Rs55 a share and delist the company from the Indian stock exchanges. This offer was made soon after GKN Automotive Gmbh (a subsidiary of GKN Plc) purchased International Finance Corporation's 14.09 percent stake in the subsidiary. These relentless deals reflected GKN's aggressive strategy in bolstering its already significant market share in the CVJs sector (Autointell, 2000a).

In 2005, GKN cemented its control over Velcon (a JV company formed by GKN in 1979 with Grupo DESC, a major Mexican industrial company with an initial stake of 25 percent), by buying the remaining 51 percent of the company (renamed GKN Driveline Celaya SA) which it not already owned for US$83 million (GKN, 2005; Lorenz, 2009). This acquisition of its Mexican JV partner was executed to strengthen GKN's presence in an increasingly strategic market;

today, GKN Driveline supplies CVJs and other driveline systems to ten vehicle makers in 16 cities across Mexico and the US. Further, the acquisition is expected to significantly bolster GKN's manufacturing capacity (for CVJs) in Mexico, rising from three million systems in 2005 to an expected nine million in 2015 (GKN, 2011).[3]

Amidst this flurry of acquiring the remaining shareholdings of JV partners, there also arose opportunities for GKN to make acquisitions, due to outsourcing by automakers. For instance, in 2000, GKN Driveline acquired Nissan's in-house CVJ-manufacturing firm at Tochigi. This represented a significant breakthrough as it was the first time a Western automotive components maker had acquired a business that was a significant part of the Nissan keiretsu. This opportunity arose as the then financially-troubled Nissan was focusing its limited financial resources on its core assembly activities and was thus compelled to outsource non-core activities (e.g., CVJs manufacturing) to reliable suppliers such as GKN; Nissan's Tochigi facility was producing 1.4 million CVJs annually for both domestic and export needs. The value of Nissan's Tochigi assets acquired by GKN was around nine billion yen (£56 million) and annual sales were estimated to be 16 billion yen (£100 million) (Autointell, 2000b; Lorenz, 2009). The significance of this deal was evidenced in a statement by GKN Driveline's then Chief Executive, Sarkis Kalyandjian: 'This is a very significant opportunity for GKN. Not only does the Tochigi facility supply the driveshafts for almost all of Nissan's domestic car production in Japan but the two companies will also be able to work closely together on future driveline engineering applications supporting Nissan's Revival Plan' (quoted in Autointell, 2000b).

Similarly, in 2001, GKN also acquired the CVJ production operations of Ford's Van Dyke Transmission Plant in Sterling Heights, Michigan and gained supplier rights to Ford Taurus and Mercury Sable vehicles assembled in Chicago (AFX, 2001). These acquisitions have consolidated GKN's position as the world's leading maker of CVJs. However, GKN's management felt that although their CVJs division was profitable, its long-term growth potential was limited with the company having achieved market leader status by the end of the 1990s (by 1999, GKN had 37 percent of the CVJs market) (Hughes, 1999). Further, GKN was facing increasing competition from its chief rival, NTN, the leading Japanese (also the world's second largest) maker of CVJs. NTN, which had originally relied largely on organic growth, was also becoming increasingly acquisitive in its bid to supplant GKN as industry leader in the global CVJs market.

In an industry defined by ruthless consolidation, it is no surprise that GKN itself became a takeover target. In February 2003, GKN's board received a takeover proposal from Carlyle, a private equity firm with deep political connections across governments; Carlyle has been labelled the 'ex-presidents' club' and its past business associates have included George H.W. Bush (former US President) and John Major (former British Prime Minister). Nonetheless, despite several months of intense discussions, both parties could not reach an agreement and GKN was able to maintain its independence (Burkeman and Borger, 2001; Lorenz, 2009).

GKN's increasing emphasis on organic growth (CVJs)

Despite its emphasis on acquisitions and the establishment of JVs throughout the 1980s and 1990s, GKN did not neglect organic growth. For instance, in 1976, GKN redoubled efforts to penetrate the profitable US market with the formation of GKN Automotive Components Inc. to provide CVJs for the new generation of front-wheel-drive cars. By 1977, GKN declared it would launch a new production plant, (costing US$50 million) in Sanford, North Carolina. Further, by around 1980, GKN stated that it would construct another CVJs plant (costing US$80 million) in North Carolina, Alamance County. These two plants were eventually commissioned in 1980 and 1981, giving GKN relatively significant production capabilities in the US (fundinguniverse, 2012). Due to the establishment of these two new plants, GKN was able to raise its North American revenues to £150 million by the end of the 1980s from a zero base at the dawn of the decade (Lees, 1992).

Despite having achieved a preeminent position in the CVJs market by the 1990s, GKN has continued to strengthen its grip on its dominant market share by means of organic growth in fast-growing automotive markets such as India and China; over the past decade, GKN has intensified its organic growth strategy. For instance, after securing full control of its Indian subsidiary GKN Driveshafts (India) Ltd by acquisition in 2001, GKN Driveline bolstered its rapid growth in India by launching a new manufacturing facility in August 2012 for CVJ Systems and Trans Axle Solutions in Pune, India. The new INR130 crores (£18 million) facility employed more than 200 people and was strategically located within 30 kilometres of a number of GKN Driveline customers (i.e., Fiat, General Motors, Tata, Volkswagen and Renault). The new 8,000-square-metre facility recorded an annual production capacity of more than 600,000 CVJ Systems (GKN, 2011; GKN, 2012).

GKN Driveline is particularly bullish about its prospects in China, India and North America and put in place expansion plans that have increased CVJ production by 60 percent over a short three- to four-year period. China is steadily accounting for a greater proportion of GKN Driveline's revenues. GKN has been making CVJs in China through a JV known as Shanghai GKN Drive Shaft Company (SDS) since 1988. The company formed this pioneering JV with HUAYU Automotive Systems Co. Ltd. (HASCO.), a subsidiary of SAIC with a 50 percent equity stake in that same year; after a successful collaboration spanning more than two decades, this JV was subsequently expanded in 2013 to encompass additional GKN Driveline offerings (i.e., its prized all-wheel-drive (hereafter 'AWD') and electric-drive (hereafter 'eDrive') systems) which necessitated a name change to Shanghai GKN HUAYU Driveline Systems Co. Ltd. to reflect the expanded nature of this partnership. By 2010, China accounted for nearly 9 percent of GKN Driveline's revenues, up from 7 percent in 2009; in earlier years, GKN's China revenues were too small to even rate a mention in its annual reports (GKN, 2009; GKN, 2010; GKN, 2013). It was in this watershed year that GKN assumed market leadership of the Chinese driveshafts market; Stefan Magirius, president of GKN China stated: 'We have 40 percent of the Chinese driveshaft market, we are the market leader and we are growing at the same speed as the market, which is expected to keep growing by 8–10 percent over the next five years'. In two statements that underscore GKN's commitment to organic growth in China, Magirius added: 'almost every year we have added another plant to keep up our growth' and 'we should be able to double the business in the next five years, all with organic growth' (quoted in Moore, 2010).

To capture an increasing share of the Chinese market, GKN is raising production through rapid capacity expansion. For instance, in November 2009, GKN opened its 11th plant in Wuhan, which makes CVJs for automakers based in central China. The 44,000-square-metre Wuhan facility was capable of producing 500,000 CVJs by 2010, with production rising to one million in 2011 and possibly two million by 2012. In 2011, in an effort to tighten its grip on the burgeoning Chinese automotive market, GKN established an even larger 52,000-square-metre plant (its 12th production facility in China and is run by SDS) in Changchun, Northeast China with the capacity to build one million CVJ systems annually (the first phase has been operational since June 2011, while the second phase was ready by end 2011) (GKN, 2011). The phase two expansion of the facility is estimated to have raised yearly production capacity to three million units. GKN's Changchun facility was the firm's second Chinese plant in a relatively short span of 18 months (GKN China, 2011).

In June 2012, GKN announced that it had opened a new precision forge (extensively used to produce CVJs) in Celaya, Mexico (with an investment of US$11.5 million); this is GKN's third forge in Celaya since 1979. The new 28,300-square-metre forge facility would produce over 15 million forgings (the basic building block for CVJs) annually and would employ 150 workers. The expansion of GKN's forging facility was a critical first step in GKN's three-year US$100 million expansion plans to make CVJ systems. Fidel Otake, GKN Driveline Mexico's managing director also asserted: 'The reason to celebrate this forge expansion is that it is the next stage of our growth. The forge is the beginning of the process for making CVJ Systems. But this growth is not only about forgings, but also in the machining and assembly plants, where we will continue the growth. The capacity for CVJ Systems will increase from six million in 2011 to nine million in 2013. The workforce too will increase from 1,300 last year (2011) to 1,700 this year (2012) in GKN Driveline in Mexico' (GKN, 2012). Due to increased demand (and projected sustained demand) from North American automakers, GKN has initiated plans to invest approximately US$179 million in six plants across North Carolina, US; the firm expects demand for its North American AWD segment (which CVJs are inextricably intertwined) to rise significantly from 2.4 million systems in 2015 to three million systems by 2020. GKN's considerable investment is expected to be used in the upgrading of five plants across North Carolina (the Counties of Person, Lee and Catawba respectively) while expanding production at a single facility in the state's Alamance County (McGavin, 2016).

GKN's diversification strategy (automotive-related) since the 1980s

By the 1980s, GKN swiftly diversified into other areas of the automotive industry such as powder metallurgy and torque management systems. Through a series of acquisitions, GKN turned its once lacklustre powder metallurgy division into an industry leading player. It started a series of acquisitions by purchasing Sinter Metals, one of the largest US sinter products companies, for an enterprise value of £337 million in May 1997. Over the course of 1997–1998, GKN further consolidated its sinter metals business by acquiring the connecting rod production plant of Borg-Warner, Laurel Manufacturing Inc's non-automotive bearings facility in Dubois, Pennsylvania and UK's Rigby Metal Components; these deals cost GKN around £52 million. However, it was the acquisition of Hoeganaes Corporation in 1998 that made GKN a major player in the sinter metals/powder metallurgy industry. The £348 million acquisition of Hoeganaes meant that it could supply both GKN's in-house powder metal needs (needed for the production of CVJs) and external customers (60 percent were automotive components makers) (GKN, 1998; Lorenz, 2009).

Later, GKN also made considerable effort to strengthen its position in torque management systems. For instance, in 2002, it acquired a 33.3 percent stake in Tochigi Fuji Sangyo (TFS), a Japanese supplier of automotive driveline components (focusing on torque management systems) from Nissan and other key shareholders for about £29 million (GKN, 2002). This acquisition of a stake in TFS was partly driven by GKN's desire to acquire complementary technologies and expand its market presence in Japan. GKN's familiarity with TFS' operations due to their 16-year relationship also expedited the acquisition process as it soon assumed control of TFS by raising its stake to 84 percent (for £26 million) in April 2004 (GKN, 2004). By 2005, GKN had acquired 100 percent of the company (the remaining 16 percent was acquired for £10 million) and formally changed TFS' name to GKN Driveline Torque Technology KK (The Engineer, 2002; GKN, 2005). GKN's acquisition of TFS reflects its overarching determination to position itself as a comprehensive driveline systems provider instead of being just a major CVJ maker.

In September 2011, GKN also acquired the driveline business of Getrag (a German maker of transmissions and powertrain systems) for £280 million; Getrag's driveline business encompasses the Getrag Corporation (Getrag's US JV with Dana Corporation) and Sweden-based Getrag All Wheel Drive AB (a JV with Dana Corporation and Volvo). The acquisition of Getrag driveline business was aimed at bolstering GKN's capabilities in the potentially lucrative AWD and eDrive systems (GKN, 2011).[4] GKN's acquisition of Getrag's driveline business and not the entire firm was a highly astute move, as it was only buying what it needed and not embarking on potentially value-destroying empire building acquisitions. The acquisition of Getrag's entire operations (with about 12,300 employees spread across 23 countries) would involve significantly greater effort and resources in integrating disparate human resource, IT, accounting and financial systems.

Technical progress and lean: The twin drivers of GKN's success

Contrary to its metal bashing image, the CVJ (especially the ones produced by GKN and its key competitor, NTN) is a relatively sophisticated product that results in weight reduction (along with the accompanying greater fuel efficiency) and greater torque in vehicles. Due to rising demands for lighter and more fuel-efficient vehicles, CVJs, once the preserve of front-wheel-drive vehicles, have now become standard in most vehicles; currently, most vehicles have two CVJ drive-shafts per vehicle and some SUVs have up to seven (Green Car Congress, 2009). GKN has been able to dominate the industry, by being a quick study rather than an innovator. As mentioned earlier, GKN did not invent the CVJ but moved into the industry through the acquisition of Uni-Cardan and was among the first to exploit its tremendous commercial potential. GKN has continued to cement its stranglehold on the industry by constantly developing superior versions of the CVJ; despite its low-tech image, not all CVJs are equal. GKN's revolutionary CVJ system, the CounterTrack (formally launched in 2009) is generally marketed as a game changer and supposedly reduces power loss by 30 percent, delivers at least 25 percent more torque and lowers vehicle weight by 15 percent (resulting in greater fuel efficiency). Further, it offers a compendious design which could be structured to optimise space utilisation in vehicles. All in all, this revolutionary CVJ from GKN offers significant advantages unrivalled by competing CVJ providers (GKN, 2012).

The sheer technical progress achieved by GKN is redefining the frontiers of driveshaft technology, as argued by Rob Rickell, global engineering director, sideshafts, GKN Driveline Driveshafts. Rickell also asserted: 'With the Countertrack fixed sideshaft design, the CVJs on that same mid-size V6 sedan will be more than 30 percent more efficient, more than 8 percent smaller, and 15 percent lighter than a conventional design' (quoted in Sawyer, 2006). GKN, citing independent engineering reports, also asserted that its countertrack CVJ technology was well poised to take the lead in a market increasingly concerned with fuel efficiency and emissions controls (GKN, 2009).

GKN has invested heavily in R&D for over a decade to perfect this technology. In 2000, GKN's R&D expenditure was only £77 million but by 2010 and 2011, it had steadily increased to £92 million and £103 million respectively (GKN, 2011). The significant economies of scale and scope it derives from its acquisitions and numerous JVs has enabled GKN to mitigate the considerable pressures from its increasing R&D investments. GKN's chief rival, NTN, is also cognisant of the importance of technical progress in establishing market dominance. NTN too has developed industry leading CVJs that supposedly generate 50 percent less vibration than the conventional, low vibration CVJs produced by its less renowned competitors thus significantly alleviating a vehicle's noise, vibration and harshness levels (NTN Americas, 2013).

Even long after achieving its exalted industry leader status, GKN continues to place considerable emphasis on technological superiority as a means of cementing its hard-fought position and stave off potential challengers. The firm's launching of its cutting-edge lightweight VL3 CVJ system in January 2016 is a clear indication of its relentless commitment to technical progress. GKN asserts its latest VL3 CVJ far surpasses the technological achievement of its predecessor, the CounterTrack, by delivering a four-kilogram reduction in the weight of rear-wheel systems (resulting in greater fuel efficiency) while concurrently bolstering a vehicle's torque by a significant 27 percent with no increase in space requirements. The considerable potential of GKN's latest product is underscored by its swift adoption by BMW's latest 7-series range in the same year (GKN, 2015b; GKN, 2016). It is evident that the seemingly staid CVJ industry is now embroiled in an escalating 'arms race' to develop increasingly lighter systems that minimise space requirements while delivering ever-increasing amounts of torque in vehicles.

GKN was relatively late in adopting lean business practices; it had a rudimentary continuous improvement practice sometime in the 1990s but it was not until the first decade of the twenty-first century that GKN formally implemented a comprehensive lean manufacturing programme (Lorenz, 2009). In 2003, GKN implemented lean across all its business units by launching a Lean Steering Committee and Improvement Plan. It quickly followed up with measures to train and deploy over 1,000 lean practitioners throughout its businesses, supported by Continuous Improvement Leaders (GKN, 2012). The driving force behind GKN's decision to implement lean was due to its customers' (i.e., GM, Ford and Daimler-Chrysler at that time) increasing adoption of lean operations. These automakers require mega suppliers such as GKN to deliver specified quantities of their materials to designated locations worldwide under just-in-time conditions. On top of these exacting specifications, GKN is also expected to offer products that are competitively priced (Kruse, 2004).

Further, through the implementation of lean, GKN has been able to significantly raise productivity, reduce defects and increase profitability. For instance, following the introduction of lean in its majority-owned Unidrive plant in Victoria, Australia in 2003, productivity rates rose by 21 percent and the number of parts per million classified as rejects fell into single figures by 2005; during this period, return on sales also doubled and the accident frequency rate was halved (GKN, 2005). Lean has since permeated into GKN's entire business model; this practice has moved beyond 'shop floor' manufacturing activities and has also strengthened internal business processes through the reduction of the financial month end process by 50 percent (GKN, 2012). Further, lean strengthens GKN's environmental footprint and sustainability, as it eliminates waste, minimises energy and raw material usage and optimises efficiency across all processes (GKN, 2011). Moreover, it frees up additional resources for R&D and even acquisitions.

While lean may not have contributed to GKN's rise to industry leadership in the global CVJs market in the 1990s, it has enabled GKN to cement its position as the number one player in this market (by strengthening quality, productivity and cost control), particularly in the face of intensifying competition from its key competitor, NTN and other lower-tier (and often lower-cost) competitors (from Korea, Taiwan and China).

NTN: profile

NTN, founded in March 1918, is the second key player in the duopolistic global CVJs market. The company was previously known as NTN Toyo but had changed its name to NTN Corporation by 1989 (NTN, 2006). In fiscal year 2015 (1 April 2015 to 31 March 2016), NTN accounted for an estimated 23 percent of industry sales (smaller than the 42 percent controlled by GKN); the Japanese fiscal year starts from April of the year concerned to March of the following year. NTN continues to be focused on growing its CVJ business whereas GKN prefers to focus on other sectors such as aerospace and torque management systems. For fiscal year 2015, NTN recorded revenues and net income of US$6.3631 billion and US$133.4 million respectively. As of March 2016, NTN recorded staff strength of 24,109 spread across more than 220 operating bases in 33 countries. The following Figure 5.4 indicates that in fiscal year 2015, NTN drew 70 percent (US$4.4542 billion) of its revenues from its Automotive Applications division; for that period, NTN's CVJs business (2015 fiscal year revenues: US$1.7838 billion) which falls under Automotive Applications accounted for 40 percent of divisional sales and 28 percent of overall revenues. Although the Americas is NTN's biggest market, the company remains heavily dependent on Japan (its domestic market), which alone accounted for more than a quarter (US$1.7759 billion) of

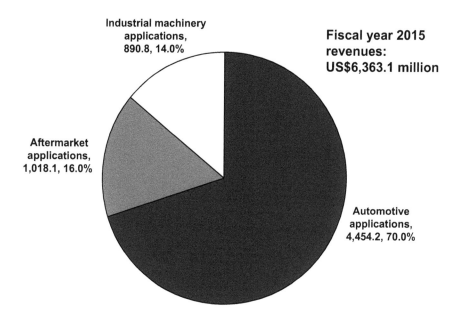

Figure 5.4 NTN's fiscal year 2015 revenues (US$ million)
Source: NTN Report 2016 for the year ended 31 March 2016
(Fiscal Year is from 1 April 2015 to 31 March 2016)

its revenues for fiscal year 2015 (Figure 5.5) (Lorenz, 2009; NTN, 2011; NTN, 2016; Edison Investment Research, 2012; GKN, 2016).

NTN's original business model in the 1960s was focused on bearings but it was able to secure licences from Birfield (via a technical tie-up with Birfield's subsidiary, Hardy Spicer Co. Ltd in 1963) to make CVJs before Birfield's acquisition by GKN. Like GKN, it too saw the potential of front-wheel-drive cars and decided to diversify into the production of CVJs (NTN, 2006; Lorenz, 2009).[5] By 2007, NTN had produced more than 400 million CVJs and the company currently has more than 18 CVJ production plants worldwide (NTN Americas, 2013); Automakers not only expect first-tier suppliers such as NTN to support their overseas expansion drives but also to locate their plants nearby to ensure smooth execution of just-in-time processes. Currently, NTN supplies CVJs to leading automakers such as GM, Daimler, Toyota, Renault-Nissan and Hyundai-Kia. Further, NTN recorded procurement expenditures of about US$1.483 billion in fiscal year 2015, somewhat less than the £1.170 billion (US$1.7901 billion) posted by GKN (NTN, 2016; GKN, 2015a); this places NTN in a disadvantageous position, as GKN with its larger procurement spend would be able to extract more concessions from its suppliers, thus lowering its cost base and improving its profitability over the long term.

In fiscal year 2015, NTN also recorded R&D expenditures of US$164.01 million, nearly twice that of its R&D expenditures of US$95.2 million in 2000, and

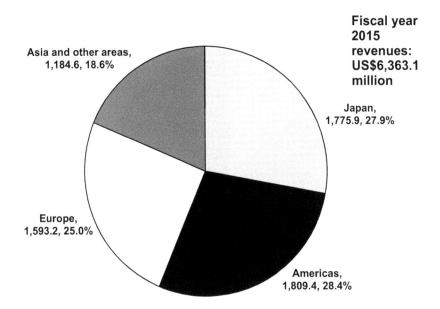

Figure 5.5 NTN's fiscal year 2015 revenues by region (US$ million)

Source: NTN Report 2016 for the year ended 31 March 2016

(Fiscal Year is from 1 April 2015 to 31 March 2016)

it is this continuous investment in R&D that has enabled NTN to develop the cutting-edge technologies needed to challenge GKN for industry leadership; it is this rapid rise in R&D expenditures over the past decade (essential to developing the technologies needed to ensure market leadership) that necessitates a constant drive to acquire critical scale economies (often via M&A). NTN's fiscal year 2015 R&D investment lags that of its only true competitor, GKN which recorded a 2015 R&D investment of £157 million (US$240.2 million) (NTN, 2011; NTN, 2016; GKN, 2015). To better support its automaker clients in both their domestic and international operations (develop products that meet their specific needs in different markets) and close the gap with GKN, NTN has established regional R&D centres in the Americas, Japan, Europe and China. To complement its increasingly globalised R&D network and augment its ability to offer technical services (e.g., design and evaluation tests) to customers, NTN, in May 2011, also established the NTN China Technical Centre in Shanghai (NTN, 2011; NTN, 2015).

Further, NTN has a more focused business model than GKN, as it has stuck to making CVJs, bearings and related products since its founding in 1918. GKN, on the other hand, has diversified into aerospace, sinter metals, powder metallurgy, land systems and torque management systems. Given NTN's more aggressive focus on growing its CVJs business, the gap between NTN and GKN in the global CVJs market is likely to close over the coming decade. In fact, this gap has been narrowing over the past few years. In 2003, GKN had a 43 percent market share in the global CVJs market but by 2015, its market share had declined to 42 percent. Conversely, NTN's global CVJs market share was just 17 percent in 2003 but has since increased to 23 percent by 2015 (GKN, 2003; GKN, 2015a; GKN, 2016; NTN, 2003; NTN, 2016).

Steady reliance on JVs

NTN, like GKN, also relied extensively on JVs to bolster its overall growth. The key difference was that NTN unlike GKN did not make as many outright acquisitions of its JV partners through most of the 1980s-1990s. In 1982, NTN entered into a JV with the Korean automaker Hyundai Motors, where Hyundai would manufacture CVJs through license from NTN. Soon after, in 1983 NTN also licensed its CVJ technology to two other foreign companies, Lepco Company of Australia and Taiway of Taiwan (NTN, 2009). NTN has steadily built up a sizeable but non-controlling stake in its Taiwanese partner, Taiway, by increasing its shareholdings in the company from its original 20 percent to its existing 36.25 percent (NTN, 2001; NTN, 2015). By 1988, NTN also co-founded Unidrive, its Australian JV CVJs manufacturer (it was 50 percent owned by BTR Nylex, with GKN and NTN accounting for the remaining 30 percent and 20 percent respectively) (Reference for Business, 2012; Unidrive, 2010; NTN, 2006).[6] NTN currently has a 40 percent equity stake in this JV while the remaining 60 percent stake is owned by GKN (NTN, 2011; Unidrive, 2010). This example highlights the fact that in a consolidating market encumbered by an ever-increasing need for scale economies, international presence and rising R&D costs, even bitter rivals are sometimes compelled to work together. Moreover, in December 1998, NTN established a JV, named NTN Transmissions Europe (hereafter 'NTE') with Renault, in Allonnes, France to make CVJs; the JV that was 80 percent owned by NTN (leaving Renault as the minority partner) commenced production in June 2000 (NTN, 2001).

By the dawn of the twenty-first century, NTN was also quick to expand its presence in China. For instance, by August 2002, NTN had established Shanghai NTN Corporation, a 95 percent NTN-owned JV in Shanghai, with Japanese trading company, Okaya & Co., Ltd., to make CVJs (90 percent of its CVJs were exported); this JV was also NTN's first production facility in China. By October 2002, NTN had also formed a JV (named NTN-Yulon Drivetrain Co., Ltd.) with Taiwan's Yulon Group in Guangzhou, to produce CVJs; NTN owns 60 percent of this JV (eBearing.com, 2003b; NTN, 2011). These two JVs function more like subsidiaries (both JVs were listed as consolidated subsidiaries in NTN's 2011 annual report), as they are among the JVs where NTN has a dominant equity stake from their very inception. The fact that NTN is strengthening its presence in Australia and China reflects the company's desire to reduce its dependence on the traditional American and Japanese markets, internationalise its operations and challenge GKN for leadership in the global CVJs market (NTN, 2006).

In September 2003, NTN also established a JV with Korea Flange Co., Ltd. (KOFCO) in Beijing (NTN had also licensed technology to KOFCO); this JV was known as Beijing NTN-Seohan Driveshaft Co. Ltd and supplies CVJs to the Hyundai Kia Automotive Group in China (NTN, 2007). In the case of Beijing NTN-Seohan Driveshaft Co. Ltd, NTN had a 40 percent share while KOFCO assumed a controlling stake of 51 percent (the remaining 9 percent stake is held by Yulon) (NTN, 2003). In that same year, NTN also formed a JV (named Asahi Forge of America Corporation (AFA)) with Asahi Forge, Co. Ltd. to produce forged parts for CVJs and hub bearings in the US (Asahi was the dominant partner with a controlling 54.1 percent stake while NTN and other investors accounted for 32.8 percent and 13.1 percent respectively). This US$17 million investment was to ensure a steady supply of 'high-quality and cost-competitive forged parts' to bolster NTN's market presence in North America (NTN, 2003). By 2005, NTN also launched an additional CVJ JV in India's fast-growing automotive market. This JV was between NTN and National Engineering Industries (NEI), a division of GP-CK Birla Group, India; NTN procured an 80 percent equity stake in the JV, effectively rendering it subsidiary status from the outset (eBearing.com, 2006; NTN, 2006).

By 2007, NTN also formed another JV with KOFCO in Alabama, in an attempt to strengthen its presence in the US market (this operation basically became NTN's second CVJ production facility in the US, following NTN Driveshaft, Inc. in Indiana) and deepen its relationship with Hyundai, an ambitious automaker bent on global expansion; NTN was the smaller partner in this JV with a 49 percent equity stake. This JV between NTN and KOFCO known as

Seohan-NTN Driveshaft USA Corporation had the primary role of supplying CVJs to Hyundai Motor Manufacturing Alabama, LLC (HMMA) (eBearing. com, 2006; NTN, 2007a).

The JVs formed by NTN are a vindication of Drucker's argument that strategic alliances, partnerships and JVs would supplant M&A and even the initiation of new wholly-owned businesses as the primary drivers of business growth and expansion worldwide (Drucker and Maciariello, 2004). Unlike acquisitions, the formation of JVs does not require the payment of significant premiums. More importantly, JVs are easier to unravel than fully acquired firms, as there are relatively less financial and legal implications involved. The acquisition and subsequent integration of companies, regardless of whether they are upstream or downstream, is a highly complex process, as it involves the merging of disparate (and increasingly complicated) accounting, human resources, legal and technological structures; the companies may also have vastly different corporate cultures which further complicates the integration process. Thus, if a company's acquisition strategy fails to produce the desired synergies, the cost of unravelling the byzantine corporate structure of the merged entities would be highly detrimental to its interests.

NTN's acquisitions: acquiring control of JVs and Assets

Throughout the 1980s-1990s, NTN had been far less aggressive than GKN in using acquisitions as a means of growing its business, preferring to rely more on JVs and organic growth (unlike GKN, NTN did not actively buy out its partners then). That explains why the relatively more acquisitive GKN was able to attain the position of market leader in the CVJs subsector despite the fact that NTN started producing CVJs earlier; NTN started producing CVJs in 1963 before GKN diversified into CVJs with its acquisition of Birfield in 1966 (GKN, 2011). In the 1980s, NTN did make several acquisitions although some of the target companies were not directly making CVJs but rather bearings, a crucial component in CVJs. For instance, in 1985, NTN formed a JV with Detroit-based Federal-Mogul Corporation (one of its US distributors) to make tapered bearings and cylindrical roller bearings. This JV was named NTN-Bower Corporation with NTN holding an initial 60 percent. However in 1987, NTN acquired full control of this JV by buying the remaining 40 percent (Reference for Business, 2012).

However, NTN in a determined bid to challenge GKN for industry supremacy, stepped up its acquisition drive in the first decade of the twenty-first century, at a time when GKN is focusing less on its CVJs business. Nonetheless, it is still very difficult for NTN to catch up with GKN in global CVJs market share (GKN's market share is nearly double that of NTN's), as GKN had gained a significant first-mover advantage with regard to acquisition in the 1980s/1990s. NTN has over the past decade adopted GKN's strategy of acquiring JV partners. For instance, in May 2006, NTN acquired an initial 25 percent stake in Germany's IFA-Antriebstechnik GmbH (IFA-AT, Germany), a key maker of CVJ bearings for Volkswagen and Audi plants globally; by 2012, NTN had raised its stake in IFA-AT to 75 percent and renamed the JV 'NTN Antriebstechnik G.m.b.H' (MarkLines, 2007; NTN, 2012). NTN asserted that its purpose in buying into IFA-AT is to forge a strong business relationship with Volkswagen. This acquisition complemented by NTN's CVJ JV with Renault (i.e., NTE) was all part of an overarching strategy to propel its CVJ business in Europe (eBearing.com, 2006). Further, NTN, through NTE, quickly acquired the Crézancy plant of the SETFORGE Group, a leading forging manufacturer of CVJ parts in France for approximately ¥400 million (US$3.8 million) in June 2008. The plant was renamed NTN Transmissions Europe Crézancy after its acquisition by NTE (NTN, 2008a). Barely a year later, NTN also raised its stake in NTE from 85 percent to 100 percent ownership (NTN, 2008b; NTN, 2009).

Moreover, NTN acquired a controlling stake in SNR Roulements (hereafter 'SNR') in 2008; SNR was a wholly-owned subsidiary of Renault that makes bearings (a critical component for making CVJs) for industrial, aeronautical and automotive applications, primarily for the European market. For SNR, NTN had basically raised its initial stake of 35 percent which it had acquired in 2007 to a controlling 51 percent by 2008 (Europa, 2007; NTN-SNR, 2011). Bolstered by it progress with SNR, NTN continued with its acquisition strategy by acquiring the assets of tedrive Sistemas de Chassis do Brasil Ltda. (the Brazilian subsidiary of tedrive Holding B.V.) for US$18.2 million in May 2010, and establishing a new company (named NTN do Brasil Produção de Semi-Eixos Ltda.) to make CVJs and expand its market share in Brazil's burgeoning automotive market (NTN, 2010; Supplier Business, 2010; NTN, 2011). Not letting up on this acquisition blitz, NTN subsequently raised its stake in SNR to 82 percent by July 2010 and the company changed its name to 'NTN-SNR Roulements'. In what was an inevitable transition, NTN achieved 100 percent ownership of NTN-SNR Roulements by March 2013 (NTN-SNR, 2011; NTN, 2011; NTN, 2013).

Historical emphasis on organic growth

Unlike its perennial competitor GKN, NTN has traditionally placed greater reliance on organic growth rather than acquisitions. In the 1980s, NTN relied heavily on organic growth by building an extensive CVJs-making facility, operated by its subsidiary, Toyo Bearing Okayama Co., Ltd. With NTN's increasing internationalisation drive, the company also established NTN Manufacturing (Thailand) Co., Ltd. in Southeast Asia for the manufacture of bearings and CVJs in 1998. In 2006, NTN launched an additional CVJ manufacturing plant (NTN's third plant in Japan), named NTN Fukuroi Corp., in Fukuroi City, Shizuoka Prefecture. That same year, NTN also announced plans to expand production capacity at existing production facilities, specifically NTN Manufacturing (Thailand) and Guangzhou NTN-Yulon Drivetrain Co., Ltd (NTN, 2006).

NTN's steadfast preference for organic growth strategies is reinforced by the firm's decision in 2011 to ramp up production of CVJs (in its assiduous bid for industry leadership) by launching the NTN NEI Manufacturing India Pvt. Ltd.

(NNMI) Chennai Plant in Chennai, southern India as its second production facility in the subcontinent. This new facility complemented NTN's other CVJs production plant in Bawal, North India. In 2012, NTN also rolled out plans to launch a new plant in the Pinthong industrial area (located in Chonburi Province) as its second production facility in Thailand. This move was to meet the increasing demands of the rapidly growing automobile market in Southeast Asia (NTN, 2012). Drawn by the significant performance-based financial incentives (e.g., up to US$4.7 million in conditional tax credits and US$300,000 in training grants) offered by Indiana Economic Development Board, NTN has also in 2015, commenced construction of a new 325,000-square-foot driveshaft facility (estimated capital investment: US$42 million) with an annual production capacity of 300,000 CVJs in the US city of Anderson, Indiana (NTN Americas, 2015; Stephens, 2016).

As NTN has been far less acquisitive than its main competitor, GKN, its growth rate (in terms of global market share) has been significantly slower. The key advantage of NTN's organic growth strategy is that the company does not have to bear the risks of acquisition or spend considerable resources in integrating the acquired companies. However, as evidenced earlier, NTN has now adopted a more acquisitive strategy to complement its organic expansion. Thus, there is a possibility that NTN could eventually buy out its partners in the various JVs it has formed, essentially emulating the strategy practised by GKN.

However, NTN could face greater difficulty in growing via acquisitions over the coming years due to increasing scrutiny by antitrust authorities in Japan and overseas. For instance, in June 2012, NTN was indicted by the Tokyo District Prosecutors Office for having allegedly violated Japan's Antimonopoly Act with regard to the sale of bearings in Japan. In 2014, NTN was also subject to heavy fines by antitrust authorities in Europe, Japan, China and Singapore for collusive price fixing; the fines imposed by the European, Japanese, Chinese and Singaporean authorities on NTN amounted to US$274.9 million, US$60.2 million, US$19.1 million, US$0.387 million respectively (NTN, 2015; Reuters, 2014).

Technical progress and lean: critical to NTN's success

NTN's focused business model, commitment to R&D and judicious acquisition strategy has enabled the firm to achieve significant technical progress in the seemingly low-tech CVJs market. For instance, NTN has developed the 'EUJ series' compact, light-weight CVJs (suitable for larger SUVs), which result in significant savings in vehicle size and weight (a 7 percent reduction in the outside diameter and an estimated 15 percent reduction in weight). NTN's 'EUJ' CVJs are also lightweight, high-efficiency eco-friendly CVJs that offer a 25 percent reduction in the loss of driving force (torque loss) transmitted from the vehicle engine to the tyres. The company has also developed another version of this CVJ (more suitable for passenger cars) known as the 'EBJ series' which promises outside diameter and weight reductions of 3 percent and 7 percent respectively. These reductions were achieved without compromising the superlative performance and efficiency of its EUJ series CVJs (NTN, 2007b).

Moreover, by 2007, NTN achieved a significant breakthrough by successfully developing and marketing 'an ultra low vibration plunging CVJ 'PTJ' (pillow journal tripod joint)' that significantly minimised plunging resistance and induced thrust; this technology basically reduces noise, harshness and vibration in vehicles. Further, NTN's ultra-low vibration CVJ products ensure greater transmission efficiency for driving force (torque). When combined with the previously mentioned EUJ and EBJ CVJs, the PTJ would further mitigate the torque loss on the driveshaft into which it is incorporated (NTN, 2007).

In its crusade to surpass GKN as industry hegemon, NTN over the ensuing years, strove indefatigably to surpass the success of its earlier EBJ and PTJ systems. In 2012, the firm declared that its newly developed 'Next Generation High Efficiency Fixed Type CVJ CFJ' is capable of significantly reducing frictional power loss (a 50 percent reduction in torque loss ratio) while concurrently lowering heat-generation by the same magnitude, vis-à-vis its earlier EBJ system; NTN asserted that its new CVJ provided the industry's highest level of transmission efficiency, effectively throwing down the gauntlet to GKN or any would be challengers. By 2015, NTN also announced its development of a 'Lightweight Driveshaft for FR (front-engine, rear-wheel-drive) vehicle', a system that is designed with the rear-wheel-drive layouts of luxury vehicles in mind. NTN's 'Lightweight Driveshaft for FR vehicle' marks a 30 percent reduction in weight compared to conventional driveshaft/CVJ systems, in the process delivering superior fuel efficiency while minimising carbon emissions; this new NTN offering is an obvious head-on competitor of GKN's VL3 CVJ system, as both appear to be designed to attract premium automakers seeking greater fuel efficiency, lower carbon emissions while optimising power delivery in vehicles (NTN, 2012; NTN, 2015).

Like many leading Japanese firms, NTN is a seasoned practitioner of lean. The concept of a lean organisation has permeated the entire firm; as illustrated by earlier case of GKN, it is important to create a 'lean culture', where employees across all departments (not just production) are committed to continuous improvement; merely adopting a few random lean practices in a few limited areas would not allow a firm to significantly eliminate waste or raise productivity across the organisation. NTN's commitment to lean has also extended to its suppliers (shrewdly referred to as business partners and not just 'mere suppliers'); NTN attempts to improve overall quality by holding supplier quality improvement meetings with its material and parts suppliers, and by conducting quality audits at supplier locations. Consequently, through this fanatical devotion to continuous improvement,[7] 34 production sites across NTN and two sales sites attained the ISO 9001 quality management system by 2011 (NTN, 2011).

NTN also clearly understands the lean concept of pull (giving customers what they want) in bolstering customer satisfaction and solving problems from customers' viewpoint. In 2006, as part of its lean strategy, NTN required extensive collaboration at all levels for all related departments in efforts to bolster customer satisfaction. These collaborative efforts included ascertaining customer needs to other endeavours such as product development, design, production and eventual delivery. Through this lean practice of pull, all NTN sales companies globally would not only assign a sales representative for each customer and sales agent (sales agents too have been co-opted into NTN's lean strategy), but also a technical manager to complete their service offering. Resultantly, NTN is able to determine the precise nature of customer needs and wants, identify problems swiftly and provide customers with the requisite solutions (NTN, 2011).

4. Consolidation among the remaining CVJs makers

In the 1980s, there were also numerous CVJs makers ranging from the two fast rising industry leaders (GKN and NTN) to the numerous smaller manufacturers emerging from China and India. Even the leading automakers, GM and Ford had in-house CVJ production facilities. Today, the two market leaders (i.e., GKN and NTN) have basically cornered the global CVJs market with an approximate two-thirds market share between the two of them. Thus, like the global tyres and seats industries analysed earlier in this book, the next round of industry consolidation is happening at the second/third-tier supplier level. There is also the possibility that some of these lower-tier suppliers could end up being acquired by the industry's number two player, NTN, as it has over the past decade strove to supplant GKN as industry leader by incorporating (somewhat late in the game) acquisition strategies into its modus operandi; GKN established a near unassailable lead via the successful deployment of an aggressive acquisitions approach throughout the 1980s/1990s.

Despite their considerable size, GM and Ford had a relatively small presence in the global CVJs market in the 1980s. In the case of GM's CVJs manufacturing operations, it was created as part of the company's in-house CVJs manufacturing operations (to ensure a steady supply of CVJs). Back in the 1980s, GM's in-house CVJs operations was GKN's chief competitor in the US (Lorenz, 2009). In 1997, GM also formed a 50–50 JV with Japan's NSK Ltd to make CVJs in Brazil. The JV was known as Delco Chassis NSK do Brasil Ltd and was based in Suzano City, Sao Paulo. However, the JV became part of Delphi's operations when Delphi was spun off from GM in 1999; Delphi subsequently ended this JV in 2001 (eBearing.com, 2001). Later in 2008, Delphi as part of its restructuring plan, sold its global steering and halfshaft business (included its CVJ operations) to Steering Solutions Corporation, an affiliate of Platinum Equity, LLC., a private equity firm (Delphi, 2008). Visteon was also an in-house supplier (includes CVJs) to Ford but like Delphi, was spun out from its parent company in June 2000 (Visteon, 2012).

It is highly unlikely these internal operations of automakers (even if they had avoided their divestitures/spin-offs) would ever become serious challengers to subsystems integrators such as GKN or NTN, as their primary objective is to ensure that the automakers have ready access to an affordable supply of CVJs. Nonetheless, the powerful forces generated by the cascade effect could eventually compel these automakers to spin off their CVJs operations (essentially a non-core activity), in order to focus their resources on higher value-added activities such as international marketing, growing their international operations and developing next-generation technologies. The CVJs production assets of these automakers could also be acquired by the industry leaders, as evidenced by GKN's acquisition of Nissan's in-house CVJs manufacturing facilities at Tochigi in 2000.

There are also several other makers of CVJs globally but they simply do not possess the economies of scale and scope or resources needed to challenge the duopolistic stranglehold of GKN and NTN. For instance, in Japan, there is NKN Ltd, not to be confused with its much larger Japanese counterpart, NTN. Further, there is also Korea's largest CVJs maker, KOFCO, which has a JV with NTN in the US. Additionally, in Taiwan, its leading domestic automaker, the Yulon Group also makes CVJs through its subsidiary, Kian Seng Metal Works Co. Ltd and a JV with NTN in Guangzhou, China (as mentioned earlier); most of the CVJs produced by Yulon's subsidiary and Chinese JV are currently meant for the domestic Chinese market and are not exported internationally to leading automakers (Liang, 2012). In China, the biggest CVJs maker is Wanxiang, which makes the component through its QC Driveline division (Wanxiang, 2012). China also has numerous other obscure CVJs makers such as Zhejiang ODM Transmission Technology Co. Ltd (a small company with sales of around US$100 million and has key clients such as Chery and SAIC) and Taizhou Hongli Automobile Parts Co. Ltd (provides CVJs to GM Wuling, Suzuki Changhe, Kia Motors, vehicles that are largely sold in China's domestic market). There are also several others (e.g., Ningbo A&F CVJ Manufacture Co., Ltd) in China that provide CVJs for the automotive aftermarket. Many of these Chinese firms have annual sales of barely US$100 million, negligible R&D budgets and limited or no experience servicing major automakers. More importantly, they do not have the scale economies needed to service the increasingly globalised operations of the leading automakers which practise highly demanding just-in-time operations.

It is unlikely that the major automakers would ever procure CVJs from these lower-tier suppliers, as they have no track record of servicing major carmakers and lack the necessary resources to conduct significant R&D. There is also a significant quality differential between the CVJs created by NTN compared to the ones from the smaller players. Further, the major automakers would not want to incur any significant reputational risk resulting from using suppliers that they do not trust. This emphasis on having credible suppliers is evidenced by the following statement from Bill Taylor, the former CEO of Mercedes-Benz US: 'in an operation like ours, the suppliers will make you or break you' (quoted in Chappell, 2005). These remaining players in the global CVJs market are currently in a situation, where they are being compelled by the disruptive forces of the cascade effect to merge amongst themselves, in order to secure the economies of scale and scope needed to compete against the industry duopolists. If these lower-tier suppliers do not merge and gain the necessary scale economies, they could end up becoming the takeover targets of the two dominant companies, or risk going out of business altogether.

Alternatively, they could also survive as niche players in the aftermarket (or act as suppliers to the industry leaders) but it is unlikely they would ever pose a threat to the dominance of the duopolists. Unlike the earlier tyre and seat industries mentioned in this book, there are no credible second-tier players in the global CVJs market that have the potential to supplant the existing leading players.

5. Conclusion

The global CVJs market has reached a highly consolidated state since the 1980s, with the two leading players, GKN and NTN having achieved duopolistic control of the market. GKN was able to achieve its predominant status by quickly acquiring its JV partners and competitors alike whenever the opportunity presented itself. Further, the company was highly adaptable and quick to capitalise on the latest, most profitable trends (e.g., the increasing popularity of front-wheel vehicles and the subsequent need for CVJs). GKN's case highlights the importance of corporate agility in ensuring organisational longevity; this approach refers to the need to acquire businesses that work and/or are potentially lucrative and divest those that do not contribute to a firm's long-term profitability.

NTN, GKN's closest competitor in CVJs, took a more conservative approach (utilising organic growth and the formation of JVs) since the 1980s; NTN is however more acquisitive nowadays (even acquiring controlling stakes in its JVs and converting them into subsidiaries), in an attempt to narrow the gap with GKN. Both companies have used or are deploying JVs as a methodical means of acquiring a company, a contrast to the outright acquisitions carried out by the leading subsystems integrators in the global tyres and automotive seats sectors. The use of JVs as a springboard to acquisition strategy gives the potential acquirer time to familiarise itself with the targeted firm's culture, operations, finances and the market in which it operates. However, as noted earlier, NTN is far more focused on making CVJs and related products while GKN has adopted a more conglomerate model, spread across CVJs, powder metallurgy, land systems and aerospace. This has resulted in NTN narrowing the gap with GKN although GKN is still significantly ahead in terms of global CVJs market share.

Moreover, the other players in the global CVJs market simply do not possess the economies of scale and scope needed to pose a threat to the dominance of these duopolists. The only way these remaining players can ensure their long-term survival would be to merge amongst themselves and gain the necessary scale economies; economies of scale and scope are of the utmost importance in the CVJs industry (or any other automotive components subsector for that matter), as companies need to be able to support the demanding global operations of their automaker clients. Mainstream thinkers such as Thomas Friedman, are mistaken in their belief that small companies are able to compete effectively against the reigning industrial giants in this newly-globalised 'flat' world (Friedman, 2006). This is because these small firms are simply outclassed by their larger counterparts in every aspect from R&D expenditure to their marketing budgets.

Even though there are only two key players in the global CVJs market, they continue to contest fiercely for market share. Under this competitive duopoly, the profits of the key players are constantly changing thus preventing the onset of industry stasis. Further, in this climate of intense competition, weaknesses such as operational inefficiency and strategic ineffectiveness prevalent in large companies are also kept in check (Chandler and Hikino, 1999). Contrary to its undeserved image as a monolithic 'metal basher', the CVJ's industry has become one committed to relentless technical progress where the reigning duopolists are locked in an ever-escalating technological 'arms race' to stay the critical one-step ahead of the competition. However, it is highly unlikely that the global CVJs industry could become monopolistic, as GKN and NTN would find each other too expensive to acquire and existing tightening legislation (i.e., antitrust laws) render any potential acquisitions predatory and possibly illegal; cross-shareholdings in Japan also make companies like NTN extremely hard to acquire. Due to the sheer duopolistic market power wielded by GKN and NTN, it is inevitable that they would come under increasing scrutiny by regulators, thus they could experience increasing difficulty in executing their acquisition strategies in the CVJs and related bearings markets; this situation is likely to affect NTN more greatly, as it is trying to close the gap with GKN by way of acquisitions.

Moreover, successful enterprises such as GKN have long proven that it is far more profitable over the long term to sell entire systems (i.e., GKN's Driveline solutions that combines its AWD, bearings, CVJs and eDrive systems) instead of relying on just one successful product (i.e., CVJs). Further with rising maturity of the global CVJs market, industry leaders such as GKN are in a way, compelled to source for or expand their presence in different businesses (e.g., torque management systems, aerospace) to ensure their long-term survival and profitability. The profits generated from GKN's steady CVJs business could be used to finance forays (via acquisitions or JVs) into these potentially more lucrative ventures.

Notes

1 GKN also greatly expanded its presence in the aerospace industry through the £284 million acquisition of Westland, a leading aerospace and helicopters maker in 1994 (GKN, 2016; The Economist, 2012).
2 Invensys was then Unidrive's largest shareholder with a 50 percent stake in the firm (GKN, 2000).
3 The importance of this acquisition was highlighted by Fidel Otake, GKN Driveline Mexico's managing director, who asserted 'Mexico is a very important growth market for GKN Driveline' and 'we have invested over US$100 million (1.4 billion Pesos) in our Mexican operations since 2005. This has allowed us to more efficiently serve our growing customer base throughout the region' (GKN, 2011).
4 eDrive systems refer to secondary electrically driven axles which facilitate AWD capability and enhanced fuel efficiency (GKN, 2015a).
5 Trevor Bonner, then head of Uni-Cardan (a GKN subsidiary) also validated NTN's strategic move into CVJs (CVJs facilitated front-wheel drive) as evidenced by the following statement: 'Given the particular demographics of Japan, and also the infrastructure or lack of it at the time, most of the vehicles produced were small cars with front-wheel drive (thus needing CVJs)' (Lorenz, 2009:227).
6 BTR Nylex merged with Siebe plc to form Invensys in February 1999, resulting in Invensys controlling 50 percent of Unidrive. In May 2000, Invensys sold its

50 percent stake to GKN and NTN, with GKN taking another 30 percent (increasing its overall stake to 60 percent) and NTN taking the remaining 20 percent (increasing its overall stake to 40 percent) (GKN, 2000; TDK-Lambda, 2013).

7 Continuous improvement occupies an exalted position in the hierarchy of lean practices and has been described by industry analysts as a 'pillar' of lean (Lorenz, 2009).

References

Automotive Intelligence (2000a) GKN strengthens position in Brazilian automotive market, *autointell.com* [internet] Available at: www.autointell.net/supplier/supplier_news/gkn-add.htm [Accessed on 20 February, 2012].

Automotive Intelligence (2000b) Nissan: Manufacturing, Smyrna, Tenn., *autointell.com* [internet] Available at: www.autointell.com/asian_companies/nissan/nissan-facilities/nissan-us-facilities.htm [Accessed on 31 January, 2011].

Birmingham Post & Mail Ltd (1998) Boots and GKN unveil ventures in the Far East, Birmingham Post & Mail Ltd [internet] Available at: http://www.thefreelibrary.com/Boots+and+GKN+unveil+ventures+in+the+Far+East.-a060778737 [Accessed on 19 July, 2012].

Burkeman, O. and Borger, J. (2001) The ex-presidents' club, *The Guardian* [internet] Available at: www.guardian.co.uk/world/2001/oct/31/september11.usa4 [Accessed on 13 June, 2012].

Chandler, A.D. and Hikino, T. (1999) The large industrial enterprise and the dynamics of modern economic growth, in Chandler, A., Amatori, F. and Hikino, T. (eds), *Big Business and The Wealth of Nations*, Cambridge: Cambridge University Press.

Chappell, L. (2005) Boosting M-class quality is US plant's top challenge: Mercedes plant CEO turned to suppliers to improve SUV, *Automotive News* [internet] Available at: www.autonews.com/article/20050711/SUB/507110799?template=print [Accessed on 30 August, 2016].

Delphi Corporation (2008) Delphi receives final court approval for sale of global steering business, *Delphi* [internet] Available at: http://delphi.com/about/news/media/pressReleases/2008/pr_2008_02_21_002/ [Accessed on 16 July, 2012].

Drucker, P.F. and Mariariello, J.A. (2004) The Daily Drucker: 366 Days of Insight and Motivation for Getting the Right Things Done, New York: HarperCollins Publishers.

eBearing.com (2001) Delphi exits NSK joint venture in Brazil for hub assemblies, *eBearing.com* [internet] Available at: www.ebearing.com/news2001/news362.htm [Accessed on 13 May, 2012].

eBearing.com (2003a) GKN Automotive becomes GKN Driveline, *eBearing.com* [internet] Available at: www.ebearing.com/news2003/091102.htm [Accessed on 13 May, 2012].

eBearing.com (2003b) NTN establishing more joint ventures in China, *eBearing.com* [internet] Available at: www.ebearing.com/news2003/111901.htm [Accessed on 12 May, 2012].

eBearing.com (2006a) NTN acquires IFA Stake, *eBearing.com* [internet] Available at: www.ebearing.com/news2006/052501.htm [Accessed on 13 May, 2012].

eBearing.com (2006b) NTN in New Japanese CV manufacturing venture, *eBearing.com* [internet] Available at: www.ebearing.com/news2006/071901.htm [Accessed on 12 May, 2012].

Edison Investment Research (2012) *Outlook: GKN*, London: Edison Investment Research.

Funding Universe (2012) GKN plc History, Funding Universe [internet] Available at: http://www.fundinguniverse.com/company-histories/gkn-plc-history/ [Accessed on 22 December, 2012].

Europa (1999) Case No COMP/M.1587-DANA/GKN, *Europa* [internet] Available at: http://ec.europa.eu/competition/mergers/cases/decisions/m1587_en.pdf [Accessed on 20 February, 2012].

Europa (2007) Case No COMP/M.4346 -NTN/SNR, *Europa* [internet] Available at: http://ec.europa.eu/competition/mergers/cases/decisions/m4346_20070327_20310_en.pdf [Accessed on 16 July, 2016].

Foley, S (1999) GKN buys Opel plant in drive to work closer with GM, *The Independent* [internet] Available at: www.independent.co.uk/news/business/news/gkn-buys-opel-plant-in-drive-to – work-closer-with-gm-740840.html [Accessed on 15 July, 2012].

Friedman, T. (2006) The World Is Flat: The Globalized World in the Twenty-First Century, New York: Farrar, Straus and Giroux.

GKN (1998) GKN plc Annual Report 1998, Worcestershire: GKN plc.

GKN (2000) GKN increases its shareholding in Unidrive in Australia to 60%, *GKN* [internet] Available at: http://tools.morningstar.co.uk/uk/stockreport/default.aspx?tab=3&vw=story&SecurityToken=0P00007OCX]3]0]E0WWE$$ALL&Id=0P00007OCX&ClientFund=0&CurrencyId=GBP&story=7829725424853 [Accessed on 30 November, 2011].

GKN (2001) *GKN plc 2001*, Worcestershire: GKN plc.

GKN (2002) GKN plc 2002, Worcestershire: GKN plc.

GKN (2003) *GKN plc Annual Report 2003*, Worcestershire: GKN plc.

GKN (2004) *GKN plc Annual Report 2004*, Worcestershire: GKN plc.

GKN (2005) *GKN plc Annual Report 2005*, Worcestershire: GKN plc.

GKN (2009) *GKN plc Annual Report and Accounts 2009*, Worcestershire: GKN plc.

GKN (2010) *GKN plc Annual Report and Accounts 2010*, Worcestershire: GKN plc.

GKN (2011a) The drive to automotive, *GKN* [internet] Available at: www.gkn250.com/1925.html [Accessed on 30 November, 2011].

GKN (2011b) GKN Driveline production expansion and new technology for China, GKN [internet] Available at: www.gkn.com/media/News/Pages/GKN-Driveline-production-expansion-and-new-technology-for-China.aspx [Accessed on 30 November, 2011].

GKN (2011c) GKN plc Annual Report and Accounts 2011, Worcestershire: GKN plc.

GKN (2012a) GKN plc Annual Report and Accounts 2012, Worcestershire: GKN plc.

GKN (2012b) Potential suppliers, *GKN* [internet] Available at: www.gkndriveline.com/drivelinecms/opencms/en/suppliers/potential-suppliers.html [Accessed on 7 June, 2012].

GKN (2013) GKN announces major expansion of its joint venture in China, *GKN* [internet] Available at: www.gkn.com/en/newsroom/news-releases/group/2013/gkn-announces-major-expansion-of-its-joint-venture-in-china/ [Accessed on 21 January, 2017].

GKN (2015a) GKN plc Annual Report and Accounts 2015, Worcestershire: GKN plc.

GKN (2015b) New GKN CV joint system helps make premium vehicles lighter and more efficient, *PRNewswire* [internet] Available at: www.prnewswire.com/news-releases/new-gkn-cv-joint-system-helps-make-premium-vehicles-lighter-and-more-efficient-300175931.html [Accessed on 22 January, 2017].

GKN (2016a) All-new GKN sideshaft system debuts with Premium Automaker, *PR Newswire* [internet] Available at: www.prnewswire.com/news-releases/all-new-gkn-sideshaft-system-debuts-with-premium-automaker-300211531.html [Accessed on 22 January, 2017].

GKN (2016b) Berenberg European corporate conference, *GKN* [internet] Available at: www.gkn.com/globalassets/downloads/results-and-presentations/2016/berenberg-european-conference-uk-5-december-2016.pdf [Accessed on 17 February, 2017].

GKN (2016c) Our heritage: 1986–2001, *GKN* [internet] Available at: www.gkn.com/aboutus/ourheritage_old/Pages/1986-2001.aspx [Accessed on 16 July, 2016].

GKN China (2011) Changchun plant opening, *GKN China* [internet] Available at: www.gknchina.com/news/changchun-plant-opening [Accessed on 30 November, 2011].

GKN Land Systems (2012) New generation of GKN developed countertrack CV joints reaches the independent repair market, *GKN* [internet] Available at: www.gkn.com/landsystems/brands/gkn-pss/about-us/news/Pages/New-generation-of-GKN-developed-countertrack-CV-joints.aspx [Accessed on 20 June, 2012].

Green Car Congress (2009) GKN Driveline Says Countertrack Constant Velocity Joint Technology Saves Fuel, Green Car Congress [internet] Available at: http://www.greencarcongress.com/2009/07/gkn-2009717.html [Accessed on 20 March, 2012].

Hotten, R. (1994) GKN to spend pounds 50m on Italian plant in joint venture with Fiat, *The Independent* [internet] Available at: www.independent.co.uk/news/business/gkn-to-spend-pounds-50m-on-italian-plant-in-joint-venture-with-fiat-1412246.html [Accessed on 15 July, 2012].

Hughes, C. (1999) Corporate Profile: Your move, Mr Chow, The Independent [internet] Available at: http://www.independent.co.uk/news/business/corporate-profile-your-move-mr-chow-1111974.html [Accessed on 20 February, 2012].

International Organization for Standardization (2011) *ISO/TS 16949:2009*, iso.org [internet] Available at: www.iso.org/iso/catalogue_detail?csnumber=52844 [Accessed on 7 June, 2012].

Kruse, E. (2004) Why does GKN run Lean? *SCRC* [internet] Available at: http://scm.ncsu.edu/scm-articles/article/why-does-gkn-run-lean [Accessed on 20 March, 2012].

Lees, D. (1992) From Steel to Services: An Account of Change in GKN in the 1980s, Cambridge: Magdalene College.

Liang, Q. (2012) Kian Shen to expand production capacities in China, *The Taiwan Economic News* [internet] Available at: www.thefreelibrary.com/Kian+Shen+to+expand+production+capacities+in+China.-a0282824785 [Accessed on 15 September, 2012].

Lorenz, A. (1997) UK: GKN hits its stride, *Management Today* [internet] Available at: www.managementtoday.co.uk/news/411124/UK-GKN-HITS-ITS-STRIDE/?DCMP=ILC-SEARCH [Accessed on 26 December, 2011].

Lorenz, A. (2009) *GKN: The Making of a Business 1759–2009*, Chichester: John Wiley & Sons Ltd.

MarkLines Co., Ltd (2007) Japanese Parts Suppliers in Europe Focusing on Products Related to Diesel Engines, Marklines [internet] Available at: http://www.marklines.com/en/report/rep569_200705 [Accessed on 21 February, 2012].

McGavin, S.H. (2016) GKN Driveline plans to invest $179 million in 6 N.C. plants, *Automotive News* [interne] Available at: www.autonews.com/article/20161220/

OEM10/161229985/gkn-driveline-plans-to-invest-$179-million-in-6-n.c.-plants [Accessed on 11 January, 2017].

Moore, M. (2010) Britain's GKN rides China's high-speed advance, *The Telegraph* [internet] Available at: www.telegraph.co.uk/finance/china-business/7958867/Britains-GKN-rides-Chinas-high-speed-advance.html [Accessed on 3 February, 2012].

Nolan, P. (2008) Capitalism and Freedom, The Contradictory Character of Globalisation, London: Anthem Press.

NTN Americas (2013) Products: Constant velocity joints, *NTN Americas* [internet] Available at: www.ntnamericas.com/en/products/constant-velocity-joints [Accessed on 8 March, 2013].

NTN Americas (2015) 2015-11-18 Press release, *NTN Americas* [internet] Available at: www.ntnamericas.com/en/about-ntn/media-and-resources/208-2015-11-20-press-release [Accessed on 11 January, 2017].

NTN Bearing Corporation of America (2009) *Ball and Roller Bearings Catalogue A-1000-XI*, NTN Bearing Corporation of America.

NTN Corporation (2001) *Annual Report 2001*, Osaka: NTN Corporation.

NTN Corporation (2003) *Annual Report 2003 Year Ended March 31, 2003*, Osaka: NTN Corporation.

NTN Corporation (2006) *Annual Report 2006 Year Ended March 31, 2006*, Osaka: NTN Corporation.

NTN Corporation (2007a) NTN Creates New Joint Venture for CVJ Production in Alabama, USA, *NTN Corporation* [internet] Available at: www.ntn.co.jp/english/news/news_files/press/news20070302.html [Accessed on 10 May, 2012].

NTN Corporation (2007b) *NTN Technical Review No. 75*, Osaka: NTN Corporation.

NTN Corporation (2008a) *Annual Report 2008 Year Ended March 31, 2008*, Osaka: NTN Corporation.

NTN Corporation (2008b) NTN expands European CVJ Business by acquiring SETFORGE's Crézancy Plant, *NTN Corporation* [internet] Available at: www.ntn.co.jp/english/news/news_files/press/news200800005.html [Accessed on 10 May, 2012].

NTN Corporation (2009) *Annual Report 2009 Year Ended March 31, 2009*, Osaka: NTN Corporation.

NTN Corporation (2010a) NTN Establishes CVJ Production Base in Brazil: Production of CVJ s to Begin in June 2011, *NTN Corporation* [internet] Available at: www.ntn.co.jp/english/news/news_files/press/news201000030.html [Accessed on 11 May, 2012].

NTN Corporation (2010b) *NTN Report 2010 for the Year Ended, March 31*, Osaka: NTN Corporation.

NTN Corporation (2011a) 2nd Production base established in Southern India [Production of CVJs and 3rd generation hub bearings to begin in April 2012], *NTN Corporation* [internet] Available at: www.ntn.co.jp/english/news/news_files/press/news201100014.html [Accessed on 10 May, 2012].

NTN Corporation (2011b) *NTN Report 2011 for the Year Ended, March 31*, Osaka: NTN Corporation.

NTN Corporation (2012a) Development of "Next Generation High Efficiency Fixed Type CVJ CFJ", *NTN Corporation* [internet] Available at: www.ntnglobal.com/en/news/new_products/news201200039.html [Accessed on 22 January, 2017].

NTN Corporation (2012b) NTN to establish second production base in Thailand for automotive products [Developing a local integrated production system in the Southeast Asian region], *NTN Corporation* [internet] Available at: www.ntn.co.jp/english/news/news_files/press/news201200011.html [Accessed on 11 May, 2012].

NTN Corporation (2015) Development of "Lightweight Driveshaft for FR vehicle", *NTN Corporation* [internet] Available at: www.ntnglobal.com/en/news/new_products/news201500074.html [Accessed on 22 January, 2017].

NTN Corporation (2016a) Consolidated Financial Results for Year Ended March 31, 2016: May 17, 2016, Osaka: NTN Corporation.

NTN Corporation (2016b) *Financial Results for the Year Ended March 31, 2016*, Osaka: NTN Corporation.

NTN-SNR (2011) Corporate press release: NTN-SNR ROULEMENTS, *NTN-SNR* [internet] Available at: www.ntn-snr.com/portal/ru/ru-ru/file.cfm/NTN_SNR_DP_GB_opt.pdf?contentID=6331 [Accessed on 15 July, 2016].

PMR (2005) GKN beefs up its operations in Poland, *PMR* [internet] Available at: www.polishmarket.com/29713/GKN-beefs-up-its-operations-in-Poland.shtml [Accessed on 15 July, 2012].Reference for Business (2012) NTN Corporation, *Reference for Business* [internet] Available at: www.referenceforbusiness.com/history2/90/NTN-Corporation.html [Accessed on 12 September, 2012].

Reuters (2014) Singapore fines Japanese ball bearing firms S$9.3 million for price-fixing, Reuters [internet] Available at: http://www.reuters.com/article/singapore-antitrust-japan-idUSL3N0OC0OY20140527 [Accessed on 9 December, 2016].

Sawyer, C. (2006) Rethinking constant velocity joints, *Automotive Design and Production* [internet] Available at: www.autofieldguide.com/articles/rethinking-constant-velocity-joints [Accessed on 16 May, 2012].

Stephens, C. (2016) Madison County business: Looking ahead, looking up, *The Herald Bulletin* [internet] Available at: www.heraldbulletin.com/news/local_news/madison-county-business-looking-ahead-looking-up/article_1a9618ca-377f-58fd-a923-af183055df8c.html [Accessed on 11 January, 2017].

Sturgeon, T.J. and Lester, R.K. (2003) The New Global Supply-Base: New Challenges for Local Suppliers in East Asia, MIT Working Paper IPC-03-006, MA: MIT.

Supplier Business (2010) NTN to purchase tedrive Sistemas' constant-velocity joints business in Brazil, *Supplier Business* [internet] Available at: www.supplierbusiness.com/news/10884/ntn-to-purchase-tedrive-sistemas-constant-velocity-joints-business-in-brazil [Accessed on 4 August, 2013].

TDK-Lambda (2013) BTR plc and Siebe plc merge to create leading electronics and engineering group, *TDK-Lambda* [internet] Available at: www.us.tdk-lambda.com/hp/News/news3.htm [Accessed on 19 April, 2013].

The Economist (2000) Confucius rules at GKN, The Economist [internet] Available at: www.economist.com/node/368280 [Accessed on 13 September, 2012].

The Economist (2012) Word on a wing: A long-established global innovator shows how British firms can make it in modern manufacturing, The Economist [internet] Available at: www.economist.com/node/21556582 [Accessed on 16 July, 2016].

The Engineer (2002) Managing Torque, The Engineer [internet] Available at: www.
    theengineer.co.uk/issues/22-march-2002/managing-torque/ [Accessed on 16 July,
    2016].

Toh, A. (2014) CORRECTED-Singapore fines Japanese ball bearing firms S$9.3 mln
    for price-fixing, *Reuters* [internet] Available at: www.reuters.com/article/singa
    pore-antitrust-japan-idUSL3N0OC0OY20140528 [Accessed on 15 July, 2016].

Unidrive Pty Ltd (2010) About Unidrive Pty Ltd: Our History, Unidrive [internet]
    Available at: http://www.unidrive.com/about-us.html [Accessed on 28 Novem-
    ber, 2011].

Visteon Corporation (2012) Frequently asked questions: Investors, *Visteon* [internet]
    Available at: www.visteon.com/faq/investors.html#11 [Accessed on 12 Septem-
    ber, 2012].

Wanxiang America Corporation (2012) QC Driveline, *Wanxiang* [internet] Available
    at: www.wanxiang.com/driveline.html [Accessed on 13 March, 2012].

6 The global braking systems industry

1. Introduction

The global braking systems industry comprises two components, namely high-tech braking systems and foundation brakes.[1] Unlike their predecessors a generation or two earlier, many of today's braking systems are increasingly sophisticated systems complete with hydraulic brakes which are then supported by technologies such as Anti-lock Braking Systems (ABS), Electronic Stability Control (ESC) and Traction Control Systems (TCS)[2]; they extend far beyond plain-vanilla foundation brakes (encompasses the primary low-tech components of calipers, rotors, drums, vacuum boosters and master cylinders) (Murphy, 2009a). Such high-tech braking systems used to be the preserve of luxury vehicles but are now becoming increasingly prevalent in the average car. Jason Forcier, president of Robert Bosch LLC's North America, automotive electronics division has described vehicle safety (incorporating high-tech and even predictive braking systems) as 'the next frontier for automotive electronics' (quoted in Bosch, 2008). In North America, ESC has already gained ubiquity and 100 percent of new vehicles are believed to be ABS, ESC and TCS equipped by 2013 and 2014 respectively (Continental, 2015). The brakes industry has evolved considerably over the past decade and has now become a highly advanced safety systems platform comprising ultra-efficient brakes, cutting-edge sensors and automated driving assistance technologies (the lynchpin of tomorrow's autonomous vehicles).

Today, the approximately €19.3 billion (US$21.1 billion) global braking systems market is dominated by three key German companies, namely Continental, Bosch and ZF. These oligopolists control a stupendous 76.7 percent of the global braking systems market.[3] Nonetheless Continental and ZF still have significant capabilities in foundation brakes while Bosch has exited this business. They are followed by the next rung of second-tier suppliers (i.e., Akebono, Mando, Hitachi, Brembo, ADVICS, Chassis Brake International (hereafter 'CBI') and Hyundai Mobis) who are largely focused on foundation brakes and possess some capabilities in high-tech braking systems. These second-tier suppliers are in turn followed by a sizeable number of third-tier suppliers who mostly supply basic-foundation brakes and their related components. This highly oligopolistic industry structure is the result of considerable industry consolidation since the 1980s, triggered by the unrelenting forces of the cascade effect.

Industry pioneer, Bosch which for decades had the largest market share in the braking systems industry ceded its number one position following the gradual divestment of its foundation brakes business over the 2009–2012 period. In 2009, Bosch divested its North American foundation brakes business (the deal encompassed relatively low margin braking components such as brake calipers, disk brakes and drum brakes) to Japan's Akebono (Associated Press, 2009). However, in March 2011, Akebono declined to buy the rest of Bosch's braking systems business, arguing that it did not fit well with their overall business strategy (Reuters, 2011). Nonetheless, Bosch did succeed in selling the remnants of its foundation brakes business to KPS Capital Partners (hereafter 'KPS'), a US private equity firm in January 2012 for a rumoured US$255.56 million (this figure is considerably lower than Bosch's initial asking price of US$700 million, reflecting the low value that the market now attaches to the foundation brakes business) (Wilson and Bryant, 2012; Huebner and Burger, 2012). Bosch felt that foundation brakes have become highly commoditised components (unlike ABS, TCS and ESC that have far higher margins), that have to be spun off to lower-tier suppliers with a lower cost structure. Further it wanted to focus its attention and resources on capturing the more lucrative yet increasingly capital intensive high-tech braking systems market. The sheer cost/risk involved in developing these new technologies is one of the key reasons why even first-tier suppliers have to continue acquiring their smaller competitors in order to capture any emerging disruptive technologies (small firms are often the source of new technologies) and also to secure the increasing economies of scale and scope needed to mitigate these rising cost pressures (Quinn, 1953); despite the argument that small firms are often leading innovators, they, unlike multinationals such as Bosch, do not possess the financial muscle and scale economies needed to successfully commercialise their technologies, exploit their fullest potential through relentless product development and deliver them swiftly to the global market with the requisite marketing and distribution support.

Bosch's main rival in the braking systems business, Continental, has overtaken it in terms of overall market share (foundation brakes along with other high-tech braking systems), as it has not only held onto its foundation brakes business but has also made considerable headway in the advanced braking systems market by means of acquisition; Continental (better known for its tyres) is now the world's largest maker of braking systems while ZF ranks third in this sector (Murphy, 2012). Continental is determined to stay in the foundation brakes business, as indicated by Ralf Cramer, head of Continental's Chassis & Safety division: 'we won't exit the foundation-brake business' and 'we will stay in it very strongly' (quoted in Murphy, 2012); the company is of the opinion that foundation brakes remain a crucial building block for developing the overall braking systems business.

TRW (now part of ZF), in its earlier existence as an independent company, also expressed similar views to Continental's (unlike Bosch, TRW found the foundation brakes profitable). The company reaffirmed this belief by continuing to invest and secure innovations in foundation brakes. For instance, TRW had achieved considerable success with its new rear electric park brake, which is integrated with the caliper (part of foundation brakes) and also could be installed on a vehicle's front axles to facilitate customer requests for inexpensive drum brakes on the rear (Murphy, 2012). ZF, through its acquisition of TRW in 2015, was able to capitalise on TRW's earlier efforts and become the third largest braking systems company in the world; prior to its acquisition of TRW, ZF was primarily a maker of steering systems and powertrains.

The braking systems market, despite being dominated by three leading oligopolists, is still experiencing considerable consolidation, as the second and third-tier players are compelled to merge among themselves to secure much-needed scale economies. These lower-tier suppliers sometimes also find themselves becoming the acquisition targets of the larger first-tier braking systems suppliers; this trend has been unfolding over the past few decades, with first-tier firms such as Bosch acquiring a 14.7 percent stake in Akebono, a rising second-tier supplier in 1988 (Reuters, 1988).[4] Further, Mando, a Korean second-tier supplier was the acquisition target of both Continental and TRW (Korean Herald, 2005). This industry consolidation is not expected to cease in the medium term, as eroding margins, cost pressures (resulting from increasing technological complexity in braking systems) and intensifying competition tighten their grip on the industry. The major obstacle to this unrelenting consolidation trend is the rising scrutiny of antitrust authorities worldwide, that seem increasingly resolved in stemming the onset of a Thucydidean world where the strong (i.e., oligopolists) impose their will on the markets with impunity.

2. The cascade effect's impact on braking systems makers

Driven by the cascade effect, automakers have generally divested their internal brake production facilities and outsourced the production of brakes and related components to external suppliers. For instance, in 1999, GM spun off its brake operations as part of Delphi, which later sold the business in early 2008 (Klier and Rubinstein, 2008). Further, its Japanese competitor, Mazda divested its subsidiaries that made braking systems to focus resources on higher value-added activities that could potentially increase the market share of their core business (i.e., assembling cars). The automakers have in turn placed considerable pressure on their brakes suppliers to meet their increasing demands, which range from meeting their demands in 'just-in-time' practices to price discounts. These pressures have greatly eroded margins in the braking systems industry, particularly in the relatively commoditised foundation brakes segment. Consequently, first-tier suppliers such as Delphi have exited the brakes business entirely. In 2007, Delphi sold its brake hose business to Harco Manufacturing Group LLC for US$9.8 million (along with some considerations) (Rubber & Plastics News, 2007). Not long after this sale, Delphi also divested its North American brake components, machining and assembly assets to TRW in early 2008 for US$40 million and disposed the remnants of its global brake business to China's Beijing West Industries for US$100 million in 2009 (this deal also included the remainder of Delphi's global suspension business) (Murphy, 2012).

In an increasingly commoditised market (particularly with regard to foundation brakes) and strong automaker power, the impact of the cascade effect is especially forceful. Even long-time braking systems pioneer, Bosch, has made the decision to divest its foundation brakes business, citing a lack of profitability caused by rising material prices and its earlier mistaken assumption that automakers would buy complete brake systems from a single source (unfortunately, in the brakes market, automakers may use components made by different suppliers). However, the other leading global braking systems companies, Continental and ZF are still keen in the foundation brakes business, thus they have focused their attention on acquiring the smaller players in this segment and even their own suppliers.

Due to the intense pressures generated by the cascade effect, the global braking systems market is still witnessing considerable M&A. This is attributable to the steady transformation of the braking systems industry into an increasingly technologically driven safety systems platform; as indicated in the following sections, firms as Continental are starting to acquire non-traditional firms with expertise in software development. The consolidation pressures are also mounting at the second and third-tier level. Second-tier suppliers such as Akebono are compelled to consolidate in order to gain much needed economies of scale and scope to survive in a rapidly evolving industry. Through its acquisition of Bosch's North America foundation brakes business in 2009, Akebono became the largest player in the global foundation brakes business (covers disc and drum brakes) with a near 40 percent market share; Bosch's divestment had allowed Akebono to leapfrog the competition. Industry titans, ZF and Continental now rank second and fourth in the foundation brakes business, with significantly lower market shares of approximately 16 percent and 8 percent respectively. Other players in the foundation brakes market include Mando, Hitachi, Brembo and ADVICS which record estimated market shares of 11 percent, 7 percent, 7 percent and 6 percent respectively. This already volatile state of affairs was upended again when the remnants of Bosch's former foundation brakes business was reconstituted by its private equity owner KPS and re-launched as CBI in mid-2012; CBI, the seeming 'arriviste', asserts that it is among the world's top three foundation brakes makers (Edison Investment Research, 2012; Murphy, 2012; CBI, 2016).

3. The leading braking systems makers

Continental: profile

Continental founded in 1871, is now the world's second largest automotive components suppliers, after Robert Bosch. With the arrival of 2016, the company having surmounted the monumental struggles of the automotive industry, also stood unflinchingly as the world's largest braking systems supplier (possesses an estimated 31.1 percent global market share) and fourth largest tyre company. Its success is predicated on the uncanny ability to exploit the considerable synergies between the two areas, as the tyre in its role as the 'neural connection' between the road and the vehicle chassis could provide significant information for today's increasingly sophisticated braking systems (i.e., ABS, TCS, ESC).

In 2015, Continental recorded revenues of €39.2 billion (US$43.5 billion) and a net income of €2.7 billion (US$3.0 billion). By the end of 2015, Continental had approximately 207,899 employees spread across 55 countries (Continental, 1998; Continental, 2015a). Continental's braking systems business is part of its Chassis & Safety division which accounted for 21.5 percent (about €8.4 billion) of the company's overall 2015 revenues (Figure 6.1); for that year, the firm's braking systems segment alone generated an estimated €6.01 billion (US$6.6759 billion) in revenues, which comprised 71.4 percent and 15.3 percent of divisional and overall revenues respectively. The Chassis & Safety business is Continental's second largest division after its tyres division (Continental, 2015a). This massive division alone operates more than 70 plants, research centres and test tracks in 20 different countries, supported by over 6000 engineers (Continental, 2016). A global presence of this magnitude is sine qua non, as Continental now supplies most of the major automakers (e.g., Ford, Volkswagen, BMW, Daimler), who have effectively internationalised their operations and require their brake suppliers to be located close to their assembly operations (to facilitate just-in-time measures); for instance, to supply its automaker customers in China alone (the world's largest automotive market), Continental's Chassis & Safety division had, by 2015, established ten production and R&D facilities in the country (Continental 2015). The provision of close customer support is

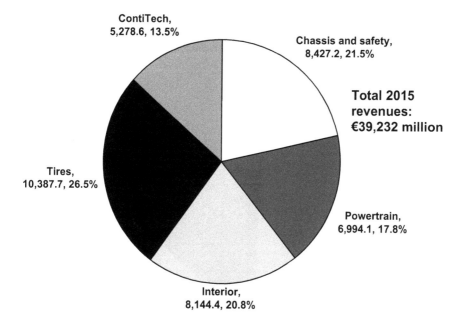

Figure 6.1 Continental's 2015 annual revenues (€ million)

Source: 2015 Continental AG Annual Report

essentially viewed by Continental as an article of faith underscoring its international growth strategy, as evidenced by the following statement: 'local closeness to our customers and global knowledge management are translated into successful products on a daily basis' (Continental, 2011).

Continental is also exposed to significant automaker pressure in other areas such as quality and pricing (Continental, 2011). Given these pressures, there is inevitably growing pressure for Continental to seek further acquisitions to gain additional economies of scale and scope (needed to secure 'operating efficiencies' and 'reduced expenditures'). Further, Continental with its 2015 procurement expenses of €17.4 billion (US$19.3 billion) is in a position to exert overwhelming pressure on its own suppliers, illustrating the powerful forces cascading through this global value chain (Continental, 2015a); Continental's procurement budget has more than doubled since 2008 (its 2008 procurement budget was around €8.5 billion) due to the firm merging its purchasing operations with that of its acquirer, Schaeffler in 2009 (just-auto.com, 2009).

As evidenced in Figure 6.2, Continental is still very much dependent on Germany (its domestic market) and the European region, which, in 2015, accounted for 21.4 percent (€8.38 billion) and 28.1 percent (€11.04 billion) of its overall revenues respectively. Its Chassis & Safety division (which its braking systems business is embedded) follows a similar trend, with Germany accounting for 24 percent (€2.02 billion) of overall divisional revenues in 2015 (Continental, 2015).

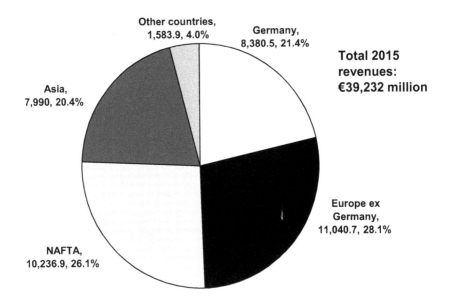

Figure 6.2 Continental's 2015 revenues by region (€ million)

Source: 2015 Continental AG Annual Report

Continental's acquisitions over the past two decades

In 1998, Continental greatly augmented its then relatively small brakes business by acquiring ITT Industries Automotive Brake and Chassis' (B) operations for US$1.93 billion. The acquisition was a turning point in Continental's history, as it transformed from being just a tyre maker to a world-class supplier of complete braking/safety systems. ITT itself had become a leading brakes supplier by acquiring Germany's Alfred Teves in 1967 (Klier and Rubinstein, 2008).

Continental has been relentless in executing its acquisition strategy over the past two decades. For instance, Continental acquired two Japanese brakes makers in 2001. The two companies were Shin-Ei and ShinTec, former subsidiaries of the Mazda Motor Corporation. Continental's Board Member, Dr. Wolfgang Ziebart had asserted these acquisitions were crucial steps in achieving Continental's goal of 'becoming a system supplier for mechanical and electronic brake systems in the markets of Japan and Korea' (quoted in tyrepress.com, 2001). Further, in July 2007, Continental acquired its long-time supplier, Automotive Products Italia (SV) S.r.l. (hereafter 'AP') from the Australian Pacifica Group Limited. AP, founded in 1984, was a maker of drum and park brakes for passenger and commercial vehicles and had approximately 500 employees. In 2006, the company recorded sales of around € 79 million and its list of clients included leading automakers such as Fiat, Ford, Renault/Nissan, Toyota, Land Rover, Mazda and GM. The acquisition enabled Continental to not only strengthen its capabilities in high-tech and cost-effective braking systems (i.e., drum brakes) but also augment its presence in Asia. Further, AP had been a long-time supplier to Continental, thus making the decision to acquire the firm even easier. Continental is now aiming to become a full-service provider in braking systems, a role that it is trying to achieve via acquisitions (Murphy, 2012).

However, it was really Continental's US$15.7 billion acquisition of Siemens VDO in 2007 that bolstered the company's market share and capabilities. The acquisition of Siemens VDO not only positioned Continental to challenge Bosch as the world's largest automotive components company but also augmented its capabilities in high-tech braking systems and sensors. For instance, Continental's acquisition of Siemens VDO allowed it to secure control of the company's revolutionary 'wedge' braking systems technology which is a high-tech electronic brake-by-wire system that has dispensed with traditional components such as the hydraulic lines, vacuum booster, fluid reservoir, parking-brake assembly/cable, mechanical pedal and the master cylinder; Siemens VDO had ambitiously planned to use this new technology to dominate the braking systems market (Murphy, 2005). Continental's strategic intent was to integrate Siemens VDO's technologies and evolve its own market dominating product (named ContiGuard) (Thiel and van Loon, 2007; Continental, 2007); this breakthrough technology combined with the sheer economies of scale and scope (along with the technological synergies) from Continental's sizeable tyre division could position Continental as the leader in automotive safety systems; this strategy gives Continental greater product differentiation and the opportunity to charge a premium for a cutting-edge product.

However, this ambitious acquisition of Siemens VDO left Continental financially vulnerable in the event of a hostile takeover, as it had assumed €9.5 billion
of debt to finance the takeover, in the process, causing its share price to plunge
by 50 percent. Resultantly, Continental itself was acquired by an opportunistic
Schaeffler (a family-owned German maker of ball bearings that was a third of
its size) for about €12 billion in 2008; the acquisition was deemed hostile by
Continental's management but was eventually completed with an agreement by
Schaeffler to keep its equity stake at 49.99 percent for four years and increasing
its offer from €70.12 to €75 per share (Mason, 2008). The hostility surrounding Schaeffler's bid is evidenced by Continental's then CEO Manfred Wennemer
accusing Schaeffler's management of behaving 'egotistically, high-handedly and
irresponsibly' (quoted in Drives and Controls, 2008). Wennemer also accused
Schaeffler of wanting to split up Continental and eventually resigned after
Schaeffler's acquisition of the firm; Continental's board, possibly enticed by the
significant premium offered by Schaeffler, compelled Wennemer to resume negotiations and go through with the acquisition (Schäfer, 2008). Despite Schaeffler's
subsequent acquisition of Continental, there has been no more formal merger
between the two firms and Continental continues to operate as an 'independent'
entity. Nonetheless by 2015, Schaeffler still retained a significant 46 percent stake
in Continental valued at €19.7 billion (Bryant, 2015, Continental, 2015).

Despite the fracas presented by its acquisition, Continental has continued to
pursue an aggressive acquisition strategy (albeit the size of its acquisitions is relatively small compared to earlier buyouts). In March 2012, Continental acquired
its partner, Rico Auto Industries Limited's 50 percent stake in their JV, Continental Rico Hydraulic Brakes India Ltd (in the process, converting the JV into a
fully-owned subsidiary of Continental) (Continental, 2012). This relentless drive
to gain size and scale economies is not without its problems. Scherer argues that
in the automotive industry, size does come with its accompanying impediments
which include bureaucracy, convoluted decision making structures and the loss
of organisational agility (Scherer, 1996). However, with the advent of email and
other modern means of instantaneous communication, the ill-effects of increasing
organisational size and bureaucracy have been alleviated (to some extent). Moreover, there is increased scrutiny by antitrust regulators due to the rising number
of acquisitions in the global automotive components industry. For instance, Continental has made at least 12 acquisitions (not just in braking systems) since 2000.

In its relentless acquisition drive, Continental acquired Elektrobit Automotive
Group, the automotive software business of Elektrobit Corporation for €600 million (US$680 million) in July 2015; the acquisition would enable the addition
of 1,900 software professionals to Continental's already robust 11,000 software
team. This acquisition was executed to augment Continental's capabilities in
advanced driver assistance systems and autonomous vehicle technology (Behrmann, 2015; Continental, 2015). Further, this merger reflects the ascendance of
what was once a low-tech, plain-vanilla brakes industry into today's increasingly
sophisticated safety systems market, where cutting-edge technological competence is rapidly becoming the arbiter of market success.

Continental's JV strategy

Over the last two decades, Continental has also relied on JVs as a means of complementing its aggressive acquisition strategy, securing greater scale economies and growing its global market share. As indicated by the above case of Continental Rico Hydraulic Brakes India, it is also often a useful springboard towards outright acquisition, particularly after an investor has acquired sufficient local knowledge and market share, and the local regulatory framework has become more favourable. In 1994, Continental established Shanghai Automotive Brake Systems Co., Ltd., a significant JV with SAIC. Additionally, Continental formed another JV with Japan's Nisshinbo Industries in 2000. This JV known as Continental Teves Corporation, (hereafter 'Continental Teves') was a full-system supplier of brakes and chassis; Continental had a 51 percent stake while Nisshinbo held the remaining 49 percent shareholding in the JV. This JV was formed to strengthen both companies' presence in the Japanese and Korean markets; Continental has since increased its stake in Continental Teves to 100 percent, converting this former JV into a wholly-owned subsidiary (Continental, 2014; Nisshinbo, 2016).

Since the establishment of Continental Teves, the company continued to use JVs as a growth strategy. In 2010, Continental established a new JV named Continental Brake Systems (Shanghai) Co., Ltd. with Chinese automotive components supplier, HASCO. This JV was 51 percent owned by Continental and augmented the company's position as a key supplier of hydraulic brake systems in China (Continental, 2010). Nonetheless, JVs are not always plain sailing. This is particularly so in China, where automotive components firms such as HASCO can and often have concurrent JVs with multiple partners. Currently, HASCO has JV arrangements with both Continental and its key rival, ZF. Thus, there is always the risk of Continental's commercial secrets ending up in the hands of ZF and vice-versa. Further, there is the danger of Continental breeding its own competition (i.e., HASCO) which could potentially use the company's technology against it in the future. However, in the no-holds-barred tussle to stake a claim in the world's largest automotive market (i.e., China), it could be argued that Continental has little choice but to trade its coveted technology for precious market share.

Continental's twin drivers of success: technical progress and lean

As mentioned earlier, Bosch's exit of the foundation brakes business had paved the way for Continental's dominance of the global braking systems industry. However, this is not to suggest Continental had obtained its position by chance. The company, has over the past few decades, been a key innovator in the industry. For instance, Continental asserts that it was the first supplier to place the microprocessor-based ABS through series production in 1984, underscoring its confidence in what was then perceived to be unproven newfangled technology (Continental, 2006). Continental is now attempting to cement its grip on the global braking systems market through its latest ContiGuard technology. The company asserts that its ContiGuard technology integrates safety technologies, sophisticated sensors and advanced telematics in a modular platform, with a high degree of scalability. Moreover, Continental mentions that ContiGuard is able to exploit the full potential of safety components like ABS, ESC and driver assistance systems. It adds that through collating all relevant data on road conditions, ContiGuard is also capable of giving early warnings of hazardous situations. Over the past few years, ContiGuard's situational awareness has taken a leap forward through the introduction of a 360° surround view system, which is an intricate amalgamation of radar and camera technology. The sophisticated features evident in Continental's increasingly intelligent ContiGuard system are essentially the cornerstones for the company's still in development autonomous vehicle system (Continental, 2012; Continental, 2017; Crowe, 2013).

Continental was able to evolve this cutting-edge technology at a rapid pace partly due to its judicious acquisition of Siemens VDO. Further, the company's relentless investment in R&D has also given it a considerable competitive advantage; between 2000 and 2015, Continental's R&D investment increased nearly seven fold from €374.2 million to €2.4496 billion (US$2.7191 billion) (Continental, 2000; Continental 2015). Leveraging on this expanded, bountiful R&D war chest, Continental has continued its unyielding drive to push the very frontiers of technical progress. In April 2016, Continental launched its new high-efficiency braking system, the MK C1; this new system can generate tremendous braking pressure significantly faster than conventional hydraulic brakes, in the process, delivering not only considerably faster braking but also significantly reduced braking distances. MK C1's remarkable breaking qualities also make it ideal in supporting the development of Continental's increasingly automated driving systems. Further, the unconventionally light MK C1 reduces a vehicle's overall weight, granting it greater fuel efficiency and lower carbon emissions; these traits are coveted by mainstream automakers, in their race to market increasing numbers of fuel-efficient and environmentally-friendly vehicles to the general motorist, who desires the aforementioned qualities (with fuel efficiency usually at the top of the pecking order) (Continental, 2016).

Despite being a relatively late adaptor of lean (Continental adapted it only in 2006), Continental has effectively leveraged lean to great effect. Continental's Regensburg facility now ranks among the best plants across Europe when it comes to implementing lean production. Since the implementation of lean at the Regensburg facility, set-up times for its manufacturing cells (from 2009 to 2011) have declined to nearly half their previous levels. Further, its manufacturing cells have been designed to enable scalability, so they can be easily configured for variations in demand levels; this practice is fundamentally driven by the lean philosophy of eliminating waste and optimising the use of resources/processes (Continental, 2011; Womack and Jones, 2003). Continental's staunch commitment to lean is evidenced by the fact that from 2009–2011, it sent more than 2,000 employees to the various courses offered by the Lean Academy (Continental, 2011).

Bosch: profile

Bosch is currently the world's largest automotive components supplier, with approximately 375,000 employees worldwide (by 31 December 2015), easily dwarfing Continental and ZF. The company traces its roots back to 1886 when Robert Bosch founded the 'Workshop for Precision Mechanics and Electrical Engineering' in Stuttgart. By the commencement of 2016, Bosch was the world's second largest braking systems supplier with an estimated global market share of 27.6 percent; the company possesses significant expertise in automotive electronics and high-tech braking systems. In 2015, Bosch posted overall revenues of about €70.6 billion (US$78.4 billion), eclipsing those of its key rivals, Continental and ZF. In terms of revenue, Bosch is in fact considerably bigger than some automakers such as PSA and Renault which recorded 2015 revenues of €54.7 billion and €45.3 billion respectively. The company also recorded a 2015 net income of €3.537 billion (US$3.926 billion). Bosch's braking systems business is part of its Mobility Solutions division, which alone generated nearly 60 percent (about €41.7 billion) of total 2015 revenues (Figure 6.3); this leviathan's braking systems business posted estimated 2015 revenues of €5.33 billion, which comprised 12.8 percent and 7.6 percent of divisional and overall revenues respectively (Bosch, 2015). Despite having 440 subsidiaries in some

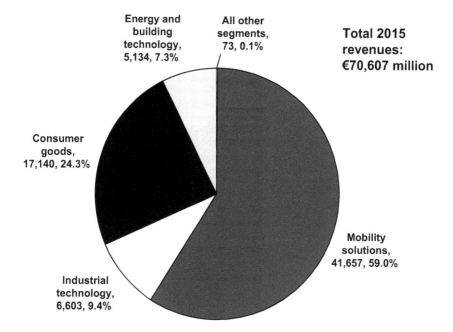

Figure 6.3 Bosch's 2015 annual revenues (€ million)

*The Mobility Solutions division includes braking systems

Source: 2015 The Bosch Group Annual Report

60 countries (if its trading and service partners are included, Bosch is represented in about 150 countries), Bosch drew a disproportionate 52.9 percent (about €37.3 billion) of its revenues from Europe in 2015 (Figure 6.4) (Bosch, 2015; PSA, 2015; Renault, 2015).

In 2015, Bosch's R&D expenditures amounted to €6.378 billion (US$7.0796 billion), significantly higher than the DM2.04 billion (about US$1.19 billion) it recorded in 1990 (Bosch, 2015; Bosch, 1991). This exponential increase in its research costs is one of the key reasons Bosch must embark on a relentless acquisition campaign to seek ever-increasing economies of scale and scope. Up until 2012, Bosch was the world's largest supplier of braking systems. However in September 2009, Bosch divested its North American foundation brakes business (the deal encompassed relatively low margin braking components such as brake calipers, disk brakes and drum brakes) with estimated revenues of US$580 million to Japan's Akebono for a relatively low US$10 million (Associated Press, 2009; Beene, 2009; TireBusiness.com, 2009). In January 2012, Bosch divested the remaining parts of its foundation brakes business (it had 2010 sales of €850 million (US$1.1 billion)) to KPS for €200 million (US$255.56 million) (Huebner and Burger, 2012). The fact that Bosch was willing to divest its entire foundation brakes business for relatively low prices underscored its lack of confidence in the growth prospects of this business; Bosch is of the opinion braking systems which encompasses high-tech brakes, sensors and driver assistance systems are sui generis and could prove extremely lucrative.

Nonetheless, it is still too early to conclude whether Bosch has made the right decision to leave the foundation brakes business (after all, they are regarded as

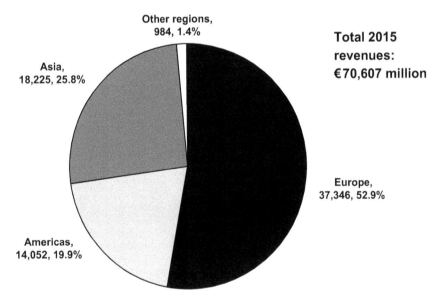

Figure 6.4 Bosch's 2015 revenues by region (€ million)

Source: 2015 The Bosch Group Annual Report

a critical building block for developing high-tech braking systems such as ABS, ESC and TCS). It is possible Bosch could be sacrificing short-term market share for long-term growth, as it is focusing increasing resources on cutting-edge braking systems and electronics that could give the company a significant competitive advantage in the future; being the world's largest automotive components company also gives it the immense financial wherewithal to pursue its ambition and any strategy which it deems necessary. Further, the fact that Bosch still retains easy access to foundation brake technologies through its 9.3 percent equity stake (making it the second largest shareholder after Toyota) in Akebono, the buyer of its North American foundation brakes business probably explains its lack of concern over exiting the business (TireBusiness.com, 2009; Akebono, 2015).

Moreover, Bosch with its yearly procurement spend of €27 billion (US$29.97 billion) is in an unassailable position to exert inordinate pressure on its own suppliers, in a manner akin to automakers assertively flexing their financial muscle in price negotiations (a clear illustration of the cascade effect) (Bosch, 2016); Bosch's procurement budget is not only the largest among the braking systems makers but also the highest among all the five subsectors covered in this book. However, with first-tier suppliers such as Bosch accounting for an increasing value of today's automobile and their rising procurement budgets (due to acquisitions), there is possibly a steady shift in the 'balance of power' with automakers no longer being able to exert the same degree of influence on these gargantuan suppliers. For instance, following the eruption of the global financial crisis in 2007, many automakers dramatically cut back production but with the unexpected resurgence of global demand (particularly in North America) in 2010, they suddenly found themselves short of components. In such instances, according to an industry analyst, some suppliers actually told their automaker clients: 'either you pay our price or we will not deliver' (Schafer, 2011); this situation provides irrevocable evidence of the arrival of the age of mega suppliers, with their increasing power to dictate the rules of the game in the global automotive value chain.

Bosch's acquisitions since the 1980s

Bosch has made several acquisitions over the past two decades. In fact, the company has a venture capital division (Robert Bosch Venture Capital) to make strategic acquisitions, targeting specifically smaller companies with innovative new technologies; this, to some degree, concurs with TK Quinn's argument that small companies, not big corporations, are the source of innovation (Bosch, 2011; Quinn 1953). Bosch had reportedly allocated €8 billion in net cash at the beginning of 2010 to fund acquisitions although it appears to be more selective nowadays (Urquhart, 2010). Since 1996, Bosch has acquired several companies with significant expertise in all the components that braking systems comprise. For instance, Bosch acquired the brake systems division (the light vehicle hydraulic brakes and ABS) of Allied Signal in 1996 for US$1.5 billion. Through this acquisition, Bosch secured another 24 production facilities employing about 11,000 people in Brazil, France, Italy, Mexico, Poland, Portugal, Spain, Turkey and the US, and through JVs in China, India and Korea. These plants manufactured disc and drum brakes, master cylinders, proportioning valves, vacuum pumps and boosters, rotors and hubs, foundation brakes and ABS.

This acquisition of Allied Signal's braking systems division is not only one of Bosch's biggest acquisitions over the last two decades but also represents one of its most significant steps towards becoming a vertically integrated company in braking systems. This acquisition was crucial for ensuring Bosch's long-term competitiveness in the braking systems subsector, as Bosch's then key ABS competitors, ITT Automotive, Lucas Industries Inc., Varity Kelsey-Hayes and GM's Delphi Automotive Systems were already offering complete braking systems. Additionally, this acquisition established Bosch as the world's leading ABS supplier with more than a third (about 35 percent) of the braking systems market (includes ABS and foundation brakes), placing it significantly ahead of its nearest competitor, ITT, which then had 28 percent of this market; ITT's automotive brake and chassis operations were subsequently acquired by Continental for a reported US$1.93 billion in 1998 (WardsAuto, 1996; Continental, 1998). Despite the pioneering work Bosch had done in ABS, it, like its other key competitors, still had to rely heavily on acquisitions to bolster their respective market positions in the then rapidly growing ABS and braking systems market.

This relentless consolidation in the braking systems industry during the mid to late-1990s was largely driven by demands from automakers looking for first-tier suppliers with a global footprint, as they expanded their operations beyond their traditional stomping grounds of Europe and North America (Bloomberg, 1996). This trend was reaffirmed by the following statement from Victor Rice, Varity's Chief Executive who also became CEO of the then newly-formed LucasVarity PLC: 'I don't believe you can compete in the auto-parts business unless you're a global supplier'. Rice also commented on the limited reach of Lucas and Varity prior to their merger: 'if you look at Varity, it was a North American supplier. And at best, Lucas was a European supplier' (quoted in Bloomberg, 1996). This is further evidenced by the fact, that prior to their merger, Varity's key brake customers were the American automakers comprising GM, Chrysler and Ford, while Lucas' major customers were the European carmakers made up of Volkswagen, BMW and Renault (Bloomberg, 1996).

Later, in 2005, Bosch secured majority control of its JV partner, Kalyani Brakes Ltd by raising its stake in the company from 40 percent to 79 percent in a deal valued at US$63.9 million; Kalyani's case validates again the increasing use of JVs as a first step towards acquisition (Upadhyaya, 2005). Kalyani Brakes was a manufacturer of conventional braking systems and components for passenger cars, tractors, three-wheelers and two-wheelers in its plants in Jalgaon, Chakan and Manesar; at its acquisition, Kalyani employed about 1,800 associates and in the fiscal year 2004/2005 generated revenues of €63 million. Moreover, Bosch acquired its Melbourne-based brake components supplier Pacifica Group in two key stages; the first stage involved acquiring 75.3 percent share in Melbourne-based Pacifica Group for AUS$235m (US$182.19 million) in 2007 while the second stage culminated in the acquisition of Pacifica's remaining shares in 2009. In Australia, Pacifica was a supplier of braking systems for Toyota, Ford, GM's Holden unit and Mitsubishi. It also supplied brakes to GM in North America for light trucks and had plants in China and Thailand, as well as the US and Europe.

Further, in 2007, Bosch bolstered its brakes business in the Americas by acquiring Delphi Corporation's brake components business in Saltillo, Mexico for US$15 million (Bosch was able to secure control of Delphi's brake components business in Mexico for this discounted price, as Delphi had entered Chapter 11 in 2005 and was still undergoing restructuring in 2007) (Delphi, 2005; Automotive News, 2007). Through these acquisitions, Bosch was able to bolster its market share and potential bargaining position in future negotiations with leading automakers. Moreover, in 2007, Bosch acquired the brake friction business of Chicago-based Morse Automotive Corporation; this division of Morse produced pads for disc brakes and linings for drum brakes, as well as brake calipers, mainly for the North American market (Rauwald, 2008). The acquisition of Morse's brake friction facilitated Bosch's entry into the production of brake pads. Bosch's push into the brake pads market is driven by the increasing aftermarket demand for these components. To meet this rising demand, Bosch has increased the production of brake pads by 12 million units at its plant in Juarez, Mexico towards the end of 2011; the company, in 2016, also commenced a US$30 million expansion of its brake plant in Aguascalientes, Mexico to augment existing production of ABS and stability control systems. It has also constructed a new €120 million plant in Nanjing, China which produces an estimated 80 million brake pads annually from 2015 (Bosch, 2011; Bosch, 2013; Sedgwick, 2016).

These successive acquisitions greatly bolstered Bosch's vertically integrated structure, giving it capabilities at virtually every stage of the braking systems industry, while strengthening its market share in Australia, India and the US; these bolt-on acquisitions (ranging from US$15 million to around US$200 million) are also generally considerably smaller than Bosch's acquisitions in earlier years and this trend of making smaller targeted purchases (to acquire new technologies, capabilities and markets) instead of outright multi-billion-dollar acquisitions is also exhibited in the other sectors analysed in this book. Although Bosch had painstakingly built up its braking systems business (comprising foundation brakes, ABS, TCS and ESC) over the past few decades, it has proven equally ruthless in carving out the low-margin foundation brakes business in 2012, in order to focus resources on the more lucrative ABS, TCS, ESC and predictive braking systems. To bolster its competences in high-tech braking systems, Bosch acquired ZF's 50 percent stake in a 50:50 ZF-Bosch JV known as ZF Lenksysteme GmbH (ZFLS) in January 2015; this JV, which was formed in 1999, generated 2014 revenues of €4.4 billion. The JV has been incorporated into Bosch and is now known as Robert Bosch Automotive Steering GmbH (Boston, 2014; Bosch, 2015). The acquisition highlights the effectiveness of using JVs as a springboard to eventual acquisition, as it allows potential acquirers to evaluate their desired partners, products and markets.

Key to Bosch's market dominance: cutting-edge technical progress and lean

Bosch has consistently occupied a dominant role in the global braking systems industry by playing the role of industry pioneer. For instance, it was the first to launch the ABS system in 1978 (it was introduced through the Mercedes-Benz-S class in that same year) and produced its 200 millionth ABS system by 2009; today, Bosch is the number one supplier of ABS to automakers (Bosch, 2003; Ganesh, 2010; Bosch, 2009). When Bosch first introduced the ABS in 1978, the automakers were generally not receptive and Bosch endured losses in the first decade of introducing the ABS (Muller, 2005). The company followed up quickly in the field of high-tech braking systems by introducing the TCS in 1986. It subsequently pioneered the ESC in 1995 and was also the first supplier to introduce ESC through the Mercedes-Benz S-Class sedan in 1995 (Liebemann et al., 2005). By 2003, Bosch had delivered more than 100 million ABS worldwide and barely two years later, it accounted for 30 percent of ABS systems found in cars globally (Muller, 2005). Riding this rising innovation wave, Bosch easily accounted for 32 percent of the global ESC market by 2007 (iSuppli, 2008).

Despite having ceded the position of industry leader to Continental, Bosch intends to remain the market leader in the far more lucrative, ABS, TCS and ESC segments as they evolve into more advanced active safety and collision avoidance technologies with significantly greater prevalence and profitability. Due to increasingly stringent government requirements, these braking systems that Bosch pioneered invariably experienced significant rises in their installation rates between 2010 and 2015. For instance, by 2015, 90 percent of all new vehicles globally would be equipped with ABS, up from 75 percent in 2010 (Murphy, 2009b; Bosch, 2011); by November 2014, ESC would also be fitted as standard equipment in all new vehicles throughout the EU (in 2012, 72 percent of all newly registered cars and light commercial vehicles in Europe were equipped with ESC) (Bosch, 2012). Bosch's strategic intent of focusing on these high value-added braking systems is confirmed by its 2012 press release which stated: 'Bosch's brake operations will be focused on brake boosters and brake control systems (i.e., ABS, TCS and ESC)' (Bosch, 2012).

By 2016, Bosch had made and delivered around 150 million ESC/ESP systems, since it started producing it in 1995. Moreover, the company has over 600 engineers working on the above technologies (European Patent Office, 2016). Today, Bosch strives assiduously to be at the forefront of predictive braking systems development, by transforming existing (albeit relatively sophisticated) driver assistance systems into next-generational game-changing automated driving technology, unimaginable a decade earlier. Bosch asserts that its predictive emergency braking system can prevent up to two-thirds of rear-end crashes (at speeds not exceeding 30 km/h) that could result in injury and vehicular damage; in avoidable incidents with casualties (assuming comparable velocities with the former scenario), the company declares an impressive prevention rate of up to 72 percent. The tremendous strides made by Bosch in developing these automated braking systems are essentially paving the way for a future dominated by autonomous vehicles (Bosch, 2017). This strategy of making increasingly intelligent components has become sine qua non among the contesting first-tier suppliers seeking higher margins and industry hegemony; the unrelenting rise of this digitisation trend as industry dogma is evidenced in the following statements from market analysts: 'increased electronics content is especially important to high-tech suppliers' and 'driverless cars provide an opportunity to either make or lose an awful lot of money. The companies that understand and best prepare for this new world will win over those that don't' (Klier and Rubenstein, 2008: 362; Mui, 2013: 2). However, the increasing complexities of these technologies would unremittingly exacerbate the already astronomical cost of developing them. This would, in turn, drive firms such as Bosch to make further acquisitions to secure greater scale economies.

Bosch has also successfully applied its cutting-edge technology to the now increasingly prevalent lean manufacturing system. For instance, Bosch augmented its just-in-time process by integrating radio-frequency identification (RFID) to raise production accuracy and reliability, monitor progress and alleviate the cost of collating data involved in churning out smaller batches. This application of RFID to just-in-time was first tried out at Bosch's Homburg plant, in the process further reducing inventories which were already low by lean manufacturing standards. Subsequent inventory replenishment was achieved through the automatic capture of production information by 27 RFID gates that are connected to core SAP software, which reports the precise location (with the exact timing) where intermediate goods are required. The required materials are then delivered just-in-time from a warehouse four miles away, thus further reducing the need for costly buffer inventories. With this system in place, Bosch was able to plan its replenishment route for the Homburg plant with relative ease (SAP, 2009). Bosch quickly deployed this augmented lean solution at its Bamberg plant and was able to replicate the success it had with the Homburg plant. Using eight RFID gates, products are registered as they pass designated points and this information is immediately forwarded to Bosch's enterprise resource planning (ERP) system. Consequently, the entire production process at Bosch's Bamberg plant was rendered more transparent, and the planning process was greatly simplified. Since the introduction of this system in 2008, Bosch has saved more than US$1.4 billion annually (SAP, 2009); these considerable savings could be used for further R&D and/or acquisitions.

ZF: profile

ZF was founded in September 1915 as a maker of gears and transmissions for aircraft, boats and vehicles (ZF, 2015a). However, ZF became the third largest global braking systems supplier (with an estimated 18 percent market share) through its bold €10.09 billion all cash acquisition of TRW in May 2015; the acquisition was the largest in ZF's corporate history and the merged entity, ZF TRW, became a ZF division. The fact that ZF was willing to make an all cash offer for TRW underscored the confidence which the company had in this acquisition; financial research asserts that cash offers not only indicate the significant value which the acquirer associates with its bid but also the confidence that the target company would be a profitable entity with the desired synergies once it is assimilated into its fold (Fishman, 1989).

With this acquisition, ZF was able to gain control of a braking systems empire which TRW spent the past two decades building. This acquisition also nearly doubled ZF recorded revenues to approximately €29.2 billion (about US$32.5 billion) in December 2015 from €18.4 billion in the same period the earlier year. From 2014 to 2015, the firm's net income also nearly doubled, growing from €672 million to €1.019 billion (US$1.135 billion). ZF's braking systems business is part of its Active & Passive Safety Technology division (the firm's biggest business segment) which accounted for 30.7 percent (€ 8.94 billion) of its total revenues in 2015 (Figure 6.5); for that year, the firm's braking systems business alone generated €3.49 billion in revenues, which comprised 39 percent and 12 percent of divisional and overall revenues respectively. Unlike Bosch which focuses on high-tech braking systems and related electronics, ZF still retains significant foundation brakes operations. On 31 December 2015, ZF had 138,269

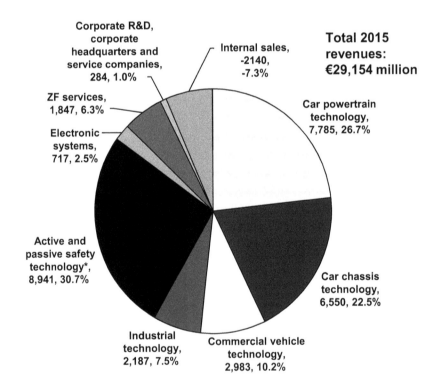

Figure 6.5 ZF's 2015 annual revenues (€ million)

*The Active & Passive Safety Technology division includes braking systems

Source: 2015 ZF Annual Report

full-time employees spread across 230 facilities in 40 countries (ZF, 2014; ZF, 2015b; **ZF, 2015c**).

In 2015, ZF drew nearly half of its revenues (47.4 percent or €13.82 billion) from Europe, as evidenced in Figure 6.6. The remaining regions, North America (NAFTA), South America, Asia Pacific and Africa accounted for 27.8 percent (€8.12 billion), 2.2 percent (€0.63 billion), 21.8 percent (€ 6.36 billion) and 0.8 percent (€0.22 billion) of overall sales respectively (Figure 6.6) (ZF, 2015b).

In 2015, ZF's purchasing expenditure of €18.056 billion (US$20.11 billion) was smaller than Bosch's €27 billion (US$29.97 billion) but larger than Continental's €17.4 billion (US$19.3 billion) (ZF 2015b; Bosch, 2015; Continental, 2015). Over a single financial year (from 2014 to 2015), ZF's purchasing spend had increased by over €7 billion. This significant rapid increase in ZF's purchasing expenditure was the product of its TRW acquisition. However, this massive spike in ZF's purchasing spend also greatly extended its leverage over its suppliers; in an industry faced with ever-increasing operational costs, this considerable market leverage is now sine qua non in lowering a firm's cost base and increasing its overall profitability.

ZF/TRW's acquisitions since the 1990s

ZF's current market position in the braking systems industry is undeniably due to its assimilation of TRW's operations and technology. The company's acquisition of TRW was a bold 'bet-the-firm' strategy in an industry, where M&A strategies nowadays typically involve bolt-on acquisitions (valuations rarely exceed a

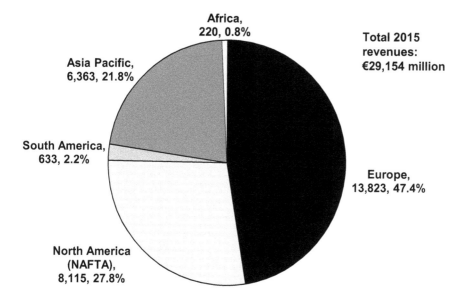

Figure 6.6 ZF's 2015 revenues by region (€ million)

Source: 2015 ZF Annual Report

few hundred million dollars) in which the acquirer tends to buy only divisions which it needs. However, it could be argued that ZF and TRW were essentially compelled to merge, as it is the only way that they could swiftly gain scale economies needed to compete against significantly larger rivals, Continental and Bosch. Even after the merger, ZF is still markedly smaller than Continental and Bosch; in terms of overall 2015 revenues, Bosch is still easily double that of ZF's, which gives the former a distinct edge in an industry where financial muscle is increasingly the arbiter of success (ZF, 2015b; Bosch, 2015). The following sections present TRW's earlier acquisition and JV strategies which were instrumental to the rise of its acquirer, ZF as a marquee braking systems supplier.

Like its acquirer ZF, TRW had entered the braking systems industry via a sizeable acquisition. TRW had penetrated the market through its acquisition of LucasVarity PLC (then the world's second largest maker of automotive brakes after Bosch) in 1999 for a then whopping US$6.6 billion, outbidding a competing offer from the Federal-Mogul Corporation; this proved that a timely acquisition could facilitate a company's entry into a new sector (The New York Times, 1999). LucasVarity itself was a product of a relentless centralisation of capital: UK's Lucas Industries Inc. had acquired Varity Corp. of the US for US$2 billion in June 1996, forming LucasVarity PLC (the deal combined Varity's Kelsey-Hayes ABS and truck diesel-engine expertise with Lucas' strength in diesel parts and disc brakes) (Bloomberg, 1996). TRW's acquisition of LucasVarity gave it the ability to provide entire front-end systems for cars by combining LucasVarity brakes and TRW's steering and suspension parts, thus making TRW's products more appealing to automakers that are increasingly looking for suppliers capable of supplying entire modular systems (The New York Times, 1999).

By acquiring LucasVarity, TRW also gained control of the brake operations of Kelsey-Hayes which was earlier acquired by Varity in 1987 for US$577 million in cash and securities. However, with the acquisition of Varity by Lucas Industries in 1996, Kelsey-Hayes was reorganised as a subsidiary of LucasVarity (International Directory of Company Histories, 1999); despite its revamped status as a LucasVarity subsidiary, Kelsey-Hayes still did not have the scale economies to compete in the fast-consolidating braking systems market and the company could not sustain its competitiveness in the fast-expanding ABS market whose products were becoming cheaper by the day (Klier and Rubenstein, 2008). The tremendous scale economies needed to compete in the increasingly complex global braking systems markets (particularly in the then burgeoning ABS market) eventually led to the acquisition of LucasVarity by TRW. However, this acquisition of LucasVarity pushed TRW's debt load to a colossal US$9.3 billion (Reference for Business, 2016).

Even over the past decade, TRW continued to push ahead with its strategy to become a comprehensive brake systems provider, as opposed to Bosch which had already divested its foundation brakes business. For instance, in 2008, TRW acquired part of Delphi's North American brake component machining and module assembly assets (encompasses production inventory) for around US$40 million. Further, TRW has leased part of Delphi's former brake manufacturing facility in Saginaw, Michigan (TRW, 2008). This acquisition not only boosted TRW's assets but also strengthened its capabilities and human capital, demonstrating that acquisitions are an effective means of securing the talent needed to compete in an increasingly technologically complex braking systems market. TRW's acquisition strategy appears to be highly-focused, suggesting that its management did not have any empire-building tendencies; the company's acquisitions greatly augmented its braking systems capabilities despite adding on considerable debt.[5]

ZF/TRW's JV strategy

Besides acquisitions, TRW also utilised JVs to advance its overall growth strategy and secure greater scale economies. TRW formed a JV in India (through TRW's Lucas subsidiary) as far back as 1962. This Indian JV known as Brakes India Limited was forged with TVS Sundram Group; in 2011, TRW had a 49 percent in this JV, which generated an annual revenue of US$688.6 million (TRW, 2010; TRW, 2011). Further, in 1996, TRW forged a 50–50 JV (known as SM-Sistemas Modulares Ltda.) with Dana Limited in Brazil (TRW, 2011; Dana, 2011). Moreover, in 2005, TRW formed a 50–50 JV (known as CSG TRW Chassis Systems Co., Ltd.) with China South Industries Group Corporation to make advanced braking and steering systems for China's burgeoning automotive market (TRW, 2005). However, as mentioned earlier in the Continental analysis, there is also considerable intellectual property risk involved in JVs, particularly if there is a significant technical/commercial expertise gap between the two partners. Further, there is the issue of control, particularly if TRW is not the controlling partner in the JV. Nonetheless, as evidenced in the earlier analysis of GKN, JVs could serve as a first step to eventual acquisition if circumstances permit (e.g., relaxation of regulations, a partner that is willing to divest).

ZF/TRW's technical progress and pragmatic lean strategy

TRW being a highly-focused braking systems provider (compared to the far more diversified Bosch) had achieved significant technical progress in braking technologies. Its technical achievements ranged from seemingly plain-vanilla foundation brakes (includes calipers) to high-tech ESC systems. TRW's technical progress was also the outcome of its commitment to R&D; its R&D expenses rose nearly five-fold, from US$167 million in 2000 to an untenable US$957 million in 2014; it was also this exponential rise in much needed R&D investment that compelled TRW to seek further acquisitions to gain increasing economies of scale and scope (TRW, 2003; TRW, 2014). After its subsequent acquisition by ZF, the merged company's R&D expenditure rose even further to €1.39 billion (US$1.51 billion), a critical expense in an increasingly technologically exacting industry, which an independent TRW could no longer afford on its own.

In the case of calipers, TRW developed two caliper designs (the 'FBC' and the 'Opposed Piston Caliper') in recent years to meet increasing requirements for greater brake output and improved performance with regard to the mitigation of noise, vibration and harshness. Besides providing superior brake performance, both calipers are made of aluminium or composite to achieve the lowest weight possible, and they also come with residual drag reducing features; this design facilitates CO2 emission reduction and promotes greater fuel efficiency (TRW, 2012b).

TRW's superior innovation also enabled it to become the first firm to develop and market the Electric Park Brake (EPB) on a mass production vehicle in 2001 (there are more than 10 million TRW EPB systems on today's roads globally). With TRW's EPB, vehicles would not only dispense with the parking brake lever or pedal but also experienced gains in vehicle styling, space management and crashworthiness. It also interacts with stability control to enable a full four-wheel ABS stop. Further TRW's EPB system is designed to reduce drag and save weight (greatly improving fuel efficiency) as opposed to traditional mechanical parking brake systems that do not have this feature. Moreover, TRW's ESC system is an intelligent system capable of applying automatic brake pressure to the relevant wheels and even reducing (if necessary) engine throttle to realign the vehicle with the driver's intended route, if it detects a potential loss of vehicle control. Additionally, TRW's latest ESC system (i.e., the EBC460) offers more technical capabilities, such as the reduction of noise, vibration and harshness along with the promotion of increased motor lifetime and interactivity with other ESC sensors. It also enables regenerative braking, which not only recovers a significant amount of the vehicle's kinetic energy but also transforms it into electricity that could be used to recharge its batteries (TRW, 2012a; Lampton, 2012). Given these superlative technical specifications, it is evident that these products are not only geared towards promoting greater safety but also increasing fuel efficiency (TRW, 2012a).

Flushed with exuberance and enhanced financial muscle following the merger between ZF and TRW in 2015, the newly consolidated firm pressed forward with its overriding ambition to scale the technical heights of this increasingly sophisticated braking systems industry. In October 2015, ZF announced that its innovative Integrated Brake Control System (IBC) would be commercially available by 2018. This state-of-the-art system, developed to supplant existing ESC and vacuum brake boosting systems, can bolster conventional safe-braking and semi-automated driving capabilities; through the IBC, vehicles can generate extreme brake pressure in less than 150 milliseconds (the industry average is about 300–400 milliseconds), significantly reducing braking distances. Further, the IBC is designed to address the significant technical demands of autonomous vehicles, should they enter the mainstream in the near future (ZF, 2015d; ZF, 2016; Meyer, 2015).

In its earlier form as TRW, the company, like its key competitors, actively used lean to lower costs and bolster its productivity and competitiveness. The company adopted lean in the 2000–2001 period. For instance, during this period, TRW restructured its caliper remanufacturing line by replacing the batch production approach (this approach has large amounts of work-in-progress (WIP) between each process operation, thus needing a larger floor area) with the lean manufacturing system. This revamp quickly removed all WIP between each process, enabling better control and operator utilisation throughout each line. Moreover, lean has improved material handling and process flow at TRW. For instance, packing was shifted to the end of each line when it was previously carried out in a central packaging area, which occasionally led to finished assemblies being placed in the wrong boxes. The new layout brought about by lean has saved at least 750 miles of forklift traffic per year. Resultantly, TRW began shipping daily to its distribution sites in Chicago and New Jersey direct from the end of the new assembly lines, thus reducing the possibility of double handling to and from the warehouse and prime pick areas (TRW, 2001). The significant achievements rendered by lean are evidenced in the following statements by David Bourne, manufacturing development manager, TRW: 'we reduced the number of assembly lines from ten to seven and increased capacity from 250,000 to 309,000 units per shift' and 'this reduction of assembly lines enabled us to open up 11,400 square feet of floor space for future development – a major improvement', and 'overall team morale has appreciably improved' (quoted in TRW, 2001).

Superior technical innovation (coupled with superlative processes) has become a critical means of product differentiation for TRW and its competitors. However, to stay at the forefront of this technological innovation, TRW would need to continue investing increasing funds in R&D. This would also entail securing ever-increasing scale economies (to alleviate rising cost pressures) and new capabilities (via acquisitions), further compounding the cascade effect. Given this situation, it was clear that TRW was no longer capable of competing effectively against its larger rivals (i.e., Continental and Bosch) with their significantly larger R&D budgets and this inevitably led to its merger with ZF.

4. Consolidation among the lower-tier braking systems makers

Over the past two-three decades, the global braking systems industry has experienced considerable consolidation, resulting in today's highly oligopolistic industry structure dominated by three major players. These three oligopolists are increasingly focusing their resources on developing high-tech (and higher margin) braking systems (hydraulic brakes supported by ABS, ESC and TCS), while giving relatively less attention to the relatively low-margin foundation brakes business. In the case of Bosch, it has exited the foundation brakes business entirely in January 2012. However, it is now the lower-tier suppliers such as Akebono, Hyundai Mobis, Mando, Hitachi, Brembo, ADVICS and CBI that are experiencing relatively greater consolidation, as they strive to gain the economies of scale and scope needed to compete in an increasingly oligopolistic market structure plagued by declining profit margins; unlike the 'big three' (i.e., Continental, Bosch and ZF), they are mostly focused on foundation brakes but have weaker expertise in high-tech braking systems.

Akebono, founded in 1929, has relied largely on organic growth since its inception and achieved revenues of US$2.1 billion in 2015 (Akebono, 2015).

It has made a few acquisitions since the 1990s. In 1996, Akebono acquired a 30 percent stake in P.T. Tri Dharma Wisesa in Indonesia. However, it increased its stake in the firm to 50 percent in 2006 and eventually changed its subsidiary's name to PT Akebono Brake Astra Indonesia to reflect its new status as an Akebono facility. Nonetheless, it was Akebono's US$10 million acquisition of Bosch's North American foundation brakes business in 2009 that proved to be a turning point in the company's history[6]; the fact that Bosch was willing to divest its North American foundation brakes business for only US$10 million reflected the company's disillusionment with the foundation brakes business and its resolve to focus its resources on developing its significantly higher-margin high-tech braking systems business (TireBusiness.com, 2009; Akebono, 2012). With this acquisition, Akebono quickly positioned itself to become the world's largest producer of foundation brakes (with a 40 percent market share), a position once occupied by Continental. However, it is important to note that Bosch has been the second largest shareholder in Akebono since 1999 (Bosch currently holds a 9.3 percent stake, making it the largest shareholder after Toyota, which has a 11.4 percent shareholding) (Akebono, 2015). Thus, the above divestment could represent 'just a transfer' of assets to an affiliate company. Bosch's equity stake also indicates the fact that the major industry leaders are already targeting the second-tier suppliers in the global braking systems market, in a ruthless centralisation of capital. Akebono is acutely aware of the importance of securing increasing scale economies in an era of rising automaker demands thus it is not letting up on its acquisition trail. In July 2014, Akebono acquired the remaining 45.7 percent stake in a JV (known as 'Sanyo Manufacturing') established along with Mitsubishi Motors, Hiruta Kogyo Co., Ltd and Asagoe Machine Mfg. Co., Ltd, in the process converting the JV into a fully-owned subsidiary. Upon conversion, the fully-owned subsidiary is expected to have desired synergies such as faster decision making. Moreover, it is positioned as Akebono's leading manufacturing facility in western Japan, with significant capabilities in the making of drum brakes and presses (Akebono, 2014).

In Korea, Hyundai Mobis, a leading supplier of braking systems to Hyundai and Kia (its affiliate companies), has over the past decade turned to acquisitions to spur growth; Hyundai Mobis is owned by Hyundai Motor Group and its affiliate, Kia Motors Corp (Hyundai Mobis, 2012; Courtenay, 2007). In 2005, Hyundai Mobis acquired the China-based brakes and steering division of Seohan Industry Company (the division was renamed Wuxi Mobis Automotive Parts Co. Ltd) in an attempt to bolster its presence in China, the world's fastest growing automotive market (Hyundai Mobis, 2008). That same year, the company also acquired a 38.3 percent stake in its smaller domestic competitor Korea Automotive Systems Co. (Kasco), a maker of braking, steering and power train systems for US$25.4 million; Hyundai Mobis eventually acquired the rest of Kasco in March 2007 and secured control of around 50 percent of the brakes market in Korea (Hyundai Mobis, 2005; Courtenay, 2005; Courtenay, 2007). Further, Hyundai Mobis' top domestic competitor, Mando was sold by South Korea's Halla Engineering & Construction to CCMP Capital Asia for approximately

US$446 million in 2000, soon after the 1997–1998 Asian financial crisis (Jin, 2008). However, Halla regained control of Mando in January 2008 when it acquired a 72.4 percent stake in the firm. Halla's renewed interest was sparked by Mando's profitability and significant operations in China and India, where its biggest customer, Hyundai Motor (accounted for 70 percent of Mando's sales in 2007) is one of the best-selling automakers. Earlier, Hyundai and US private equity firm, KKR had also expressed their interest in acquiring the firm (Tucker and Song, 2008).

Amidst this rampant consolidation, some second-tier braking system makers such as Hitachi have shrewdly rebranded themselves as lucrative niche players; Hitachi has positioned itself as a specialist provider of brake hoses. This is evidenced by its acquisition of the automotive brake-hose operations of a US-based Coupled Products LLC (a subsidiary of China-controlled Wanxiang (USA) Holdings) in February 2008. Following this acquisition, the company was renamed Hitachi Cable Florida, Inc. Hitachi launched the acquisition with the intent of strengthening its business with the Big Three automakers (i.e., GM, Ford, Chrysler) in North America. Through this acquisition, Hitachi was able to raise its sales of automotive hose assemblies in North America to an estimated US$180 million in 2008 from its earlier US$120 million. The acquisition also enabled Hitachi to secure control of 40 percent of the North American brake hose market and 20 percent of the overall global market for this component; by 2016, its share of the North American brake hose market rose to above 50 percent (Hitachi Cable, 2008; Meyer, 2008; ProMéxico, 2016). This specialisation strategy is becoming increasingly popular among large low-cost suppliers, who grow revenues via mass production of specific components (e.g., brake hoses), and derive profitability through the effective application of lean principles in their operations (Klier and Rubenstein, 2008).

In its drive to become a specialist brakes components supplier, Hitachi (in January 2012) tightened its control over Japan Brake Industrial Co. Ltd. (a maker of disc brake pads) by acquiring the 21.1 percent stake of Nissin Kogyo Co., Ltd.; prior to this acquisition, Hitachi already had a 73.4 percent stake in the company (Reuters, 2012). Due to its considerable 20 percent market share in the highly specialised brake hose market, Hitachi along with its alleged conspirators were charged by the US Justice Department antitrust division in 2014 with price fixing and bid rigging for the 2004–2009 period. Hitachi eventually pleaded guilty and paid a US$1.25 million fine (Tire Business, 2014). This incident reveals the dark side of rising market consolidation as increasing market power could lead to collusive cartel-like behaviour amongst firms. These circumstances would invariably trigger increasing regulatory scrutiny, and the corresponding punishment meted out for such corporate malfeasance.

Some industry players, however, have always been niche providers, developing exceptional capabilities that automakers are more than willing to pay premium prices for. For instance, Brembo, an Italian supplier, has traditionally focused on supplying braking systems to high-end European automobiles (particularly high performance vehicles) and prides itself as the widely-acknowledged creator of disc brakes for today's automobiles (Brembo, 2012a). The company is also one of the leading providers of brakes to Formula 1 and its superlative brake calipers have become indispensable to high-end sports cars such as Ferrari 488 GTB, Nissan GT-R, Lamborghini Aventador and the Dodge Viper SRT (Brembo, 2017). This niche approach has greatly limited its size compared to its larger rivals who target the mass market; Brembo's 2015 revenues of around €2.07 billion and pool of around 10,000 employees are a mere fraction of the financial resources and human capital wielded by the industry oligopolists (Brembo, 2015). The company for the most part of its existence has relied on organic growth. Brembo itself was not spared from the rising consolidation in the industry, when Kelsey-Hayes, a US brakes manufacturer acquired a significant stake in the firm; Brembo had agreed to this investment in the hope of gaining further scale economies needed to grow internationally. However, this partnership did not work out, and Brembo bought back Kelsey-Hayes' stake in 1993 (Brembo, 2012a).

By the beginning of this century, the company had decided to adopt acquisitions as a means of increasing its market presence. In early 2000, Brembo made an outright acquisition of Alfa Real Minas, to acquire superior capabilities in the development of automobile brake discs and engine flywheels assembly. Later that year, Brembo also acquired the British company AP Racing Limited for US$43 million to bolster its capabilities in the making of brake and clutch systems for high-performance sports vehicles, race cars and motorcycles (Brembo, 2012b; Grand Prix, 2000). In 2011, Brembo acquired another firm, Perdriel S.A., an Argentinian manufacturer of brake discs for €3.3 million. Perdriel S.A. had a workforce of about 150 and estimated revenues of €20 million (Brembo, 2011). Brembo had hoped to complement its increasing investment in Brazil (where it has 60 percent of the market for brake discs and drums) with this investment in Argentina, in the process strengthening its presence in South America (Brembo, 2011). To augment its presence in the critical Chinese market, Brembo also acquired a majority 66 percent stake in ASIMCO Meilian Braking Systems (Langfang) Co. Ltd. (a cast-iron brake discs maker based in Langfang in China's Hebei province) for an estimated €78 million in May 2016 (Brembo, 2016).

Japan's ADVICS, founded in 2001, is among one of the more aggressive second-tier brakes manufacturers that have turned to acquisitions to strengthen its market presence. The company recorded consolidated sales of US$4.4 billion in 2015 (ADVICS, 2016; Bloomberg, 2016). It was jointly founded by Aisin Seiki, Denso, Sumitomo Electric Industries and Toyota, to develop and sell braking systems and related components. Aisin Seiki has a 40 percent stake in ADVICS, while DENSO, Sumitomo Electric Industries Ltd and Toyota each have a 20 percent stake. This arrangement also reflects the convoluted nature of Japan's cross-shareholdings system, making acquisition by foreigners relatively difficult. In February 2003, ADVICS through its North American subsidiary made a 100 percent acquisition of Sumitomo Electric Industries Brakes Inc. and SAFA L.L.C. which are located in Ohio (US) and Georgia (US) respectively. Both companies were subsidiaries of its shareholder, Sumitomo Electric Industries Ltd, which probably facilitated ease of transaction (ADVICS, 2003; Supplier Business, 2008). These two acquisitions greatly bolstered ADVICS' capabilities and market presence in the US.

In February 2008, ADVICS acquired an 80 percent stake in Sumiden Brake S & E Inc. (S & E) from Sumitomo Electric Industries, Ltd. Prior to its acquisition, S & E was engaged in the sale of aftermarket components in Japan (ADVICS, 2008; Supplier Business, 2008). This acquisition significantly augmented ADVICS' presence in its domestic aftermarket. Soon after in July 2008, ADVICS' China subsidiary, ADVICS Tianjin Automobile Parts Co., Ltd. merged with Tianjin AISIN Automobile Parts Co., Ltd, with ADVICS holding a near controlling stake of 50.1 percent (ADVICS, 2007; ADVICS, 2010). This merger was executed to enable ADVICS to gain greater economies of scale and scope needed to compete in an increasingly competitive Chinese brakes market. ADVICS next acquired the Kariya plant (Aichi, Japan) and AS Brake Systems Inc. (Itami, Hyogo, Japan) from Aisin Seiki Co., Ltd in April 2010. It quickly followed up by acquiring AISIN Brake & Chassis, L.L.C. from Aisin Seiki Co., Ltd in July 2010 (ADVICS, 2010). The fact that Aisin Seiki was the single largest shareholder in ADVICS virtually ensured the smooth acquisition of these firms. Further by outsourcing the braking systems to ADVICS, Aisin Seiki could focus on its higher margin transmission (the company's core business) and navigation business. In ADVICS' case, there is no doubt that the company would not have been able to grow at this pace, if not for its aggressive acquisition strategy and the strong support of Aisin Seiki.

This industry has also borne witness to remarkable second acts, as evidenced by the phoenix-like regeneration of CBI. The aforementioned firm basically emerged from Bosch's divestment of the remnants of its foundation brakes business to US private equity firm, KPS in 2012. Barely after its formal inception in June 2012, CBI quickly acquired Autocast & Forge Pty Ltd, an Australian cast iron foundry, illustrating the firm's vertical integration strategy in the manufacture of foundation brakes; the ability to make specialised castings is a critical step in foundation brakes manufacturing. Despite its upstart status, CBI is now one of the world's top three foundation brakes owing to the strong foundations laid by Bosch. In 2015, CBI recorded revenues of €860 million. Today, CBI has 5,300 employees, along with 14 manufacturing facilities globally. Moreover, it has R&D technical centres in Europe, China, India, Brazil and Australia. CBI remains controlled by its acquirer, KPS, a private equity firm with over US$6 billion in assets under management (Australian Government Productivity Commission, 2012; CBI, 2015; CBI, 2016). The rise of CBI is also indicative of the increasing presence of non-traditional players (i.e., private equity) in the automotive components industry. Drawn by the sheer volume of M&A activity and the alluring prospect of significant returns in the automotive components industry, it is inevitable that private equity firms would be keen to enter the industry; in 2015 alone, the automotive components industry experienced a staggering US$32.9 billion worth of M&A transactions, far exceeding the relatively modest US$4.4 billion witnessed in 2010 (PwC, 2015).

From the above evidence, it is clear that there has been considerable consolidation even among the second-tier suppliers of braking systems for the last two to three decades. The degree of consolidation is already intensifying at an accelerated pace, as these suppliers scramble desperately to merge amongst themselves, in attempts to gain greater scale economies to alleviate rising pressures from automakers and defend themselves from the acquisition strategies of the first-tier suppliers (or even well-financed emerging market players keen to acquire well-honed technical capabilities); LucasVarity, prior to its acquisition by TRW, attempted to acquire Korea's Mando in 1998 (The Birmingham Post, 1998). However, it is doubtful that they would be able to compete against the likes of Continental and Bosch who have garnered overwhelming economies of scale and scope. These three oligopolists were able to gain their considerable market strength as they were the first to realise the importance of pursuing an aggressive acquisition strategy, which also allowed them to gain access to new technologies, markets and distribution channels.

The significantly larger revenues of the industry oligopolists also allow them to commit more resources to cutting-edge research, aggressive marketing campaigns and strengthening their brand value, thus augmenting their already considerable market strength. With the advent of the Global Business Revolution, firms from the emerging economies (e.g., China) have not been spared from the impact of the cascade effect. They too have been compelled to seek greater economies of scale and scope, better technologies, new distribution channels and markets in order to compete and survive in an increasingly oligopolistic global brakes market; in fact, the need to secure these factors is even more intense for firms from the emerging markets, as they need to breach an ever-increasing gap with their first and second-tier rivals from the developed markets.

5. Conclusion

The global braking systems industry has consolidated at a relentless pace since the 1980s. The leading players of the 1980s (e.g., Varity, ITT, Kelsey-Hayes) no longer exist as independent companies as they have been consolidated into the fold of their bigger and more aggressive competitors (i.e., Continental and ZF). Back in the 1980s, the global braking systems industry was still relatively fragmented, with several large independent brakes manufacturers such as Bosch, Delphi, Lucas, Varity, ITT and Kelsey-Hayes along with an even larger pool of smaller companies with insignificant market strength.

Today, the industry is highly oligopolistic, dominated by three key players that continue to strengthen their market power by means of acquisition and strong organic growth; as mentioned earlier, some first-tier suppliers basically entered the global brakes business by acquiring their competitors (e.g., TRW acquired the then newly combined LucasVariety in 1999). The smaller second-tier suppliers in the industry are the ones that failed to leverage on the acquisition wave of the 1980s/1990s; they were either too dependent on slower organic growth or did not have the financial muscle to make the necessary acquisitions. Some of them were also too specialised in their respective niches to gain the necessary scale economies needed for growth (e.g., Brembo was a specialist provider of brakes to high performance cars for most of its existence). However, in an increasingly oligopolistic market, some of these second-tier suppliers (e.g., Akebono, Brembo, ADVICS) are now becoming increasingly acquisitive, having recognised the importance of M&A as a means of securing economies of scale and scope, and gaining much-needed new technologies, distribution channels and market share. Further, a number of these second-tier suppliers (e.g., Hitachi) have used acquisitions to become specialist providers of high-volume yet critical brake components; they do not possess the financial muscle to compete head-on with the tier-one suppliers in the production of entire braking systems; thus, specialisation is a viable means of ensuring their survival. In view of the above evidence, it is clear that there is still considerable room for consolidation at the second-tier supplier level.

Despite their cognisance of the need for increasing acquisitions, it is questionable whether these second-tier suppliers would ever catch up with their first-tier counterparts. The first-tier suppliers have significant first-mover advantages in utilising acquisitions as a means of complementing their aggressive organic growth strategies. These acquisitions have allowed them to swiftly gain and exploit the economies of scale and scope needed to bolster their already considerable market shares. Further, their increased scale economies enabled them to strengthen their capabilities in all aspects (i.e., production, distribution, purchasing, R&D, finance and general management) (Chandler, 2004). To compete, the second-tier suppliers would have to make acquisitions of similar size (or make as many acquisitions) as these oligopolists. However, this would be extremely difficult, given that they do not have the requisite financial strength.

Further, even if these smaller suppliers were successful in making the desired acquisitions, they would still be considerably behind the existing oligopolists who have long since worked out all the bugs in the system (includes production, marketing, finance, R&D, international expansion). These oligopolists would again invest the considerable profits derived from their significant market positions into further acquisitions, expansion (e.g., building newer and more advanced facilities to boost production in new overseas markets, and establishing additional support infrastructure in these markets) and aggressive marketing activities which bolster their already dominant positions. However, the rapid consolidation in the global automotive components industry has not escaped the watchful eye of increasingly zealous regulatory authorities in the US, Europe and Japan, who are now actively monitoring the industry for collusive behaviour and related anti-competitive activities.

Notes

1 Foundation brakes remain the basic framework on which other braking systems could be developed. A foundation brake comprises the brake drum, spring actuator and the mechanical brake mechanism (encompasses both the brake shoes and friction material) (Ontario Ministry of Transportation, 2013; Catalog Auto, 2016).

2 ABS prevents the locking of wheels in the event of braking and maintains the vehicle's stability, thus ensuring that it comes to a quick but safe stop. ESC works by neutralising potential skidding (skidding and the subsequent lateral impact is one of the primary causes of severe and fatal road crashes) through vehicle stabilisation (this is achieved through the application of braking pressure to relevant wheels and if necessary, cutting engine power). TCS basically prevents wheel spin; in the event of a vehicle's wheels spinning, TCS works by reducing the engine's torque and if needed applying braking pressure surgically to individual wheels, so as to maintain the optimal slip of the driven wheels (Bosch, 2012).

3 The market shares of key players (i.e., Continental, Bosch and ZF) are estimates of an increasingly complex market which now encompasses various components such as foundation brakes, ABS, ESC, TCS, automatic brakes, hydraulic brakes, predictive brakes, regenerative brakes and their related sensors and actuators.

4 Bosch's stake in Akebono has since fallen to 9.3 percent, suggesting that it is not easy for Western firms to acquire a significant interest in Japanese firms with their convoluted cross-shareholding structures (Akebono, 2015).

5 This is opposed to the unfocussed and overly-aggressive acquisition strategies of empire-builders which often proved ruinous for their firms. William Durant, GM's founder was the 'classic empire-building financier'. Analysts are often scathing of Durant's strategy, asserting: 'He had absolutely no idea how to manage anything once he bought it. He therefore wound up with a dozen car companies, each managed separately with a high degree of product overlap' (Womack, Jones and Roos, 2007: 38).

6 Although Bosch North American foundation brakes business generated sales of US$580 million in 2009, it was reportedly unprofitable (TireBusiness.com, 2009; Murphy, 2012).

References

ADVICS Co., Ltd (2003) Acquisition of production plants in U.S.A., *ADVICS* [internet] Available at: www.advics.co.jp/eng/news/press_030226.html [Accessed on 12 July, 2012].

ADVICS Co., Ltd (2007) Merger of automotive brake business in China, *ADVICS* [internet] Available at: www.advics.co.jp/eng/news/press_071205.html [Accessed on 12 July, 2012].

ADVICS Co., Ltd (2008) Acquisition of the stocks of Sumiden Brake S & E, *ADVICS* [internet] Available at: www.advics.co.jp/eng/news/press_080204.html [Accessed on 12 July, 2012].

ADVICS Co., Ltd (2010) History, *ADVICS* [internet] Available at: www.advics.co.jp/eng/company/enkaku.html [Accessed on 12 July, 2012].

ADVICS Co., Ltd (2012a) Company summary, *ADVICS* [internet] Available at: www.advics.co.jp/eng/company/gaiyou.html [Accessed on 12 July, 2012].

ADVICS Co, Ltd (2016) Company Summary, ADVICS [internet] Available at: http://www.advics.co.jp/eng/company/outline.html [Accessed on 12 December, 2016].

ADVICS North America Inc (2011) Parent company, *ADVICS North America* [internet] Available at: www.advics-na.com/AdvicsPages/profile.aspx [Accessed on 12 July, 2012].

Akebono Brake Industry Co., Ltd (2010) *Akebono Report 2010 Business & CSR Activities*, Tokyo: Akebono Brake Industry Co., Ltd.

Akebono Brake Industry Co., Ltd (2012) Akebono history, *Akebono* [internet] Available at: www.akebono-brake.com/english/corporate/history/index.html [Accessed on 17 March, 2012].

Akebono Brake Industry Co., Ltd (2014) Akebono Brake makes west Japan manufacturing base a fully owned subsidiary, *Akebono* [internet] Available at: www.akebono-brake.com/static/news/2014/07/31/ne20140731_01.html [Accessed on 17 July, 2016].

Akebono Brake Industry Co., Ltd (2015) *Akebono Report 2015 Business & CSR Activities*, Tokyo: Akebono Brake Industry Co., Ltd.

Akustica (2009) Bosch to Acquire Akustica, Inc., *Akustica press release*, Available at: www.cmu.edu/cttec/News/2009-news/Akustica%20Acquistion.html [Accessed on 3 May, 2012].

Associated Press (2009) Bosch sells American brakes unit to Akebono, *Associated Press* [internet] Available at: www.highbeam.com/doc/1A1-D9ATNP7O3.html [Accessed on 03 March, 2012].

Australian Government Productivity Commission (2012) Australia Automotive Component Manufacturer: Chassis Brakes International (Australia) Pty Ltd (ACN 006 530 427) Submission, Canberra: Australian Government Productivity Commission.

Automotive News (2007) Bosch to buy Delphi brake parts business, Automotive News [internet] Available at: http://connection.ebscohost.com/c/articles/25587712/bosch-buy-delphi-brake-parts-business [Accessed on 11 March, 2012].

Beene, R. (2009) Bosch Group may sell part of brake business to Akebono Brake, Crain's Detroit Business [internet] Available at: http://www.crainsdetroit.com/article/20090828/FREE/908289997/bosch-group-may-sell-part-of-brake-business-to-akebono-brake [Accessed on 15 March, 2012].

Behrmann, E. (2015) Continental to buy Elektrobit software unit for $680 million, *Bloomberg.com* [internet] Available at: www.bloomberg.com/news/articles/2015-05-19/continental-ag-agrees-to-buy-elektrobit-unit-for-680-million [Accessed on 18 February, 2017].

Bloomberg (1996) Britain's Lucas Industries buys Varity Corp. of U.S. Consolidation to create 'global force' in brakes, *Bloomberg.com* [internet] Available at: http://articles.baltimoresun.com/1996-06-01/business/1996153078_1_varity-corp-brakes-lucas-industries [Accessed on 19 July, 2012].

Bloomberg (2016) Company overview of Advics Co. Ltd., *Bloomberg.com* [internet] Available at: www.bloomberg.com/research/stocks/private/snapshot.asp?privcapId=9648410 [Accessed on 23 July, 2016].

Bosch (1991) Annual Report 1991, Stuttgart: Bosch.

Bosch (2003) 25th Bosch ABS anniversary: 1978–2003, *Bosch.com* [internet] Available at: www.bosch.com/assets/en/company/innovation/theme03.htm [Accessed on 11 March, 2012].

Bosch (2007) Following expiration of offer period: Bosch acquires 75.3 percent share in Pacifica Group, *Bosch.com* [internet] Available at: www.bosch.com.au/content/language1/html/4700.htm [Accessed on 8 August, 2012].

Bosch (2008) Bosch predicts vehicle safety is the next frontier for automotive electronics, *Bosch.com* [internet] Available at: http://us.bosch-press.com/tbwebdb/bosch-usa/en-US/PressText.cfm?CFID=58772390&CFTOKEN=c19d7a66b5caef91-E4164106-F30C-6090-DC785855DDFC1E71&nh=00&Search=0&id=335 [Accessed on 1 September, 2016].

Bosch (2009) *Bosch Annual Report 2009*, Stuttgart: Bosch.

Bosch (2010) *Bosch Annual Report 2010*, Stuttgart: Bosch.

Bosch (2011a) *Bosch Annual Report 2011*, Stuttgart: Bosch.

Bosch (2011b) Bosch Packaging Technology, 150 Years of Packaging Experience, Customers Have Benefited From the Technological Competence, Power of Innovation and Reliability of Bosch Packaging Technology for Decades, Stuttgart: Bosch.

Bosch (2011c) Robert Bosch venture capital GmbH, *Bosch.com* [internet] Available at: www.rbvc.com/content/language1/html/55_ENU_XHTML.aspx [Accessed on 3 November, 2011].

Bosch (2012) Automotive technology, *Bosch.com* [internet] Available at: www.bosch-presse.de/presseforum/details.htm?txtID=5557&locale=en [Accessed on 11 April, 2012].

Bosch (2012a) Akustica leaps into high-volume mobile device market with new analog MEMS Mic, *Bosch.com* [internet] Available at: www.bosch-press.com/tbwebdb/bosch-usa/en-US/PressText.cfm?CFID=11236813&CFTOKEN=2fe04a1666f5371a-0865FDCD-D980-7224-1127D99942FE29C0&nh=00&Search=0&id=490 [Accessed on 3 May, 2012].

Bosch (2012b) Bosch automotive technology: Active safety, *Bosch.com* [internet] Available at: www.bosch-automotivetechnology.com/en/de/driving_safety/driving_safety_systems_for_commercial_vehicles/active_safety_1/active_safety_3.html [Accessed on 6 February, 2012].

Bosch (2012c) Bosch automotive technology: ESP® – your electronic guardian angel, *Bosch.com* [internet] Available at: www.bosch-automotivetechnology.us/en_us/us/specials_1/specials_for_more_driving_safety_1/bosch_esp_4/esp_start page___3_texts___3_pictures_7.html [Accessed on 6 February, 2012].

Bosch (2012d) Predictive brake assist PBA: Prepared for braking, before you are, *Bosch.com* [internet] Available at: http://rb-kwin.bosch.com/en/safety_comfort/drivingsafety/predictivesafetysystemspss/pba.html [Accessed on 6 February, 2012].

Bosch (2012e) Trends in automotive technology, *Bosch.com* [internet] Available at: www.bosch-presse.de/presseforum/details.htm?txtID=5482 [Accessed on 11 April, 2012].

Bosch (2013) Bosch Automotive Aftermarket opens new plant in Nanjing, China, Bosch.com [internet] Available at: http://www.bosch-presse.de/pressportal/de/en/bosch-automotive-aftermarket-opens-new-plant-in-nanjing-china-42133.html [Accessed on 18 December, 2016].

Bosch (2014) A lifesaver's anniversary: 100 million Bosch ESP systems, *Bosch.com* [internet] Available at: www.bosch-presse.de/presseforum/details.htm?txtID=6718&tk_id=108&locale=en [Accessed on 8 August, 2016].

Bosch (2015) *Bosch Annual Report 2015*, Stuttgart: Bosch.

Bosch (2016) Purchasing and logistics, *Bosch.com* [internet] Available at: http://purchasing.bosch.com/en/de/home/start.html [Accessed on 8 August, 2016].

Bosch (2017) Predictive emergency braking system, *Bosch.com* [internet] Available at: www.bosch-mobility-solutions.com/en/products-and-services/passenger-cars-and-light-commercial-vehicles/driver-assistance-systems/predictive-emergency-braking-system/ [Accessed on 26 January, 2017].

Boston, W. (2014) Bosch agrees to buy German auto-parts supplier's share in steering venture, wsj.com [internet] Available at: www.wsj.com/articles/bosch-agrees-to-buy-german-auto-parts-suppliers-share-in-steering-venture-1410774792 [Accessed on 22 July, 2016].

Brembo S.p.A. (2011) Brembo reinforces its leadership in the brake disc sector in South America agreement for the acquisition of the Argentinian Company Perdriel signed, *Brembo* [internet] Available at: www.brembo.com/en/Press/Comunicati-stampa/Documents/Comunicati%20Stampa%202011/2011%2008%2001%20 Closing%20Perdriel_en.pdf [Accessed on 12 June, 2012].

Brembo S.p.A. (2012a) Brembo Group, *Brembo* [internet] Available at: www. brembo.com/en/investors/gruppo-Brembo/Pages/default.aspx [Accessed on 12 June, 2012].

Brembo S.p.A. (2012b) Brembo reconfirms its leadership in technological challenge in World Championship Formula 1 2012, *Brembo* [internet] Available at: www.brembo. com/en/Press/Comunicati-stampa/Documents/Comunicati%20Stampa%20 2012/Brembo%20F1%20World%20Championship_2012.pdf [Accessed on 12 June, 2012].

Brembo S.p.A. (2015) *Brembo Annual Report 2015*, Stezzano: Brembo S.p.A.

Brembo S.p.A. (2016) Acquisition of a 66% stake in ASIMCO Meilian Braking Systems Finalised, *Brembo* [internet] Available at: www.brembo.com/en/company/ news/brembo-brakes-acquisition-of-asimco [Accessed on 23 July, 2016].

Brembo S.p.A. (2017a) Calipers, *Brembo* [internet] Available at: www.brembo.com/ en/car/original-equipment/products/calipers [Accessed on 19 February, 2017].

Brembo S.p.A. (2017b) Formula 1, *Brembo* [internet] Available at: www.brembo. com/en/car/formula-1 [Accessed on 19 February, 2017].

Bryant, C. (2015) Continental deal turns good for Germany's Schaeffler family, ft.com [internet] Available at: https://www.ft.com/content/6c5fab52-1337-11e5-ad26-00144feabdc0 [Accessed on 20 November, 2016].

Catalog Auto (2016) Definition of a foundation brake, *Catalog Auto* [internet] Available at: www.catalogauto.com/spare-parts/definition-of-a-foundation-break [Accessed on 1 September, 2016].

Chandler, A.D. (2004) *Scale and Scope: The Dynamics of Industrial Capitalism*, Seventh Printing, Cambridge, MA: Harvard University Press.

Chassis Brakes International (2015) Chassis Brakes International group acquires business of autocast and forge PTY limited, *Chassis Brakes International* [online] Available at: www.chassisbrakes.com/chassis-brakes-international-group-acquires-business-of-autocast-and-forge-pty-limited/ [Accessed on 23 July, 2016].

Chassis Brakes International (2016) Group at a glance, *Chassis Brakes International* [online] Available at: www.chassisbrakes.com/quality-charter/ [Accessed on 23 July, 2016].

Continental, AG (1998) Continental buys 'Brake and Chassis' Unit from ITT Industries, *Continental AG* [online] Available at: www.conti-online.com/generator/ www/com/en/continental/portal/themes/ir/news_adhoc/archive/ad_hoc/ ad_hoc_1998_07_27_1_en,version=10.html [Accessed on 6 February, 2012].

Continental, AG (2000) *Annual Report 2000*, Hanover: Continental AG.

Continental, AG (2006) Continental Automotive Systems: 100 Years. Forward Thinking, *Continental AG* [online] Available at: www.conti-online.com/gen erator/www/jp/jp/cas/cas/themes/press_services/hidden/press_releases/ company/economy_slash_business/strategies/pr_2006_10_02_100_years/ pr_2006_10_02_100_years_en.html [Accessed on 1 September, 2016].

Continental, AG (2007a) Continental Harnesses Forces as Purchase of Siemens VDO Ushers in New Era, *Continental AG* [online] Available at: www.continental-corporation.com/www/portal_com_en/themes/ir/news_adhoc/archive/news/071205_day_one_en.html [Accessed on 20 July, 2012].

Continental, AG (2007b) Continental to Acquire 51 Percent of Matador Rubber Group, *Continental AG* [online] Available at: www.conti-online.com/generator/www/de/en/continental/automobile/themes/news/archive/2007/goto_pr_2007_04_11_matador_en.html [Accessed on 20 July, 2012].

Continental AG (2010) Continental Establishes a New Joint Venture, Continental Brake Systems (Shanghai) Co., Ltd., Continental AG [online] Available at: http://www.continental-corporation.com/www/pressportal_com_en/themes/press_releases/3_automotive_group/chassis_safety/press_releases/pr_2010_10_25_brake_systems_china_en.html [Accessed on 7 December, 2016].

Continental, AG (2011) *Annual Report 2011*, Hanover: Continental AG.

Continental, AG (2012a) Continental Acquires Joint-Venture Shares from RICO Auto, *Continental AG* [online] Available at: www.conti-online.com/generator/www/in/in/continental/pressportal/themes/press_releases/3_automotive_group/chassis_safety/goto_pr_2012_03_09_indien_jv_rico_en.html [Accessed on 12 April, 2012].

Continental, AG (2012b) Corporate History, *Continental AG* [online] Available at: www.conti-online.com/generator/www/us/en/continental/pressportal/themes/basic_information/140_years_continental/hidden/goto_geschichte_en.html [Accessed on 12 April, 2012].

Continental, AG (2014) List of share property of the Continental Corporation as of December 31, 2014, *Continental AG* [online] Available at: www.continental-corporation.com/www/download/portal_com_en/themes/ir/events/an_shareholder/subsidiary_list_2014_en.pdf [Accessed on 27 February, 2017].

Continental, AG (2015a) *Annual Report 2015*, Hanover: Continental AG.

Continental, AG (2015b) Continental Closes Acquisition of Elektrobit Automotive, *Continental AG* [online] Available at: www.continental-corporation.com/www/pressportal_com_en/themes/press_releases/2_corporation/acquisitions_joint ventures/pr-2015-07-01-elektrobit-en.html [Accessed on 18 February, 2017].

Continental, AG (2015c) *Fact book 2015*, Hanover: Continental AG.

Continental, AG (2016) Chassis & Safety division, Hanover: Continental AG.

Continental, AG (2017) Surround View/ Contiguard, *Continental AG* [online] Available at: www.continental-its.com/www/its_de_EN/themes/ITS_Continental/verkehrsmanagement_surround_view_de.html [Accessed on 26 January, 2017].

Courtenay, V. (2005) Hyundai Mobis acquires Korean parts supplier, *WardsAuto* [internet] Available at: http://wardsauto.com/news-amp-analysis/hyundai-mobis-acquires-korean-parts-supplier [Accessed on 15 June, 2012].

Courtenay, V. (2007) Hyundai Mobis, Kasco to merge, *WardsAuto* [internet] Available at: http://wardsauto.com/news-amp-analysis/hyundai-mobis-kasco-merge [Accessed on 15 June, 2012].

Crowe, P. (2013) Cars doing stop & go driving autonomously by 2016, *HybridCars.com* [internet] Available at: www.hybridcars.com/cars-doing-stop-go-driving-autonomously-by-2016/ [Accessed on 1 September, 2016].

Dana Holding Corporation (2011) *Dana Solutions for South America*, Ohio: Dana Holding Corporation.

Delphi Corporation (2005) Form 10-K, Troy, Michigan: Delphi Corporation.

Drives & Controls (2008) Schaeffler wins control of Continental with a minority stake, *Drives & Controls* [internet] Available at: www.drives.co.uk/fullstory. asp?id=2368 [Accessed on 9 March, 2012].

Edison Investment Research (2012) *Outlook: GKN*, London: Edison Investment Research.

European Patent Office (2016) Anton van Zanten (The Netherlands, Germany): Winner of the European Inventor Award 2016, *European Patent Office* [internet] Available at: www.epo.org/learning-events/european-inventor/finalists/2016/vanzanten.html [Accessed on 8 August, 2016].

Fishman, M. (1989) Preemptive bidding and the role of the medium of exchange in acquisitions, *Journal of Finance*, 44(1): 41–57.

Ganesh (2010) Bosch sets up manufacturing facility for antilock braking system at Chakan plant, *Machinist* [internet] Available at: http://machinist.in/index.php?option=com_content&task=view&id=2542&Itemid=2 [Accessed on 20 July, 2012].

Grand Prix (2000) Italian brake manufacturer Brembo seal AP Racing takeover, Grand Prix [internet] Available at: http://www.grandprix.com/ns/ns02870.html [Accessed on 17 March, 2012].

Groupe Renault (2015) 2015 Annual Report, Boulogne-Billancourt Cedex: Groupe Renault.

Hitachi Cable (2008) Hitachi Cable establishes new automotive brake hose company in United States, *Hitachi Cable* [internet] Available at: www.hitachi-cable. com/i_r/news/__icsFiles/afieldfile/2008/03/24/080307e.pdf [Accessed on 22 March, 2012].

Huebner and Burger (2012) Bosch sells low-tech brakes ops to buyout firm, *Reuters.com* [internet] Available at: www.reuters.com/article/2012/01/10/us-robert boschgmbh-kps-idUSTRE80919X20120110 [Accessed on 23 March, 2012].

Hyundai Mobis (2005) Mobis acquires auto parts maker in China, *Hyundai Mobis* [internet] Available at: www.mobis.co.kr/Eng/PR/News/View.aspx?idx=162&page=6&si=&st= [Accessed on 12 March, 2012].

Hyundai Mobis (2008) Hyundai Mobis and Subsidiaries, Notes to Consolidated Financial Statements, December 31, 2008 and 2007, Seoul: Hyundai Mobis.

Hyundai Mobis (2012) Stock information: Shareholders, *Hyundai Mobis* [internet] Available at: www.mobis.co.kr/Eng/Company/Investor/Stock/StockHolders. aspx [Accessed on 19 October, 2012].

Interntional Directory of Company Histories (1999) TRW Automotive Holdings Corp., Michigan: St James Press.

iSuppli Corporation (2008) MEMS in automotive: How regulatory issues will reshape the market, El Segundo, California: iSuppli Corporation.

Jin, R. (2008) Halla to Buy Back Mando After 10 Years, The Korea Times [internet] Available at: http://www.koreatimes.co.kr/www/news/biz/2012/09/123_17675.html [Accessed on 23 March, 2012].

Klier, T.H. and Rubenstein, J.M. (2008) *Who Really Made Your Car? Restructuring and Geographic Change in the Auto Industry*, Kalamazoo, MI: W.E. Upjohn Institute for Employment Research.

Korean Herald (2005) Continental, Siemens, TRW bid to buy Mando, *Korean Herald* [internet] Available at: http://eng.edaily.co.kr/press/View.asp?m=1&seq=3317&page=1 [Accessed on 2 August, 2012].

Lampton, C. (2012) How Brake Calipers Work?, HowStuffWorks, Inc [internet] Available at: http://auto.howstuffworks.com/auto-parts/brakes/brake-parts/brake-calipers.htm [Accessed on 28 March, 2012].

Liebemann, E.K., Meder, K., Schuh, J. and Nenninger, G. (2005) Safety and performance enhancement: The Bosch Electronic Stability Control (ESP), *Enhanced Safety Vehicles*, ESV Paper No: 05–0471. Washington D.C.

Mason, R. (2008) Schaeffler family buys out tyre giant Continental for €12bn, The Telegraph [internet] Available at: http://www.telegraph.co.uk/finance/newsby sector/transport/2795163/Schaeffler-family-buys-out-tyre-giant-Continental-for-12bn.html [Accessed on 2 August, 2012].

Meyer, B. (2008) Hitachi acquires hose unit, *Rubber & Plastics News* [internet] Available at: http://connection.ebscohost.com/c/articles/31791419/hitachi-acquires-hose-unit [Accessed on 20 March, 2012].

Meyer, M. (2015) Automotive expert discusses brake system trends, *Machine Design* [internet] Available at: http://machinedesign.com/automotive/automotive-expert-discusses-brake-system-trends [Accessed on 2 February, 2017].

Mui, C.K. (2013) Driverless car ripple effects – as far as the eye can see (Part 2), *Forbes.com* [internet] Available at: www.forbes.com/sites/chunkamui/2013/01/24/googles-trillion-dollar-driverless-car-part-2-the-ripple-effects/#5cde4e7c6ce8 [Accessed on 27 January, 2017].

Muller, J. (2005) Parts for the sensitive car, *Forbes.com* [internet] Available at: www.forbes.com/forbes/2005/1128/204.html [Accessed on 6 August, 2012].

Murphy, T. (2005) SiemensVDO Wedges Into Brake Sector, WardsAuto.com [internet] Available at: http://wardsauto.com/news-analysis/siemensvdo-wedges-brake-sector [Accessed on 11 December, 2012].

Murphy, T. (2009a) Bosch changes direction on brake operations, *WardsAuto* [internet] Available at: http://wardsauto.com/ar/bosch_brake_operations_090730 [Accessed on 6 August, 2012].

Murphy, T. (2009b) Foundation brakes still unprofitable for Bosch, *WardsAuto* [internet] Available at: http://wardsauto.com/news-amp-analysis/foundation-brakes-still-unprofitable-bosch [Accessed on 6 August, 2012].

Murphy, T. (2012) Brake market faces big squeeze, *WardsAuto* [internet] Available at: http://wardsauto.com/suppliers/brake-market-faces-big-squeeze [Accessed on 6 August, 2012].

The New York Times (1999) TRW, outbidding federal-mogul, to buy Lucas varity of Britain, *nytimes.com* [internet] Available at: www.nytimes.com/1999/01/29/business/trw-outbidding-federal-mogul-to-buy-lucas-varity-of-britain.html [Accessed on 23 December, 2012].

Nisshinbo (2013) Agreement on establishment of joint venture with Continental Automotive Holding Co., Ltd. for manufacturing Electronic Brake Systems (EBS) component in China, *Nisshinbo* [internet] Available at: www.nisshinbo.co.jp/english/news/news20131106_1065.html [Accessed on 21 July, 2016].

Nisshinbo (2016) History, *Nisshinbo* [internet] Available at: www.nisshinbo.co.jp/english/profile/history.html [Accessed on 21 July, 2016].

Ontario Ministry of Transportation (2013) Types of foundation brakes, *Ministry of Transportation* [internet] Available at: www.mto.gov.on.ca/english/handbook/airbrake/section6-1-0.shtml [Accessed on 1 September, 2016].

ProMéxico (2016) Hitachi Cable: unstoppable growth, *ProMéxico* [internet] Available at: http://negocios.promexico.gob.mx/english/04-2013/art06.html [Accessed on 23 July, 2016].

PSA Peugeot Citroën (2015) *2015 Annual Results*, Paris: PSA Peugeot Citroën.

PwC (2015) Driving Value: 2015 Automotive M&A Insights, New York: PwC.

Quinn, T.K. (1953) Giant Business: Threat to Democracy: The Autobiography of an Insider, New York: Exposition Press.

Rauwald, C. (2008) Bosch plans to acquire Morse Grp's brake friction ops, *Dow Jones Newswires*, 3 September.

Reference for Business (2016) TRW Automotive Holdings Corp. – company profile, information, business description, history, background information on TRW Automotive Holdings Corp., *Reference for Business* [internet] Available at: www.referenceforbusiness.com/history2/93/TRW-Automotive-Holdings-Corp.html [Accessed on 20 July, 2016].

Reuters (1988) Bosch's Stake in Japan, nytimes.com [internet] Available at: http://www.nytimes.com/1988/07/20/business/bosch-s-stake-in-japan.html?n=Top%2fReference%2fTimes%20Topics%2fSubjects%2fF%2fFinances [Accessed on 6 August, 2012].

Reuters (2011) Akebono abandons talks on buying Bosch's brake ops, *Reuters.com* [internet] Available at: http://in.reuters.com/article/2011/03/04/akebono-bosch-announcement-idINTKG00705820110304 [Accessed on 08 April, 2012].

Reuters (2012) Nissin Kogyo Co., Ltd. divests stake in Japan Brake Industrial Co., Ltd, *Reuters.com* [internet] Available at: www.reuters.com/finance/stocks/4217.T/key-developments/article/2471956 [Accessed on 08 April, 2012].

Rubber & Plastics News (2007) Delphi reaches deal to sell brake hose unit, *Rubber & Plastics News* [internet] Available at: http://connection.ebscohost.com/c/articles/24194996/delphi-reaches-deal-sell-brake-hose-unit [Accessed on 15 February, 2012].

SAP AG (2009a) Lean manufacturing with RFID-enabled Kanban at Bosch, SAP AG [internet] Available at: www.sap.com/community/showdetail.epx?ItemID=17699 [Accessed on 11 August, 2012].

SAP AG (2009b) Robert Bosch: Leaner Manufacturing Processes with RFID Data Capture, Germany: SAP AG.

Schäfer, D. (2008) Continental reaches deal with Schaeffler, *FT.com* [internet] Available at: www.ft.com/cms/s/0/df93572a-6f49-11dd-986f-0000779fd18c.html#axzz2OBVPLmBt [Accessed on 18 February, 2012].

Schäfer, D. (2011) Lack of parts hits VW production, *FT.com* [internet] Available at: www.ft.com/intl/cms/s/0/ebef9264-2a3f-11e0-b906-00144feab49a.html#axzz2ZyJTg1j6 [Accessed on 25 July, 2013].

Scherer, F.M. (1996) Industry Structure, Strategy and Public Policy, New York: HarperCollins College Publishers.

Sedgwick, D. (2016) No. 1 global supplier sees big opportunity with new technology, *Automotive News* [internet] Available at: www.autonews.com/article/20160620/OEM10/306209989/bosch-still-finds-n.-america-fertile [Accessed on 22 July, 2016].

Supplier Business (2008) *ADVICS Braking and Safety Systems*, London: Supplier Business.

The Birmingham Post (1998) LucasVarity eyes Korean brake maker, The Birmingham Post [internet] Available at: www.thefreelibrary.com/LucasVarity+eyes+Korean+brake+maker.-a060780431 [Accessed on 21 March, 2012].

Thiel and van Loon (2007) Continental to buy Siemens VDO unit for $15.7 billion (Update2), *Bloomberg.com* [internet] Available at: www.bloomberg.com/apps/news?pid=newsarchive&sid=aW_sxjc9m6C0 [Accessed on 10 May, 2012].

TireBusiness.com (2009) Akebono buying Bosch brake assets in N. America, *Tire-Business.com* [internet] Available at: www.tirebusiness.com/article/20090925/NEWS/309259996/akebono-buying-bosch-brake-assets-in-n-america [Accessed on 31 August, 2012].

Tire Business.com (2014) Hitachi pleads guilty in brake hose price fixing probe, *Tire-Business.com* [internet] Available at: www.tirebusiness.com/article/20141112/NEWS/141119955 [Accessed on 23 July, 2016].

TRW Automotive Holdings Corp. (2001) TRW Revamps caliper Reman line for over-all operations improvement: Company Institutes lean manufacturing techniques, *TRW* [internet] Available at: http://trw.mediaroom.com/index.php?item=134 [Accessed on 13 June, 2012].

TRW Automotive Holdings Corp. (2003) *2003 Annual Report*, Michigan: TRW Automotive Holdings Corp.

TRW Automotive Holdings Corp. (2005) TRW and China South Group announce Chassis joint venture, *TRW* [internet] Available at: http://ir.trw.com/release detail.cfm?releaseid=270415 [Accessed on 13 June, 2012].

TRW Automotive Holdings Corp. (2008) TRW completes purchase of Certain North American braking machining and module assembly assets from Delphi, *TRW* [internet] Available at: http://ir.trw.com/releasedetail.cfm?releaseid=285974 [Accessed on 13 June, 2012].

TRW Automotive Holdings Corp. (2010) TRW to partner with Brakes India for local rollout of slip control systems, TRW [internet] Available at: http://trw.media room.com/index.php?s=32950&item=110415 [Accessed on 3 November, 2012].

TRW Automotive Holdings Corp. (2011) *2011 Annual Report*, Michigan: TRW Automotive Holdings Corp.

TRW Automotive Holdings Corp. (2012a) Foundation brakes, *TRW* [internet] Avail-able at: http://207.82.198.115/braking_systems/foundation_brakes [Accessed on 13 June, 2012].

TRW Automotive Holdings Corp. (2012b) High performance calipers, *TRW* [inter-net] Available at: http://207.82.198.115/braking_systems/foundation_brakes/high_performance_calipers [Accessed on 13 June, 2012].

Tucker and Song (2008) Halla takes the wheel at Mando again, *FT.com* [inter-net] Available at: www.ft.com/intl/cms/s/0/8432e02c-c840-11dc-94a6-0000779fd2ac.html#axzz2NhHsOvgE [Accessed on 15 August, 2012].

Tyrepress.com (2001) Acquisition Of Two Japanese Brake Manufacturers By Con-tinental, Tyrepress.com [internet] Available at: http://www.tyrepress.com/2001/11/acquisition-of-two-japanese-brake-manufacturers-by-continental/ [Accessed on 10 December, 2012].

Upadhyaya, R. (2005) Robert Bosch to up stake in India Kalyani Brakes, *Dow Jones Newswires*, 12 July.

Urquhart, T. (2010) Bosch On Target for Record 2010 Revenues, IHS Global Insight Daily Analysis, 17 December 2010.

WardsAuto (1996) AlliedSignal brakes put Bosch in systems business, WardsAuto [internet] Available at: http://wardsauto.com/news-amp-analysis/alliedsignal-brakes-put-bosch-systems-business [Accessed on 20 March, 2012].

Wilson, J. and Bryant, C. (2012) Bosch sells brakes unit to private equity buyer, *ft.com* [internet] Available at: www.ft.com/cms/s/0/8de35146-3ba1-11e1-a09a-00144feabdc0.html#axzz1tpIaWkv0 [Accessed on 23 March, 2012].

Womack, J.P. and Jones, D.T. (2003) *Lean Thinking: Banish Waste and Create Wealth in Your Corporation*, London: Simon & Schuster UK Ltd.

Womack, J.P., Jones, D.T. and Roos, D. (2007) *The Machine That Changed the World: How Lean Production Changed the World*, London: Simon and Schuster UK Ltd.

ZF Friedrichshafen AG (2014) Annual Report 2014, Friedrichshafen: ZF Friedrichshafen AG.

ZF Friedrichshafen AG (2015a) 100 Years ZF Friedrichshafen AG: Global Group in its anniversary year, *ZF* [internet] Available at: www.zf.com/china/media/en_cn/china/regional_content_china/news_cn/auto_shanghai/press_release/tx03_autoshanghai15_zf_anniversary_year_en.pdf [Accessed on 21 July, 2016].

ZF Friedrichshafen AG (2015b) *Annual Report 2015*, Friedrichshafen: ZF Friedrichshafen AG.

ZF Friedrichshafen AG (2015c) ZF completes acquisition of TRW automotive, *ZF* [internet] Available at: www.zf.com/corporate/en_de/press/press_releases/press_release.jsp?newsId=22096936 [Accessed on 23 July, 2016].

ZF Friedrichshafen AG (2015d) ZF TRW's innovative integrated brake control system to launch in high volume in 2018, *ZF* [internet] Available at: www.prnewswire.com/news-releases/zf-trws-innovative-integrated-brake-control-system-to-launch-in-high-volume-in-2018–300156608.html [Accessed on 26 January, 2017].

ZF Friedrichshafen AG (2016) Integrated brake control: Enhancing safety, *ZF* [internet] Available at: www.zf.com/corporate/en_de/magazine/magazin_artikel_viewpage_22186537.html [Accessed on 26 January, 2017].

7 The global automotive semiconductor business

1. Introduction

Today's automobiles contain 50 to more than 100 microprocessors, critical components in parking brakes, engine control units, entertainment systems, stability control and power steering (Greimel, 2011; Osawa, 2011; Pagliery, 2014). These microprocessors are essentially tiny computers and are also known as 'ECUs'. Information from these microprocessors is basically stored on semiconductors made from silicon chips. The ever-increasing complexity of today's automobiles, surrounded by its bewildering array of high-tech driving systems, is fuelling an insatiable hunger for semiconductors of equal if not greater sophistication. Moulded by this technological rapacity, the automobile has become the most advanced computer a household could own; in fact, the communications and networking technologies of vehicles being rolled out over the coming decade would easily exceed that of any device consumers own (Shapiro, 2015; O'Donnell, 2016). In 2005, before the complex wave of networking technologies (e.g., GPS, telematics) made their way into the vehicular mainstream, the global automotive semiconductor business was already valued at a considerable US$18 billion, accounting for almost 50 percent of the total global electronics market (Gupta, 2005; Klier and Rubenstein, 2008; Hammerschmidt, 2012).

Back in this relatively 'analogue' era of 2005, about a third of automotive semiconductors were used in automotive interior systems, with another one-fourth each in powertrain and exterior systems and the remainder in chassis systems (Webber, 2005; Webber, 2006). However, the industry soon received its digital awakening, with the introduction of new legislation aimed at improving vehicle safety/security and moderate automotive emissions. This legislation coupled with rising customer expectations invariably bolstered demand for highly-sophisticated microprocessors, which have since made their way into every nook and cranny of the automobile (Infineon, 2006b). Over the ensuing decade of rapid digitisation, this industry generally experienced untrammelled growth, reaching an estimated US$29 billion by 2015 (IHS, 2016). As we stand tremulously on the cusp of this artificial intelligence powered era, increasingly sophisticated microprocessors are now needed to execute tens of millions of lines of software code in today's automobiles, controlling everything from the brakes to the volume of the radio; as astounding as it may sound, the average automobile today (e.g., a Ford Taurus) has about 10 million lines of software code (reaching a high of 100 million lines in the average luxury car) compared to 6.5 million lines in a Boeing 787 (Charette, 2009). The dependence on these high-powered chips (and the concomitant demand for them) is expected to rise even further, with the escalating importance of automotive electronics (e.g., driver information and communication systems, in-car entertainment electronics, automated braking and driving systems) as differentiators in an increasingly competitive automotive market desperately chasing the favour of its customers. The sheer ferocity of this digitisation current has resulted in chip designers possibly supplanting mechanical engineers as the primary human capital needed in automotive components manufacturing (Klier and Rubenstein, 2008).

When the industry was in its infancy (in the 1980s), automotive semiconductors were produced largely by the divisions of Hitachi, Mitsubishi, Siemens AG, Motorola whose core business was not making such semiconductors. However, these divisions were eventually spun off (between 1998 and 2004) and through a relentless centralisation of capital became powerful oligopolists in a fast-consolidating industry. Being the spin-offs of gargantuan electronics multinationals, these divisions began life with strong, technical foundations, considerable financial resources, a ready pool of customers and reasonable global presence.

Emerging from the consolidation tsunami of the past few decades are the following industry titans: NXP, Infineon, Renesas and STM. Together, they accounted for over two-fifths of the global automotive semiconductor market (by revenues) in 2015 (Semicast, 2012). The global automotive semiconductor industry comprises these oligopolists who produce highly sophisticated microprocessors and microcontrollers,[1] their lower-tier competitors and the foundry chip makers, who themselves have garnered a significant market presence through consolidation triggered by the cascade effect. Although this book looks extensively at these oligopolists, the industry has actually been consolidating long before these oligopolists were formed (their previous incarnations were already merging or forming JVs in the 1980s to secure economies of scale and scope). For instance, before STM assumed its current identity in May 1998, it was known as SGS-Thomson Microelectronics (itself the result of a merger between Italy's Microelecttronica and France's Thomson Semiconducteurs in 1987) (EE Times, 1998). By 2011, Renesas assumed the position of industry leader with a 13.6 percent market share while Infineon, STM and Freescale accounted for 9.8 percent, 8.9 percent and 8.1 percent respectively. Trailing these industry oligopolists was NXP with a respectable 6.9 percent of this market. After nearly two-three decades of consolidation, the industry seemed to have largely consolidated with the above five firms dominating the top positions since 2006 (Barnden, 2012). However, this seemingly stratified ranking order was upended when fifth-placed NXP acquired fourth-placed, Freescale in 2015 in a daring bet-the-firm bid. Through this acquisition, NXP emerged as the new industry leader with a global market share of 14.4 percent, easily surpassing Infineon, Renesas and STM which recorded 9.27 percent, 9.2 percent and 7.2 percent respectively. In a tumultuous landscape buffeted by violent disruptive M&A forces, this ranking order is inevitably subject to considerable fluidity. This is evidenced by Qualcomm's sudden announced acquisition of NXP in October 2016 (NXP, 2016c). Further stirring of this volatile mix is virtually assured, as the remaining incumbents are fighting tooth and nail to survive and strengthen their market presence; currently fifth-placed Texas Instruments (hereafter 'TI') with its 6.7 percent global market share appears to be focusing greater resources in the automotive semiconductor market, indicating a desire to strengthen its presence in an industry poised to play a pre-eminent role in the age of autonomous driving (TI, 2015).

The global automotive semiconductor industry is still relatively fragmented at the third-tier levels, with considerable room for consolidation among these players, who tend not to specialise in automotive semiconductors. Most of the so-called third-tier players in the global automotive semiconductor industry (i.e., Bosch and Toshiba) are market leaders in other fields; Bosch is the world's largest automotive components supplier, with significant capabilities in high-tech braking systems and automotive electronics, while Toshiba is a well-known consumer electronics producer. To put it simply, Bosch and Toshiba could easily and rapidly expand their market share in the automotive semiconductor arena, if they choose to. Further consolidation in this industry appears to be accelerating, as these firms are driven to secure ever-increasing economies of scale and scope needed to alleviate rising R&D costs (a consequence of rising complexity in today's automobiles). Rising R&D costs and the ever-increasing need to secure greater economies of scale and scope (via mergers, JVs or strategic alliances) have become truisms in the automotive semiconductor industry.

It is possible the industry leaders could acquire the automotive semiconductors divisions of the 'third-tier' players as they turn their focus to their core businesses. However, in recent years, JVs have also become significant growth drivers among the industry oligopolists as they enable them to secure greater scale economies and penetrate new growth markets, without risking as much capital (this lower risk would of course mean less control and lower profitability). In addition, JVs also draw less attention from antitrust authorities, who have in recent years, increased their scrutiny of acquisitions. Unlike the other sectors covered in this book, the pace of consolidation in the automotive semiconductor industry was relatively slow in the 1980s and the industry was still relatively fragmented at the dawn of the twenty-first century (the top four players today did not exist then).

Since then, the pace of consolidation in the automotive semiconductor industry has accelerated, resulting in the formation of the top four industry oligopolists (in their current forms) by 2015. The catalyst for this consolidation was increasing technological complexity and the all-important need to secure the economies of scale and scope vital to alleviating the cost pressures resulting from attempts to meet the increasing technological demands of automakers and even tier-one mega supplier clients (e.g., Delphi, Bosch).

2. The cascade effect's impact on automotive semiconductor makers

The powerful forces generated by the cascade effect have resulted in automakers and first-tier mega suppliers intensifying their pressure on their semiconductor suppliers (i.e., NXP, Infineon, Renesas and STM) to deliver increasingly complex microprocessors capable of powering systems of rising technological sophistication; although these semiconductor makers are considered second-tier players in the global automotive value chain, they now possess unprecedented market power, as increasingly chip-dependent automakers and their first-tier suppliers are unable to finish their products without them. Further, these semiconductor suppliers must be able to supply these chips on a 'just-in-time' basis to these automakers on an increasingly globalised basis. To meet the rising production, logistical and research cost resulting from producing these microprocessors, these suppliers are compelled to secure ever-rising economies of scale and scope (in R&D, purchasing, human resources and subsystems integration) by means of consolidation (Nolan, 2008). To acquire the cutting-edge R&D and organisational skills needed to dominate the industry, these suppliers are also constantly compelled to make the acquisitions needed to secure the best 'human capital'; as mentioned earlier, the right 'human capital' is vital to fully extract the economies of scale and scope (along with the requisite technical and management expertise) desired in acquisitions (Chandler and Hikino, 1999).

Concurrently these suppliers would also divest non-core businesses in attempts to focus their resources on growing their core segments. These suppliers, in turn, also exert similar, if not greater pressure (e.g., demands for discounts, assuming a larger portion of the production and research process) on their suppliers. Consequently, these lower-tier suppliers are also compelled by cascading forces to merge and attain greater economies of scale and scope. Even the so-called lower-tier suppliers (e.g., Bosch, Toshiba) in the global automotive semiconductor industry are themselves gargantuan multinationals with annual revenues exceeding US$10 billion. They are smaller than the industry oligopolists in the automotive semiconductor segment because they have chosen to specialise in other product segments. However, the overall revenues of these 'lower-tiers' could be significantly larger than the key players in the global automotive chip segment.

As for the lowest-tier foundry chip suppliers (e.g., Taiwan Semiconductor Manufacturing Company Limited (TSMC), United Microelectronics Corporation (UMC) and GLOBALFOUNDRIES Inc. (hereafter 'GLOBALFOUNDRIES')), they are also sizeable multinationals in their own right; foundries such as TSMC are not engaged in product development like Renesas, as they focus strictly on making semiconductors in their own plants for higher-tier chip suppliers, who service the automakers and tier-one suppliers (Ballhaus, Pagella and Vogel, 2009). TSMC, GLOBALFOUNDRIES and UMC recorded 2015 revenues of US$25.7 billion, US$4.673 billion and US$4.417 billion respectively (TSMC, 2015; Gartner, 2016; UMC, 2015). These three oligopolists are all suppliers to the leading automotive semiconductor makers (i.e., NXP, Infineon, Renesas and STM); TSMC, UMC and GLOBALFOUNDRIES (the so-called 'lower-tier' foundry chip makers) have accumulated so much market power that they accounted for nearly three-quarters of global foundry chip revenues in 2015 (TSMC, 2015; UMC, 2015; Gartner, 2016); this market was valued at US$48.8 billion in 2015, even larger than the US$29 billion recorded by its client industry, the global automotive semiconductor subsector (Gartner, 2016; IHS, 2016). The required investment, barriers to entry, R&D expenditure and economies of scale and scope needed to survive in the foundry chips business and the automotive semiconductor industry are possibly the highest in the automotive components industry; a semiconductor fabrication plant can cost up to US$5 billion to build and develop. Moreover, the cost involved in building semiconductor 'fabs' or fabrication facilities, has been escalating over the years, with every major technological advancement necessitating increasingly complex and financially prohibitive production processes. This trend has resulted in many US chip companies focusing their efforts on design while relying on lower-tier contract manufacturers to make the products. Nonetheless, this trend proved enticing and eventually immensely profitable to Asian companies like Taiwan's TSMC which made significant investments in sprawling new facilities, frequently financed by considerable government coffers (Randewich, 2012). The chip companies' increasing reliance on contract manufacturers is a clear indication of the cascade effect at work, with the leading suppliers focusing more on coordinating and planning the supply chain rather than non-core relatively low value-added manufacturing (Nolan, 2009).

The increasing ubiquity of sophisticated automotive electronics has resulted in extraordinary cost pressures in the automotive semiconductor industry, as the key players are easily compelled to spend upwards of US$500 million annually on R&D for the past decade. This sizeable R&D investment has become critical in ensuring a company's competitive advantage, where technological obsolescence would easily compromise its lead. Although industry consolidation may not fully alleviate these pressures, it remains the most viable option (arguably the only option) for these automotive semiconductor manufacturers. The fact that Renesas, Fujitsu and Panasonic contemplated a merger for their system large-scale-integration (LSI) chip operations (the system LSI chip is also known as the 'system-on-chip' (hereafter 'SoC')),[2] barely three years after Renesas' merger with Hitachi and Mitsubishi in 2009 reinforces the inevitability of the consolidation trend in the global automotive semiconductor industry (Yasu, 2012; Renesas, 2012; Osawa, 2012; Murakami, 2006). With the predicament of the above Japanese players in mind, NXP's US$11.86 billion acquisition of its larger competitor, Freescale would not seem audacious but rather one driven by the need to secure ever-increasing scale economies, essential in buffering the significant cost pressures plaguing the industry.

The impact of the cascade effect on the global automotive semiconductor industry (and indeed the semiconductor as a whole) has been far greater than previously imagined. Today, leading semiconductor firms such as Renesas are actually striving to become fabless companies that focus on the high-end of the value chain which involve mainly the design and development of semiconductors (Ballhaus, Pagella and Vogel, 2009). This is a natural progression, as the plain old manufacturing of semiconductors is a high-cost and low-margin business. To achieve this aim, these firms have or are in the process of outsourcing their foundry operations, choosing instead to focus on chip design. Further, they must master the systems integration skills of the leading automakers and larger mega suppliers (e.g., Bridgestone, Continental) mentioned in earlier chapters.

3. The leading automotive semiconductor makers

NXP: profile

NXP (spun off from electronics giant, Philips in 2006) used to be the world's fifth largest automotive semiconductors maker with a 6.4 percent market share in 2014 (Semicast, 2012; Buksh, 2016). Through its previous existence as a Philips division, NXP had already gathered more than 50 years of experience in making semiconductors. Despite NXP's relative 'youth' (as an independent company), it has quickly executed a strategy (comprising both acquisitions and JVs) to secure critical economies of scale and scope. On 7 December 2015, NXP vaulted to the top of the pecking order in the global automotive semiconductor industry, through its bold US$11.86 billion (cash/stock) acquisition of Freescale, then the world's fourth largest semiconductor maker; with this approximate US$12 billion valuation, NXP effectively paid no premium for its acquisition of the embattled Freescale, which only returned to profitability in 2014, after a string of successive net losses amounting to a crippling US$1.77 billion (from 2010–2013) (Auchard, 2015; Freescale, 2014). Before the dust could settle in the trail of this disruptive acquisition, NXP soon became the target of Qualcomm, which announced its takeover of the former in October 2016, barely a year after the initial merger between NXP and Freescale. Qualcomm has traditionally drawn the bulk (approximately 90 percent) of its revenues from making microchips for smart phones and tablets. However, drawn by the siren call of controlling a lucrative future dominated by highly-networked autonomous vehicles with their insatiable need for increasingly intelligent microchips, Qualcomm decided to stage an audacious acquisition of NXP in 2016; Qualcomm agreed to pay US$110 (a significant premium of 34 percent) for each NXP share in a cash/debt bid valuing the deal at a staggering US$47 billion (Clark & Higgins, 2016; NXP, 2016c). Pending regulatory approval, this acquisition (the largest in Qualcomm's history) is expected to be concluded by the end of 2017, in the process creating a juggernaut with outsized revenues in excess of US$30 billion (Waters, Fedor and Thomas, 2016).

By the end of 2015, NXP had assumed the pre-eminent position of the world's largest automotive semiconductor maker with an estimated global market share of 14.4 percent (US$4.178 billion); it also had operations in over 35 countries. Through its acquisition of Freescale, NXP effectively doubled its automotive semiconductor revenues and market share (Buksh, 2016; Webber, Fitzgerald and Doliner, 2016). The firm posted 2015 overall revenues of US$9.779 billion (combined adjusted figure), dwarfing the top-lines of its closest rivals, Infineon, Renesas, STM, which were US$6.473 billion, US$5.730 billion and US$6.897 billion respectively. As indicated in Figure 7.1, the High Performance Mixed Signal (includes application specific semiconductors and system solutions for the automotive industry) segment accounted for 85.3 percent (around US$8.340 billion) of NXP's overall 2015 revenues; for that year, NXP's US$4.178 billion in automotive semiconductor sales accounted for 42.7 percent of overall revenues. The newly-merged NXP and Freescale subsequently posted 2016 revenues of US$9.498 billion; it is evident the merged entity's overall 2016 revenues was not only significantly less than the US$10 billion plus revenues it projected earlier but also lower than the US$9.779 billion it delivered a year earlier. NXP's top-line underperformance coupled with its 2016 net loss of US$133 million not only proves that mergers do not always live up to hyped expectations but also illustrates the hard truth that size alone does not ensure profitability (NXP, 2015a; NXP, 2017; Infineon, 2015a; Renesas, 2016; STM, 2016a).

As of 31 December 2015, NXP had 44,000 employees worldwide. NXP is the most China dependent among the top four automotive semiconductor makers,

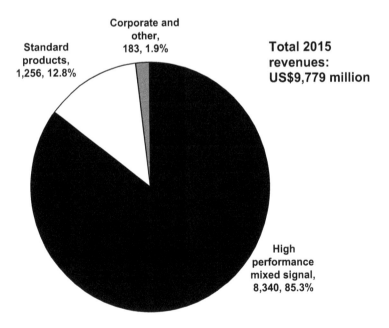

Figure 7.1 NXP's 2015 annual revenues (US$ million)

Source: NXP Semiconductors Reports Fourth Quarter and Full-Year 2016 Results

drawing over half of its revenues from this country alone. The company's largest customers are Bosch, Continental, Delphi, Hella, Hyundai and Visteon. Further, none of these customers represented more than 10 percent of NXP's revenues in the years 2014–2015. In 2015, NXP also recorded procurement expenditure of about US$1.879 billion, giving it considerable leverage over its suppliers (NXP, 2015a). The company's procurement spend is expected to increase exponentially after its assimilation into Qualcomm, further augmenting its already considerable market power. This potential boost in leverage is critical to NXP, as it now faces the problem of dealing with an increasingly powerful supplier (e.g., UMC), thus its strategy of squeezing such foundry suppliers for concessions has become a thing of the past; conversely, it may have to learn how to work with these gargantuan foundry suppliers as partners rather than continuing the traditional top-down client/supplier relationship (an example of this shift in power dynamics would be the Renesas and TSMC partnership discussed in the subsequent section).

By 2016, NXP operated 14 manufacturing facilities in Asia, Europe and the United States (seven are wafer fabrication facilities while the other half comprised assembly and test facilities) (NXP, 2016a). Through its now dominant market share, NXP has become the leading automotive chip supplier in areas spanning car entertainment, chassis & safety, in-vehicle networking, powertrain and secure car access. These capabilities position NXP as a significant player with considerable influence over the development of driver-assistance and autonomous vehicle systems.

NXP and Freescale: a ruthless centralisation of capital

Like the other industries covered earlier in this book, NXP has used JVs towards eventual acquisition (or at least a dominant stake). For instance, in 2006, NXP acquired a 10.7 percent stake in Systems on Silicon Manufacturing Co. Pte. Ltd. (SSMC), a leading semiconductor maker by buying it from Singapore's EDBI for US$185 million; at that time, SSMC was a JV between Philips (50.5 percent), TSMC (32 percent) and EDBI (17.5 percent). By November 2006, NXP had increased its stake in SSMC to a controlling 61.2 percent through a US$113 million cash payment (NXP, 2006b; NXP, 2012b). The company has also forged other JVs and alliances to secure greater scale economies in semiconductor manufacturing. These other JVs and alliances include Advanced Semiconductor Manufacturing Co. Ltd. (formed in 1995), Suzhou ASEN Semiconductors Co. Ltd (formed in 2007), Datang NXP Semiconductors (formed in 2013) Cohda Wireless Pty Ltd (formed in 2013) and WeEn Semiconductors (formed in 2016) where NXP holds stakes of 27 percent, 40 percent, 49 percent, 23 percent and 49 percent respectively; its former JV, Jilin NXP Semiconductors Ltd (formed in 2003) was merged with its 2016 cooperative effort, WeEn Semiconductors (NXP, 2012b; NXP, 2015b; WeEn Semiconductor, 2017). Advanced Semiconductor Manufacturing Co. Ltd. and Jilin NXP Semiconductors Ltd were formed through NXP's former parent, Philips, underscoring the firm foundations it laid for NXP (NXP, 2010). Given the rapid consolidation in the global semiconductor industry, NXP could target the acquisition of the remaining stakes in some of these JVs.

In April 2012, NXP acquired 100 percent of Dutch-based Catena Group, an electronic design and IP company. NXP asserts that the acquisition of Catena would not only bolster its innovation capabilities but also augment its already robust positions in the automotive analogue mixed signal solutions business and the wireless car connectivity field. The value of Catena's acquisition is highlighted by NXP's CEO, Rick Clemmer: 'Combining the core competencies of both teams enables us to further strengthen our leadership in wireless connectivity in automotive and other sectors. Catena has already made a significant contribution to NXP becoming the number one chip supplier for the global car entertainment market . . .' (Clemmer, 2012). However, in an industry plagued by ever-increasing demands for scale economies and the threat of technological obsolescence, NXP saw the urgent need to join the ranks of the top-tier automotive semiconductor makers. Thus, in December 2015, NXP made a 'bet-the-firm' move by acquiring Freescale (traditionally slightly ahead of it in terms of market share), a firm that was controlled by leading private equity player, Blackstone and its investment partners. NXP's 'bet-the-firm' acquisition strategy is in direct contrast to the more conservative bolt-on acquisition strategy favoured by today's firms; bolt-on strategies are financially less risky, as they allow acquirers to target specific assets while avoiding the significant legacy issues surrounding the assimilation of entire corporations.

Through this ruthless centralisation of capital, NXP not only gained control of Freescale's market share but also reaped the fruit of its earlier acquisition efforts. Like its acquirer (i.e., NXP), Freescale was the result of a spin-off. In 2004, Freescale was created when Motorola spun off its semiconductor products division. Freescale had a strong start, as it was able to leverage on the significant breakthroughs achieved by its former parent, Motorola. Despite its more sterling reputation in telecommunications, Motorola was, in fact, a pioneer in automotive semiconductors. For instance, Motorola introduced the first mass-produced semiconductors for use in car radios as early as 1957. More importantly, the first significant application of Motorola's microprocessors was an automotive ECU in 1980. Due to the firm foundations laid by Motorola, Freescale began life as the third largest independent semiconductor company in the US, with a significant global footprint (it had R&D, manufacturing and sales operations spread across 30 countries). This was further augmented by over 50 years of experience of manufacturing semiconductors as part of Motorola, Inc. In its drive to obtain greater scale economies and new technologies, Freescale acquired Canada-based Seaway Networks Inc. a private fabless semiconductor supplier of content processing technology in August 2005 (Bloomberg, 2012); Seaway's expertise and intellectual property in content processing, advanced networking and traffic management complemented Freescale's expertise in communications processors (Freescale, 2012c). The acquisition was relatively swift and smooth, as the two companies had complementary technologies (Seaway's content processing solutions used Freescale's processors which contained PowerPC cores) and strong ties formed long before the acquisition (Seaway was a Freescale design alliance partner); buying out one's long-time partner or supplier is an effective way of ensuring a successful acquisition (Freescale, 2005).

Freescale itself became engulfed by this wave of consolidation, as it was soon acquired by a consortium of private equity firms led by Blackstone in 2006 for US$17.6 billion; the other private equity firms included Carlyle, Permira Funds and Texas Pacific Group (Kraeuter, 2006; Klier and Rubenstein, 2008). Following its acquisition by Blackstone, Freescale pressed on with its acquisition strategy to gain greater scale economies; around this time, a Freescale executive cynically described his company as 'a platform for participating in the consolidation of the industry through acquisitions' (quoted in Brown and Linden, 2009). In 2008, Freescale acquired SigmaTel Inc for about US$110 million in cash. The acquisition was executed to augment Freescale's strengths in automotive infotainment microprocessors and consumer electronics (Electronic Design, 2008). In that same year, Freescale also acquired privately-held Intoto, Inc., a leading provider of software platform products for networking and communications equipment manufacturers. This acquisition not only gave Freescale greater scale economies but also strengthened its capabilities in cutting-edge multicore chip (chips that are not only high-powered but also extremely energy efficient) development (Freescale, 2008a). These acquisitions also enabled Freescale to secure control of valuable patents which would allow the firm to augment its intellectual property with additional legal protection; very often, these patents can be used strategically against competitors by accusing them of infringement. The acquisition of smaller firms by Freescale also supports the earlier argument by TK Quinn that small firms, not multinationals, are often the source of cutting-edge innovations (Quinn, 1953). However, Quinn fails to note that it is only large multinationals such as Freescale that are capable of commercialising revolutionary technologies on a global scale and further develop their potential (Chandler and Hikino, 1999); this is especially so in the case of the automotive semiconductor industry where capital and R&D expenditures can easily amount to billions of dollars.

Private equity firms such as Blackstone have become an undeniable force in the automotive semiconductor industry. However, they are financial investors (i.e., acquiring firms they believe to be undervalued and selling them for profit later), rather than long-term strategic investors. These private equity firms also tend to make acquisitions through assuming a significant amount of debt (these acquisitions are usually 60–90 percent debt financed) and often use the cash of acquired firms to service the massive debt. In some cases, private equity firms might even saddle the firms with more debt after acquisitions, to pay themselves special dividends later; during this period, these firms often lay off significant numbers of people from the acquired firms to reduce costs. Despite the controversial nature of such acquisitions, it is sometimes argued these financiers are incentivised to promote greater efficiency (sometimes, they could merely introduce cosmetic changes such as layoffs to reduce overheads), as they want to 'flip' the acquired firm to another buyer later for significant profit (Kaplan and Stromberg, 2009; The Economist, 2012).

Nonetheless, strategic investors (non-private equity acquirers) are not always better, as they tend to be more hesitant in terminating underperforming projects as they believe themselves to be investing in the business for the long haul (Arping and Falconieri, 2007). Proponents of private equity firms also argue they play a critical role in separating the wheat from the chaff (they have to first determine that the target firms are indeed firms with growth potential, and then ensure that the acquired firms have the right management, and are in the right markets with the right products), as they are, after all, risking a significant amount of money (Morrill et al., 2009).

In a sign that suggests greater antitrust scrutiny in the global automotive components industry, Freescale voiced the following concern in its 2011 annual report: 'Our ability to acquire targets may also be limited by applicable antitrust laws and other regulations in the US, the EU and other jurisdictions in which we do business' (Freescale, 2011). Given the dominant market power wielded by the merged NXP and Freescale, regulators are even more likely to scrutinise their operations microscopically for evidence of anticompetitive behaviour. Moreover, automakers fearful of the increasing power of their suppliers have also begun monitoring them for signs of collusion and in some cases, have taken legal action against such behaviour. For instance, several automakers have taken legal action against their windshield glass suppliers (Asahi, Pilkington, Saint-Gobain and Soliver) after the European Commission found them guilty in 2008 of anticompetitive collusive behaviour. With the intensifying power struggle between carmakers and their mega suppliers, it is a matter of time before suppliers in other subsectors face similar punitive measures from their clients (Simon, 2011).

NXP and Freescale: technical progress and process improvement

Notwithstanding increasing competition and cost pressures, NXP continues to underscore its commitment to technical progress, by investing US$592 million in R&D in 2015; one could argue that it has no choice, as the player with relatively obsolete technology would be quickly eliminated in an increasingly high-tech industry. Further, as of December 2015, NXP had around 8,831 R&D related staff (8,481 of these research employees work in its High Performance Mixed Signal segment while the remaining 350 support the firm's Standard Products businesses) (NXP, 2015a).

Through its acquisition of Freescale, NXP not only gained significant technical expertise but perhaps equally important expertise in deploying process improvements (usually through lean practices) in mitigating production costs and sustaining profit margins. Despite being the smallest of the top four automotive semiconductor makers, Freescale was a key innovator in the industry, a position made possible by exemplary industry-leading process innovation. In 2011 alone, Freescale was able to expand its Qorivva automotive microcontroller portfolio, by launching the Qorivva 32-bit microcontroller based on Power Architecture technology which was created to increase the accessibility of surround-camera parking assist systems (once the preserve of luxury vehicles) to a wider range of vehicles; this chip basically conveys high-resolution visual data over Fast Ethernet, facilitating an all-around view of the vehicle's immediate surroundings, rendering safer and greater ease in parking (Freescale, 2011). In that same year, Freescale was also able to triple the performance of its market-leading integrated circuits to deliver the considerable processing capabilities which have become critical in powering sophisticated direct fuel-injection components and increasingly advanced hybrid and electric vehicles.

In 2011, Freescale was also able to launch its new multicore i.MX 6-series of applications processors for the next generation of automotive infotainment devices; Freescale's i.MX chip currently is the 'brains' behind the driver infotainment and telematics systems in more than ten of the top automakers (Freescale, 2011). Moreover, in April 2012, Freescale introduced its multicore Qorivva MPC5746M microcontroller which was developed to meet rising demand for superior performance in automotive powertrains while concurrently addressing increasingly sophisticated safety and application security needs. This chip also provides optimal performance for a broad range of automotive systems which include internal combustion engines, hybrid systems and transmission systems. Further it recognises and prevents electronics system faults and also protects vehicles from potential hackers as vehicles become increasingly connected (Freescale, 2012b). Through its 2015 acquisition of Freescale, NXP was thus attempting to integrate this superlative chip technology into its portfolio, without having to go through the usual expensive but not necessarily fruitful product development cycle.

Further, Freescale forged collaborations with other industry players to keep pace with the rapid advances and rising customer expectations in the automotive semiconductor industry. For instance, through its collaboration with Macronix (a specialist in Serial Flash Technology), Freescale would be able to equip its Qorivva microchip with Macronix's Serial Flash technology which enables superior high-resolution colour, 'Thin Film Transistor' dual displays and video input capabilities for more advanced automotive dashboard displays (resulting in greater driver safety) (Macronix, 2011). Freescale could have undoubtedly developed this technology on its own but it would further sap its relatively weak financial resources (compared to its larger competitors) in an increasingly competitive industry plagued by ever-increasing costs and customer expectations. Freescale was also part of an industry cooperative effort known as the 'OPEN Alliance Special Interest Group' (OPEN SIG) which aims to drive the rapid adoption of Ethernet in automobiles, given the rising connectivity of today's vehicles. The other members of the alliance include NXP (Freescale's eventual acquirer), Broadman (the leading provider of semiconductor solutions for wired and wireless communications) and Haman (a provider of infotainment solutions for the automotive and consumer markets). This alliance endeavoured to work on industry standards and needs for strengthening ride comfort, in-vehicle safety and infotainment while fostering efforts to attenuate network complexity and associated cabling costs (Hammerschmidt, 2011). Such alliances could become more commonplace, as the sheer development costs of in-vehicle networking technologies could prove too much for any semiconductor firm on its own.

Barely catching a breath from its blitzkrieg-like acquisition of Freescale, NXP has continued to press the boundaries of technical progress in what has become a winner-takes-all market. In May 2016, NXP launched its ultra-sophisticated BlueBox platform which was developed with the expressed purpose of assisting automakers in the manufacture and testing of autonomous vehicles. Through this platform, NXP would be able to define the technology that automakers (their suppliers included) need to meet the exacting safety, power and processing performance preconditions in an increasingly technology-driven automotive industry (Korosec, 2016; NXP, 2016b); simply put, if NXP is able to successfully implement its agenda, it would be able to set the standards and define the rules of the game in the near future.

In its earlier existence as Freescale, the firm strove tenaciously to secure process improvements as a means of mitigating ever-rising costs. In 2007, Freescale began to ramp up its adoption of lean production. For instance, it commenced the reinvention of its Oak Hill facility in Austin, Texas, converting it from a fab making five to ten high-volume products (working with around 20 active mask sets) to one making a broad range of low-volume products, using more than 250 active mask sets. This conversion would normally have cost Freescale at least US$100 million and clients typically were reluctant to bear part of the conversion cost. However, it managed to pull off this conversion at a fraction of the cost, without client support. According to Chris Magnella, director of Freescale's Oak Hill fab operations, this was achieved through a shift to a lean manufacturing culture, which was about deploying suitable engineers where they are most needed. He also added that Freescale basically invested mainly on areas where it could use existing equipment and slash costs innovatively. For instance, Freescale's engineers purchased a standard Maytag dishwasher from Home Depot and converted it into a MEMS (microelectromechanical systems) box washer used at the Oak Hill facility (Hand, 2010); MEMs enable tiny electrical and mechanical components to be built onto a single chip and is used by companies such as Freescale to make acceleration, pressure and other sensors (Freescale, 2012a). The above innovative cost-saving measures were particularly important for Freescale, as it did not have the financial muscle of its much larger competitors such as Renesas and Infineon which easily have automotive semiconductor revenues two or three times that of Freescale's; however in an industry driven by ever-increasing economies of scale and scope and relentless consolidation, such process ingenuity was still insufficient and Freescale's survival as an independent entity, even at that point, seemed uncertain.

Freescale had also incorporated the lean practice of pull, which involves giving customers what they want and not wasting resources in trying to convince them that the product is what they require; this is best exemplified by Freescale's cutting-edge Qorivva microchip (cited earlier) which was developed in cooperation with one of its automaker customers, BMW (product development involving customers is the most direct way of giving them what they want) (Womack and Jones, 2005). Further, Freescale married its lean practices with that of 'six sigma' to work towards a 'zero defect' culture; the firm's six sigma system identifies misaligned processes that require the necessary adjustment and also ensures that specification limits are deployed to assess the accuracy of product design as per design stipulations. Resultantly, Freescale asserts that through this 'zero defect' methodology, products are subject to optimal quality scrutiny throughout the various production stages of design, wafer fabrication, assembly and testing, and eventually delivering the uncompromising quality expected by its customers (Freescale, 2011).

Infineon: profile

Backed by its superlative technology and sheer competitive tenacity, the German chip juggernaut, Infineon has carved for itself the hard-fought rank of the world's second largest producer of automotive semiconductors in the early days of 2016 (predicated on its 9.27 percent (US$2.69 billion) 2015 full-year global market share). In 2015, Infineon posted overall revenues of €5.795 billion (US$6.473 billion) and a net profit of €634 million (US$724.8 million). Infineon's automotive division was its largest business segment, generating 40.6 percent (€2.351 billion or US$2.69 billion) of its total revenues (Figure 7.2); its automotive semiconductor revenues have nearly tripled since

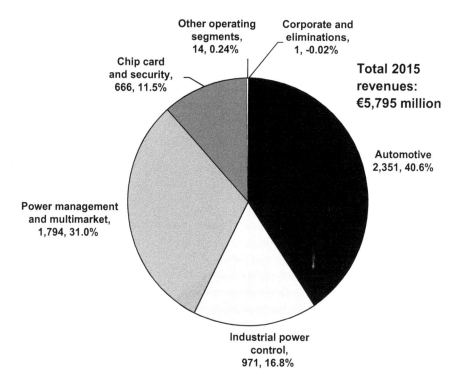

Figure 7.2 Infineon's 2015 annual revenues (€ million)

Source: 2015 Infineon Annual Report

2000 (Infineon's automotive revenues in 2000 was €880.2 million) (Infineon, 2000; Infineon, 2015a). The following Figure 7.3 indicates that Infineon generates nearly half of its overall revenues (€2.666 billion) from the Asia Pacific region. China is now Infineon's single largest market, as it alone accounted for 23.1 percent (€1.337 billion) of Infineon's 2015 revenues; the country became Infineon's largest single market in 2014 owing to its burgeoning middle class (growing at 10 million annually) and their rising demand for automobiles.

Infineon's major customers include Autoliv, Bosch, BYD, Continental, Delphi, Denso, Hella, Lear, Mando, Omron, Tesla, Valeo and ZF. It also supplies directly to automakers such as BYD, Hyundai, Mitsubishi and Tesla (Infineon, 2015a). To support the global expansion strategies of these automakers, Infineon has established 19 production sites across 11 countries. In February 2012, Infineon also constructed a new 100,000-sq.m. semiconductor plant in Kulim, Malaysia; this facility augmented its production capacity for power semiconductors (used extensively in hybrid and electric vehicles). This Kulim site was further expanded in 2015 to meet increasing demand for the aforementioned power semiconductors. As of September 2015, Infineon had around 35,400 employees worldwide (Solid State Technology, 2012; Infineon, 2015a).

In 2015, Infineon recorded procurement expenses of €2.469 billion (US$2.823 billion), the highest among the top four automotive semiconductor makers. Consequently, as in the case of its key rival, Renesas, Infineon enjoys significant leverage over its suppliers. However, the balance of power between Infineon and its foundry suppliers (e.g., UMC) is also shifting, as companies

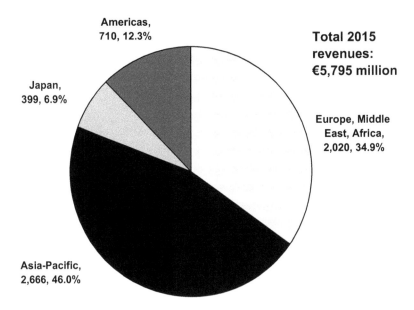

Figure 7.3 Infineon's 2015 revenues by region (€ million)

Source: 2015 Infineon Annual Report

such as UMC have also consolidated and become multi-billion companies with considerable market power themselves (UMC recorded 2015 overall revenues of US\$4.417 billion, which is more than Infineon's US\$2.69 billion automotive semiconductor business for that year) (UMC, 2015; Infineon, 2015a).

Infineon's acquisitions over the past decade

Infineon, the world's second largest producer of automotive semiconductors was spun off from Siemens in 1999 (Floerecke, 2005). The spun-off division, previously known as Siemens Semiconductors was a significant operation, with 1998 revenues of US\$3.8 billion, and had around 25,000 employees worldwide (Ascierto, 1999). Infineon's illustrious origins laid solid foundations for the launch of Infineon, as it began life with sizeable revenues, advanced technology and a global footprint. Since its inception, the company has continuously strived to boost its range of semiconductor offerings in the automotive industry, aided by a series of acquisitions and JVs. In May 2001, Infineon formed a JV with Saifun Semiconductors Ltd. (the JV firm was known as Ingentix) to make flash memory products (according to Dr. Boaz Eitan, Saifun Semiconductors' then CEO, these chips also have automotive applications) based on Saifun's patented technology (this suggests that JVs like outright acquisitions could be an effective means of securing control of the latest technologies). Through a US\$17 million investment, Infineon became the controlling partner with a 51 percent stake in this JV (Infineon, 2001). However, this JV was subsequently renamed Infineon Technologies Flash as Infineon steadily increased its shareholding in the JV and eventually bought out Saifun's entire stake in January 2005 (Infineon acquired Saifun's remaining 30 percent stake for US\$46 million and secured a licence to use Saifun's proprietary technology) (Infineon, 2004; Infineon, 2006a). This strategy is similar to GKN's strategy in using JVs as a springboard to eventual acquisition.

Further, in 2003, Infineon acquired SensoNor ASA for about US\$56 million, in an attempt to augment its position in automotive semiconductor sensors; SensoNor produced and marketed tyre pressure and acceleration sensors. The acquisition of SensoNor made Infineon the leader of the tyre pressure sensor segment (EDN, 2003; Infineon, 2006b). This acquisition also highlights Infineon's resolve to grow its automotive semiconductor offerings via acquisitions.

To achieve the ever-increasing economies of scale and scope needed to survive the withering competition in a fast consolidating industry, Infineon has persisted with its acquisition drive. In 2008, Infineon acquired Primarion, a leader in power management systems. This acquisition was executed to secure power management capabilities that would complement Infineon's semiconductor manufacturing strengths. In the semiconductor industry, the above examples indicate that the main driver of consolidation is economies of scale. The importance of scale economies is also stressed by Peter Wennick, CFO of ASML Holding N.V. who commented: 'Market consolidation in the semiconductor industry is an inevitable trend which actually started at the end of the last decade and will continue. The main driver for consolidation is the need for economies of scale.

R&D costs are ever-increasing and only by achieving production economies of scale can firms cover their R&D expenses' (quoted in Balhaus, Pagella and Vogel, 2009); Wennick was right on most counts except for his analysis that consolidation had begun in the late 1990s, as the previous corporate forms (as divisions of leading electronics multinationals) of the industry oligopolists had spent decades building up these semiconductor businesses through a combination of mergers and organic growth strategies.

However, in 2010, Infineon sold its wireless chips business to Intel (for an estimated US$1.4 billion) to focus on its core business of automotive chips, which accounts for two-fifths of its revenues; the funds raised from the sale were expected be used to finance acquisitions in key areas such as automotive microchips (Infineon, 2010; Virki, 2011). The need for greater economies of scale has also led to the growth of JVs, which allow firms to gain scale economies without incurring the significant risks and costs involved in outright acquisitions; acquisitions usually involve paying a significant premium (the acquisition of a public firm usually involves paying a premium of 15–50 percent over the existing share price) and are harder to unravel (after acquisition, different accounting, human resources, finance and supply chain systems are merged thus unravelling is considerably more complex), if the desired merger synergies are not achieved; acquisitions are also costly, as they involve significant legal and due diligence costs (numerous lawyers, accountants, bankers and consultants are typically involved) (Kaplan, 1989; Kaplan and Stromberg, 2009; Bargeron et al., 2008). Such partnerships also allow firms to fuel growth in new markets and alleviate rising research costs. For instance, in 2009, Infineon forged a partnership with TSMC to develop cutting-edge 65 nanometre embedded flash (eFlash) process technology targeting next-generation automotive, chip card and security applications (Whytock, 2009).

In a sign that it is not slowing down on its acquisition campaign, Infineon indicated in June 2011 that it would retain some of its more than €2 billion (US$2.9 billion) in net cash for opportunistic acquisitions. However, Infineon did suggest that automotive semiconductor firms were getting more expensive to acquire (making strategic alliances a more viable option) (Klemming and Kjetland, 2011). Earlier in May 2011, Infineon, in its drive to secure even more scale economies, had acquired the cleanroom and manufacturing facilities of Qimonda for approximately US$144 million (EE Times Asia, 2011). This acquisition was expected to give Infineon added capabilities in the production of power semiconductors that are used in electric vehicles and a host of consumer electronics. These acquired facilities were also located in an area that bordered Infineon's premises in Dresden, Germany, affording the company greater synergies in coordinating its supply chain (Infineon, 2011). This transaction reinforces the argument that it is sometimes better for an acquirer to purchase only the assets of a firm (it is only buying what it needs) instead of making an outright acquisition. This bolt-on approach is not only more cost-effective but also limits the acquirer's obligations; once an acquirer secures full or majority control of a firm, it also assumes full responsibility of its legal and financial obligations, which could be obscured by the legalese of its financial statements.

In January 2015, Infineon also completed its approximately US$3 billion all cash acquisition of US-based International Rectifier Corporation, a maker of power semiconductors (with recorded revenues of US$ 1.1 billion in June 2014). The price which Infineon paid for International Rectifier represented a 50 percent premium, underscoring the considerable synergies which Infineon is confident of reaping from this acquisition. The acquisition not only gave Infineon much need economies of scale but also a stronger presence in Asia and the United States. More importantly, the deal greatly augmented Infineon's capabilities in power semiconductors, (critical components in increasingly popular hybrid and electric vehicles) and expertise in power conversion (De La Merced, 2014; Infineon, 2014; Infineon, 2015c). In its relentless acquisition campaign, Infineon soon acquired Cree Inc's Wolfspeed Power and Radio Frequency division for an approximated US$850 million in cash in January 2016; Cree is a US-based maker of semiconductors for power and radio frequency applications. Infineon viewed this acquisition as complementary to its earlier takeover of International Rectifier, as it bolstered the company's capabilities in making semiconductors for premium markets in electric cars, renewable energy and cutting-edge cellular network pertaining to the 'Internet of Things'[3] (this infrastructure would also involve the 'connected' car) (Infineon, 2016a; Geiger and Henning, 2016). Not letting up on this unremitting consolidation wave, Infineon soon acquired Innoluce BV, a Nijmegen headquartered fabless semiconductor company in October 2016. This acquisition was executed to give Infineon much needed capabilities in MEMS-based lidar (light detection and ranging)[4] technologies, an increasingly critical component in semi-automated and fully autonomous vehicles (Infineon, 2016b). This MEMS lidar which has the capability of scanning 5,000 data points for every scene on a per second basis, is also effective up to 250 metres. This cutting-edge lidar technology is expected to form part of a sophisticated network of integrated safety systems (ultrasonic sensors, lidar, radar and digital cameras) that would provide autonomous vehicles with an enveloping 'safety cocoon' (Bornefeld, 2016; The Economist, 2016).

Infineon's technical progress and adoption of lean principles

Technical progress and innovation lies at the heart of Infineon's strategy. To secure technological leadership in this rapidly evolving market, Infineon spent around 12.4 percent (€717 million or US$819.7 million) of its 2015 revenues on R&D and this considerable investment in R&D has contributed to its intellectual property holdings (in 2015, Infineon had more than 25,000 patent and patent applications, with 2,200 of them coming from its acquired firm, International Rectifier). The firm's R&D facilities span 32 sites across 13 countries, supported by 5,778 personnel (about 16 percent of its total workforce) (Infineon, 2015a). To stay at the cutting-edge of automotive semiconductor development, Infineon also works with leading educational institutions such as the Graz University of Technology, Vienna University of Technology, Bochum University and Erlangen University.

Infineon asserts that its innovators concentrate on 'energy efficiency, mobility and security, three of the great global challenges of our age'. Further it is this commitment to innovation that gives Infineon its competitive advantage (Infineon, 2011). Infineon's innovation has enabled the firm to dominate the increasingly complex field of automotive semiconductors. For instance, in 2010, Infineon launched its new AUDO MAX family of 32-bit microcontrollers for automotive powertrain and chassis applications; this range of microcontrollers facilitates the creation of engine management systems in compliance with stringent Euro 5 and Euro 6 emission standards for combustion vehicles while also enabling the powering of powertrains used in electrical vehicles (Infineon, 2010); this expertise in producing chips for increasingly fuel-efficient and environmentally-friendly engine management systems is a key competitive advantage in a regulatory environment that is actively promoting the use of vehicles equipped with such systems (includes hybrids and electric vehicles). Semiconductor companies such as Infineon are positioned to benefit from this trend, as the semiconductor content per car (for engine management systems) is approximately valued at around US$600-US$700 in hybrid and electric vehicles, as opposed to just US$250-US$300 in combustion engine vehicles. Further, combustion engine vehicles themselves are getting increasingly fuel-efficient, thus they too could demand increasingly fuel-efficient technologies powered by Infineon chips; for internal-combustion powered cars, Infineon also has an AUDO MAX chip that is capable of determining the optimal fuel-air mixture and the appropriate fuel injection and ignition timing for each individual cylinder (Infineon, 2010).

Further, Infineon's XC2200 microcontroller family fulfils the demanding requirements of a vehicle's 'Body Control Module' applications such as car access, door modules, internal and external lighting systems. It also meets the requirements of the vehicle's Central Gateway applications that run on-board internal interfaces (e.g., dashboard or convenient control, motor management, in-car entertainment) and the interaction with external interfaces for after-sales software updates along with 'Heating, Ventilation and Air-Conditioning' (hereafter 'HVAC') applications. Moreover, these highly-integrated microcontrollers not only offer superior performance but also feature very low power consumption in stand-by and operation mode (Avnet, 2012; Infineon, 2007). Over the last five years, Infineon has been focusing its considerable resources on developing the technology needed to serve as the 'brains' of semi-automated and automated systems. By 2015, Infineon had achieved significant breakthroughs in radar chips capable of measuring the distance between vehicles and their relative velocities; with this capability in place, these intelligent systems are able to give drivers early warning and even trigger emergency braking when needed (Infineon, 2015c). These cutting-edge technologies are not just an outcome of Infineon's commitment to R&D but also due to its ability to harness the various technologies it secured through acquisitions (see earlier section) over the past two decades. According to Infineon's CFO, Dominik Asam (in 2011), the company was prepared to spend another €1 billion on acquisitions with particular interest in firms with energy efficiency capabilities (this would augment Infineon's already strong capabilities in energy efficient yet high performance microchips). Asam also added that given Infineon's strong finances, the company could conduct smaller acquisitions with its existing cash reserves alone (Sheahan, 2011); this emphasis on smaller acquisitions is in keeping with recent industry trends of acquiring bolt-ons (e.g., Infineon's purchase of Qimonda's cleanroom and manufacturing facilities) rather than making 'bet-the-farm' multi-billion-dollar acquisitions. Further, in a volatile market where revolutionary technologies are now unfolding at a breakneck pace, Infineon has little choice but to deploy M&A as the primary vehicle in securing proven technologies which it could readily commercialise. Without the acquisition of smaller firms such as Innoluce (cited earlier), it would have taken Infineon years to develop the lidar technology which it is now incorporating into its already considerable automated systems portfolio.

Infineon is also not averse to working with rivals such as Bosch (also a customer) and STM, in order to gain much needed economies of scale and scope, along with next-generation technologies (e.g., power semiconductors) (Infineon, 2009). Going forward, Infineon and Bosch will work jointly on the development of enabling technologies for the production of power semiconductors. Through its cooperation with Bosch, Infineon would not only expand its share of the automotive semiconductor market, it would also become Bosch's preferred supplier of power semiconductors (Infineon, 2009). Infineon and Bosch have actually been collaborating in chip development for several years. A further indication of this ingrained relationship is that Infineon has received the 'Bosch Global Supplier Award' five times (the last occasion was 2015) for various categories spanning over a decade (Infineon, 2009; Infineon, 2015b). Infineon has also worked with one of its key rivals, STM in the development of power semiconductors. This collaboration has yielded significant breakthroughs, as indicated in the following statements from Maurizio Giudice, the Marketing Director of STM's Power Transistor Division who described the resulting power semiconductor as 'the most advanced in the industry' and 'will deliver the highest power density and efficiency among devices of comparable voltage rating' (STM, 2010a). Although rising research costs and ever-increasing demands for scale economies necessitate such intimate collaborations between rivals, there is also heightened risk of negative spillovers such as acrimonious disputes over intellectual property (unless ownership terms are clearly specified and enforceable) and industrial espionage.

In an effort to strengthen process improvement, Infineon has adopted some aspects of lean enterprise (e.g., just-in-time, kaizen/continuous improvement). For instance, Infineon has been operating an internal idea management system for several years to facilitate continuous improvement. According to Infineon, this system known as 'Your Idea Pays' (YIP) is critical in encouraging a steady flow of suggestions from employees. The company also has a 'Voice of Customer' programme to understand the needs of the customer at the transactional level (known as 'Gemba' in lean) through constant engagement, with the aim of taking corrective action immediately and ultimately better meeting customer needs (lean is about giving customers what they want and not about spending additional resources to convince them about what they need) (Womack and Jones, 2005). Infineon has even appointed specially designated 'Lean Manufacturing Managers' across their various plants (Infineon, 2012). Nonetheless, Infineon's lean programme lacks the comprehensive nature of its closest rival, Renesas, which now has several contingency measures in place to address any potential lapses. However, Renesas' seemingly water-tight lean manufacturing programme is the result of being the victim of the 2011 earthquake which exposed fundamental weaknesses in lean. Further, Infineon does not have a centralised lean programme, in the same vein as Bridgestone's (Chapter 3), thus making it harder to spread lean principles effectively across all levels of an increasingly large organisation.

Renesas: profile

Defying the wildly disruptive acquisition upheavals coursing through this industry, Renesas stoically earned a hard-fought place as the world's third largest producer of automotive semiconductors (includes microcontrollers, SoC solutions) in the first quarter of 2016 (based on an estimated 9.2 percent global market share (US$2.66 billion) in 2015) (IHS, 2016; Renesas, 2016). As evidenced in Figure 7.4, Renesas recorded revenues of approximately US$5.73 billion

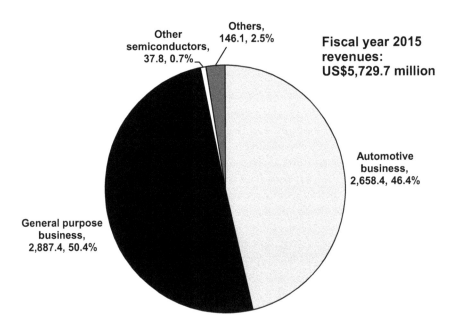

Figure 7.4 Renesas' fiscal year 2015 revenues (US$ million)

Source: Renesas Financial Report 2016, Year Ended 31 March 2016

(Fiscal Year is from 1 April 2015 to 31 March 2016)

for fiscal year 2015 (1 April 2015 to 31 March 2016), with the automotive business accounting for a significant 46.4 percent (US$2.66 billion) of Renesas' total sales; the Japanese fiscal year starts from April of the year concerned to March of the following year. Microcontrollers accounted for approximately 90 percent (US$2.4 billion) of Renesas' 2015 automotive business. In the case of automotive microcontrollers,[5] Renesas' global market share was a near hegemonic 40 percent stake in 2015 (by industry revenues) (Nelson, 2015; Databeans, 2012; Databeans, 2016). For fiscal year 2015, Renesas also recorded a net profit of US$713.2 million. Despite Renesas' position as one of the industry leaders, it is still highly dependent on its domestic market, drawing 43.8 percent (US$2.5 billion) of its revenues from Japan (Figure 7.5).

Further, despite Renesas' significant market share in automotive semiconductors, it faces considerable difficulty in making profits, reinforcing the fact that not all leading subsystems integrators are profitable. From fiscal years 2010 to 2015, Renesas reported net losses in three out of the six years. As indicated in Table 7.1, Renesas in the fiscal years 2010, 2011 and 2013 suffered successive net losses of approximately US$1.3372 billion, US$792.4 million and US$53 million respectively. Renesas only regained its profitability in the fiscal years 2014 and 2015, posting net incomes of US$763 million and US$713.2 million; this profitability came at a hefty price as it involved extensive restructuring which

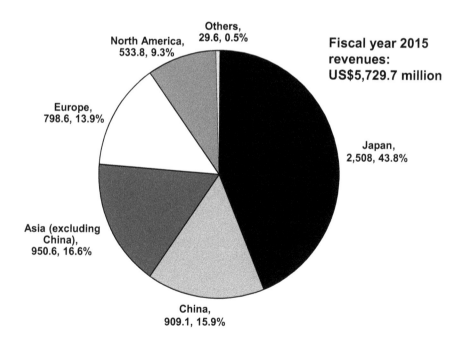

Figure 7.5 Renesas' fiscal year 2015 revenues by region (US$ million)

Source: Renesas Financial Report 2016, Year Ended 31 March 2016

(Fiscal Year is from 1 April 2015 to 31 March 2016)

Table 7.1 Renasas' net income (loss) 2010–2015 (US$ million)

Year	Net Income (Loss)
2010	(1,337.2)
2011	(792.4)
2012	2,043.9
2013	(53)
2014	763
2015	713.2

Source: Renasas Annual Reports

involved the elimination of over 20,000 jobs and the closure of several plants in Japan (Renesas, 2016).

In 2011 and 2012, Renesas' losses were to some extent due to its under-performing consumer electronics division, which faced declining demand for its system LSI chips, used for processing images for TV screens. Renesas remains relatively profitable for automotive microcontrollers (about 10 percent profit margin) owing to its dominant global market share (Amano, 2012; Renesas, 2012). The highly-cyclical nature of the automotive industry also contributes to the considerable volatility in Renesas' profitability.

As of March 2016, Renesas had 19,160 employees worldwide. In that period, Renesas had nine manufacturing and engineering service, five design and applica-tion technologies and 14 sales companies worldwide (Renesas, 2016). Renesas is controlled by a Japanese government -backed investment firm, INCJ, which has an approximate 70 percent stake in the firm (Uranaka and Yamazaki, 2016). The company supplies all the major Japanese automakers (e.g., Toyota, Nissan and Honda) along with leading American automakers such as GM and Ford (Dishman, 2012). Moreover, in 2016, Renesas recorded procurement expenses of US$1.552 billion (Renesas, 2016). With this significant purchasing spend, Renesas wields considerable market power over its suppliers, enabling it to extract concessions such as discounts (a power that it is likely to use more often, as Renesas experiences increasing pressure from the automakers). However, this approach of squeezing suppliers looks increasingly untenable, as Renesas' suppli-ers are themselves consolidating and have become multi-billion-dollar enterprises themselves. For instance, Renesas now refers to its foundry supplier, TSMC as a partner rather than supplier, and it has outsourced partial microcontroller pro-duction (those using 90 nanometre eFlash process technology) to TSMC. In May 2012, the two firms even signed an agreement to extend their partnership to include next-generation automotive and consumer applications (Solid State Technology, 2012).

Renesas, a product of relentless consolidation

Renesas Technology was formed in April 2003 as a JV between Hitachi Ltd and Mitsubishi Electric Corp which owned 55 percent and 45 percent respectively

(Klier and Rubenstein, 2008). The JV had 27,200 employees (upon its establishment) and recorded estimated revenues of 900 billion yen (about US$7.33 billion) in 2003. Further, the two partners moved their respective microcomputer, memory (includes flash memory, static random access memory (hereafter 'SRAM')), logic, analogue and discrete devices operations into Renesas (Clarke, 2002).[6] This JV also had 7 percent of the global semiconductor market and was the leading microcontroller supplier (Klier and Rubenstein, 2008). This earlier version of Renesas was also not profitable, posting estimated net losses of US$858.03 million and US$603.8 million in 2009 and 2010 respectively (Renesas, 2010). However, in a relentless drive to secure greater economies of scale and scope, Hitachi and Mitsubishi (the existing shareholders of Renesas Technology) agreed to merge with NEC Corp (the parent of NEC Electronics) in 2009 to form a new entity, Renesas Electronics Corp (operational by April 1, 2010). This merger was financed by Renesas issuing its common stock to NEC Corp, Hitachi and Mitsubishi in exchange for an investment of about 134.6 billion yen (US$1.44 billion) (Renesas, 2010).

Nonetheless, NEC would have the largest equity stake of 33.97 percent while Hitachi and Mitsubishi would have smaller stakes of approximately 30.7 percent and 25.1 percent respectively; the remaining 1.5 percent is held by Japan Trustee Services Bank, Ltd. (The Associated Press, 2009; Renesas, 2012). The new Renesas became the world's third largest semiconductor company by revenues (about US$14 billion) upon inception (ranking just behind Intel and Samsung Electronics Co.), positioning it for the eventual dominance of the global automotive microcontroller industry. The newly merged Renesas also had 47,000 employees spread across 20 subsidiaries worldwide (Renesas, 2012). Through this merger, both NEC Electronics and Renesas Technology received a much-needed capital infusion of around US$2.2 billion (Kachi and Maxwell, 2009). Soon after this merger, Renesas continued with its acquisition campaign. In July 2010, Renesas Electronics acquired Nokia's wireless modem business for about US$200 million. The critical nature of this acquisition is evidenced in this statement by Kai Oistamo, Executive Vice President, Nokia: 'wireless modems are an integral part of today's chipset solutions' (quoted in Renesas, 2010). The deal also includes an alliance to conduct long-term joint research on future radio technologies. Further, this arrangement not only reflects the increasing popularity of alliances in securing additional scale economies and new technologies but also an effective means of spreading the high risks (and costs) involved in developing next-generational technologies. This acquisition ties in with Renesas' belief in the rising convergence of products from automotive and mobile areas. More importantly, it reflects Renesas' desire to dominate this burgeoning market for microchips used in the automotive (particularly automotive infotainment) market. Renesas' acquisition and growth strategy is fundamentally driven by its 'Smart Society' vision that users increasingly desire a seamless integration of internet and email access, text messages as well as personal information data into automobiles, physical infrastructure (e.g., homes and offices) and mobile telephony (Renesas, 2010; Renesas, 2012).

Renesas is also steadily adopting a systems integration business model, similar to that of the leading automakers and their tier-one suppliers. For instance, Renesas, in March 2012, divested Renesas Northern Japan Semiconductor (its wholly-owned subsidiary for automotive microcontrollers) to Fuji Electric Co., Ltd. as part of its strategy to focus more on higher-value added chip design and development. It also outlined plans to sell its Tsuruoka fab in Yamagata Prefecture (a 300mm wafer fab for SoC LSIs) (Semiconductor Portal, 2012). The divestment of these lower value-added fab operations would enable the firm to focus more resources on its more lucrative chip design operations. It would also enable Renesas to make more acquisitions in this upper stratum of the semiconductor value chain, in the process gaining greater economies of scale and scope needed to succeed in this more profitable segment. Nonetheless, burdened by ever-increasing R&D costs, coupled with the crippling repair costs (amounting to US$575.6 million) brought about by the 2011 Japanese earthquake (the incident devastated 40 percent of Renesas' chip production capacity) and declining profitability in its consumer electronics unit wrought by intensifying competition from fast-rising rivals such as Samsung Electronics, Renesas became increasingly vulnerable to acquisitions; Renesas' flagship automotive microcontroller division, with an operating profit margin of at least 10 percent and accounting for approximately 18–19 percent of group revenues, was its only ray of hope amidst this sea of troubles (Renesas, 2011; Savitz, 2011; Electronics.ca, 2012; Fujimura, 2012).

In August 2012, leading private equity firm, KKR, detecting the opportunity presented by Renesas' weakened state, attempted to acquire a controlling stake of more than 50 percent in Renesas for US$1.27 billion, a move that illustrated again the increasing role of 'finance capital' in the global automotive semiconductor industry (Saito, 2012; Soble and Sender, 2012; Hilferding, 1910). Despite the tremendous costs involved in the semiconductor industry, Renesas was a highly attractive acquisition for KKR, whose controversial modus operandi involves buying undervalued companies, turning them around (i.e., selling unprofitable divisions and laying off their employees) and then selling them for a significant profit; despite posting 2011 revenues of US$13.2 billion and total assets of US$13.3 billion, Renesas' market capitalisation was valued at around US$1.4 billion, enabling a successful acquirer to control what was then the world's largest automotive semiconductor supplier at a 'considerable bargain' (Renesas, 2011; Google Finance, 2012).

However, KKR's acquisition attempt was soon displaced in October 2012 by a higher bid (US$2.55 billion) from Japanese state-backed INCJ and a consortium of Japanese multinationals (comprises Toyota, Nissan, Honda, Denso, Nikon, Canon, Panasonic and Yaskawa Electric Corporation (a maker of robots used in car manufacturing)) it was leading at the time. KKR officially withdrew its bid for Renesas on 13 October 2012 (AltAssets, 2012). This government intervention was executed to ensure that strategic technologies (e.g., automotive chip and related technologies) did not fall into foreign hands and compromise Japan's dominance in the global automotive industry; this urgency is exacerbated by the increasing reliance of automakers on sophisticated microchips. This government intervention is not just a bailout, as it also marks the resurgence of industrial policy as a tool in ensuring the strength of a country's key industries. In Renesas' case, its chips were not only used by Japan's automotive makers but also by her world-leading consumer electronics industry (this explains the participation of consumer electronics firms such as Panasonic, Canon and Nikon in Japan's recent bailout of Renesas) (Schlesinger and Frischkorn, 2012).

Following its acquisition by INCJ and the accompanying Japanese consortia, Renesas has been compelled to undergo a painful restructuring which saw its workforce shrink dramatically from 46,430 to 21,083 employees over the 2011–2015 period (Renesas, 2011; Renesas, 2015). In March 2014, Renesas also divested its integrated chip factory in northern Japan to Sony Corp for US$67.4 million. A year later, the company also sold its subsidiary, Renesas SP Drivers Inc (an Apple Inc supplier) to Synaptics Inc for US$475 million (Knight and Murai, 2014; Nikkei Asian Review, 2014; Renesas, 2015). By 2015, an extensively restructured Renesas with its renewed focus on automotive semiconductors, stronger finances and cutting-edge technology is positioning itself to regain market share which it ceded to competitors over the past few years. In September 2016, the re-energised Renesas agreed to acquire Intersil Corp, a California-based chipmaker (with strengths in automotive, mobile, infrastructure and industrial applications) in an all-cash takeover for US$3.2 billion. Renesas is paying a significant premium of 43.9 percent for Intersil, outbidding a competing US suitor Maxim Integrated Products Inc in the process. This considerable premium along with the all-cash nature of the acquisition is indicative of the confidence which Renesas has in reaping the desired synergies of the merger (for example, bolster its capabilities in making semiconductors with autonomous driving features) (Beckerman and Mochizuki, 2016; Yamazaki, 2016). It could also be argued that Renesas has no choice to pay a sizeable premium for Intersil, if it wants to regain its market leader status in an industry where the pace of consolidation is tightening and the demand for new technologies and scale economies nearly insatiable. A fund manager who owns Renesas shares commented that 'they might be over-paying just a little, but if Renesas doesn't buy Intersil they will struggle to supply customers in the US'. He also added 'if they (i.e., Renesas) want to be a top auto-industry component maker they have to do this' (quoted in Yamazaki, 2016).

Technical progress and lean: key to Renesas' initial success

Despite its considerable financial woes and recent extensive restructuring efforts, Renesas continues to invest heavily in R&D. In fiscal year 2016, Renesas recorded R&D expenditures of US$804.8 million, the second highest among the top four automotive semiconductor makers, trailing only Infineon's €717 million (US$819.7 million) (Renesas, 2016). It is this steadfast commitment to R&D (even in the face of overwhelming financial adversity) that has enabled the firm to dominate technological development in the increasingly complex field of automotive microcontrollers (Renesas, 2012). As mentioned earlier, Renesas is the world leader in automotive microcontrollers (the 'brains' of the car) with over two-fifths of global market share by revenue. It has been able to achieve dominance of this industry by being among the first semiconductor companies to deliver microcontrollers optimised for the automotive market (with functions ranging from electric power steering to airbag control). Due to its significant R&D investment and relentless acquisition drive, Renesas has developed industry leading expertise in multicore technology which delivers superior chip performance while utilising less energy. To facilitate greater connectivity among the various microcontrollers found in today's automobiles, Renesas has developed an extensive range of 'system-in-a-package' (hereafter 'SiP') products that merge an MCU with different arrays of analogue components. The SiPs produced by Renesas include devices capable of coordinating body control with embedded controller area and local interconnect networks, which would include the ones for managing the electric motors in power windows and automated door closing systems (Renesas, 2012). Additionally, Renesas has also developed cutting-edge SoC technology that forms the backbone of automotive information systems (includes car navigation systems) (Renesas, 2010).

Since 2010, Renesas has continued to make significant strides in chip technology, particularly in areas which support the now increasingly likely advent of autonomous vehicles. In December 2015, the company declared its creation of a new dual-port on-chip SRAM technology for in-vehicle infotainment SoCs in the 16 nanometre and subsequent generations; this new technology provides unrivalled speed and stability, qualities that are being compromised in an increasingly delicate semiconductor fabrication process bound on an inextricable path to ever-finer feature sizes. Moreover, this state-of-the-art technology not only serves as video buffer memory in automotive infotainment SoCs but also delivers the critical real-time image processing capabilities required by driverless vehicle systems; on top of these superlative traits, this technology has lower power consumption vis-à-vis competing systems. Barely a year later in December 2016, Renesas also announced the successful development of four new MCUs (its RH850/P1L-C group), designed to optimise the capabilities (i.e., increased security, energy efficiency and reliability) of chassis and safety systems in advanced driver assistance systems, particularly those of autonomous vehicles (Renesas, 2015; Renesas, 2016).

Renesas' industry-beating technology is partially the result of sustained intensive R&D investment over the years; however, it is questionable whether it would have achieved this technological leadership without a commensurate acquisition strategy to secure the latest emerging technologies (as evidenced in the earlier section); an active acquisitions strategy is also needed to secure ever-increasing demands for economies of scale and scope which has become the hallmark of the industry. For instance, Renesas' acquisition of Nokia's wireless modem business in July 2010 was a critical first step towards developing semiconductors capable of empowering automotive information systems with networking capabilities. Renesas undoubtedly could have developed these technologies on its own but it would have taken considerably more time and investment in an increasingly competitive industry; the actual development cost could potentially greatly exceed the US$200 million it spent on its acquisition of Nokia's wireless modem business. To stay ahead of its rivals in this intensifying race to build the 'brains' behind tomorrow's autonomous vehicles, Renesas is also working with non-traditional automotive players such as BlackBerry QNX (its parent company, BlackBerry, is better known for its once best-selling phone) to develop an autonomous driving technology platform, which integrates an intricate network of hardware, software and sensors, delivering superlative capabilities in obstacle detection, road signs and cross traffic (at intersections) recognition and the smooth execution of safe automatic lane changes (Marketwired, 2017).

Renesas' use of lean techniques (e.g., just-in-time) has greatly contributed to its rise to the top of the global automotive semiconductor industry. For instance, Renesas' quality assurance strategy is driven by the principle of delivering to its clients the product they procured with the exact specifications and quality mandated under the premise of just-in-time management. However, the Japanese earthquake in March 2011 has exposed the vulnerability of such traditional lean approaches (Wassener and Nicholson, 2011); Renesas also incurred a special loss of around US$598 million due to the earthquake but actual losses could be significantly higher due to a loss of customer confidence and goodwill (Renesas, 2011). Renesas has launched several measures (collectively known as the Renesas Business Continuity Plan) to mitigate the deficiencies in a just-in-time system, once thought to have been honed to perfection. These measures included:

- Building stronger and more quake-resistant factories that could resume operations a month after being hit by a similar earthquake,
- Establishing a multi-fab manufacturing framework which facilitates quick response to disasters by quickly switching output to alternate factories,
- Reinforcing the supply chain by improving the efficiency of the procurement process and ensuring more effective control of inventories of work in process and finished products. Renesas would also secure raw materials from multiple suppliers and ensure more efficient management of risk information extending to even secondary suppliers (Renesas, 2011).

Renesas is evidently a world leader in automotive semiconductors and microcontrollers. Its abysmal financial performance in its earlier years (just prior to its acquisition by INCJ) was largely due to an over-expansion strategy spanning all areas from consumer electronics to automotive technologies, untimely shocks (i.e., the earthquake) and ever-increasing cost structure generated by the cascade effect in a technologically demanding industry.

STM: profile

In this volatile sea of internecine rivalry between anxious incumbents and ambitious 'upstarts', STM has steadfastly defended its perennial rank as the world's fourth largest automotive semiconductor maker at the dawn of 2016, recording a global market share of 7.2 percent (US$2.096 billion) in 2015 (STM, 2016a; IHS, 2016). The company posted overall 2015 revenues of about US$6.897 billion and a net profit of US$104 million. As of 31 December 2015, it had about 43,183 employees spread across 13 main manufacturing sites worldwide, providing effective support for the increasingly international operations of automakers (STM, 2016a). STM's Automotive Products Group (APG) comprised the bulk of its Sense & Power and Automotive Products (SP&A) division which accounted for 63.8 percent (US$4.401 billion) of the company's total revenues in 2015 (Figure 7.6). STM's APG alone generated US$1.727 billion in 2015 revenues, which was about 39.2 percent and 25 percent of SP&A's and STM's overall revenues respectively. However, by combining APG's revenues with that generated by STM's automotive microcontrollers business (and related technologies), STM's total automotive semiconductor revenues was around US$2.096 billion, which constituted approximately 30.4 percent of its total revenues. Although STM was ranked fourth worldwide for automotive semiconductors, it is the least dependent on the automotive industry. However, the above automotive revenues indicate that STM in recent years is focusing more on its automotive business, as its automotive revenues now account for nearly a third of total revenues, a significant increase over the earlier years; in 2010, STM drew about 13.7 percent of its revenues from the automotive industry while in 1998, it derived 12 percent of its revenues from its automotive business. The company's leading automotive customers are Bosch and Continental which were also ranked within STM's top ten customers in 2015 (STM, 2016a; STM, 1998; IHS, 2016).

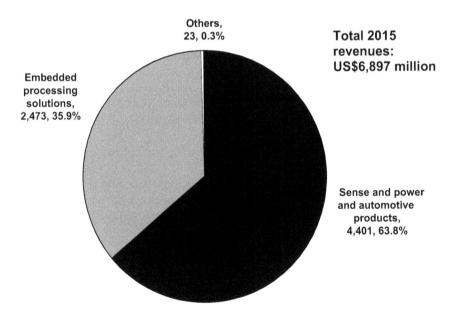

Figure 7.6 STM's 2015 annual revenues (US$ million)

Source: 2016 STM Form 20-F

While these automakers and first-tier suppliers exercise considerable market power over it, STM is also able to exert significant pressure over its own suppliers owing to its colossal US$1.251 billion purchasing budget. However, STM may not be able to squeeze its suppliers (e.g., TSMC) for long, as they too have consolidated and become industrial titans in their own right; in the case of TSMC, its 2015 revenues of US$25.7 billion was not only significantly larger than STM's US$6.897 billion but also larger than that of STM's key rivals (i.e., NXP (US$9.779 billion), Infineon (US$6.473 billion) and Renesas (US$5.730 billion)) combined; more importantly, TSMC's 2015 net income of US$9.236 billion also dwarfed that of STM, Infineon and Renesas which reported figures of US$104 million, US$724.8 million and US$713.2 million respectively (TSMC, 2015; STM, 2016a; NXP, 2015a; Infineon, 2015a; Renesas, 2015). TSMC is perhaps one of the few instances where a lower-tier supplier is not only bigger (in terms of revenue) but also far more profitable than its customers, who are ironically higher-tier suppliers in the automotive components industry. STM is the most Asia-centric among the four leading makers of automotive semiconductors, drawing 57.5 percent of its revenues (US$3.969 billion) from the region; the company procures 12.5 percent (US$863 million) and 45 percent (US$3.106 billion) of its revenues from Japan-Korea and Greater China-South Asia respectively (Figure 7.7). The company's Asian-centric strategy best positions it to benefit from these growing economies, particularly that of China and India (STM, 2016a).

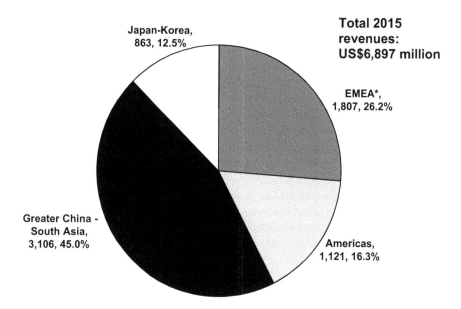

Figure 7.7 STM's 2015 revenues by region (US$ million)

*EMEA- Europe, the Middle East and Africa

Source: 2016 STM Form 20-F

STM's expansion over the years has greatly increased costs (particularly R&D costs); its R&D costs in 2015 stood at US$1.425 billion, compared to just US$532.3 million in 1996. Moreover, STM's allocates nearly a fifth of its workforce (8,304 personnel) to supporting its R&D efforts. Thus STM, like its peers, has been compelled (as evidenced in the following section) to seek greater economies of scale and scope by means of acquisitions, JVs and even cooperation with one of its closest rivals, Freescale (now part of NXP) to finance the increasing R&D investments crucial for survival in an oligopolistic market with intensifying demands for technological progress.

STM's M&A attempts since the 1980s

STM's history is one marked by consolidation. The company itself was the result of a merger between Italy's Microelecttronica and France's Thomson Semiconducteurs in 1987, and it was known as SGS-Thomson Microelectronics before it assumed its current name in May 1998. Further, in 1998, STM acquired Peripheral Technology Solutions, the semiconductor operations of Adaptec for US$73 million in cash (EE Times, 1998). Since then, STM has embarked on a series of acquisitions to secure the scale economies needed to compete effectively in the global automotive semiconductor industry. For instance, in 2000, it secured full-ownership of the Portland Group Inc (PGI), a vendor of compilers and software development tools to the high-performance parallel computing market, for US$17.1 million. This acquisition not only augmented STM's strength in automotive chip solutions but in other areas such as wireless, wireline, data storage and multimedia (STM, 2000).

Moreover, in 2002, STM acquired (for about US$343 million) Belgium-headquartered Alcatel Microelectronics (a subsidiary of France's Alcatel Group), a key player in the design, manufacture and marketing of semiconductor components with a focus on automotive, telecommunications and peripheral markets (STM, 2010a; EE Times, 2002). On top of this acquisition, STM was also able to secure even greater scale economics and access to cutting-edge DSL technologies by forging a JV with Alcatel. Since then, STM has persisted with its acquisition strategy, to secure technologies needed to give it an edge in an increasingly competitive market. In 2011, the company acquired the semiconductor assets and intellectual property of Arkados, a firm with strengths in powerline communication and smart grids (needed to enable the charging of electric vehicles). The technologies procured through this acquisition could enable utilities and consumers to manage the process of charging Plug-In Electric Vehicles (STM, 2011b).

The drive to alleviate ever-increasing research costs and secure scale economies has also compelled STM to work with one of its key rivals, Freescale (now part of NXP); from 1996 to 2015, STM's R&D expenditure has been rising steadily at a CAGR of 5 percent (STM, 1996; STM, 2016a). For instance, in February 2006, STM initiated a joint development programme with Freescale to develop microcontroller products with considerable power and augmented intelligence across many car electronics segments. These chips are suitable across a stream of automotive safety applications which encompass ABS, active suspension (superior dynamics and drive performance), electric power steering (enhanced vehicle efficiency) and radar (adaptive cruise control) (Freescale, 2009).

This cooperation yielded significant advances in automotive semiconductor development, as evidenced by the following statement from a key Freescale executive: 'our common microcontroller architectural platform has enabled Freescale and STM to accelerate the goal of making Power Architecture technology the leading automotive microcontroller core' (quoted in Freescale, 2008b). This level of cooperation is rare in the automotive components industry where competition between rivals is akin to an escalating arms race; one does not see Adient cooperating with Lear in seating systems development, or Goodyear working with Bridgestone to develop a new line of tyres. This cooperation is driven purely by necessity in an industry where development costs (driven by increasing technological complexity) have nearly spiralled out of control. Although such cooperation gives firms such as STM far less control and scale economies, it involves significantly less investment and risks. STM has cited the following as examples of risks it is concerned with in the event of acquisitions:

- Integration risks, especially when the acquired company has a vastly different corporate culture;
- Diversion of management's attention from key strategic issues;
- Inadequate intellectual property rights or inaccuracies in the ownership with regard to this issue;
- Incurring potential liabilities (disclosed or undisclosed) associated with the acquired firm, where liabilities could exceed the amount of indemnification available from the seller;
- Possible inaccuracies in the financials of the acquired firm;
- Acquired business may not be able to keep up with the quality of products and services historically provided by the acquirer;
- Potential difficulties in attracting and retaining qualified management for the acquired business;
- Potential difficulties involved in retaining customers of the acquired firm;
- Social and other costs linked to post-acquisition restructuring plans. Some of the acquired firm's employees may have to be laid off after acquisition, thus significant severance packages must be paid. Laying off employees after acquisition also involves some reputational risks (STM, 2011a).

Thus, cooperation with other firms in research ventures tends to avoid the risks involved in acquisitions or JVs. Moreover, collaborative efforts are not subject to the same degree of scrutiny by antitrust authorities, which tend to further increase the costs involved in outright acquisitions.

STM's technical progress and lean practice

STM has long since recognised the importance of technical progress (includes innovation) and process improvements (through lean) in ensuring its survival and growth in an increasingly oligopolistic industry. This is evidenced in

STM's 2011 annual report where it states: 'There is no assurance that we will be able to maintain or grow our market share if we are unable to accelerate product innovation, identify new applications for our products, extend our customer base, realise manufacturing improvements and/or otherwise control our costs' (STM, 2011a:8). Automakers, in their bid for market share, are compelled to increase the number of convenience features for the driver and passengers. This pressure is invariably transferred to suppliers such as STM. STM is well-placed to meet such automaker demands due to its unique SoC technology which enables advanced automotive features supported by highly integrated microelectronics for mechatronic capabilities such as door applications or single chip system integrated circuits for mirrors (Costlow, 2012). This example also highlights the fact that STM is trying to position itself as a solutions provider rather than just a maker of high-tech microchips; being a solutions provider is potentially far more lucrative, as evidenced by IBM which successfully made the transition from PC maker to IT solutions provider. STM's desire for technological leadership is further underscored by the fact that it spent a significant 20.7 percent of its revenues (US$1.425 billion) on R&D in 2015; for that year, STM invested more in R&D than any of its key rivals (STM, 2016a).

In 2011, STM also launched its Teseo II, a new generation of SoCs for Portable Navigation Devices, in-car navigation and telematics applications; STM prefers to call them stand alone 'chip solutions' so as to raise their market value and its pricing power in negotiations with automakers. These SoCs were marketed as pioneering devices with the capacity to detect signals from various satellite navigation systems. STM's Teseo II chips integrate virtually unerring positioning accuracy and increased indoor sensitivity with superior processing capabilities and design flexibility. Resultantly, STM asserts these chips have the ability to acquire speed, position and time data from all key navigation systems worldwide and this significantly augments position accuracy and navigation even in reduced satellite visibility conditions (includes urban canyons) (STM, 2011c).

To capture the latest technologies in a rapidly advancing automotive semiconductor market and alleviate rising cost pressures, STM has also turned to forming collaborations with its suppliers. For instance, in 2010, STM formed a collaborative effort with its supplier, Mentor Graphics, an electronic hardware and software design solutions provider. This three-year collaboration, known as 'DeCADE' was forged with the specific purpose of developing advanced design solutions for SoC technology utilised in digital and analogue designs. STM had formed this alliance to strengthen its lead in the ability to create customer-focused semiconductors and associated technologies (STM, 2010b). On the part of Mentor Graphics, it gets to deepen its relationship with its customer while acquiring advanced technical knowledge useful in moving up the value chain (it otherwise would have to make considerable investment to develop this technology on its own). Sometimes, such collaborations could be a prelude to an acquisition, as indicated by the automotive seats industry (e.g., JCI and Lear both acquired their respective fabric suppliers, Michel Thierry and New Trend Group); it is easier for an acquirer to buy out its former suppliers or partners as they are more familiar with the operations, culture and finances of the target.

In view of the tremendous progress attained by its immediate competitors in producing microchips meant to compete in an increasingly probable age of driverless vehicles, STM is also working intensely with Mobileye (a firm with significant expertise in computer vision) to develop a next-generational SoC (known as the EyeQ 5), with the capacity to act as the central processor for fully-autonomous driving; this pioneering technology is capable of providing super-computing computational abilities while minimising power consumption. Similarly, STM is also working with Autotalks, a vehicle-to-everything (V2X) chipset maker to develop a global navigation satellite system when supported by V2X chips would offer unerring positioning and vehicle-to-vehicle networking capabilities; V2X technology is meant to augment road safety and traffic management (STM, 2016b). Like its competitors, STM has been consumed by the gold-rush of autonomous driving, and is funnelling ever-increasing amounts of 'blood and treasure' to ensure its victory in this tussle for market share. Given the spiralling and increasingly unmanageable cost of cutting-edge R&D, in-depth partnerships across firms with seemingly different specialisations (like the above) are fast becoming de rigueur.

In further attempts to bolster its competitiveness (through process improvement) in an increasingly competitive automotive semiconductor market, STM launched a centralised 'Lean Initiatives Programme' in 2008 to supplant its earlier Total Quality Management programme; STM has been using some aspects of lean (e.g., just-in-time) since 1998 but a centralised lean system, as evidenced earlier, is far more comprehensive and easier to promote across all levels of an organisation (not limited to just production) (STM, 1998). Like all other comprehensive lean programmes (e.g., Renesas', Bridgestone's and JCI's), it is driven by the premise of eradicating waste and inefficiencies in continuous efforts to strengthen business performance. Further, STM was quick to realise that for lean to succeed, it had to rely on all its employees throughout the organisation and not just the manufacturing staff. To expedite the successful implementation of its lean programme, STM quickly launched a comprehensive training programme on lean principles which involved all production employees from management staff to operators. STM's lean programme has since spread to the rest of the organisation and its primary objective is to reinforce all its employees' engagement to deliver to its customers the best quality and service at the most competitive price (STM, 2008). STM has reaped the benefits of its centralised 'Lean Initiatives Programme'. For instance, it has achieved savings in packing/shipping as shipped volume (by inference, shipping costs) fell by 3.3 percent (around 30 containers) in 2011 compared to 2010. Since then, STM has generated annual savings of US$ 450,000 in freight and material costs, a reduction of 725 m^3 in volume and 220 tons of CO_2 emission reduction (STM, 2011d). As lean continues to permeate through every layer of STM's organisational structure, it is expected to reap further gains in productivity (through the reduction of waste) and cost savings. Further, lean could facilitate greater technical progress as it frees up resources for cutting-edge R&D and even acquisitions, which could add new technologies to STM's intellectual property.

4. Other players in the global automotive semiconductor industry

Beyond the top four oligopolists, there are still a number of third-tier players in the global automotive semiconductor industry; the industry is still relatively fragmented at the third-tier level, with significant room for consolidation. These firms are TI, Bosch, Toshiba, Fujitsu, Panasonic and ON Semiconductor (hereafter 'ON'). In an industry that is undergoing consolidation, some of these firms have already embarked on acquisition programmes to bolster their scale economies. Further, some of them (i.e., Bosch, Fujitsu and Panasonic) are not very keen in the global automotive semiconductor segment as their primary business is in other automotive components or consumer electronics.

STM is followed by TI and Bosch (the world's leading automotive components supplier with relatively strong chip making facilities of its own) which respectively account for about 6.7 percent and 5.1 percent of the global automotive semiconductor market (IHS, 2016; TI, 2015). TI is relatively acquisitive, having grown its semiconductor business through a series of acquisitions since 1996; from 1996 to 2011, TI made 33 semiconductor-related acquisitions while Bosch mostly focused on growing its semiconductor business organically (TI, 2016). Like many chip makers, TI has, in recent years, identified automotive semiconductors as a key growth market. In 2015, TI drew about 15 percent (US$1.95 billion) of its revenues from its automotive semiconductor business, while in 2011, it secured about 8.3 percent (US$1.135 billion) of its revenues from this segment; this increased dependency is indicative of TI's rising focus on the automotive semiconductor business. With 2015 revenues of US$13 billion (larger than any of the top four oligopolists in the automotive semiconductor makers), TI has the financial muscle and technical knowledge to penetrate the highest echelons of the global automotive semiconductor industry. However, TI's different market positioning has resulted in the company possessing smaller market shares than the industry oligopolists in the global automotive semiconductor business. TI still places considerable emphasis on making chips meant for consumer electronics, as indicated by the fact that Apple (TI's single biggest customer) alone accounted for 11 percent (US$1.43 billion) of its total 2015 revenues (TI, 2015).

Bosch, being the world's largest automotive components supplier clearly has the wherewithal to dominate the automotive semiconductor business (if it chooses) but prefers to compete in the higher value-added automotive electronics segments such as high-tech braking, driver assistance and autonomous vehicle technology. The company has been producing semiconductors in its Reutlingen plant since 1971 (Bosch, 2010). It has also turned to acquisitions to secure further scale economies in an increasingly consolidated industry, confronted by rising costs. In 2009, Bosch acquired Akustica, Inc., an innovator in the application of CMOS and MEMS technology; CMOS is a semiconductor technology that requires less power and subsequently produces lower heat output than competing technologies, thus facilitating higher circuit density (Gartner, 2012). Bosch believes that this acquisition would further augment its world-leading MEMS technologies, which facilitate low power, high performance processing (increasingly important in automotive electronics) (Bosch, 2012; Freescale, 2012a).

In recent years, Bosch has turned to further organic growth to bolster its automotive semiconductor production. For instance, in 2010, Bosch opened a new semiconductor production line in Reutlingen, Germany 2010. Bosch's new 200mm production line represented its largest single investment ever, costing €600 million (about US$825 million). Unlike other semiconductor vendors which have outsourced chip production to foundries, Bosch has adopted a vertically integrated approach of keeping most of its semiconductor production inhouse. A Bosch spokesperson asserted that 'the proximity of chip production, electronics development and ECU production has proved to be very fruitful'. He also made the following comment in reference to companies such as Daimler and Porsche that are headquartered in the vicinity: 'some of our customers happen to be based nearby which also helps to keep communications processes simple and fast' (quoted in Hammerschmidt, 2010). Bosch's organic growth strategy seems to be one that is aimed at ensuring a steady supply of semiconductors for its own specific applications and not one that is aimed at competing directly with the industry oligopolists (Kallenbach, 2011). This strategy also ensures increased operational efficiency, resulting in greater customer satisfaction (particularly in the case of customers such as Daimler and Porsche that are located nearby). By sticking to an organic growth strategy in this regard, Bosch avoids the exacting costs of exorbitant target premiums and significant post-acquisition integration efforts.

There is also a relatively lower-profile and smaller firm known as ON that has successfully carved out a niche in the automotive semiconductor industry; In 2015, ON had a 3.98 percent market share (US$1.153 billion) in the global automotive semiconductor industry (ON, 2015a). ON derives a significant 33 percent of its 2015 revenues (US$1.153 billion) from its automotive business; the automotive segment comprises the bulk of ON's revenues. Like the industry oligopolists, ON was spun off from a major electronics multinational in 1999 (in its case, Motorola) (ON, 2011). To secure the massive economies of scale and scope needed to survive in this industry, ON has also embarked on several acquisitions since its inception. In 2000, ON completed the acquisition of Cherry Semiconductor (for US$250 million), which specialised in the production of analogue Integrated Circuits (ICs) for the automotive and power management markets. The acquisition not only strengthened ON's revenue base (increasing it to about US$1.75 billion from its original US$1.62 billion in 1999) but also augmented its capabilities in automotive chips (The Power Pulse.Net, 2000). The company further consolidated its acquisition drive by acquiring LSI Logic Corporation's wafer fabrication facility and other semiconductor manufacturing equipment for about US$105 million, in April 2006. Through this acquisition, ON was able to gain not only competent process development engineers but also significant operational expertise and process development know-how (ON, 2006). This transaction supports the assertion that it is sometimes better for an acquirer to purchase only the assets (the ones it desires) of a firm instead of making an outright acquisition.

Further, ON in its relentless quest to secure further scale economies and augment its capabilities in automotive semiconductors, soon acquired AMI Semiconductor through a stock swap valued at US$915 million (ON's biggest acquisition to date); an ON spokesperson had stated that the company had hoped to achieve 'significant cost savings' through this acquisition (Manufacturing.net, 2007). ON quickly followed up with the acquisition of Catalyst Semiconductor in that same year, in a stock swap valued at US$115 million (Kress, 2008). The acquisition further strengthened ON's technical capabilities in custom application-specific circuits (ASIC) and power products, proving again that acquisitions is often driven by a need to secure the latest technologies. ON could have developed these new technologies on its own but it would have involved considerably more time and risk. The time and energies invested in developing these new technologies is better invested in growing the company's brand and market share, particularly in the fast-moving semiconductor industry.

Not letting up on its acquisition campaign, ON acquired Pulsecore Semiconductor for about US$17 million (in an all-cash transaction) in 2009. The acquisition not only augmented ON's technical capabilities in electromagnetic interference reduction but also enabled ON to break into the burgeoning Indian automotive market (proving again the effectiveness of acquisitions in penetrating new growth markets) (Lapedus, 2009). In that same year, ON also announced its acquisition of California Micro Devices for around US$108 million (ON, 2009). Further in 2011, ON acquired SANYO Semiconductor Co., Ltd. (a subsidiary of SANYO Electric) and other assets listed under SANYO Electric's semiconductor business. To finance the acquisition, ON paid US$144 million in cash and assumed a US$378 million loan from SANYO Electric. ON executed the acquisition as a means of penetrating the Japanese market and deepening its expertise in semiconductors (particularly in automotive semiconductors used in car stereo systems, where SANYO has considerable expertise). Moreover, in August 2014, ON acquired Aptina, a maker of sophisticated image sensors for automotive and industrial markets for US$454 million (all cash); this acquisition gave ON significant capabilities in making image sensors for the automotive industry (ON, 2014; ON, 2015a). In an audacious bid which dwarfed its earlier acquisition efforts, ON soon embarked on a US$2.4 billion (all cash) takeover of Fairchild Semiconductors in November 2015, with the intention of creating a US$5 billion entity, capable of challenging the marquee players in the automotive semiconductor industry. Fairchild's US$2.4 billion valuation is not significantly smaller than ON's (2015 market capitalisation and revenues of US$4.038 billion and US$3.496 billion respectively) thus this is indicative of the boldness and confidence embodied in ON's all cash acquisition (GuruFocus.com, 2016; ON, 2015b).

It is apparent from the above evidence, that ON is as acquisitive if not more so than the leading industry players. In fact, the scale of its acquisitions reveal a 'bet-the-firm' daring, unmatched by many second-tier companies. However, in a rapidly consolidating industry defined by relentless acquisitions and an ever-increasing demand for scale economies, it is highly possible that second-tier firms such as ON could also soon become the acquisition target of the larger firms, keen to expand their technological capabilities, market shares and consolidate their positions.

Given the increasing pace of consolidation in the global automotive semiconductor industry, the smaller players (i.e., Micron, Toshiba, Osram) could choose to grow their automotive chip businesses by means of acquisition or risk being put out of business (at least for their automotive businesses) by the industry oligopolists who have secured tremendous scale economies in their fight for market dominance; by 2015, Micron, Toshiba and Osram still did not move beyond bit player status in this industry, posting relatively small market shares of 2.3 percent, 2.2 percent and 2.2 percent respectively (IHS, 2016). However, firms such as Toshiba have the financial means to catch up with the oligopolists if they choose to; for example, Toshiba had total revenues of about US$50.2 billion (financial year starting 1 April 2015 to 31 March 2016), larger than the revenues recorded by any of the four key players in the global automotive semiconductor industry put together (Toshiba, 2016).

Between the years 2011–2012, the other key Japanese players, Fujitsu and Panasonic, also discussed merger plans with Renesas for their system LSI chip (widely used in vehicles) operations in an increasingly tough environment, plagued by rising costs and an ever-growing need for economies of scale and scope; LSI chips not only have high development costs which erode profit margins but also require constant remodelling which further exacerbates cost pressures (Yasu, 2012; Osawa, 2012). The overwhelming need for consolidation is particularly evident in Japan's semiconductor industry, which is experiencing a steady loss of its once exalted competitiveness. In 1987, six Japanese semiconductor companies namely Matsushita, Panasonic, Mitsubishi, Hitachi, NEC Fujitsu and Toshiba were ranked among the world's top ten semiconductor producers. However, by 2012, only Renesas and Toshiba were in the global top ten (Manners, 2012). The increased economies of scale and scope gained from a merger would enable the new firm to compete more effectively against their fast-rising Korean rivals (e.g., Samsung) and cement their lead over emerging ones from China.

In March 2015, Fujitsu and Panasonic eventually merged their LSI chip operations into an independent company known as Socionext, which has approximately 2,600 employees; Renesas, which was undergoing a significant restructuring, declined the merger offer (Clarke, 2015). Even with this merger, the automotive semiconductor manufacturing assets of firms such as Fujitsu and Panasonic could still become acquisition targets of the oligopolists. Although Fujitsu and Panasonic have a relatively small presence in the global automotive semiconductor industry, they do possess cutting-edge technologies, which are highly attractive to oligopolists seeking to augment not only their scale economies but also their technological capabilities through acquisition. However, as proven in Renesas' case, it is extremely difficult for foreign firms to acquire a controlling stake in Japanese firms.

Amidst this cascading consolidation swirl, the industry cause célèbre was perhaps the 2012 entry of chip titan, Intel (the world's biggest chip maker with 2015 revenues of US$55.4 billion), the global brand more commonly associated with personal computers. Intel's then CEO, Paul Otellini, had identified the automotive semiconductor industry as an opportunity to diversify beyond the personal-computer business, which now generates more than 90 percent of its revenues; the company's confidence in the growth potential of the automotive chip industry is further evidenced by the following statements from Ton Steenman, vice president of Intel's intelligent systems group: 'the industry is in the middle of this very significant transition to bring much richer connectivity into the vehicle' and 'we are beyond the pivot point of this becoming a significant business' (quoted in King, 2012). Intel, which has already landed deals with Daimler, BMW and Nissan, is also trying to convince more automakers that high-tech features such as in-car information and entertainment systems (an increased demand for such high-tech features would invariably increase demand for Intel's high-powered chips) can act as key differentiators in an increasingly competitive car market (King, 2012). In July 2016, Intel announced plans to work with BMW and Israel's Mobileye to develop driverless car technology, with Intel developing sophisticated semiconductors intelligent enough to make its way through heavy traffic and avoid accidents (Taylor, 2016).

Intel's steady entry into the global automotive semiconductor industry is a game-changer, as it would not only compel the industry oligopolists but also the lower-tier automotive chip makers to seek even greater economies of scale and scope in an already intensely competitive market. A smaller but equally ambitious non-traditional entrant into the automotive semiconductor market would be Nvidia, one of the world's leading developers of graphic processors used in video game consoles and laptops. The company entered the industry through a contract with Audi to develop the chips powering the 3-D navigation system display in the Audi A8 that was launched in 2011. Nvidia despite lacking Intel's financial muscle has also landed contracts to produce chips used in the Lamborghini and Tesla S models; Nvidia's recorded 2015 revenues of US$5.01 billion is merely a fraction of Intel's US$55.4 billion for the same year.[7] The company's cutting-edge Tegra processors are currently used to power the infotainment and navigation systems in select Audi, Lamborghini and Tesla models; Nvidia's chips are used in over 10 million cars worldwide. Drawn by the immensely lucrative prospect of dominating a future potentially populated by autonomous vehicles, this upstart firm is pulling out all the stops in its relentless drive to control this specific chip market with its Drive PX chip, which is designed specifically for the driverless car (Lienert, 2015; Shilov, 2015; Nvidia, 2016). The entry of these new players, with their significant technological prowess would inevitably accelerate the cascade effect (and pace of consolidation) in the industry, with the weaker players being assimilated into their more successful counterparts or weeded out of the market completely.

Rise of the foundry chip makers

Over the past two decades, the leading automotive semiconductor makers have also become increasingly reliant on their three key suppliers (i.e., TSMC, UMC and GLOBALFOUNDRIES) who now control around 74 percent of global foundry chip production. TSMC, the dominant foundry chip supplier with a global market share of 52.7 percent (2015 revenues: US$25.7 billion) in 2015, was founded as a JV between the Taiwan government, which wanted to promote the development of the island's semiconductor industry, and Philips Electronics NV; the Taiwanese government, Phillips, and local private investors held 49 percent, 27 percent and 24 percent equity stakes respectively (Meaney, 1994; TSMC, 2015; Gartner, 2016). TSMC is also immensely profitable with 2015 net income of US$9.236 billion, far more than the net profits of the top four automotive semiconductor makers combined (TSMC, 2015). The company has also turned to acquisitions to secure the ever-increasing economies of scale and scope needed to survive and compete in an increasingly duopolistic/oligopolistic environment. In June 1999, TSMC acquired a 30 percent stake in Acer Semiconductor Manufacturing, Inc. (ASMI), subsequently renaming the facility 'TSMC-Acer Manufacturing Corporation' (TASMC) (TSMC, 1999).

Although Acer remained the largest shareholder in TASMC, it had ceded effective management of the manufacturing facility to TSMC (since June 1999), which not only converted it into a pure-play foundry but also integrated its operations into TSMC by December 1999. By January 2000, TSMC had acquired most of Acer's remaining 70 percent stake in TASMC, via a stock swap valued at US$90 million (leaving Acer with an insignificant 2 percent stake). Acer was quick to offload its stake in TASMC, as it was starting to position itself as a systems integrator, focused on growing its core business of assembling personal computers and peripherals (TSMC, 1999; Kanellos, 1999). The merger was engineered to bolster TSMC's efficiency and service quality; this was indicated by Morris Chang, TSMC's chairman: 'the merger of TSMC and TASMC will further improve operational efficiency through integration, enabling more timely service to our customers' (Carroll, 2000).

In its bid for greater economies of scale and scope, TSMC swiftly followed up with the acquisition of Worldwide Semiconductor Manufacturing Corporation (WSMC) in June 2000, which boosted its production capacity by a significant 21 percent (increasing its annual production capacity of 8-inch equivalent wafers from 2.8 million in 1999 to 3.4 million in 2000) (TSMC, 2000). This acquisition of WSMC was financed by TSMC's issuance of 1.15 billion new shares valued at US$6.45 billion in an all-stock transaction. According to industry analysts, TSMC's acquisitions strategy enabled it to bolster capacity more rapidly and economically than through organic strategies such as building new facilities; even back in 2000, the costs of building a fabrication plant had reached astronomical levels (e.g., in 2000, the cost of building an 8-inch fab plant from scratch had reached US$1.5 billion) (Bloomberg, 2000). Through this ruthless consolidation, TSMC has achieved considerable economies of scale and scope, along with superior technological prowess, and is now widely known as the world's largest contract chipmaker (BBC, 2012). Its strengths have been recognised by Renesas, which has even outsourced the production of its cutting-edge microcontrollers (using 40 nanometre embedded flash (eFlash) process technology) to TSMC; microcontrollers made using the 40 nanometre process are able to achieve higher speed, lower power consumption and are more than 50 percent smaller compared with those using the more conventional 90 nanometre process (these strengths make Renesas' latest microcontrollers well-suited for next-generation automotive applications).

It could also be argued that Renesas embroiled in a technological arms race (to produce smaller, and more powerful and energy efficient chips at lower prices) with its rivals has no choice but to outsource the production of its latest proprietary microcontrollers (described by some analysts as Renesas' 'crown jewel'); by gaining access to Renesas' technology, TSMC would also significantly bolster its intellectual property portfolio (Liao, 2012; Yoshida, 2012). Through this outsourcing, Renesas would be able to focus more resources on developing next-generational technologies needed to win this technological arms race.

Further, Renesas' 'sharing' of this technology with TSMC is the company's first step towards creating an ecosystem for this new technology, in the process widening its potential customer base (Liao, 2012). Moreover, Renesas and TSMC have collaborated to develop advanced microcontroller technologies by combining Renesas' sophisticated, high-speed MONOS (metal-oxide-nitride-oxide-silicon) technology capable of reliable and superlative technical support with TSMC's superior CMOS (complementary metal-oxide-semiconductor) process capabilities and flexible production facilities (Renesas, 2012; Shilov, 2012); Renesas' MONOS technology enables far greater reliability and scalability in microcontrollers, making it best suited for automotive and other technically challenging applications that require highly-integrated and reliable microcontrollers (Renesas, 2013). In September 2016, TSMC and Renesas also announced plans to collaborate in the development of 28 nanometre embedded flash process technology, critical for making microcontrollers used in advanced electric, hybrid and driverless car systems (TSMC, 2016). These collaborations indicate that the sheer technological complexity and development costs involved in the industry are now compelling automotive semiconductor makers to engage in increasingly equal partnerships with their supposedly lower-tier suppliers. In a bid to control spiralling R&D and operational costs, TSMC has also turned to working closely with its equipment suppliers.[8] For instance, in August 2012, TSMC invested about US$1.4 billion to acquire a 5 percent stake in its supplier, ASML, a Dutch firm that attaches circuit patterns onto chips (this could be regarded as a form of vertical integration). TSMC added that it regards this investment in ASML as a 'co-investment programme' to develop future technology that would enable TSMC to rein in its costs in the long run (BBC, 2012).

Further, TSMC asserted that its investment in ASML would enable the firm to develop equipment that could deal with larger circular wafers where the chips are sliced. Currently, industry analysts state that chipmakers globally are attempting to increase the size of the wafers to 450mm, from the existing size of 300mm; an increase in the size of these wafers would translate into significant cost alleviation for the chipmakers, as a larger quantity of chips could be derived from them (BBC, 2012). TSMC has persisted in its relentless drive to secure economies of scale and scope, by acquiring the Taiwanese facility (Taoyuan county) of Qualcomm, the US mobile chip giant for US$85 million in November 2014 (Wu, 2014). In terms of strategy, TSMC typically uses a bolt-on acquisition approach to secure much needed economies of scale and scope. It tends to target smaller firms with comparable technological capabilities, thus avoiding the significant premiums paid in acquisitions of large firms with high-end technological expertise. Moreover, it works with its client, Renesas in the development of next-generational semiconductor technology, thus avoiding the massive investments required in this technological arms race, if one were to go it alone. This strategic approach has enabled TSMC to rein in its cost base and in the process raise its overall profitability.

In recent years, a new player, GLOBALFOUNDRIES Inc. has risen quickly to challenge the stranglehold of TSMC. The company is now the world's second largest foundry chips maker with an estimated 9.6 percent (2015 revenues: US$4.673 billion) global market share (Gartner, 2016). GLOBALFOUNDRIES was formed in March 2009 through the spin-off of AMD's manufacturing arm as a JV operation with Advanced Technology Investment Co. (ATIC), an investment fund controlled by the Abu Dhabi government; ATIC (renamed Mubadala Technology in May 2014) had paid US$700 million for a 65.8 percent stake in the JV (Mubadala, 2014). There were two key objectives for this divestiture: (i) AMD had decided in 2009 to become a fabless operation focused on higher value-added chip design (Shah, 2012) (ii) it was part of AMD's ongoing restructuring plan intended to regain profitability and raise much-needed cash needed to compete with its significantly stronger rival, Intel (Lemon, 2009). Nonetheless, AMD still owned 34.2 percent of GLOBALFOUNDRIES at the time of the spin off but steadily reduced its stake over the next three years. In March 2012, AMD sold its remaining 9 percent stake to ATIC, giving it full ownership of GLOBAL-FOUNDRIES (McGrath, 2012; Reuters, 2012).

The fact that GLOBALFOUNDRIES was spun off from AMD, the world's second largest microprocessors maker granted it significant economies of scale and scope, a global footprint and considerable technological capabilities. These strengths were subsequently bolstered by its acquisition (through ATIC) of Singapore's Chartered Semiconductors for US$3.9 billion in late 2009 (GLOBAL-FOUNDRIES, 2009); like TSMC and UMC, it quickly realised that acquisitions was a quicker and cheaper growth strategy than building new plants from scratch. This strong start quickly enabled it to become the world's third largest foundry chip maker, after TSMC and UMC (its global market share of 12 percent in 2011, placed it narrowly behind UMC, the industry number two which posted a 13.1 percent market share in the same year) (GLOBALFOUNDRIES, 2011; UMC, 2011a). GLOBALFOUNDRIES is also cognisant of the growth potential in the automotive foundry chip subsector and asserts that its technology and processes are well-suited to compete in this market; the firm asserts that its latest BCDlite foundry technology is designed for a broad range of automotive applications such as audio amplifiers, displays, LED driver integrated circuits and power management devices and that all its 200mm fabs in Singapore are certified to ISO/TS16949 automotive quality standards (the acknowledged benchmark for automotive quality system standards), giving it the capability and credibility needed to compete in an increasingly demanding automotive semiconductor industry (GLOBALFOUNDRIES, 2011; Morgan, 2010). It is evident that GLOBALFOUNDRIES' critical technologies (i.e., ISO/TS16949-certified 200mm fabs) came with its acquisition of Chartered Semiconductors in 2009, validating again the value of acquisitions in securing valuable technologies and quality systems (GLOBALFOUNDRIES, 2011; Morgan, 2010). In July 2015, GLOBALFOUNDRIES also completed its acquisition of IBM's microelectronics business which not only augmented the company's capabilities in semiconductor development and manufacturing but also gave it control over 16,000 patents and applications. In addition, this acquisition enabled GLOBALFOUNDRIES to supplant UMC as the world's second largest foundry chips maker (GLOBALFOUNDRIES, 2015; Gartner, 2016).

UMC, founded in Taiwan in May 1980, is a distant third to TSMC in the foundry chip market; by end 2015, UMC had a 9.1 percent (US$4.417 billion) market share compared to TSMC's 52.7 percent and GLOBALFOUNDRIES' 9.6 percent. In terms of profitability, UMC's 2015 net income of US$354 million is also significantly behind TSMC's staggering US$9.236 billion for the same period. The company had also utilised acquisitions as a means of expanding and consolidating its position in the pure-play foundry market. It started its acquisition campaign by purchasing Holtek semiconductor (renamed UTEK Semiconductor Corp) in April 1998. That same year, UMC acquired a controlling 56 percent in Nippon Steel Semiconductor Corp. in September for US$11 million; it renamed the company, UMC Japan (UMCJ) in 2001 (UMC, 1998; UMC, 2011a; TSMC, 2011b). Further, in 2000, in an attempt to close the gap with its key rival, TSMC, UMC integrated four of its affiliates, namely United Semiconductor Corp (USC), United Integrated Circuits Corp (UICC), United Silicon Inc (USI) and UTEK Semiconductor Corp via a series of share swaps (UMC, 1999; UMC, 2000). UMC's consolidation of its affiliate companies, in 2000, is driven by both an increasing need for scale economies and customer demands (i.e., increasingly globalised automakers and first-tier suppliers who require worldwide support) (Business Wire, 2000). Peter Chang, UMC's CEO of Foundry Operations, expressed that the consolidation would result in the following benefits: 'a better service interface for customers with production at multiple UMC fabs, better synergies in our technology development efforts, faster process deployment between fabs, as well as across-the-board improvements in efficiency' (quoted in Business Wire, 2000).

From 2009 to 2011, UMC assiduously pursed an acquisition strategy in attempts to close the gap with TSMC. For instance, in October 2009, it acquired the remaining shares in UMCJ (for US$76.3 million) which it did not own and made it a fully UMC-owned subsidiary (Cyber Media, 2009). Further, in October 2011, UMC acquired a 35.03 percent stake in Best Elite International Limited (through a partial cash acquisition), the holding company of Chinese contract chip maker Hejian Technology (Suzhou) Co, indirectly making UMC the largest shareholder in Hejian; this partial acquisition is UMC's springboard to a complete acquisition of Hejian (subject to regulatory approval). This deal was executed, despite the fact that UMC's earlier attempt to merge with Hejian (via share issuance) in November 2010 was blocked by regulatory hurdles in Taiwan which forbid the issuance of new shares in acquisitions (the more likely reason for this obstruction is to limit the technology flow to China) (UMC, 2011b; Kwong, 2010). UMC also has a history of working with its clients to develop new technologies. For instance, in 2002, UMC worked with Infineon and AMD to develop 65/45 nanometre manufacturing platform technologies for the high-volume production of semiconductor logic products on next-generation 300 millimeter wafers. The advantages of this collaboration was that it not only enabled the sharing of cost and risk, but also facilitated the pooling of technical capabilities and resources in the joint development of common technological platforms which could be customised to address each company's individual production specifications (AMD, 2002).

5. Conclusion

In the 1980s, automotive semiconductors were largely produced by the divisions of Hitachi, Mitsubishi, Siemens and Motorola. To these firms, this was essentially a peripheral business. These divisions were eventually spun off between 1998 and 2004; without the strong technical and economic foundations established by their previous corporate forms, it is doubtful whether these firms would have grown at their current pace. Further, with the increasing complexity of automotive components and the subsequent demand for sophisticated microprocessors to run these parts, the automotive semiconductor industry grew by leaps and bounds over the ensuing decades. The spun-off divisions of multinationals such as Hitachi, Mitsubishi, Siemens, and Motorola competed fiercely for leadership in this 'new' industry. A relentless series of M&A resulted in the formation of four leading industry titans, namely NXP, Infineon, Renesas and STM which together accounted for over 40 percent of the global automotive semiconductor market. This industry has also attracted the attention of opportunistic, private equity firms, who have undeniably become key players in this ruthless centralisation of capital. Further, as evidenced earlier, JVs and even collaborations between close rivals (e.g., STM and Freescale) have become alternative means of securing additional economies of scale and scope, and access to new technologies and markets. However, such efforts often come at the expense of control and accidental technological spillovers (i.e., critical technologies landing in the hands of one's competitor).

The consolidation process in the global automotive semiconductor industry is far from over. Rather, it has intensified exponentially over the past decade, with no signs of slowing down. The increasing demand for high-tech automotive components (e.g., autonomous driving technology, hybrid and electric vehicle engines, and advanced infotainment systems) spurred by rising regulatory demands and consumer demands, has also resulted in an unprecedented convergence of once disparate technologies. Moreover, the sheer commercial opportunity promised by this overwhelming confluence of technologies has drawn the attention of non-traditional players (e.g., Qualcomm, Intel and Nvidia). These 'upstarts' despite their lack of automotive engineering experience, are more than able to give the reigning oligopolists a run for their money; they are also able to expedite their growth by acquiring the incumbents and upend the status quo owing to their superior financial and technological firepower (both qualities supersede automotive expertise as prerequisites for success in this increasingly digitised, artificial intelligence driven industry).

The breakneck development of this evolving subsector has invariably triggered an insatiable demand for increasingly powerful (yet energy-efficient) automotive microchips with superior networking capabilities. The unquenchable thirst for these ultra-sophisticated microchips (once confined to the realm of science fiction a mere decade ago) has inevitably raised R&D costs exponentially. To mitigate these escalating costs, the industry oligopolists are compelled to embark on further consolidation efforts to gain ever-increasing economies of scale and scope and the latest technologies. They are also increasingly outsourcing non-core activities to the lower-tiers and in many cases, asking them to assume more of the costly R&D work. Thus, the leading automotive semiconductor makers are fast acquiring system integration skills, in the process becoming more like the automakers and their first-tier suppliers.

The pressure is even more intense among the lower-tier automotive semiconductor suppliers. Smaller suppliers such as ON are constantly acquiring smaller firms to augment their scale economies, gain new technologies, develop new product segments and penetrate new markets. Even with active acquisition strategies, it is extremely difficult for lower-tier suppliers like ON to maintain their independence (the firms they acquire tend to be very small and do not add a lot of scale) in a rapidly consolidating environment dominated by the oligopolists and plagued by an ever-increasing demand for scale economies. Even the so-called lowest-tier foundry chip suppliers have been compelled by the cascade effect to merge with their rivals to secure ever-increasing economies of scale and scope along with the latest emerging technologies; the threat of technological obsolescence and the accompanying economic demise is felt more strongly here than any other sector mentioned in this book. Currently, the top three foundry chip makers (i.e., TSMC, GLOBALFOUNDRIES and UMC) control an unprecedented near three-quarters of the market; their sheer market presence and increasing financial strength (e.g., TSMC) has compelled the leading automotive semiconductor makers to treat them as strategic partners rather than mere suppliers. Given a little more time, they would be able to effectively resist the pricing pressure placed on them by the major automotive semiconductor makers, as they essentially control the basic chip making infrastructure and expertise (i.e., the backbone of the industry).

Notes

1 Microcontrollers are customised semiconductors with added specifications and are thus placed further up the value chain than plain-vanilla semiconductors (Vidyasagar, 2013). These chips are bespoke 'tiny computers' running the complex code in today's vehicles and information from these microcontrollers is stored on semiconductors (Klier and Rubenstein, 2008; Pollack and Lohr, 2011; Balhaus, Pagella and Vogel, 2009). Microcontrollers are typically made by higher-tiers such as Renesas while 'generic' semiconductors are produced by lower-tier foundry chip makers such as TSMC.

2 A SoC amalgamates in its entirety the various constituents (i.e., microprocessor, memory and other specialised circuitry) of an electronic system into a single integrated circuit, in the process gaining the capacity to deliver superior processing performance, energy efficiency and minimal space requirements (qualities that have resulted in its extensive deployment across automobiles) (Palomar Technologies, 2017).

3 The 'Internet of Things' works on the premise of machine-to-machine communication, leveraging on extensive communication networks, sophisticated sensors and cloud computing. Through this ecosystem, smart devices would communicate with one another. For instance, the sensors in a bridge, covered in icing, would warn incoming vehicles, which could then proceed to warn the driver to reduce speed or even take the initiative itself (Burrus, 2014).

4 Lidar involves using laser scanning and ranging to develop accurate three-dimensional images of objects. This technology even works on small objects and in relative darkness. However, it may encounter difficulties in dense vegetation or foggy conditions. Lidar-based systems could also be deceived into thinking that there are objects ahead of them, and consequently interfering with their operational effectiveness (Bureau of Economic Geology, 2004; The Economist, 2016; Gibbs, 2015).

5 Although microcontrollers are only a subset of the global semiconductor market, they are the most sophisticated and highest value-added segment (microcontrollers alone accounted for 21 percent of semiconductor sales in 2009) (Balhaus, Pagella and Vogel, 2009).

6 SRAM and 'Dynamic Random Access Memory' are responsible for storing data (SiliconFarEast.com, 2005).

7 Nvidia's fiscal year is from February to January of the following year (MarketWatch, 2016)

8 This escalating cost trend is highlighted by Shang-yi Chiang, TSMC's co-chief operating officer, who asserted that one of the industry's biggest challenges was 'how to effectively control the escalating wafer manufacturing cost' (quoted in BBC, 2012).

References

Advanced Micro Devices (2002) AMD, Infineon and UMC to jointly develop advanced manufacturing platform technologies, *AMD* [internet] Available at: www.amd.com/us/press-releases/Pages/Press_Release_37942.aspx [Accessed on 19 July, 2012].

Amano, T. (2012) Renesas surges 31% as Japan fund may counter KKR offer, *Bloomberg. com* [internet] Available at: www.businessweek.com/news/2012-09-23/japan-s-rescue-fund-may-counter-kkr-bid-for-chipmaker-renesas [Accessed on 12 October, 2012].

Arping, S. and Falconieri, S. (2007), Strategic versus Financial Investors: The role of strategic complementarities in financial contracting, *Ente Einaudi*, Rome, Working Paper No: 51 Rome: Ente Einaudi.

Ascierto, J (1999) Siemens names new semi division Infineon technologies: Spin-off moves toward its own goal of going public in near future, *Electronic News*, 22 March, p. 16.

Auchard, E. (2015) NXP completes deal to buy Freescale and create top auto chip-maker, *Reuters* [internet] Available at: www.reuters.com/article/us-autos-semi conductors-nxp-semicondtrs-idUSKBN0TQ1IK20151207 [Accessed on 28 January, 2017].

Avnet Inc (2012) Body control module integrated CAN bus, *Avnet* [internet] Available at: www.em.avnetasia.com/Products/DesignSolutionShow.aspx?pagesId=27& MasterPageId=17&ID=60 [Accessed on 20 February, 2017].

Balhaus, W., Pagella, A. and Vogel, C. (2009) *A Change of Pace for the Semiconductor Industry? PricewaterhouseCoopers*, Germany: Kohlhammer und Wallishauser GmbH, Druckerei und Verlag, Hechingen.

Bargeron, L.L., Schlingemann, F.P., Stulz, R.M. and Zutter, C.J. (2008) Why do private acquirers pay so little compared to public acquirers? *Journal of Financial Economics*, 89: 375–390.

Barnden, C. (2012) Semicast ranks automotive semiconductor suppliers, Semicast Research [internet] Available at: http://www.automotive-electronics.co.uk/Arti cleItem.aspx?Cont_Title=Semicast+ranks+automotive+semiconductor+suppliers [Accessed on 16 June, 2012].

BBC (2012) TSMC eyes future technology with $1.4bn ASML investment, *BBC News Business* [internet] Available at: www.bbc.co.uk/news/business-19144379 [Accessed on 6 August, 2012].

Beckerman, J. and Mochizuki, T. (2016) Renesas to buy Intersil for $3.2 billion, *wsj.com* [internet] Available at: www.wsj.com/articles/renesas-to-buy-intersil-for-3-2-billion-1473728419 [Accessed on 5 October, 2016].

Bloomberg (2000) US$6.4bn merger plan keeps TSMC in top spot, *Bloomberg.com* [internet] Available at: www.taipeitimes.com/News/front/archives/2000/01/08/0000018708 [Accessed on 19 July, 2012].

Bloomberg (2012) Semiconductors and semiconductor equipment: Company overview of Seaway Networks, Inc., *Bloomberg.com* [internet] Available at: http://invest ing.businessweek.com/research/stocks/private/snapshot.asp?privcapId=2220615 [Accessed on 13 August, 2012].

Bornefeld, R. (2016) Driverless cars: Eyes on the road, *The Economist*, 421(9021): 107–108.

Bosch (2010) Largest single investment at Bosch, Bosch.com [internet] Available at: http://www.bosch.com.cn/en/cn/newsroom_4/news_4/news-detail-page_ 14543.php [Accessed on 16 December 2012].

Bosch (2012) Akustica leaps into high-volume mobile device market with new analog MEMS Mic, *Bosch.com* [internet] Available at: www.bosch-press.com/tbwebdb/ bosch-usa/en-US/PressText.cfm?CFID=11236813&CFTOKEN=2fe04a1666 f5371a-0865FDCD-D980-7224-1127D99942FE29C0&nh=00&Search=0& id=490 [Accessed on 3 May, 2012].

Brown, C. and Linden, G. (2009) Chips and Change: How Crisis Reshapes the Semiconductor Industry, Cambridge, MA: The MIT Press.

Buksh, A.A. (2016) Automotive semiconductor market grows slightly in 2015 while ranks shift, IHS says, *IHS Markit* [internet] Available at: https://technology.ihs. com/580273/automotive-semiconductor-market-grows-slightly-in-2015-while-ranks-shift-ihs-says [Accessed on 20 February, 2017].

Bureau of Economic Geology (2004) Mapping Mustang Island with Lidar and EM: Lidar advantages and limitations, *The University of Texas at Austin* [internet]

Available at: www.beg.utexas.edu/resprog/nsg/mustang/lidar_advantage.htm [Accessed on 30 December, 2016].

Burrus, D. (2014) The internet of things is far bigger than anyone realizes, *Wired* [internet] Available at: www.wired.com/insights/2014/11/the-internet-of-things-bigger/ [Accessed on 1 August, 2016].

Business Wire (2000) UMC completes consolidation of joint ventures; company strengthens position as a world leader in foundry services – new corporate structure already in place, *Business Wire* [internet] Available at: www.thefreelibrary.com/UMC+Completes+Consolidation+of+Joint+Ventures%3B+Company+Strengthens ...-a058501642 [Accessed on 20 July, 2012].

Carroll, M. (2000) TSMC buys out Acer fab, *EE Times* [internet] Available at: www.eetimes.com/electronics-news/4167466/TSMC-buys-out-Acer-fab [Accessed on 16 July, 2012].

Chandler, A.D. and Hikino, T. (1999) The large industrial enterprise and the dynamics of modern economic growth, in Chandler, A., Amatori, F. and Hikino, T. (eds), *Big Business and The Wealth of Nations*, Cambridge: Cambridge University Press.

Charette, R.N. (2009) This car runs on code, *IEEE Spectrum* [internet] Available at: http://spectrum.ieee.org/green-tech/advanced-cars/this-car-runs-on-code [Accessed on 19 October, 2010].

Clark, D. and Higgins, T. (2016) Qualcomm to buy NXP semiconductors for $39 billion, *wsj.com* [internet] Available at: www.wsj.com/articles/qualcomm-to-buy-nxp-semiconductors-1477565063 [Accessed on 28 January, 2017].

Clarke, P. (2002) Hitachi, Mitsubishi to merge chip businesses in "Renesas" venture, EE Times [internet] Available at: http://eetimes.com/electronics-news/4097480/Hitachi-Mitsubishi-to-merge-chip-businesses-in-Renesas-venture [Accessed on 13 August, 2012].

Clarke, P (2015) Fujitsu-Panasonic chip spinoff socionext opens doors, *Electronics360* [internet] Available at: http://electronics360.globalspec.com/article/5074/fujitsu-panasonic-chip-spinoff-socionext-opens-doors [Accessed on 3 August. 2015].

Clemmer, R. (2012) NXP Semiconductors Acquires the Catena Group, NXP [internet] Available at: http://www.marketwired.com/press-release/nxp-semiconductors-acquires-the-catena-group-nasdaq-nxpi-1640214.htm [Accessed on 10 February, 2013].

Costlow, T. (2012) STMicroelectronics chip saves door space, cost, SAE International [internet] Available at: http://articles.sae.org/10692/ [Accessed on 10 February, 2013].

Cyber Media (2009) United Micro to buy outstanding shares of UMC Japan, *Cyber Media* [internet] Available at: http://archive.ciol.com/Biz-Watch/News-Reports/United-Micro-to-buy-outstanding-shares-of-UMC-Japan/301009127080/0/ [Accessed on 12 December, 2012].

Databeans (2012) Microcontroller market share: In 3 dimensions, *Databeans* [internet] Available at: www.databeans.net/microcontroller-market-share-in-3-dimensions/ [Accessed on 10 August, 2016].

Databeans (2016) Microcontroller market, *Databeans* [internet] Available at: www.databeans.net/downloads/category/trackers/microcontroller-market/ [Accessed on 10 August, 2016].

De La Merced, M.J. (2014) Infineon to buy international rectifier, a chip maker, for $3 billion, *nytimes.com* [internet] Available at: https://mobile.nytimes.com/blogs/dealbook/2014/08/20/infineon-to-buy-international-rectifier-a-chip-maker-for-3-billion/ [Accessed on 20 February, 2017].

Dishman, L. (2012) How A Semi-Conductor Plant Rebooted After The Japanese Earthquake And Saved Car Manufacturers Everywhere, Fast Company [internet] Available at: http://www.fastcoexist.com/1678441/how-a-semi-conductor-plant-rebooted-after-the-japanese-earthquake-and-saved-car-manufacturer [Accessed on 26 June, 2012].

EDN (2003) Infineon Buys SensoNor in Automotive Push, EDN [internet] Available at: http://www.edn.com/article/481021-Infineon_Buys_SensoNor_in_Automotive_Push.php [Accessed on 20 March, 2012].

EE Times (1998) STMicroelectronics buys adaptec chip unit, *EE Times* [internet] Available at: www.eetimes.com/electronics-news/4115732/STMicroelectronics-Buys-Adaptec-Chip-Unit [Accessed on 22 March, 2012].

EE Times (2002) ST buys Alcatel Micro, then sells mixed-signal portion, *EE Times* [internet] Available at: www.eetimes.com/electronics-news/4094952/ST-buys-Alcatel-Micro-then-sells-mixed-signal-portion [Accessed on 23 March, 2012].

EE Times Asia (2011) Infineon buys Qimonda assets, expands fab capacity, *EE Times Asia* [internet] Available at: www.eetasia.com/articleLogin.do?artId=8800642329&fromWhere=/ART_8800642329_765245_NT_c7df3a1e.HTM&catId=765245&newsType=NT&pageNo=null&encode=c7df3a1e# [Accessed on 23 March, 2012].

Electronics.ca Research Network (2012) Microcontroller Market Share: In 3 Dimensions, Electronics.ca [internet] Available at: http://www.electronics.ca/press center/articles/1720/1/Microcontroller-Market-Share-In-3-Dimensions/Page1.html [Accessed on 11 September, 2012].

Electronic Design (2008a) Freescale boosts multimedia portfolio, *Electronic Design* [internet] Available at: http://electronicdesign.com/analog/freescale-boosts-multimedia-portfolio [Accessed on 11 September, 2012].

Electronic Design (2008b) Freescale completes acquisition of SigmaTel, *Electronic Design* [internet] Available at: http://electronicdesign.com/boards/freescale-completes-acquisition-sigmatel [Accessed on 11 September, 2012].

Floerecke, K-D. (2005) Infineon's goal: Be the top semiconductor supplier, *Automotive News*, October 31, p. 22JJ.

Freescale Semiconductor (2005) Frequently asked questions about Freescale's acquisition of the assets of seaway networks, *Freescale Semiconductor* [internet] Available at: www.freescale.com/files/netcomm/doc/support_info/FSL_OTTAWA_FAQ.pdf [Accessed on 20 March, 2012].

Freescale Semiconductor (2008a) Freescale Completes Acquisition of Intoto to Expand Embedded Multicore Development Support, Freescale Semiconductor [internet] Available at: http://www.businesswire.com/news/home/20081008006164/en/Freescale-Completes-Acquisition-Intoto-Expand-Embedded-Multicore [Accessed on 29 March, 2012].

Freescale Semiconductor (2008b) STMicroelectronics and Freescale Joint-Design Efforts Deliver on Promise of "First Silicon", Freescale Semiconductor [internet] Available at: http://investors.st.com/phoenix.zhtml?c=111941&p=NewsArticle_pf&id=1112165 [Accessed on 29 March, 2012].

Freescale Semiconductor (2009) Automotive safety-critical systems leap forward with next-generation microcontrollers from STMicroelectronics and Freescale, Freescale Semiconductor [internet] Available at: http://media.freescale.com/phoenix.zhtml?c=196520&p=irol-newsArticle_print&ID=1338824&highlight= [Accessed on 29 March, 2012].

Freescale Semiconductor (2011) *2011 Annual Report*, Austin: Freescale Semiconductor.

Freescale Semiconductor (2012a) MEMS-based sensor technology, *Freescale Semiconductor* [internet] Available at: www.freescale.com/webapp/sps/site/overview.jsp?code=SNSMEMSOVERVIEW [Accessed on 3 May, 2012].

Freescale Semiconductor (2012b) The multifaceted world of multi-core processing, *Freescale Semiconductor* [internet] Available at: www.freescale.com/webapp/sps/site/overview.jsp?code=IFNWMULTICORE [Accessed on 28 March, 2012].

Freescale Semiconductor (2012c) Frequently Asked Questions about Freescale's Acquisition of the Assets of Seaway Networks, Austin: Freescale Semiconductor.

Freescale Secmiconductor (2014) Form 10-K, *Freescale Semiconductor* [internet] Available at: www.sec.gov/Archives/edgar/data/1392522/000139252215000003/a201410-k.htm [Accessed on 28 January, 2017].

Fujimura, N. (2012a) NEC, Hitachi plan to provide support for Japan Chipmaker Renesas, *Bloomberg News* [internet] Available at: www.businessweek.com/news/2012-06-20/nec-hitachi-plan-to-provide-support-for-japan-chipmaker-renesas [Accessed on 10 September, 2012].

Fujimura, N. (2012b) Renesas surges on report of $1.3 billion KKR stake: Tokyo mover, *Bloomberg.com* [internet] Available at: www.businessweek.com/news/2012-08-28/renesas-shares-surge-on-report-of-1-dot-3-billion-kkr-investment [Accessed on 13 September, 2012].

Gartner (2012a) CMOS (complementary Metal-oxide Semiconductor), *Gartner* [internet] Available at: www.gartner.com/it-glossary/cmos-complementary-metal-oxide-semiconductor/ [Accessed on 12 December, 2012].

Gartner (2012b) Gartner says semiconductor foundry market grew 5.1 percent in 2011 to reach $29.8 billion, *Gartner* [internet] Available at: www.gartner.com/newsroom/id/1970115 [Accessed on 20 July, 2012].

Gartner (2016) Worldwide semiconductor foundry market grew 4.4 percent in 2015, according to final results by Gartner, *Gartner* [internet] Available at: www.gartner.com/newsroom/id/3281630 [Accessed on 1 August, 2016].

Geiger, F. and Henning, E. (2016) Infineon to buy Cree's wolfspeed unit for $850 million, *wsj.com* [internet] Available at: www.wsj.com/articles/infineon-close-to-announcing-acquisition-of-crees-wolfspeed-unit-1468490049 [Accessed on 30 December, 2016].Gibbs, S. (2015) Hackers can trick self-driving cars into taking evasive action, *The Guardian* [internet] Available at: www.theguardian.com/technology/2015/sep/07/hackers-trick-self-driving-cars-lidar-sensor [Accessed on 30 December, 2016].

GLOBALFOUNDRIES (2009) ATIC makes bid to acquire chartered semiconductor, *GLOBALFOUNDRIES* [internet] Available at: www.globalfoundries.com/newsroom/2009/20090906.aspx [Accessed on 19 July, 2012].

GLOBALFOUNDRIES (2011) GLOBALFOUNDRIES offers BCDlite technology process for applications in the automotive industry, *GLOBALFOUNDRIES* [internet] Available at: www.globalfoundries.com/newsroom/2011/20110912.aspx [Accessed on 20 July, 2012].

GLOBALFOUNDRIES (2015) GLOBALFOUNDRIES Completes Acquisition of IBM Microelectronics Business, GLOBALFOUNDRIES [internet] Available at: https://www.globalfoundries.com/news-events/press-releases/globalfoundries-completes-acquisition-of-ibm-microelectronics-business [Accessed on 3 November, 2016].

Google Finance (2012) Renesas Electronics Corporation, Google Finance [internet] Available at: http://www.google.com/finance?cid=685772 [Accessed on 11 September, 2012].

Greimel, H. (2011) The big threat: Chip shortage, *Automotive News* [internet] Available at: www.autonews.com/apps/pbcs.dll/article?AID=/20110411/OEM01/304119958/1117&template=printart [Accessed on 24 November, 2011].

Gupta, B.L. (2005) World Automotive Semiconductor Markets, BCC Report SMC054A, May, Wellesley, MA: BCC Research.

GuruFocus.com (2016) ON Semiconductor Corp (NAS: ON) market cap, *GuruFocus.com* [internet] Available at: www.gurufocus.com/term/mktcap/ON/Market-Cap/ON-Semiconductor-Corp [Accessed on 3 September, 2016].

Hammerschmidt, C. (2010a) Bosch launches 200mm wafer fab, *EE Times* [internet] Available at: www.electronics-eetimes.com/en/bosch-launches-200mm-wafer-fab.html?cmp_id=7&news_id=222901029# [Accessed on 3 April, 2012].

Hammerschmidt, C. (2010b) Bosch launches fab for automotive semiconductors, *EE Times* [internet] Available at: www.eetimes.com/electronics-news/4196815/Bosch-launches-fab-for-automotive-semiconductors [Accessed on 3 April, 2012].

Hammerschmidt, C. (2012) Freescale pitches Vybrid MCU line to automotive infotainment, EE Times Europe [internet] Available at: http://www.automotive-eetimes.com/en/freescale-pitches-vybrid-mcu-line-to-automotive-infotainment.html?cmp_id=7&news_id=222902320 [Accessed on 7 July, 2012].

Hand, A. (2010) Manufacturers use creative solutions to reinvent fabs, *mysemicondaily.com* [internet] Available at: www.mysemicondaily.com/blog/?currentPage=40 [Accessed on 12 August, 2012].

Hilferding, R. (1981) *Finance Capital: A Study of the Latest Phase of Capitalist Development*, London: Routledge & Kegan Paul Ltd (First Published in 1910).

IHS (2016) Automotive semiconductor market grows slightly in 2015 while ranks shift, IHS says, *IHS* [internet] Available at: http://press.ihs.com/press-release/technology/automotive-semiconductor-market-grows-slightly-2015-while-ranks-shift-ihs-s [Accessed on 1 August, 2016].

Infineon Technologies AG (2000) Annual Report 2000, Neubiberg, Germany: Infineon Technologies AG.

Infineon Technologies AG (2001) Annual Report 2001, Neubiberg, Germany: Infineon Technologies AG.

Infineon Technologies AG (2004) *Annual Report 2004*, Neubiberg, Germany: Infineon Technologies AG.

Infineon Technologies AG (2006a) *Annual Report 2006*, Neubiberg, Germany: Infineon Technologies AG.

Infineon Technologies AG (2006b) Infineon's automotive electronics business grows faster than the market – number two position in the global market improved, *Infineon* [internet] Available at: www.infineon.com/cms/en/corporate/press/news/releases/2006/185624.html [Accessed on 2 May, 2012].

Infineon Technologies AG (2007) Infineon introduces powerful and scalable XC2200 microcontroller family for automotive body applications offering significant savings in development costs, *Infineon* [internet] Available at: www.infineon.com/cms/en/corporate/press/news/releases/2007/220277.html [Accessed on 10 October, 2012].

Infineon Technologies AG (2009) Infineon and Bosch sign a collaboration contract for power semiconductors, *Infineon* [internet] Available at: www.infineon.

com/cms/en/corporate/press/news/releases/2009/INFATV200903-045.html [Accessed on 02 May, 2012].

Infineon Technologies AG (2010) Infineon launches new automotive microcontroller family; offering powerful compute capability and advanced features to achieve strict efficiency and safety standards, *Infineon* [internet] Available at: www.infineon. com/cms/en/corporate/press/news/releases/2010/INFATV201007-061.html [Accessed on 03 July, 2012].

Infineon Technologies AG (2011) *Annual Report 2011*, Neubiberg, Germany: Infineon Technologies AG.

Infineon Technologies AG (2012) Lean manufacturing manager, *Infineon* [internet] Available at: www.jobstreet.com.my/jobs/2012/8/i/20/3167202.htm?fr=J [Accessed on 3 July, 2012].

Infineon Technologies AG (2014) Infineon Technologies AG to Acquire International Rectifier Corporation for US-Dollar 40 per share, approximately US-Dollar 3 billion in cash, Infineon [internet] Available at: http://www.infineon.com/cms/en/about-infineon/press/press-releases/2014/INFXX201408-056.html [Accessed on 3 July, 2016].

Infineon Technologies AG (2015a) *Annual Report 2015*, Neubiberg, Germany: Infineon Technologies AG.

Infineon Technologies AG (2015b) Bosch honors Infineon with award for innovation, *Infineon* [internet] Available at: www.infineon.com/cms/en/about-infineon/press/press-releases/2015/INFATV201507-070.html [Accessed on 7 September, 2016].

Infineon Technologies AG (2015c) Radar chips in cars save lives: Infineon innovation nominated for the Deutscher Zukunftspreis 2015, the German President's award for innovation in science and technology, *Infineon* [internet] Available at: www.infineon.com/cms/en/about-infineon/press/press-releases/2015/INFXX 201509-082.html [Accessed on 28 January, 2017].

Infineon Technologies AG (2016a) Infineon to acquire Wolfspeed for US Dollar 850 million in cash, *Infineon* [internet] Available at: www.infineon.com/cms/en/about-infineon/press/press-releases/2016/INFXX201607-071.html [Accessed on 30 December, 2016].

Infineon Technologies AG (2016b) Infineon strengthens leading position in automated driving through acquisition of Innoluce BV, *Infineon* [internet] Available at: www.infineon.com/cms/en/about-infineon/press/press-releases/2016/INFATV201610-002.html [Accessed on 30 December, 2016].

Kachi, H. and Maxwell, K. (2009) NEC, Renesas Get Injection Of $2.2 Billion for Chip Deal, wsj.com [internet] Available at: http://online.wsj.com/article/SB125310310748815617.html [Accessed on 16 July, 2012].

Kallenbach, R. (2011) Power electronics – a key to the electromobility of the future, Bosch.com [internet] Available at: http://www.bosch-presse.de/presseforum/details.htm?locale=en&txtID=5159 [Accessed on 12 May, 2012].

Kanellos, M. (1999) TSMC picks up remainder of Acer's chip operations, *CNET* [internet] Available at: http://news.cnet.com/TSMC-picks-up-remainder-of-Acers-chip-operations/2100-1001_3-235056.html [Accessed on 12 September, 2012].

Kaplan, S.N. (1989) The effects of management buyouts on operating performance and value, *Journal of Financial Economics*, 24(2): 217–254.

Kaplan, S.N. and Stromberg, P. (2009) Leveraged buyouts and private equity, *Journal of Economic Perspective*, 23(1): 121–146.

King, I. (2012) Nissan to use Intel Chips for car entertainment systems, *Bloomberg.com* [internet] Available at: www.bloomberg.com/news/2012-04-05/nissan-vehicle-entertainment-systems-to-include-intel-chips-1-.html [Accessed on 12 July, 2012].

Klemming, L. and Kjetland, R. (2011) Infineon's Bauer to Keep Cash for Acquisition Opportunities, Bloomberg News [internet] Available at: http://www.businessweek.com/news/2011-06-01/infineon-s-bauer-to-keep-cash-for-acquisition-opportunities.html [Accessed on 10 September, 2012].

Klier, T.H. and Rubenstein, J.M. (2008) *Who Really Made Your Car? Restructuring and Geographic Change in the Auto Industry*, Kalamazoo, MI: W.E. Upjohn Institute for Employment Research.

Knight, S. and Murai, R. (2014) Renesas says may cut more jobs, but restructuring past halfway, *Reuters* [internet], Available at: http://in.reuters.com/article/us-renesas-electron-restructuring-idINKBN0GX1KA20140902 [Accessed on 1 August, 2016].

Korosec, K. (2016) NXP pushes into self-driving car market with BlueBox computing platform, *Fortune* [internet] Available at: http://fortune.com/2016/05/16/nxp-self-driving-car-bluebox/ [Accessed on 30 January, 2017].

Kraeuter, C. (2006a) Blackstone buys freescale, *Forbes.com* [internet] Available at: www.forbes.com/2006/09/15/blackstone-freescale-buyout-tech-cx_ck_0915freescale.html [Accessed on 26 October, 2012].

Kraeuter, C. (2006b) Why private money likes chips, *Forbes.com* [internet] Available at: www.forbes.com/2006/09/14/chip-lbo-equity-tech-cx_ck_0915chip.html [Accessed on 26 October, 2012].

Kress, A. (2008) ON Semiconductor to buy Catalyst Semiconductor in $115 million deal, Phoenix Business Journal [internet] Available at: http://www.bizjournals.com/phoenix/stories/2008/07/14/daily51.html [Accessed on 13 August, 2012].

Kwong, R. (2010) Oops: key China-Taiwan deal blocked, *FT.com* [internet], Available at: http://blogs.ft.com/beyond-brics/2010/11/18/oops-key-china-taiwan-deal-blocked/#axzz20wifAPgC [Accessed on 18 July, 2012].

Lapedus, M. (2009) On semi buys EMI firm, enters India design front, *EE Times* [internet] Available at: www.eetimes.com/electronics-news/4085766/On-Semi-buys-EMI-firm-enters-India-design-front [Accessed on 20 May, 2012].

Lemon, S. (2009) AMD's Manufacturing Spinoff Renamed GlobalFoundries, PCWorld [internet] Available at: http://www.pcworld.com/article/160655/amds_manufacturing_spinoff_renamed_globalfoundries.html [Accessed on 18 July, 2012].

Liao, G. (2012) TSMC, Renesas announce agreement on cooperation, *Taipei Times* [internet] Available at: www.taipeitimes.com/News/biz/archives/2012/05/29/2003533958 [Accessed on 18 July, 2012].

Lienert, P. (2015) Nvidia wants to leap from video games to self-driving cars, Reuters [internet] Available at: http://www.reuters.com/article/nvidia-autos-idUSL2N0XE11L20150514 [Accessed on 9 November, 2016].

Macronix (2011) Macronix's serial flash to be used with Freescale's Qorivva(TM) MPC5645S microcontroller for automotive dashboard display, *Macronix International Co. Ltd* [internet] Available at: www.bloomberg.com/article/2011-12-15/aQy9Oj_J2eX4.html [Accessed on 26 October, 2012].

Manners, D. (2012) Panasonic, Fujitsu, Renesas talk merger, ElectronicsWeekly.com [internet] Available at: http://www.electronicsweekly.com/articles/08/02/2012/52920/panasonic-fujitsu-renesas-talk-merger.htm [Accessed on 17 September, 2012].

Manufacturing.net (2007) ON Semiconductor To Buy AMI Semiconductor, Manufacturing.net [internet] Available at: http://www.manufacturing.net/news/2007/12/on-semiconductor-to-buy-ami-semiconductor [Accessed on 17 September, 2012].

MarketWatch, Inc. (2016) Nvidia Corp, *MarketWatch, Inc.* [internet] Available at: www.marketwatch.com/investing/stock/nvda/financials [Accessed on 3 September, 2016].

Marketwired (2017) BlackBerry QNX and Renesas electronics America collaborate to develop an automotive-grade technology platform for autonomous driving, *Marketwired* [internet] Available at: www.marketwired.com/press-release/blackberry-qnx-renesas-electronics-america-collaborate-develop-automotive-grade-technology-nasdaq-bbry-2186274.htm [Accessed on 30 January, 2017].

McGrath, D. (2012) AMD relinquishes stake in Globalfoundries, *EE Times* [internet] Available at: www.eetimes.com/electronics-news/4237431/AMD-relinquishes-stake-in-Globalfoundries [Accessed on 19 July, 2012].

Meaney, C.S. (1994) State policy and the development of Taiwan's semiconductor industry, in Aberbach, J.D., Dollar, D. and Sokoloff, K.L. (eds), *The Role of the State in Taiwan's Development*, New York: M.E. Sharpe Inc.

Morgan, T.P. (2010) AMD's GlobalFoundries consumes chartered semi rival, *The Register*, Available at: www.theregister.co.uk/2010/01/14/globalfoundries_chartered_combo/ [Accessed on 13 December, 2012].

Morrill, N., Macleod, G., Berkowitch, M. and Lloyd, D. (2009) Talking turnarounds, *Real Deals Europe* [internet] Available at: www.rutlandpartners.com/articles/Talking-turnarounds.pdf [Accessed on 8 April, 2012].

Mubadala Development Company PJSC (2014) Advanced Technology Investment Company (ATIC) to become Mubadala Technology, *Mubadala* [internet] Available at: www.mubadala.com/en/news/advanced-technology-investment-company-atic-become-mubadala-technology [Accessed on 2 August, 2016].

Murakami, J. (2006) Summary of Fujitsu SoC technology and related business, *Fujitsu Scientific and Technical Journal*, 42(2) (April): 171–180.

Nelson, G. (2015) Restructured Renesas seeks its footing on platforms: Japanese supplier shifts to back-end vehicle software, *Automotive News* [internet] Available at: www.autonews.com/article/20151123/OEM06/311239993/restructured-renesas-seeks-its-footing – on-platforms [Accessed on 1 August, 2016].

Nikkei Asian Review (2014) Sony buying Renesas chip plant to boost image sensor output, *Nikkei Asian Review* [internet] Available at: http://asia.nikkei.com/Business/Deals/Sony-buying-Renesas-chip-plant-to-boost-image-sensor-output [Accessed on 1 August, 2016].

Nolan, P. (2008) Capitalism and Freedom, The Contradictory Character of Globalisation, London: Anthem Press.

Nvidia Corp (2016) *Form 10-K (Annual Report)*, Santa Clara: Nvidia Corp.

NXP Semiconductors N.V. (2006a) *Annual Report 2006*, Netherlands: NXP Semiconductors N.V.

NXP Semiconductors N.V. (2006b) NXP Semiconductors raises stake in SSMC to more than 60 percent, *NXP* [internet] Available at: www.nxp.com/news/press-releases/2006/11/nxp-semiconductors-raises-stake-in-ssmc.html [Accessed on 23 July, 2012].

NXP Semiconductors N.V. (2008) *Annual Report 2008*, Netherlands: NXP Semiconductors N.V.

NXP Semiconductors N.V. (2010) Statutory Annual Report for the Financial Year Ended December 31, 2010, Netherlands: NXP Semiconductors N.V.

NXP Semiconductors N.V. (2012a) *Company Presentation February 2012*, Netherlands: NXP Semiconductors N.V.

NXP Semiconductors N.V. (2012b) *Factsheet*, Netherlands: NXP Semiconductors N.V.

NXP Semiconductors N.V. (2015a) *Annual Report For the Financial Year Ended December 31, 2015*, Netherlands: NXP Semiconductors N.V.

NXP Semiconductors N.V. (2015b) *NXP Company Factsheet*, Netherlands: NXP Semiconductors N.V.

NXP Semiconductors N.V. (2015c) NXP and Freescale Announce Completion of Merger, *NXP* [internet] Available at: http://investors.nxp.com/phoenix.zhtml?c=209114&p=irol-newsArticle&ID=2120581 [Accessed on 2 August, 2016].

NXP Semiconductors N.V. (2016a) *NXP at a Glance*, Netherlands: NXP Semiconductors N.V.

NXP Semiconductors N.V. (2016b) NXP demonstrates complete autonomous vehicle platform using NXP Silicon at each ADAS node, *NXP* [internet] Available at: http://media.nxp.com/phoenix.zhtml?c=254228&p=irol-newsarticle&id=2168393 [Accessed on 30 January, 2017].

NXP Semiconductors N.V. (2016c) Qualcomm to acquire NXP, *NXP* [internet] Available at: http://media.nxp.com/phoenix.zhtml?c=254228&p=irol-newsArticle&ID=2216426 [Accessed on 28 January, 2017].

NXP Semiconductors N.V. (2017) NXP semiconductors reports fourth quarter and full-year 2016 results, *NXP* [internet] Available at: http://investors.nxp.com/phoenix.zhtml?c=209114&p=irol-newsArticle&ID=2241494 [Accessed on 3 February, 2017].

O'Donnell (2016) Car wars: The battle for automotive tech, *Recode* [internet] Available at: www.recode.net/2016/7/7/12107608/car-wars-automous-automotive-tech-intel-mobileye [Accessed on 28 July, 2016].

ON Semiconductor Corporation (2006) ON semiconductor completes $105 million acquisition of LSI logic corporation's Gresham, Ore., 8-Inch Wafer Fab, *ON Semiconductor* [internet] Available at: http://news.thomasnet.com/companystory/ON-Semiconductor-Completes-105-Million-Acquisition-of-LSI-Logic-Corporation-s-Gresham-Ore-8-Inch-Wafer-Fab-486007 [Accessed on 12 July, 2012].

ON Semiconductor Corporation (2009) ON semiconductor to acquire California micro devices for $4.70 per share in an all-cash tender offer, *ON Semiconductor* [internet] Available at: www.onsemi.com/PowerSolutions/newsItem.do?article=2219 [Accessed on 12 July, 2012].

ON Semiconductor Corporation (2011) *2011 Annual Report*, Arizona: ON Semiconductor Corporation.

ON Semiconductor Corporation (2014) ON semiconductor to acquire Aptina imaging, *ON Semiconductor* [internet] Available at: www.onsemi.com/PowerSolutions/newsItem.do?article=3116 [Accessed on 1 August, 2016].

ON Semiconductor Corporation (2015a) *2015 Annual Report*, Arizona: ON Semiconductor Corporation.

ON Semiconductor Corporation (2015b) ON Semiconductor to acquire Fairchild Semiconductor for $2.4 billion in cash, *ON Semiconductor* [internet] Available at: www.onsemi.com/PowerSolutions/newsItem.do?article=3452 [Accessed on 1 August, 2016].

Osawa, J. (2011) Chip maker runs at half speed: Japan quake slows Renesas plants involved in producing key components used by car industry, *wsj.com* [internet]

Available at: http://online.wsj.com/article/SB1000142405274870451740457 6222053226363360.html [Accessed on 24 November, 2011].

Osawa, J. (2012) Update: Renesas, Fujitsu, Panasonic in talks to integrate system chip development ops – source, *wsj.com* [internet] Available at: http://online.wsj.com/article/BT-CO-20120207-720702.html [Accessed on 6 April, 2012].

Pagliery, J. (2014) Your car is a giant computer – and it can be hacked, *CNNMoney* [internet] Available at: http://money.cnn.com/2014/06/01/technology/security/car-hack/ [Accessed on 30 July, 2016].

Palomar Technologies (2017) System on a Chip (SoC), *Palomar Technologies* [internet] Available at: www.palomartechnologies.com/applications/system-on-a-chip [Accessed on 3 February, 2017].

Pollack, A. and Lohr, S. (2011) A Japanese plant struggles to produce a critical auto part, *nytimes.com* [internet] Available at: www.nytimes.com/2011/04/28/business/global/28chip.html?_r=1&pagewanted=all [Accessed on 10 August, 2011].

Quinn, T.K. (1953) Giant Business: Threat to Democracy: The Autobiography of an Insider, New York: Exposition Press.

Randewich, N. (2012) Insight: As chip plants get pricey, U.S. risks losing edge, *Reuters.com* [internet] Available at: www.reuters.com/article/2012/05/01/us-semiconductors-manufacturing-idUSBRE8400N920120501 [Accessed on 4 May, 2012].

Renesas (2010a) *Annual Report 2010: Year Ended March 31, 2010*, Tokyo: Renesas Electronics Corporation.

Renesas (2010b) Renesas Electronics to acquire Nokia's wireless modem business; Companies to form strategic business alliance for modem technology development, *Renesas* [internet] Available at: www.renesas.com/press/news/2010/news20100706.jsp [Accessed on 12 September, 2012].

Renesas (2010c) Renesas Electronics announces growth strategies for its SoC business targeting mobile and multimedia applications, *Renesas* [internet] Available at: http://am.renesas.com/press/news/2010/news20100909.jsp [Accessed on 12 September, 2012].

Renesas (2011) *Annual Report 2011: Year Ended March 31, 2011*, Tokyo: Renesas Electronics Corporation.

Renesas (2012) Renesas Electronics and TSMC collaborate to construct ecosystem for microcontrollers: Aiming to expand MCU market by integrating the companies' world-leading technologies, *Renesas* [internet] Available at: www.renesas.com/press/news/2012/news20120528.jsp [Accessed on 12 September, 2012].

Renesas (2013a) Providing the fast-access flash memory required by high-performance MCUs, *Renesas* [internet] Available at: http://am.renesas.com/edge_ol/special/01/index.jsp [Accessed on 17 April, 2013].

Renesas (2015b) Renesas Electronics announces development of an on-chip SRAM to enable real-time image processing required in the autonomous-driving cars era, *Renesas* [internet] Available at: www.renesas.com/en-sg/about/press-center/news/2015/news20151209.html [Accessed on 28 January, 2017].

Renesas (2016a) *Financial Report 2016: Year Ended March 31, 2016*, Tokyo: Renesas Electronics Corporation.

Renesas (2016b) Renesas Electronics announces completion of safety microcontroller lineup suitable for system platform development to accelerate realization of autonomous driving, *Renesas* [internet] Available at: www.renesas.com/en-sg/about/press-center/news/2016/news20161215.html [Accessed on 30 January, 2017].

Reuters (2012) UPDATE 1-AMD sells stake in GlobalFoundries; restructures supply deal, *Reuters.com* [internet] Available at: www.reuters.com/article/2012/03/05/amd-idUSL4E8E55XG20120305 [Accessed on 13 December, 2012].

Saito, M. (2012) Japan's Renesas expects worst-ever annual loss of $1.9 billion, *Reuters.com* [internet] Available at: http://uk.reuters.com/article/2012/08/02/oukin-uk-renesas-earnings-idUKBRE87109E20120802 [Accessed on 10 September, 2012].

Savitz, E. (2011) Japan quake knocked out 25% of global silicon wafer production, *Forbes* [internet] Available at: www.forbes.com/sites/ericsavitz/2011/03/21/japan-quake-knocked-out-25-of-global-silicon-wafer-production/ [Accessed on 11 September, 2012].

Schlesinger, J.M. and Frischkorn, B. (2012) Japan govt-backed fund mulls bid for Renesas to counter KKR offer – source, *wsj.com* [internet] Available at: http://online.wsj.com/article/BT-CO-20120922-700853.html [Accessed on 28 October, 2012].

Semicast (2012) Renesas Electronics leads OE automotive semiconductor vendor ranking in 2011; freescale falls to fourth behind STMicroelectronics, *Semicast* [internet] Available at: www.ecnmag.com/news/2012/03/renesas-electronics-leads-oe-automotive-semiconductor-vendor-ranking-2011-freescale-falls-fourth-behind-stmicroelectronics [Accessed on 24 September, 2012].

Semiconductor Portal Inc. (2012) Renesas earmarks 155 billion yen for restructuring in fight for survival, *Semiconductor Portal* [internet] Available at: www.semiconportal.com/en/archive/news/main-news/120807-renesas-restructuring.html [Accessed on 17 September, 2012].

Shah, A. (2012) Intel warns AMD about patent breach, *PCWorld* [internet] Available at: www.pcworld.com/article/161311/intel_warns_amd_about_patent_breach.html [Accessed on 18 July, 2012].

Shapiro, D. (2015) The car of the future is 'the most powerful computer you will ever own', The Telegraph [internet] Available at: http://www.telegraph.co.uk/technology/news/11609406/The-car-of-the-future-is-the-most-powerful-computer-you-will-ever-own.html [Accessed on 2 August, 2016].

Sheahan, M. (2011) Infineon could spend 1 bln eur on M&A-CFO in paper, Reuters.com [internet] Available at: http://in.reuters.com/article/2011/12/21/infineon-acquisitions-idINL6E7NL0KR20111221 [Accessed on 20 August, 2012].

Shilov, A. (2012) TSMC to make chips for Renesas: Renesas electronics and TSMC sign pact for ecosystem for microcontrollers, *X-bit laboratories* [internet] Available at: www.xbitlabs.com/news/other/display/20120528102443_TSMC_to_Make_Chips_for_Renesas.html [Accessed on 18 July, 2012].

Shilov, A. (2015) Nvidia: We've learnt a lot from the automotive industry, *Kitguru.net* [internet] Available at: www.kitguru.net/components/anton-shilov/nvidia-weve-learnt-a-lot-from-the-automotive-industry/ [Accessed on 3 September, 2016].

SiliconFarEast.com (2005) Static Random Access Memories (SRAMs), *SiliconFarEast.com* [internet] Available at: www.siliconfareast.com/srams.htm [Accessed on 19 September, 2012].

Simon, B. (2011) Car parts makers face antitrust scrutiny, *ft.com* [internet] Available at: www.ft.com/intl/cms/s/0/1592b926-af00-11e0-bb89-00144feabdc0.html#axzz2NhHsOvgE [Accessed on 18 July, 2012].

Soble, J. and Sender, H. (2012) KKR starts talks to buy Renesas, FT.com [internet] Available at: http://www.ft.com/intl/cms/s/0/d4ffacf0-f195-11e1-bba3-00144feabdc0.html#axzz263ryXmKO [Accessed on 10 September, 2012].

Solid State Technology (2012) TSMC, Renesas aim to expand microcontroller market, LexisNexis [internet] Available at: http://www.electroiq.com/semiconductors/2012/05/28/tsmc-renesas-aim-to-expand-microcontroller-market.html [Accessed on 6 June, 2012].

STMicroelectronics N.V. (1996) *STMicroelectronics 1996 Annual Report*, France: STMicroelectronics N.V.

STMicroelectronics N.V. (1998) *STMicroelectronics 1998 Annual Report*, Geneva: STMicroelectronics N.V.

STMicroelectronics N.V. (2000) STMicroelectronics announces acquisition of Portland Group Inc., *STMicroelectronics* [internet] Available at: http://investors.st.com/phoenix.zhtml?c=111941&p=irol-newsArticle&ID=1455084&highlight= [Accessed on 10 May, 2012].

STMicroelectronics N.V. (2002) STMicroelectronics to acquire Alcatel's Microelectronics business, *STMicroelectronics* [internet] Available at: http://investors.st.com/phoenix.zhtml?c=111941&p=irol-newsArticle&ID=1454699&highlight= [Accessed on 10 May, 2012].

STMicroelectronics N.V. (2008) *Corporate Social Responsibility 08*, Geneva: STMicroelectronics N.V.

STMicroelectronics N.V. (2010a) *20-F Annual and Transition Report of Foreign Private Issuers Pursuant to Sections 13 or 15(d)*, Geneva: STMicroelectronics N.V.

STMicroelectronics N.V. (2010b) Mentor graphics to extend cooperation with STMicroelectronics for advanced chip-development design solutions, *STMicroelectronics* [internet] Available at: www.mentor.com/company/news/cooperation-with-stmicroelectronics-for-advanced-chip-development-design-solutions [Accessed on 10 May, 2012].

STMicroelectronics N.V. (2011a) *20-F Annual and Transition Report of Foreign Private Issuers Pursuant to Sections 13 or 15(d)*, Geneva: STMicroelectronics N.V.

STMicroelectronics N.V. (2011b) STMicroelectronics Expands Capabilities in Convergent Home Digital Networking and Smart Grid, STMicroelectronics [internet] Available at: http://investors.st.com/phoenix.zhtml?c=111941&p=irol-newsArticle_Print&ID=1582231 [Accessed on 10 May. 2012].

STMicroelectronics N.V. (2011c) STMicroelectronics Debuts the World's First Single-Chip Positioning Device for Multiple Global Navigation Systems, STMicroelectronics [internet] Available at: http://www.prnewswire.com/news-releases/stmicroelectronics-debuts-the-worlds-first-single-chip-positioning-device-for-multiple-global-navigation-systems-114473384.html [Accessed on 10 May. 2012].

STMicroelectronics N.V. (2011d) Sustainability Report 2011, Geneva: STMicroelectronics N.V.

STMicroelectronics N.V. (2016a) *Form 20-F*, Geneva: STMicroelectronics N.V.

STMicroelectronics N.V. (2016b) The road to full autonomous driving: Mobileye and STMicroelectronics to develop EyeQ®5 system-on-chip, targeting sensor fusion central computer for autonomous vehicles, *STMicroelectronics* [internet] Available at: www.st.com/content/st_com/en/about/media-center/press-item.html/p3832.html [Accessed on 30 January, 2017].

Taiwan Semiconductor Manufacturing Company Ltd (1999) TSMC and TASMC announce to MergeCombination to enable improved manufacturing efficiencies, increased foundry capacity and greater focus on core competencies, *TSMC* [internet] Available at: www.tsmc.com.tw/tsmcdotcom/PRListingNewsArchivesAction. do?action=detail&newsid=905&language=E [Accessed on 18 July, 2012].

Taiwan Semiconductor Manufacturing Company Ltd (2000) Financial Statements as of December 31, 2000 and 1999, Hsinchu, Taiwan: TSMC.

Taiwan Semiconductor Manufacturing Company Ltd (2011a) *Annual Report 2011*, Hsinchu, Taiwan: TSMC.

Taiwan Semiconductor Manufacturing Company Ltd (2011b) *Form 20-F*, Hsinchu, Taiwan: TSMC.

Taiwan Semiconductor Manufacturing Company Ltd (2015) *Form 20-F*, Hsinchu, Taiwan: TSMC.

Taiwan Semiconductor Manufacturing Company Ltd (2016) Renesas Electronics and TSMC announce 28nm MCU Collaboration for next-generation green and autonomous vehicles, *TSMC* [internet] Available at: www.tsmc.com/tsmcdot com/PRListingNewsAction.do?action=detail&language=E&newsid=THHIANH ITH [Accessed on 3 September, 2016].

Taylor, E. (2016) BMW to develop driverless car technology with Intel, Mobileye, *Reuters* [internet] Available at: www.reuters.com/article/us-bmw-mobileye-intel-idUSKCN0ZH4Z3 [Accessed on 2 August, 2016].

Texas Instruments Incorporated (2015) *2015 Annual Report*, Dallas: Texas Instruments Incorporated.

Texas Instruments Incorporated (2016) Acquisitions and divestitures, *Texas Instruments* [internet] Available at: www.ti.com/corp/docs/investor_relations/acquisi tions_divestitures.html [Accessed on 3 September, 2016].

The Associated Press (2009) NEC, Renesas to Merge Chip Businesses, The Associated Press [internet] Available at: https://www.wirelessweek.com/news/2009/04/ nec-renesas-merge-chip-businesses [Accessed on 7 July, 2012].

The Economist (2012) Monsters Inc? Private-equity firms may make the economy work better, but their bosses get too much cash, The Economist [internet] Available at: www.economist.com/node/21543545 [Accessed on 26 October, 2012].

The Economist (2016) Driverless cars: Eyes on the road, The Economist, 421(9021): 107–108.

The Power Pulse.Net (2000) ON semiconductor completes acquisition of cherry semiconductor, *The Power Pulse.Net* [internet] Available at: www.powerpulse.net/ story.php?storyID=1118 [Accessed on 11 January, 2013].

Toshiba Corporation (2016) *Annual Report, Year Ended March 31, 2016, Financial Review*, Tokyo, Japan: Toshiba Corporation.

United Microelectronics Corporation (1998) UMC group will take over Nippon Steel Semiconductor Corporation from Nippon Steel Corporation, *UMC* [internet] Available at: www.umc.com/english/news/1998/9809.asp [Accessed on 19 July, 2012].

United Microelectronics Corporation (1999) UMC group announces consolidation of joint ventures and acceleration of foundry capacity expansion, *UMC* [internet] Available at: www.umc.com/english/news/1999/990614.asp [Accessed on 19 July, 2012].

United Microelectronics Corporation (2000) UMC completes consolidation of joint ventures, *UMC* [internet] Available at: www.umc.com/english/news/2000/ 20000110.asp [Accessed on 19 July, 2012].

United Microelectronics Corporation (2011a) *Form 20-F Annual Report Fiscal Year Ended December 31, 2011*, Taipei, Taiwan: UMC.

United Microelectronics Corporation (2011b) UMC receives government approval to acquire stakes in He Jian, *UMC* [internet] Available at: www.umc.com/english/news/2011/20111031.asp [Accessed on 19 July, 2012].

United Microelectronics Corporation (2015) *Form 20-F Annual Report Fiscal Year Ended December 31, 2015*, Taipei, Taiwan: UMC.

Uranaka, T. and Yamazaki, M. (2016) Japan government fund INCJ plans Renesas sale; Nidec to bid: sources, *Reuters* [internet] Available at: www.reuters.com/arti cle/us-japan-renesas-idUSKCN0UT20B [Accessed on 1 August, 2016].

Vidyasagar, S. (2013) What is the difference between microcontroller and micro-processor? *Vidyasagar Sir's Web* [internet] Available at: http://vsagar.com/2013/01/16/difference-microcontroller-microprocessor/ [Accessed on 7 January, 2013].

Virki, T. (2011) Infineon profits jump on strong car industry demand, Reuters. com [internet] Available at: http://www.reuters.com/article/2011/07/28/us-infineon-idUSTRE76R36I20110728 [Accessed on 12 August, 2012].

Wassener, B. and Nicholson, C.V. (2011) In Quake's aftermath, Japanese companies try to take stock, *nytimes.com* [internet] Available at: www.nytimes.com/2011/03/12/business/global/12yen.html?pagewanted=all&_r=0 [Accessed on 20 November, 2012].

Waters, R., Fedor, L. and Thomas, N. (2016) Qualcomm buys NXP for $47bn in Europe's largest tech deal, *ft.com* [internet] Available at: www.ft.com/content/457edf86-9c33-11e6-a6e4-8b8e77dd083a [Accessed on 28 January, 2017].

Webber, C. (2005) Automotive semiconductor market continues steady growth, exceeding $16 billion in 2005, *Strategy Analytics* [internet] Available at: www.strategyanalytics.net/default.aspx?mod=PressReleaseViewer&a0=2585 [Accessed on 12 May, 2012].

Webber, C. (2006) Automotive semiconductor demand forecast 2004–2013, *Strategy Analytics* [internet] Available at: www.strategyanalytics.net/default.aspx?mod=ReportAbstractViewer&a0=3035 [Accessed on 12 May, 2012].

Webber, C., Fitzgerald, M. and Doliner, L. (2016) Strategy analytics: NXP tops automotive semiconductor vendor rankings, *Strategy Analytics* [internet] Available at: www.strategyanalytics.com/strategy-analytics/news/strategy-analytics-press-releases/strategy-analytics-press-release/2016/05/02/strategy-analytics-nxp-tops-automotive-semiconductor-vendor-rankings#.V6IUANeznh4 [Accessed on 26 July, 2016].

WeEn Semiconductors (2017) About WeEn, *WeEn Semiconductors* [internet] Available at: www.ween-semi.com/about.aspx [Accessed on 2 February, 2017].

Whytock, P. (2009) Infineon and TSMC extend collaboration on auto and chip-card apps, *Electronic Design* [internet] Available at: http://electronicdesign.com/article/news/infineon_and_tsmc_extend_collaboration_on_auto_and_chip_card_apps [Accessed on 22 March, 2012].

Womack, J.P. and Jones, D.T. (2005) Lean Solutions: How Companies and Customers Can Create Value and Wealth Together, London: Simon & Schuster UK Ltd.

Wu, D. (2014) TSMC acquires Qualcomm facility for $85M, *Nikkei Asian Review* [internet] Available at: http://asia.nikkei.com/Business/Companies/TSMC-acquires-Qualcomm-facility-for-85M [Accessed on 2 August, 2016].

Yamazaki, M. (2016) Japan's Renesas pushes into autos with $3.2 billion Intersil buy, *Reuters* [internet] Available at: www.reuters.com/article/us-intersil-m-a-renesas-idUSKCN11I2O3 [Accessed on 5 October, 2016].

Yasu, M. (2012) Renesas, Fujitsu, Panasonic rise on chip-unit merger report: Tokyo mover, *Bloomberg.com* [internet] Available at: http://mobile.bloomberg.com/news/2012-02-08/renesas-fujitsu-panasonic-rise-on-chip-unit-merger-report-tokyo-mover [Accessed on 10 April, 2012].

Yoshida, J. (2012) Renesas, TSMC tout licensable MCU platform using 40-nm eFlash, *EE Times* [internet] Available at: www.eetimes.com/electronics-news/4373900/Renesas – TSMC-tout-licensable-MCU-platform-using-40-nm-eFlash [Accessed on 18 July, 2012].

8 Comparative analysis of the five components subsectors

1. Demand for technical progress: a common trait across all five subsectors

Buffeted by the relentless consolidation wave unleashed by the cascade effect, the key players in each of the five subsectors covered in this book, have over the span of the last three decades become industry oligarchs, fast approaching the zenith of their power (the top two to four companies now control approximately 40 percent or more of their respective markets). Across the oligopolistic (sometimes duopolistic) landscapes of these subsectors, where mutually destructive price wars are anathema and once efficacious marketing campaigns have run their course, cutting-edge technical progress is now increasingly viewed by the prevailing mega suppliers as a critical means of bolstering (or at the very least cementing) their market dominance. In this context, achieving technical progress would refer to the development of technologically superior products that command premium prices owing to their superlative appeal to customers. However, as evidenced across these five subsectors, a consistent track record of significant technical progress and process innovation does not necessarily confer market success on the incumbents but a refusal to participate in this intensifying technological 'arms race' would certainly place them at a strategic disadvantage (i.e., loss of hard fought market share to existing rivals or even non-traditional upstarts possessing superior financial/technological wherewithal).

The increasing omnipresence of state-of-the-art technology is now exhibited across the tyres, seats, CVJs and brakes subsectors which are often misperceived as low-tech, industrial relics from an earlier century. For instance, the 'humble' tyre industry, unbeknownst to the general public, has evolved into a savvy technological player that incorporates sophisticated microchips in its premium products resulting in today's advanced run-flat tyres and even tyres capable of actively assessing road conditions. This cutting-edge technology is expected to diffuse into the tyre makers' mainstream offerings over the coming years, akin to the manner in which ABS became ubiquitous in today's standard family automobile despite its origins as an accoutrement once found exclusively in luxury makes; nonetheless, the pace of adoption of this advanced technology by tyre makers is expected to be far more expeditious especially with rising customer concern on road safety, and the overriding desire by the incumbents to gain a crucial competitive advantage in an increasingly hyper-competitive oligopolistic environment. Moreover, the transformative (yet not immediately perceptible) effects of technical progress are increasingly felt in the seats industry, where revolutionary light-weight metals (e.g., composites) are being used in the manufacture of seating structures, enhancing their appeal to automaker clients intent on assembling increasing numbers of these lighter vehicles (with their superior fuel efficiency and performance) desired by the general motoring public. In the seats industry, advanced technology is also used to strengthen the ergonomics of seating systems through the development of seats capable of sensing their occupants and making the requisite adjustments to suit individual morphologies and preferences; these high-tech seats could also come with automated massage technologies. In the case of the CVJs subsector, despite its struggles in jettisoning its moribund 'metal basher' image, there is also an increasing use of advanced light-weight materials, with the aim of reducing overall vehicle weight and torque loss; CVJs made from these revolutionary materials also tend to minimise noise, harshness and vibration in vehicles, thus significantly improving the driving experience.

As for the once nondescript brakes subsector, it has over the last two decades, evolved into a sophisticated braking systems industry, incorporating cutting-edge electronics that have transcended even once advanced ABS and ESC sensors; this smattering array of technological marvels (include sophisticated sensors and telematics, supported by rapidly advancing GPS, radar, lidar and digital camera technologies) now offers vehicle occupants safety standards unimaginable a mere decade earlier. Many of the above technological applications would have been impossible, without the remarkable computing power provided by increasingly powerful microchips which are still experiencing exponential increases in processing capabilities. The active deployment of microchips is not merely limited to the tyres, seats, CVJs and brakes subsectors addressed in this book but has now become the unifying theme across the entire automotive industry. This dependency on the semiconductor subsector has accorded it an importance, akin to the fossil fuels industry. With the likely advent of artificial intelligence driven autonomous vehicles and ultra-sophisticated electric vehicle engines, the demand for microchips, capable of providing the immense processing power required by these near insatiable technologies, is expected to reach stratospheric heights.

The relentless drive by leading automotive components suppliers to develop these next-generation technologies undoubtedly involves spending billions on R&D. This in turn generates tremendous cost pressures, which compel these suppliers to seek ever-increasing scale economies and new technologies (includes process innovation and human capital) via acquisitions. Acquisitions are often executed to secure emerging technologies, as developing them entirely through organic growth would involve greater investment of time and resources, potentially delaying a new product's time to market (invariably leading to a loss of market share).

As a consequence of the cascade effect, many leading suppliers are now exerting pressure on their supplier networks to shoulder some of the ever-increasing cost of cutting-edge research. Lower tier suppliers are sometimes amenable to such demands as they get to learn the advanced technology of the higher-tiers and develop skills that would enable them to move up the value chain. As evidenced in Chapter 7 (automotive semiconductors), STM has worked with its supplier, Mentor Graphics to develop next-generation semiconductor chips and platforms. Similarly, Renesas also actively works with its supplier, TSMC in the development of next-generational semiconductor technology. While this level of client-supplier cooperation is still largely confined to the automotive semiconductor industry, it is possible that with the increasing technological sophistication required to sustain the competitiveness of their products (and invariably rising capital expenditures and R&D costs), the mega suppliers in the remaining subsectors of this book could with their rising oligopolistic might, compel their suppliers to bear part of these escalating expenditures.

Despite the significant emphasis on technical progress, it is important to recognise there are considerable limitations to this costly yet increasingly critical endeavour. For instance, the tyre makers, notwithstanding their multi-billion-dollar R&D budgets and professed technological progress still cannot develop an effective synthetic substitute to natural rubber, a raw material that comes largely from the emerging markets of Indonesia, Thailand and Malaysia; this seemingly simple raw material derived from naturally occurring latex has heat-resistant properties and a malleability unmatched by its synthetic challengers, compelling tyre makers to continue spending billions annually on natural rubber purchases.

2. JVs as a stepping stone towards eventual acquisition: the case of the tyres and CVJ industry

Over the past few decades, the JV route has proven to be an effective strategy among automotive components suppliers to discretely acquire control of a targeted firm. More importantly, it enables the acquirer to study the culture, production, management practices and market of its partner before deciding on an eventual acquisition; as evidenced in the case of DaimlerChrysler and Goodyear/Sumitomo, failed acquisitions are very much like costly divorces, which are painful to unravel for both parties, as they involve the complex integration of legacy systems (includes complex accounting, financial, human resource and IT systems) and differing corporate cultures.

In the tyre industry, Michelin has deployed JVs as part of its acquisition and overseas expansion strategy. As evidenced in Chapter 3, Michelin, throughout the 1990s, methodically secured control over all its JVs with Shenyang Tyres General Factory and Shanghai Tyre and Rubber, eventually merging them into a single entity (with even greater economies of scale and scope) which cemented its market dominance in China, the world's largest automotive market.

Today, duopolistic firms GKN and NTN control nearly two-thirds of the market in CVJs, a component which is used in over 80 percent of light vehicles globally; GKN alone accounts for over 40 percent of this market. Both firms have used or are deploying JVs as a methodical means of acquiring a company, which contrasts against the outright acquisition strategies practised by their counterparts in the global tyres and automotive seats industry. The JV route to acquisition has enabled GKN to surreptitiously amass its significant market share over the past few decades. However, given the intensifying scrutiny of today's antitrust authorities, it is no longer easy for GKN to sustain this modus operandi. The fact that the US Department of Justice's Antitrust division has charged 46 companies in the automotive components industry with anticompetitive conduct and levied fines amounting to US$2.8 billion on them over the last four years shows the intense scrutiny which the industry is undergoing (The United States Department of Justice, 2016).

3. Hybrid growth strategy in strategic markets: the case of the tyres, seats and CVJ industries

The considerable emphasis on acquisitions may convey the misconception that firms have discarded organic growth strategies. However, research in this book reveals that some firms (e.g., Goodyear, Michelin, Faurecia and GKN) across the tyres, seats and CVJ industries have in fact increased their production capacities in key markets such as the US and China over the past few decades. Goodyear, for instance, has invested over US$700 million in its Pulandian plant in China, which became operational in 2013. This is often supported by judicious acquisition strategies executed to secure control of emerging technologies (includes process innovation), markets and networks. In recent years, the acquisition strategies of these firms have become bolt-on in nature, as they only buy parts of companies which they require and not the firms in their entirety. It makes little commercial sense to buy entire companies as there is considerable duplication and the cost involved is also considerably higher. Further the acquirer could unwittingly become liable for any legal obligations buried deep within the acquired firm's financial statements.

A hybrid growth strategy may be the best move forward for most firms today, as there are considerable drawbacks on becoming overly reliant on either a singular M&A or organic growth approach. As evidenced in the case of Lear in the 1990s (see Chapter 4 on seats), an overly aggressive acquisitions strategy (particularly one financed by debt) could have disastrous financial ramifications. However, if a firm were to rely strictly on organic growth, it would quickly cede precious market share to its more aggressive competitor in possession of targeted and well-executed acquisitions strategy. This is evidenced in the case of NTN, which focused on organic growth throughout the 1980s-1990s, and ended up trailing its chief competitor, GKN, in terms of the global market share for CVJs (see Chapter 5 on CVJs). In an era, where companies must release cutting-edge products at relatively quick time to market, it would be unrealistic to rely strictly on organic growth strategies, as in-house R&D takes considerable time and may not always produce the desired results.

4. Rise of private equity: the kingmakers of the automotive industry

From automakers to their components suppliers, the presence of private equity continues to be felt across the global automotive value chain over the past three decades. The automotive industry is a perennial target of private equity players as they tend to target mature industries filled with firms plagued by high capital expenditures, excessive staff numbers and relatively low growth rates. At the automaker level (see Chapter 2 on the automobile industry), Cerberus was a pivotal player, as it acquired 'Big 3' automaker Chrysler from Daimler in the 2007–2009 period (Bunkley, 2009). The traditional tyre sector has crossed paths with these financiers on multiple occasions over the past few decades. Among the highest profile of these encounters would be Sir James Goldsmith's (possibly among the first of the key private equity players) bold acquisition bid for Goodyear in 1986 (see Chapter 3 on tyres). Although Goldsmith ultimately failed in his acquisition of Goodyear, he did succeed in compelling Goodyear to buy back its own stock, in the process earning a US$93 million profit. In the 1980s, Goldsmith was regarded as a corporate raider, who bought undervalued companies, broke them up and sold off the various parts for profit. Today's private equity industry works on similar principles of identifying undervalued assets but takes a slight longer view on the divestiture of the acquired assets (about three to five years but sometimes longer) (Mercer, 1990). Following Goldsmith's audacious bid for Goodyear, the tyre industry continues to be the target of private equity. For instance, Clayton & Dubilier acquired Uniroyal Goodrich in 1987 which it subsequently sold to Michelin in 1989. In Goodyear's case, it encountered these financiers again when it sold its Engineering Products division to Carlyle in 2007 (Hicks, 1989; Goodyear, 2016).

In the braking systems industry, a private equity firm, KPS, has become a key player through its acquisition of Bosch's foundation brakes business in 2012 (see Chapter 6 on brakes) (Wilson and Bryant, 2012; Huebner and Burger, 2012). It has since reconstituted Bosch's foundation brakes business as an independent firm known as CBI with 2015 revenues of €860 million. CBI, with over 5000 employees, is now a key player in the foundation brakes business, which is the basic framework for the development of any advanced braking systems. As discussed in Chapter 6, firms such as Bosch no longer find 'nuts and bolts' businesses such as making foundation brakes lucrative and would rather focus on high-tech braking systems and related automotive electronics. This has created an opening for investors with deep pockets. If KPS could use CBI as a vehicle to acquire remaining foundation brakes makers, it could end up controlling the fundamental framework of the braking systems business, an area which is increasingly neglected due to its seeming lack of profitability. Since its 2012 acquisition of Bosch's foundation brakes business (now known as CBI), KPS has also acquired Autocast & Forge Pty Ltd, an Australian cast iron foundry, in what appears to be a vertical integration strategy aimed at strengthening the firm's control over the foundation brakes supply chain. Despite the evidence suggesting that most acquisitions ultimately fail, it is doubtful CBI would have attained these capabilities and scale economies at such a rapid pace if not for an aggressive acquisitions strategy. Moreover, it could be argued that KPS/CBI also benefitted immensely from Bosch's earlier acquisition efforts over the last two decades. Bosch's acquisition of Allied Signal's braking systems business in 1996 gave the firm a broad spectrum of capabilities in braking systems, including foundation systems. By acquiring Bosch's foundation brakes business, KPS not only started out with one of the world's largest foundation brakes business but also one where Bosch, had at one stage, spent considerable resources, time and effort assimilating and refining the efforts of the preceding organisation (i.e., AlliedSignal).

The private equity industry also played a critical role in the consolidation of the automotive semiconductor industry. As evidenced in Chapter 7, a consortium of private equity firms led by the Blackstone Group (the largest in the pack) acquired control of leading semiconductor maker, Freescale in 2006 for US$17.6 billion (US$7.07 billion in equity and the remainder in debt) (King and Kelly, 2015). Using Freescale as a springboard and investment vehicle, this investment consortium swiftly acquired other chip companies such as SigmaTel and InToto in 2008. On the back of these acquisitions, Blackstone and its partners soon took Freescale public in 2011. Although Freescale's 2011 listing raised approximately US$1 billion, the bulk of the funds were used to service its massive debt load which was in excess of US$7.5 billion (Gara, 2015). With Freescale's listing, this consortium soon liquidated a portion of their ownership, in the process reducing their original 80 percent stake in the firm to 65 percent (Kraeuter, 2006; Klier and Rubenstein, 2008; Beltran, 2015). However, these supposedly savvy dealmakers failed to secure the outsized returns they were expecting from their acquisition of Freescale; in pre-crisis 2006 (the time of Freescale's acquisition), it is not uncommon for private equity players to expect returns of 70–80 percent (Manigart and Meuleman, 2004).

With the divestment of their remaining 65 percent stake in Freescale to NXP in 2015 for US$11.76 billion, Blackstone and its partners managed to cash out with about US$7.09 billion in cash and stock. This deal also required NXP to assume Freescale's considerable US$5 billion debt obligations thus bringing the actual amount it paid to US$16.7 billion. In contrast to their usual three- to five-year investment horizon, Blackstone and its consortium had to wait nearly a decade to secure what was at best a breakeven return. It is also not clear how Freescale has benefitted from being under private equity ownership for close to a decade. Over this period, it not only failed to close the gap with its competitors (e.g., Infineon and STM) but ended up being acquired by a traditionally smaller rival in the automotive semiconductors industry. Its tenure as a private equity portfolio company also saw an exponential increase in its debt, rising from a little under US$1 billion to approximately US$5 billion at the point of its sale to NXP (Beltran, 2015; Appelbaum and Batt, 2014).

Despite their predatory nature, one could make the case that private equity firms serve a 'policing' role in preventing incompetent management; badly-managed firms often see their market capitalisations fall below their book value (the value of their assets), making them prime targets for acquisitions by private equity firms, who profess to be efficiency experts out to unlock the true value of acquired firms.

5. The strong hand of industrial policy

Government intervention, in the guise of industrial policy is apparent in the global automotive industry over the past three decades. Industrial policy is often conceived with the intention of creating 'national champions' or to ensure critical technologies remain in domestic hands in order to sustain and augment a country's competitive advantage. At the automaker level, the US government was instrumental in the bailout of GM and Chrysler in the aftermath of the 2008 global financial crisis (see Chapter 2). In the case of Renault, the French government now has a near 20 percent stake, enabling it to interfere on matters such as executive pay and possibly even the bringing back of manufacturing jobs into France to assuage France's relatively high unemployment levels.

As evidenced in Chapter 7, Japanese government-backed private firm, INCJ along with a consortium of Japanese firms effectively nationalised Renesas through the acquisition of a greater than 50 percent stake in the then crisis-stricken firm (Saito, 2012; Soble and Sender, 2012). This Japanese government bailout was executed to ensure critical semiconductor technologies do not end in foreign hands, compromising the country's status as a high-end manufacturing powerhouse. To ensure Renesas remained in Japanese hands, the government-backed INCJ even outbid KKR, a leading US private equity firm; INCJ paid US$2.55 billion to acquire Renesas which was valued at approximately US$1.4 billion (Renesas, 2011; Google Finance, 2012; AltAssets, 2012).

From a broader perspective, it could be argued that the very existence of these sophisticated automotive semiconductors (the very 'brains' of today's increasingly connected vehicles), is the result of the US government's space programme; NASA's Apollo programme in the 1960s generated significant demand for microchips and thus provided the much needed boost to the then fledgling semiconductor industry (Emblemsvåg, 2015). The same argument could be made for the GPS and telematics increasingly found in vehicles rolling off today's automobile production lines (Mazzucato, 2013). Many of these technologies (e.g., the internet, GPS) were originally conceived and developed by the military and associated entities; The internet originated from the US Defense Advanced Research Projects Agency's (hereafter 'DARPA') pioneering efforts in the 1950s-1960s to develop a communication system coordinated by a computer network while the GPS was initially developed by the US Department of Defense (hereafter 'DoD') in the 1970s (DoD, 2016; Waldrop, 2015; NASA, 2015). In addition, the Taiwanese government's drive to create a vibrant, domestic semiconductor industry, also gave rise to the creation of TSMC and UMC, who now dominate the US$48.8 billion global market for basic semiconductors. The Taiwanese government not only facilitated the availability of credit to semiconductor companies such as TSMC in the 1980s but also built critical infrastructure (e.g., Hsinchu Science Park) with the accompanying tax incentives and congregation of skilled manpower to support their growth (Gartner, 2016; IHS, 2016; Prestowitz, 2005).

The strong hand of industrial policy is also evident among today's state-owned enterprises. As evidenced in Chapter 3, Chinese state-owned enterprise, CNCC has acquired a significant stake in Italy's Pirelli. This acquisition enabled CNCC to acquire premium tyre making technology, significantly raising its technical capabilities and possibly even pricing power. To develop the technical prowess which Pirelli wields would have taken CNCC possibly decades of successful R&D investment; the monetary investment in R&D does not necessarily yield commensurate results (very often, it does not do so) and this accounts for its costly nature. With the eventual assimilation of Pirelli, CNCC might even have a chance of competing for a place among the top three tyre makers, a notion which would have been inconceivable a decade or so earlier (Arosio and Masoni, 2015). Chinese state-owned enterprises backed by ready access to cheap credit from similarly state-backed funds such as China Reform Holdings Corp and Silk Road Fund are now aggressively acquiring Western enterprises with the aim of leapfrogging the value chain; from 2015 to 2016, CNCC borrowed in excess of US$43 billion from state-backed funds and banks; Silk Road Fund itself has a 25 percent stake in Pirelli (Wu, 2016). Not content with targeting the leading components suppliers, Chinese state-owned enterprises are also looking at acquiring the resource players at the bottom of the global value chain. As evidenced in Chapter 3, Sinochem, another Chinese state-owned enterprise launched its successful acquisition of Halcyon, a Singapore-listed natural rubber supplier in early 2016 (Aravindan, 2016; Cheok, 2016). The above acquisitions suggest an industrial policy designed to secure control of the entire global tyres value chain, controlling everything from natural rubber to high-end tyre manufacturing.

6. Keeping your enemies closer: the case of the CVJ and automotive semiconductor industries

Faced with ever-increasing scale economy demands and rising costs, even rival firms, fighting tooth and nail for market leadership are sometimes compelled to work together. Moreover, there are also limits to acquisitions strategies aimed at procuring desired technologies, in view of their costs, requisite integration efforts and mounting worldwide antitrust scrutiny; in view of these factors, it might be more tenable in some cases for automotive components makers to work together through carefully crafted cooperative efforts. As mentioned in Chapter 5, arch rivals GKN and NTN formed an Australian JV, Unidrive in 1988, in their attempt to secure greater economies of scale and scope and an increased international presence (GKN, 2003; GKN, 2012; NTN, 2010). Further examples of such unusual collaborations would be that of STM (in an attempt to alleviate escalating

R&D costs) forming a joint development programme with key rival, Freescale in 2006 to develop next-generation car microcontrollers needed to sustain both their leadership positions (Freescale, 2009). Similarly, the world's second largest automotive semiconductor maker, Infineon is also partial to working with rivals such as Bosch, which is concurrently a valued client that has given the former a top supplier award multiple times (see Chapter 7) (Infineon, 2015). In an industry where intellectual property is key to survival, cooperation of this nature seems surreal and counterintuitive. However, escalating R&D running into the billions has necessitated such unlikely cooperation. The above alliances were feasible as there were visible benefits for both parties such as significant cost and risk mitigation. In the case of STM and Freescale, an alliance of this nature enabled them to develop cutting-edge products that not only grew their business ecosystem but also strengthened their competitiveness against bigger rivals, Renesas and Infineon.

However, to derive the potential benefits of such unusual cooperation, the nature of the collaboration along with intellectual property ownership must be clearly defined (i.e., who works on what? who gets what and why?) from the outset. The once foreboding notion of working with one's arch rivals is gaining traction across the entire automotive industry. Even automakers, with their significantly larger R&D budgets have come to realise that it is becoming increasingly impossible to go it alone, in an industry with an insatiable appetite for technological progress and accompanying scale economies. For instance, BMW and Toyota are working together to develop advanced lithium-ion batteries (to be used in their forthcoming electric and hybrid vehicles), hydrogen fuels, vehicle electrification and revolutionary lightweight materials (Reed and Bryant, 2012). Further, the two companies are cooperating in the development of a sports car, powered by hybrid engines; this project combines BMWs significant expertise in powerful engines with Toyota's unrivalled production capabilities (Foy, 2014). Moreover Toyota has also worked with Ford to develop gas-electric hybrid fuel systems for trucks and SUVs (Bunkley, 2011).

7. Conclusion

The relentless drive to secure innovative technical progress has been a running theme at both the automaker and subsector levels. As evidenced in this book, the five key subsectors (i.e., tyres, seats, CVJs, brakes and automotive semiconductors) are now shouldering an increasingly disproportionate share of the R&D load. For automotive semiconductors, the cost of R&D has become practically untenable for the smaller players, driving some to mount unprecedented bet-the-firm acquisitions; NXP's acquisition of its larger rival, Freescale in 2015 is a case in point.

This book also reveals the subtle acquisition strategies (in the form of JVs) deployed with significant success by the tyres and constant velocity joints industries over the past few decades. However, this covert approach to staging acquisitions may not enjoy the same level of success in the coming years, with the increasing level of scrutiny by antitrust authorities. In an industry seemingly defined by an overwhelming number of acquisitions over the past few decades, it may appear that many companies have abandoned organic growth strategies. However, this is not the case, as the various subsectors covered in this book deploy a hybrid approach, deploying an active mix of acquisition and organic growth strategies. Throughout the past three decades, finance capital in the guise of private equity and its antecedents (i.e., the corporate raiders) have also left an indelible mark on the consolidating automotive landscape and are expected to continue to do so. Moreover, research in this book reveals that governments, through active industrial policies, have played a considerable role in shaping the very technologies and strategic directions of the key corporate players. In the case of emerging countries such as China, the government, through its state-owned enterprises, is now embarking on a relentless acquisition campaign to create champions capable of competing effectively on the global stage. However, this would prove to be a challenging endeavour, as many of the top three players (i.e., the existing oligopolists) across the five subsectors covered in this book have accumulated unprecedented economies of scale and scope, supported by multi-billion-dollar R&D, purchasing and marketing budgets; the established oligopolists are still deploying bolt-on acquisition strategies to acquire desired technologies, further augmenting their already seemingly unassailable market positions.

Throughout this landscape with its multitude of players, the level of competition is intensifying, with the cascade effect spurring further consolidation at even the lowest and often invisible levels (i.e., the natural rubber suppliers) of the global value chain. Further, the intensifying competition (and the accompanying escalating costs) to develop next-generational technology needed to secure market dominance is ironically driving competitors to embark on unlikely product development alliances and overseas JVs.

References

AltAssets (2012) Japan's innovation network corp nears $2.55bn bailout for Renesas, *AltAssets* [internet] Available at: www.altassets.net/private-equity-news/by-news-type/deal-news/japans-innovation-network-corp-nears-2-55bn-bailout-for-renesas.html [Accessed on 15 November, 2012].

Applebaum, E. and Batt, R. (2014) *Private Equity at Work: How Wall Street Manages Main Street*, New York: Russell Sage Foundation.

Aravindan, A. (2016) Sinochem International, Halcyon Agri to create biggest natural rubber supply chain manager, *Reuters* [internet] Available at: www.reuters.com/article/us-hac-m-a-sinochem-intl-idUSKCN0WU04D [Accessed on 2 July, 2016].

Arosio, P. and Masoni, D. (2015) ChemChina to buy into Italian tire maker Pirelli in $7.7 billion deal, *Reuters* [internet] Available at: www.reuters.com/article/us-pirelli-chemchina-idUSKBN0MI0PQ20150323 [Accessed on 7 July, 2015].

Beltran, L. (2015) PE owners to show tiny gain on Freescale's $16.7 bln sale, *The PE Hub Network* [internet] Available at: www.pehub.com/2015/03/pe-owners-to-show-tiny-gain-on-freescales-16-7-bln-sale/ [Accessed on 5 September, 2016].

Bunkley, N. (2009) Daimler reaches deal to unload Chrysler stake, *nytimes.com* [internet] Available at: www.nytimes.com/2009/04/28/business/28chrysler. html [Accessed on 18 August, 2016].

Bunkley, N. (2011) Ford and Toyota to work together on hybrid system for trucks, *nytimes.com* [internet] Available at: www.nytimes.com/2011/08/23/business/ ford-and-toyota-to-work-together-on-hybrid-trucks.html?_r=0 [Accessed on 7 September, 2016].

Cheok, J. (2016) Halcyon, Sinochem to merge natural rubber businesses, *The Business Times* [internet] Available at: www.businesstimes.com.sg/companies-markets/hal cyon-sinochem-to-merge-natural-rubber-businesses [Accessed on 12 July, 2016].

Emblemsvåg, J. (2015) Reengineering Capitalism; From Industrial Revolution Towards Sustainable Development, New York: Springer International Publishing.

Foy, H. (2014) BMW and Toyota team up to develop sports car, *ft.com* [internet] Available at: www.ft.com/cms/s/0/030feb32-7c7d-11e3-b514-00144feabdc0. html#axzz4JXm7zqHV [Accessed on 7 September, 2016].

Freescale Semiconductor (2009) Automotive safety-critical systems leap forward with next-generation microcontrollers from STMicroelectronics and Freescale, *Freescale Semiconductor* [internet] Available at: http://media.freescale.com/phoenix. zhtml?c=196520&p=irol-newsArticle_print&ID=1338824&highlight= [Accessed on 29 March, 2012].

Gara, A. (2015) Patience pays off for private equity in NXP semiconductors $11.8B takeover of freescale, *Forbes* [internet] Available at: www.forbes.com/sites/antoine gara/2015/03/02/private-equity-nxp-freescale-semiconductor/#1b74f26e7a6d [Accessed on 5 September, 2016].

Gartner (2016) Worldwide semiconductor foundry market grew 4.4 percent in 2015, according to final results by Gartner, *Gartner* [internet] Available at: www.gartner. com/newsroom/id/3281630 [Accessed on 1 August, 2016].

GKN (2003) *Annual Report 2003*, Worcestershire: GKN plc.

GKN (2012) Potential suppliers, *GKN* [internet] Available at: www.gkndriveline. com/drivelinecms/opencms/en/suppliers/potential-suppliers.html [Accessed on 7 June, 2012].

Goodyear (2016) Our company: History, Goodyear [internet] Available at: www.good year.com/corporate/history/history_byyear.html [Accessed on 5 September, 2016].

Google Finance (2012) Renesas Electronics Corporation, *Google Finance* [internet] Available at: www.google.com/finance?cid=685772 [Accessed on 11 September, 2012].

Hicks, J.P. (1989) Michelin to acquire Uniroyal Goodrich, *nytimes.com* [internet] Available at: www.nytimes.com/1989/09/23/business/michelin-to-acquire-uniroyal-goodrich.html [Accessed on 5 September, 2016].

Huebner and Burger (2012) Bosch sells low-tech brakes ops to buyout firm, *Reu ters.com* [internet] Available at: www.reuters.com/article/2012/01/10/us-robert boschgmbh-kps-idUSTRE80919X20120110 [Accessed on 23 March, 2012].

IHS (2016) Automotive semiconductor market grows slightly in 2015 while ranks shift, IHS says, *IHS* [internet] Available at: http://press.ihs.com/press-release/ technology/automotive-semiconductor-market-grows-slightly-2015-while-ranks-shift-ihs-s [Accessed on 1 August, 2016].

Infineon Technologies AG (2015) Bosch honors Infineon with award for innovation, *Infineon* [internet] Available at: www.infineon.com/cms/en/about-infineon/ press/press-releases/2015/INFATV201507-070.html [Accessed on 7 September, 2016].

King, I and Kelly, J (2015) Private equity finally digs out of troubled freescale chip deal, *Bloomberg* [internet] Available at: www.bloomberg.com/news/arti cles/2015-03-05/private-equity-finally-digs-out-of-troubled-freescale-chip-deal [Accessed on 5 September, 2016].

Klier, T.H. and Rubenstein, J.M. (2008) *Who Really Made Your Car? Restructuring and Geographic Change in the Auto Industry*, Kalamazoo, Michigan: W.E. Upjohn Institute for Employment Research.

Kraeuter, C. (2006a) Blackstone buys freescale, *Forbes.com* [internet] Available at: www. forbes.com/2006/09/15/blackstone-freescale-buyout-tech-cx_ck_0915freescale. html [Accessed on 26 October, 2012].

Kraeuter, C. (2006b) Why private money likes chips, *Forbes.com* [internet] Available at: www.forbes.com/2006/09/14/chip-lbo-equity-tech-cx_ck_0915chip.html [Accessed on 26 October, 2012].

Manigart, S. and Meuleman, M. (2004) Financing Entrepreneurial Companies: How to Raise Private Equity as a High-Growth Company, Brussel: De Boeck & Larcier.

Mazzucato, M. (2013) The Entrepreneurial State: Debunking Public vs. Private Sector Myths, London: Anthem Press.

Mercer, R. (1990) The economic consequences of high leverage and stock market pressures on corporate management: A roundtable discussion, in Stern, J.M. and Chew D.H. Jr. (eds), The Revolution in Corporate Finance, Massachusetts: Blackwell Publishers Ltd.

NASA (2015) Global positioning system history, *NASA* [internet] Available at: www. nasa.gov/directorates/heo/scan/communications/policy/GPS_History.html [Accessed on 5 September, 2016].

NTN Corporation (2010) *NTN Report 2010 for the Year Ended, March 31*, Osaka: NTN Corporation.

Prestowitz, C. (2005) Three Billion New Capitalists: The Great Shift of Wealth and Power to the East, New York: Basic Books.

Reed, J. and Bryant, C. (2012) BMW and Toyota expand partnership, *ft.com* [internet] Available at: www.ft.com/cms/s/0/1ca4578c-c1de-11e1-8e7c-00144feabdc0. html?siteedition=intl#axzz4JXjxiH9H [Accessed on 7 September, 2016].

Renesas (2011) *Annual Report 2011: Year Ended March 31, 2011*, Tokyo: Renesas Electronics Corporation.

Saito, M. (2012) Japan's Renesas expects worst-ever annual loss of $1.9 billion, *Reuters.com* [internet] Available at: http://uk.reuters.com/article/2012/08/02/ oukin-uk-renesas-earnings-idUKBRE87109E20120802 [Accessed on 10 September, 2012].

Soble, J. and Sender, H. (2012) KKR starts talks to buy Renesas, *FT.com* [internet] Available at: www.ft.com/intl/cms/s/0/d4ffacf0-f195-11e1-bba3-00144 feabdc0.html#axzz263ryXmKO [Accessed on 10 September, 2012].

U.S. Department of Defense (2016) Open government data, *U.S. Department of Defense* [internet] Available at: http://data.defense.gov/ [Accessed on 5 September, 2016].

U.S. Department of Justice (2016) Hitachi automotive systems agrees to plead guilty to involvement in anti-competitive auto parts conspiracy, *DOJ* [internet] Available at: www.justice.gov/opa/pr/hitachi-automotive-systems-agrees-plead-guilty-involvement-anti-competitive-auto-parts [Accessed on 17 August, 2016].

Waldrop, M. (2015) *DARPA and the Internet Revolution*, Virginia: DARPA.

Wilson, J. and Bryant, C. (2012) Bosch sells brakes unit to private equity buyer, *ft. com* [internet] Available at: www.ft.com/cms/s/0/8de35146-3ba1-11e1-a09a-00144feabdc0.html#axzz1tpIaWkv0 [Accessed on 23 March, 2012].

Wu, K. (2016) ChemChina's global shopping spree is debt-fueled, *wsj.com* [internet] Available at: www.wsj.com/articles/chemchinas-global-shopping-spree-is-debt-fueled-1457616496 [Accessed on 16 August, 2016].

9 Conclusion and further research

1. Overview

Over the last three decades, increasingly gargantuan automakers buffeted by the cascade effect and confronted with the incessant demands of expanding global operations, rising competition and increasingly costly operating environments, are demanding greater support from their suppliers (i.e., suppliers capable of assembling large complex modules such as entire seating and braking systems, and fulfilling stringent lean practice requirements) as it means that they could commit less resources on supposedly lower value-added activities (i.e., production and related activities) and instead focus on higher value-added activities such as marketing, international expansion, raising finance for developing next-generation technologies and other acquisitions.

As evidenced across this book, the massive wave of outsourcing by automakers triggered by the cascade effect has led to the meteoric rise of an elite cadre of powerful mega suppliers over the past 20–30 years, which come complete with multi-billion-dollar revenues, outsized R&D budgets, and extended global value chains managed sometimes by hubristic managers with empire-building tendencies (in other words, virtual doppelgangers of their automaker clients); amidst the tumultuous merger fever which roiled the global economic landscape of the 1980s and 1990s, the oligarchs of these currently globe-trotting industries were then either opportunistic new entrants who bought their way via acquisition or aggressive fledgling players scrambling to stake their claims in the unfolding automotive outsourcing 'gold rush'. Moreover, the cascade effect has unleashed among these suppliers an unremitting drive for increasing technical progress and process innovation, further fuelling an insatiable hunger for greater economies of scale and scope; these suppliers too have embarked on acquisition campaigns over the last three decades resulting in unprecedented consolidation across the entire automotive components industry (the top two to four companies, in the five subsectors addressed in this book, now possess oligopolistic or even duopolistic control over their respective dominions). The level of consolidation (and the accompanying concentration of unprecedented market power in the hands of a select group of industry leviathans) across these components subsectors, in some cases, easily surpasses that of their already heavily consolidated automaker clients.

Technical progress and process innovation are now viewed by these components suppliers as a critical means of controlling costs, and developing superior products that command premium prices.[1] However, as revealed in Chapters 3–7, firms that achieve considerable technical progress and process innovation may not necessarily be able to augment their profitability but opting out of this escalating competition to develop next-generational technologies and techniques would consign them to obsolescence and possibly even economic oblivion. Today's mega suppliers are now confronted with the existential dilemma of whether to double down on their R&D investments in efforts to secure market leadership or seek the potential yet uncertain riches of other industries, particularly ones with less demanding capital outlays and possibly healthier profit margins.

The sheer permeating influence of cutting-edge technology is now clearly exhibited in what many may mistakably view as hidebound, antiquated industries such as the tyres, seats, CVJs and brakes subsectors. For instance, the brakes subsector is no longer about making plain-vanilla foundation brakes but one that has embarked on an escalating race to develop increasingly intelligent safety systems (e.g., predictive artificial intelligence features) that provide vehicle occupants with unprecedented levels of protection even under the most adverse road conditions (a virtual high-tech 'safety cocoon'). However, developing such cutting-edge technologies typically involves spending billions on R&D, as evidenced across Chapter 3–7. This revolutionary but inherently disruptive trend in turn generates tremendous cost pressures, which compel these seemingly established mega suppliers to persistently (sometimes quixotically) seek ever-increasing scale economies and promising new technologies (includes process innovation and highly-skilled human capital) via acquisitions. Acquisitions are often executed to secure emerging technologies, as developing them entirely through organic growth would involve greater investment of time and resources, potentially delaying a new product's time to market (invariably leading to a loss of market share).

The precipitously escalating race to seize much needed economies of scale and scope, sparked off by the cascade effect, has also culminated in many mega suppliers, flexing their considerable financial muscles (in a manner ironically reminiscent of their own demanding automaker clients), to compel their respective supplier networks to bear an increasing portion of the currently back-breaking burden of next-generational research. As evidenced in Chapter 7, some lower tier suppliers (particularly the savvy, ambitious ones) do not mind acquiescing, as they view this seeming obligation as a unique opportunity to master the premium cutting-edge technology of the higher-tiers, which in turn could prove invaluable in vaulting up this increasingly costly value chain. This mutual fulfilment of economic self-interests invariably lowers cost, spurs technological progress and grows the entire ecosystem.

Even the smaller firms (the third or four-tier suppliers) that act as suppliers to these first and second-tier suppliers have not been spared from this ruthless consolidation process born of the ravages of the cascade effect. They too are frequently either acquired or compelled to merge among themselves. As evidenced in Chapter 3, rubber suppliers (traditionally operating in a relatively unconsolidated market) to Bridgestone, Michelin and Goodyear are starting to merge to gain critical economies of scale and scope. By rapidly increasing their size through acquisitions, these relatively small rubber suppliers can increase their power in price negotiations with their customers, the significantly larger tyre industry oligopolists who are constantly squeezing them for discounts. The leading rubber suppliers (i.e., Von Bundit, Sri Trang and Sinochem) are now experiencing a consolidation wave in a hitherto sedate industry, far removed from the attention of international media and scholarly research. Despite its still relatively unconsolidated nature, the natural rubber industry is a US$33 billion behemoth, larger than the CVJs, braking systems and even the much vaunted automotive semiconductor industries which recorded 2015 revenues of US$7.5 billion, US$21.1 billion and US$29 billion respectively (Philippine Rural Development Program, 2015; GKN, 2015; IHS, 2016).

A similar trend is evidenced in the automotive semiconductor industry (Chapter 7), where lower-tier suppliers (i.e., TSMC, UMC) have become as large, if not larger than their customers, the leading second-tier suppliers (i.e., NXP, Infineon, Renesas, STM), as a consequence of a series of acquisitions triggered by the cascade effect. It is possible that suppliers such as TSMC and UMC deliberately position themselves as lower-tier firms (instead of moving up the value chain), as they do not wish to be subjected to direct pressure from automakers, preferring to leave it to their higher-tier counterparts. Due to the absence of this inexorable pressure from automaker clients, it is far more profitable for TSMC to remain an efficient low-cost maker of 'generic' semiconductors instead of the costly highly-customised microcontrollers made by higher-tiers such as Renesas. TSMC is in fact the most profitable firm amongst all the firms covered in this book.

The ever-increasing demands for R&D expenditures and scale economies triggered by the cascade effect has also compelled some firms (e.g., Goodyear, as evidenced in Chapter 3) to adopt 'a more focused R&D strategy' (as described by Goodyear's Keith Price) which involves fostering closer collaborations (in next-generation R&D and process improvement) with their suppliers, surrounding universities and government bodies. However, the superior technical innovation and significantly greater profitability (in net profit terms) of firms such as Bridgestone and Michelin still support the traditional approach of maintaining/increasing a company's R&D expenditure complemented by a judicious acquisitions strategy to quickly acquire access to emerging technologies and markets.

The effectiveness of acquisitions in securing significant gains in technical and process innovation in relatively short time is evidenced in the seats industry (Chapter 4). Pressured by leading assemblers to develop the capability to build entire seating systems supported by just-in-time processes (capabilities they did not earlier possess), JCI and Lear saw acquisitions as an effective means of acquiring these innovative technical and process capabilities. Despite the costly nature of an acquisitions strategy, the opportunity to become a trusted lieutenant in the automakers' drive for market dominance was simply too great to pass up; suppliers who met the exacting demands of the leading automakers were often awarded exclusive lucrative, long-term contracts which stretched across the life of entire car models (Klier and Rubenstein, 2008). Without these costly acquisitions, it is doubtful JCI and Lear would have been able to meet the demands of assemblers within their desired time frame (essential for securing their business in the first place) and subsequently grow to their existing size. These expectations have not subsided with time and have in fact intensified, as assemblers now expect mega suppliers to carry out cutting-edge R&D and actively support their international expansion. Providing global technical, R&D and just-in-time support (along with other lean measures) is extremely difficult and costly (seat factories world-wide are expected to be located no more than an hour's drive from assemblers' plants), thus only the largest suppliers with the greatest financial strength can meet these challenges. Today's mega suppliers (particularly those with a range of businesses) may no longer have the inclination to accept these Carthaginian terms and could resort to extreme measures to extricate themselves. For instance, JCI chose to spin off its seats and accompanying interiors businesses as a separate entity, Adient in 2016.

Escalating R&D costs and mounting automaker demands are not the only challenges confronting these automotive components suppliers. The rising ubiquity of advanced technology in these perceived traditional industries has invariably resulted in a blurring of lines between them and their high-tech counterparts residing in technological enclaves such as Silicon Valley. This accelerating disruptive trend is evidenced by the steady encroachment of technological titans (e.g., Google, Intel, Apple and Nvidia) into the once disparagingly labelled 'moribund' automotive industry. These non-traditional automotive players have been drawn by the potentially outsized returns realisable through rapidly emerging automotive technologies (e.g., driverless cars, ultra-efficient electric powered vehicles, 'connected' automobiles with their onboard artificial intelligence systems) and the chance to control the destiny of a revitalised automotive industry on the cusp of a new dawn. Despite their 'upstart' status, these technology firms generally have immense financial and technological resources which dwarf that of the incumbents. Given this rapidly unfolding situation, buffeted by various emerging technological challenges and economic uncertainties, it is perhaps too early to declare the traditional automotive mega suppliers the victors in this clash of the titans. The emergence of these unexpected rivals could also compel mega suppliers and their automaker clients to forge meaningful partnerships (born out of sheer economic necessity), marshalling the prodigious resources needed to combat this impending 'existential' challenge or risk ceding their hard-fought reins of power to these high-tech interlopers.

2. Market power does not always ensure profitability

Despite their growing market power, leading components suppliers are not always profitable, as evidenced in the case of Goodyear and Renesas. These suppliers, as a group, face a multitude of critical issues such as ever-increasing demands for economies of scale and scope, intensifying scrutiny by regulators and potential takeover attempts by predatory private equity firms. Many of them are generally burdened with increasing R&D, labour and operational costs, coupled with declining profit margins (as they are often squeezed by their automaker clients). Companies such as Goodyear, Lear and Renesas have in fact been plagued with losses for years. Ironically, the intensity of the competitive forces generated by the cascade effect often compels these firms to seek mergers and strategic alliances as a means of securing critical economies of scale and scope needed to ensure their very survival. The above three companies have also become acquisition targets (at varying stages of their existence) during moments of acute financial distress. Moreover, Lear's case exposes the vulnerabilities of an aggressive acquisitions strategy fuelled by debt. The rapid tightening up of credit conditions (due to the onset of the global financial crisis in 2008) played an equally important role as declining consumer demand in sending Lear into Chapter 11 in 2009.

Further the case of Renesas (Chapter 7) highlights the fact that merging two or three weaker companies does not necessarily create a stronger and more profitable enterprise despite supposed gain in scale economies. Merging the unprofitable Renesas Technology with the equally unavailing NEC Electronics Corporation did not result in a financially stronger Renesas Electronics Corp or eliminate the firm's inherent problems. For instance, its low-margin consumer products chips business (i.e., system chips which account for 26 percent of Renesas' total 2011 sales) was steadily eroded by emerging Korean rival, Samsung Electronics and existing rivals (i.e., Infineon and Freescale) although its automotive microcontroller division remained profitable, with relatively high profit margins of 10 percent (Fujimura, 2012).

Sometimes, even an aggressive growth strategy (via acquisitions) may not be enough to ensure a business' viability. This was evidenced in the case of Bosch, which was compelled to sell its unprofitable foundation brakes business (Chapter 6); Bosch's North American foundation brakes business was sold to Akebono while the remainder was divested to a private equity firm, KPS (reinforcing the growing role of finance capital in the automotive components industry). However, Bosch remains a market leader in the far more profitable high-tech braking systems market. Like GKN, Bosch has always been quick in discerning forthcoming industry and consumer trends, and taking the necessary steps to capitalise on them. This fleet footed quality has enabled both firms to dominate their respective industries. Further, Bosch and GKN have been able to manage their respective conglomerate business models more effectively than their rivals in part due to this organisational agility and the refusal to cling onto mature businesses that have limited growth potential.

3. Managerial and policy implications

The fact that seemingly large and powerful subsystems integrators are not necessarily profitable and are also subject to rising scrutiny by regulatory authorities has considerable managerial and policy implications. From a managerial perspective, using outright acquisition strategies would appear less attractive vis-à-vis strategies such as JVs and strategic alliances. The threat of acquisition by opportunistic strategic investors and private equity firms could also deter companies from embarking on expensive M&A campaigns that involve paying outsized premiums and are financed by the assumption of considerable debt. As evidenced in Chapter 6, Continental's debt-laden acquisition of Siemens VDO not only decimated its stock price but also rendered the firm too financially enfeebled to fend off Schaeffler's hostile acquisition attempt.

As mentioned in GKN's case (Chapter 5), JV strategies (with an eye to eventually acquiring one's partner) could be a less conspicuous approach towards securing control of a firm. As such strategies are not outright acquisitions, they do not draw the immediate attention of regulatory authorities. However, the potential acquirer needs to bide its time, as it steadily establishes control through increasing stakes in the firm over a relatively longer time. The use of JVs as a springboard to acquisition allows firms to better understand their partners (i.e., operations, corporate culture, finances and management) and the respective markets before acquiring a controlling stake or making a costly outright acquisition. Sometimes, government regulation may initially prevent outright acquisitions. Thus, JVs enable firms to establish an initial foothold and eventually stage an acquisition, in the event of a relaxation of the regulatory framework. Moreover, they involve significantly less risks and costs than outright acquisitions. As evidenced by GKN, this methodical approach would ensure a greater chance of post-merger success; GKN used this strategy for more than two decades with significant success. This strategy has enabled GKN to systematically expand its international presence and build its global market share in CVJs, in the process overtaking industry pioneer and rival, NTN. Similarly, in the tyres and brakes industries, the leading firms (i.e., Michelin and Continental) have also successfully used JVs as a stepping stone to eventual acquisition albeit less extensively than GKN.

As evidenced in the automaker, tyres and automotive semiconductor industries (Chapters 2, 3 and 7), strategic alliances have also over the years become increasingly popular among companies in the automotive industry. This is owing to the sheer financial cost of staging an acquisition (a hefty premium ranging from 15–50 percent is often incurred) and unravelling a failed one (e.g., DaimlerChrysler); there are also other costs such as the considerable effort required in integrating disparate accounting, financial, human resource and IT systems, along with distinct corporate cultures that could sometimes come into conflict. Nonetheless, in some cases, strategic alliances could just be acquisitions in all but name. For example, Renault has a 43.4 percent stake in its strategic partner, Nissan, easily making it the dominant partner in this alliance (Nissan, 2016).

Strategic alliances have been used by firms with varying degrees of success. In the case of the tyre industry (Chapter 3), Goodyear's global strategic alliance with Sumitomo yielded less than desirable outcomes, as it was too quick to unravel its 10 percent stake in its Japanese partner in 2003 (it had invested in Sumitomo in 1999) (The Japan Times, 2003). As evidenced by Goodyear's case, strategic alliances may take longer than a few years to yield desired outcomes, particularly if the partners involved are multi-billion-dollar firms with significant global operations. If Goodyear had held onto its relatively sizeable stake in

Sumitomo (notwithstanding the financial pain), it probably would have reaped a significant return on its investment. By remaining the second largest stockholder in Sumitomo, it would be able to leverage on Sumitomo's augmented technical capabilities (made possible by the earlier US$936 million investment by Goodyear to acquire 10 percent of Sumitomo), and gain greater access to the sizeable Japanese tyre market.

In the case of the global automotive semiconductor industry, ever-increasing R&D and operational costs (the highest among the five subsectors covered) have made strategic alliances essential for survival, thus creating a greater need to ensure their success. To secure greater scale economies, leading suppliers such as Renesas have formed strategic alliances with supposedly lower-tier (but far more profitable) suppliers such as TSMC (Chapter 7) in developing next-generation technologies. It is typically deployed by leading subsystems integrators to offload rising R&D costs to their lower-tier counterparts. Sometimes lower-tier suppliers such as TSMC do not mind bearing this increasing research cost, as they get to understand the relatively more advanced technologies of their customers, in the process strengthening their own capabilities. Further, lower-tier suppliers (not ones the size of TSMC) could eventually become the targets of their partners, the major automotive semiconductor suppliers (see NXP's acquisition of its partner/supplier, the Catena Group in Chapter 7). It is easier for acquirers to purchase their former suppliers/partners as they are familiar with the operations, culture and finances of the target and the associated risks. Moreover, smaller acquisitions are less likely to attract the scrutiny of antitrust regulators.

4. The firm and globalisation

This book reveals that the very nature of firms has changed in this era of globalisation. In the pre-globalisation period, automakers tend to exercise hegemonic control over their considerably smaller suppliers. However, today, some mega suppliers (e.g., Bosch and Continental) have become increasingly powerful and in some cases, possess revenues and R&D budgets that rival and even exceed that of the smaller automakers. This is because these suppliers have been able to stage aggressive international acquisitions and even forge JVs, and strategic alliances in once closed markets (e.g., China); by the 1990s, cross-border restrictions on acquisitions were removed in most countries.

Pressured by their automaker clients, these suppliers now account for an increasing amount of R&D and manufacturing in the global automotive value chain. This has resulted in the creation of mega suppliers accounting for most of the value of today's vehicles while the carmakers focus more on brand building and international expansion. The first-tier suppliers have in fact become part of a select group of aides to these carmakers, helping them manage a team of lower-tier suppliers spread across the global. In fact, these mega suppliers which now control the 'nuts and bolts' of the ecosystem, are poised to supplant the automakers as the dominant force in the global automotive value chain. Globalisation has also enabled first-tier suppliers (e.g., seats, brakes and CVJs makers) to outsource the manufacturing of rudimentary parts to lower-tier suppliers/

partners scattered globally, freeing up resources needed to indulge their ambitions of international expansion. These lower-tier suppliers are held accountable for quality through bar-coding technologies as each component is bar-coded at each level of the production process. Ironically, some of these lower-tier suppliers even think of their first-tier counterparts as assemblers and marketers rather than manufacturers, as they, like the automakers, have outsourced non-core manufacturing activities (Klier and Rubenstein, 2008).

In an age of globalisation, firms in their drive for increased competitiveness are often compelled to procure new technologies and innovation across international markets. This is often facilitated by international acquisitions. Resultantly, firm practices that used to be confined to certain countries have now diffused across the globe. For instance, lean production (originally of Japanese origin), is now practised by leading companies internationally. As evidenced in this book, some companies (e.g., JCI) acquired lean capabilities (or some lean aspects) by means of acquisition. For all the controversy surrounding the professed benefits and ills stemming from globalisation, it is nonetheless certain this trend has unleashed powerful forces that have transformed the automotive industry, significantly impacting the aspirations of businesses and individuals across the globe over the last three decades. This globalisation juggernaut has resulted in the ascension of automakers and mega suppliers to the commanding heights of the global economy. The precipitous rise of these multinationals has also created millions of jobs worldwide, invariably contributing to the growth of a global middle class with the discretionary income needed to purchase the burgeoning numbers of new vehicles rolling off the production lines of these ascendant automakers; a virtuous loop was set in motion, which enabled the automakers and their mega suppliers to build the sizeable war chests crucial in financing their global acquisitions and expansion. Moreover, over the transformative period of the last thirty years, individuals who were once denied the middle-class privilege of owning an automobile, by virtue of their residence in closed markets, were able to fulfil their car ownership aspirations by the legions.

Nonetheless, this globalisation wave has reached a critical inflexion point today, as it veers precariously on the precipice of having its legacy violently upended by the rapidly re-emerging and increasingly strident forces of populism and its undesirable offspring (i.e., right-wing nationalism, rampant protectionism, misguided autarkic policies and destructive trade wars). Under this climate of geopolitical and economic uncertainty, the incumbents of the automotive industry must reassess and recalibrate their growth strategies or risk having their previous efforts and ambitions undermined by punitive measures (e.g., hefty tariffs, trade quotas, regulations curbing foreign ownership) deployed by increasingly protectionist countries embroiled in an all-out trade war.

5. Further research

Where future research is concerned, researchers could look at other sectors in the automotive components industry such as the automotive glass, fuel injection, HVAC, infotainment and safety systems (includes airbags) markets. Further research into these other sectors would give a more complete view of the impact of the cascade effect on the level of consolidation in the automotive components industry, where components are increasingly intertwined, as a consequence of increasing microchip usage in vehicles. More research could also be done to assess the effectiveness of collaborative research (e.g., Goodyear working with its suppliers, universities and government bodies) as a means of mitigating the ever-increasing demand for R&D investment, which subsequently triggers a need for greater economies of scale and scope, resulting in a greater tendency for consolidation via mergers.

Future research could also examine the impact of the entry of non-traditional players into the automotive components industry. As analysed in Chapter 7, the entry of Intel into the automotive semiconductor business is expected to change the nature of the industry (i.e., potentially displacing existing industry leaders), owing to its ability to deploy immense financial muscle and unassailable expertise in an industry dominated by soaring costs, and an increasing need to use cutting-edge technology as a means of differentiation; innovative technology alone does not guarantee profitability but it is certainly needed to ensure a firm's survival in an increasingly ruthless market with an insatiable demand for the next technological arbiter. The entry of other non-traditional firms such as Google (with its pioneering autonomous vehicle technology) into the automotive components industry has also compounded the cascade effect and triggering further consolidation; to power the sophisticated self-drive technology of Google, increasingly advanced semiconductors would be needed, invariably exacerbating cost pressures in the automotive semiconductor sector which is already burdened with overwhelming R&D and operational costs.

Considerably more research could be done on the impact of strategic alliances in the tyres, seats, CVJs, brakes and automotive semiconductor industries. The impact of such arrangements on businesses has been mixed. Given that they are easier and far less costly to unravel than actual mergers (they do not involve extensive mergers of complex global finance, supply chain, IT and human resource systems), it is sometimes questionable whether the parties involved are sufficiently committed to achieving their desired goals. Moreover, further research could be conducted on the impact of the increasing presence of private equity firms in the sectors covered in this book; their desire to maximise their return on investment and implementing an exit strategy in three years is inimical to the more long-term strategies of most corporations. More importantly, private equity firms' tendency to implement aggressive cost cutting could sometimes run contrary to the significant investment in R&D needed in the sectors covered in this book.

More research could also be done on the transformative impact of the cascade effect which has significantly altered industry structures across all businesses. Contrary to Chandler's argument of oligopolies evolving only in capital-intensive industries, oligopolistic structures are now emerging across all sectors and non-traditional industries. They encompass accountancy practices, banks, casinos, consultancies, cosmetic giants, fashion houses, food and beverage firms, logistics, media, marketing and technology (includes internet-related firms) companies and stock exchanges. These industries now also comprise mainly powerful oligopolistic systems integrators which are able and willing to exert pressure on their supplier networks that pass on this pressure to the next rung of suppliers, resulting in rising concentration across all levels in the global value chain of these supposedly non-traditional sectors.

Note

1 Technical progress involves incorporating increasingly sophisticated microchips, cutting-edge electronics (e.g., ABS and ESC sensors, surrounding sensors, tyre pressure and acceleration sensors, GPS, telematics), advanced light-weight and environmentally-friendly fibres and metals (lightens vehicles and improves fuel efficiency), and ergonomics (e.g., massage technologies, shoulder and lumbar support in car seats). Process innovation involves incorporating lean, six sigma (and other innovative measures) to mitigate cost pressures and improve operational efficiency, in the process freeing up resources which could be used for further R&D or acquisitions.

References

Fujimura, N. (2012) NEC, Hitachi plan to provide support for Japan Chipmaker Renesas, *Bloomberg News* [internet] Available at: www.businessweek.com/news/2012-06-20/nec-hitachi-plan-to-provide-support-for-japan-chipmaker-renesas [Accessed on 10 September, 2012].

GKN (2015) GKN plc Annual Report and Accounts 2015, Worcestershire: GKN plc.

IHS (2016) Automotive semiconductor market grows slightly in 2015 while ranks shift, IHS says, *IHS* [internet] Available at: http://press.ihs.com/press-release/technology/automotive-semiconductor-market-grows-slightly-2015-while-ranks-shift-ihs-s [Accessed on 1 August, 2016].

Klier, T.H. and Rubenstein, J.M. (2008) *Who Really Made Your Car? Restructuring and Geographic Change in the Auto Industry*, Kalamazoo, MI: W.E. Upjohn Institute for Employment Research.

Nissan Motor Corporation (2016) *Alliance Facts and Figures 2016*, Yokohama: Nissan Motor Corporation.

Philippine Rural Development Program (2015) *Value Chain Analysis and Competitiveness Strategy: Rubber Sheets-Cotabato*, Cotabato: Department of Agriculture.

The Japan Times (2003) Sumitomo Rubber in share buyback, The Japan Times Online [internet] Available at:http://www.japantimes.co.jp/text/nb20030409a7.html [Accessed on 2 February, 2012].

Index

Page numbers in italic format indicate figures and tables.

For Product Safety Concerns and Information please contact our EU
representative GPSR@taylorandfrancis.com
Taylor & Francis Verlag GmbH, Kaufingerstraße 24, 80331 München, Germany